Philosophies of Islamic Education

The study of Islamic education has hitherto remained a tangential inquiry in the broader focus of Islamic Studies. In the wake of this neglect, a renaissance of sorts has occurred in recent years, reconfiguring the importance of Islam's attitudes to knowledge, learning, and education as paramount in the study and appreciation of Islamic civilization. *Philosophies of Islamic Education* stands in tandem to this call and takes a pioneering step in establishing the importance of its study for the educationalist, academic, and student alike. Broken into four sections, it deals with theological, pedagogic, institutional, and contemporary issues reflecting the diverse and often competing notions and practices of Islamic education. As a unique international collaboration bringing into conversation theologians, historians, philosophers, teachers, and sociologists of education, *Philosophies of Islamic Education* intends to provide fresh means for conversing with contemporary debates in ethics, secularization theory, child psychology, multiculturalism, interfaith dialogue, and moral education. In doing so, it hopes to offer an important and timely contribution to educational studies, as well as give new insight for academia in terms of conceiving learning and education.

Nadeem A. Memon is Director of Education at Razi Education, Ontario, Canada.

Mujadad Zaman is Visiting Research Fellow at the Center for Islamic Theology, University of Tübingen, Germany.

Routledge Research in Religion and Education

Series Editor Michael D. Waggoner, University of Northern Iowa, USA

1 **Religion in Education**
Innovation in International Research
Edited by Joyce Miller, Kevin O'Grady and Ursula McKenna

2 **Civility, Religious Pluralism, and Education**
Edited by Vincent F. Biondo III and Andrew Fiala

3 **International Perspectives on Education, Religion and Law**
Edited by Charles J. Russo

4 **Philosophies of Islamic Education**
Historical Perspectives and Emerging Discourses
Edited by Nadeem A. Memon and Mujadad Zaman

Philosophies of Islamic Education

Historical Perspectives and Emerging Discourses

Edited by
Nadeem A. Memon and Mujadad Zaman

Routledge
Taylor & Francis Group
NEW YORK AND LONDON

First published 2016
by Routledge
711 Third Avenue, New York, NY 10017

and by Routledge
2 Park Square, Milton Park, Abingdon, Oxon, OX14 4RN

Routledge is an imprint of the Taylor & Francis Group, an informa business

Library of Congress Cataloguing-in-Publication Data
Names: Memon, Nadeem A. (Nadeem Ahmed), 1980– editor of compilation. | Zaman, Mujadad, editor of compilation.
Title: Philosophies of Islamic education : historical perspectives and emerging discourses / edited by Nadeem A. Memon and Mujadad Zaman.
Description: New York, NY : Routledge, 2016. | Series: Routledge research in religion and education ; 4 | Includes bibliographical references.
Identifiers: LCCN 2015037836 | ISBN 9781138788541 (hbk) | ISBN 9781315765501 (ebk)
Subjects: LCSH: Islamic education—Philosophy.
Classification: LCC LC904 .P49 2016 | DDC 371.077—dc23
LC record available at http://lccn.loc.gov/2015037836

ISBN: 978-1-138-78854-1 (hbk)
ISBN: 978-1-315-76550-1 (ebk)

Typeset in Sabon
by Apex CoVantage, LLC

MIX
Paper from responsible sources
FSC® C013056

Printed and bound in Great Britain by
TJ International Ltd, Padstow, Cornwall

Contents

PART III
Schools, Universities, and Pedagogies

PART IV
Contemporary Debates

Foreword

The opening years of the 21st century brought increased attention to religion as an important dimension of culture and politics. Early in this period, the dramatic multi-pronged attacks of September 11, 2001, came as a jolting reminder of the potential for violent action that can have bases in religious motivations. Over the same period, we came to see an increase in religious-group activity in politics. In the United States we see this as an evolution from the Moral Majority movement led by televangelist Jerry Falwell that emerged as a force in the late 1970s as the beginning of the New Religious Right. On further reflection, however, we can see the involvement of religion extending much further back as a fundamental part of our social organization, rather than a new or emerging phenomenon. We need only recall the religious wars of early modern Europe through to the contentious development of US church and state relations as evidence of the long-standing role religion has played as a source of competing values and beliefs. That said, there has been a significant upturn in research and scholarship across many disciplines relative to the study of religion in the last decade and more. This is particularly the case in the area of the relationship of education and religion.

While religious education—study *toward formation* in a particular faith tradition—has been with us for millennia, study *about* religion as an academic subject apart from theology is more recent. Whereas theology departments proceeded from religious assumptions aiming to promulgate a faith tradition, the religious studies field emerged as a discipline that sought to bring a more disinterested social scientific approach to the study of religion. The origins of this approach date back to the European research centers that influenced U.S. scholars beginning in the 18th century. The formalization of this trend, however, is a fairly recent phenomenon, as illustrated by the 1949 formation of Society for the Scientific Study of Religion with its own scholarly journal and the creation of religious studies departments across the United States in the wake of the U.S. Supreme Court decision in 1963 that allowed teaching *about* religion (rather than *for*) in public education institutions. It was also that same year that the American Academy of Religion was born out of a group of scholars that had since 1909 been meeting under the various names related to biblical study.

It is out of this relatively recent increase in scholarly attention to religion and education that this book series arises. Routledge has long been an important presence in the respective fields of religion and of education. It seemed like a natural step to introduce a book series focused particularly on Research in Religion and Education. My appreciation extends to Max Novick for guiding this series into being, to Stacy Noto, and now Christina Chronister, for continuing Routledge's oversight.

This volume, the fifth in this series, comes to us from two scholars of Islamic education who are both editors of and contributors to this book. Dr. Nadeem Memon is Director of Education for Razi Education, a global education consulting firm with offices in Toronto and Dubai. Dr. Mujadad Zaman is a Research Fellow at the Center for Islamic Theology at the University of Tübingen, Germany.

Philosophies of Islamic Education: Historical Perspectives and Emerging Discourses comes at a propitious time. Whereas most editors hope to say that their work "fills a void" in the literature, I believe that this book does. The interest in Islam has grown significantly over the last fifteen years, as has the number of Islam/Muslim schools, colleges, chaplaincy programs, research centers in the West, and state curricula revision in Muslim-majority countries. Given this reality, as the editors note, the "post-9/11 context in the West and post-colonial context in the East" are drawing "public scrutiny of educational initiatives positioned as 'Islamic.' "

Dr. Zaman's introduction elucidates subtle and important distinctions that must be kept in mind as we engage with this topic, not the least of which is an inevitable comparison with philosophies of education in the Western liberal tradition. There are intriguing similarities, as well as challenging differences. He also cautions that we not think monolithically about "a philosophy" of Islamic education any more than we do about a singular Christian or Jewish philosophy of education. Memon and Zaman organize the book to provide needed "theological-historic" foundations then proceed to "sociological-contemporary" concerns and debates. Of particular interest here is a discussion of critical thinking in Islamic education. One cannot help but see parallels to similar debates in the West.

In *Philosophies of Islamic Education*, editors Memon and Zaman give us a timely and rich resource that should provide a knowledge base, provoke thoughtful discussion, and engender more sophisticated understanding of this major religious tradition at a time when such an understanding is profoundly needed.

Michael D. Waggoner
Professor and Series Editor, Routledge Research in Religion and Education Editor, Religion & Education

Acknowledgments

As with any such large collaborative project, we owe a debt of gratitude to a number of individuals, not least all of our contributors whose work, support, and contributions to this volume have given it its strength and value. Thanks to Routledge, especially its editorial team Christina Chronister and Katherine Tsamparlis whose guidance throughout the process has been invaluable. Other notable individuals who have provided much appreciated insight and advice include Professor Mike Waggoner, Professor Ahmad Atif Ahmad, Dr. Amina Nawaz, and Professor Mohamed Rustom.

In addition, Mujadad Zaman wishes to heartily thank the Center for Islamic Theology, University of Tübingen (especially, Professor Lejla Demiri), where as Visiting Research Fellow, he was very kindly given access to the resources necessary for the completion of this book project.

Introduction

Mujadad Zaman

Definitions of 'Islamic Education' defy simplicity of exposition. The historically diverse and confessionally rich faith societies forming the Islamic community (*ummah*) act to conceptually rebel against the potential of such designations. As a significant world civilization, discussions concerning Islam's attitudes toward education necessarily become suffused with cosmo-theological, philosophic, and socio-historical features, which revolve around the broader concerns of knowledge, learning, and instruction. Although it is not impossible to offer a clear definition, the correct balancing of these constituent features requires attention in order to appreciate fully the place of education within the Islamic imagination. It is here, in the intermingling of superintending concerns with those of formally pedagogic ones, that the modern educationalist studying Islamic education initially faces difficulties. Part of the problem lies in conceiving such learning, and its seemingly exhaustive differentiation, into a meaningful and dynamic whole. This being partly due to modern academic proclivities toward specialization which see 'education' as a discrete field of inquiry limiting the study of Islamic education, therefore, to either theological investigations, historical narratives, or examinations of social inequities, etc. All such generalizations are problematic to the degree of difficulty faced, when speaking of a 'civilizational mien' in education. The problem similarly arises when we aver, for example, of the Greek *paideia*, the Roman preoccupation with *mos maiorum* or the Christian with *de imitatione Christi.* Indeed whether we can still meaningfully speak of 'Christian' or 'Jewish' education is itself an ongoing debate within educational studies (Bryfman 2014; Piderit and Morey 2012). Although the accuracy of such generalizations are questionable, they nonetheless stand as useful ideal types of education wrought to rich (unique) worldviews, and it is in this sense that we accept the term 'Islamic education,' and all that it may mean, to help wedge open a door for further analytic investigation.

Venturing an answer as to what may unify the diversity of Islamic education is a question spawning lively debates within the literature, with most responses relying on theological precedent. The monotheistic impulse of Islamic religiosity is a well-studied feature of the faith, and its implications for education seem no less insignificant. The manner in which the concept of the indefatigable 'Oneness of God' (*tawhid*) permeates theology, observance, and aesthetic sensibilities in Islam ensures that the ostensible practices of its education as congregating in the presence of a '*tawhidic* worldview' informs and encourages its pedagogic sundry. Acting as a vista from which an appreciation of God as the ultimate source and custodian of knowledge (and being itself) is made, this principle arguably informs all subsequent attempts at learning and instruction within the religion. It is here that Islamic education, as treated in this book, takes a cautiously 'positive' nomenclatural approach. It is subsequently less concerned with what is commonly termed in the literature as 'Muslim education,' which stands as coterminous primarily with studies in contemporary systems of learning in the Muslim world (Hefner & Zaman 2007). Whereas Muslim education covers everything from traditional religious institutions to secular ones, it denotes empirical educational 'practice' which may not necessarily invoke normative Islamic thought and values. Thus the present volume broadly conceives 'Islamic education' as defined primarily in terms of its rich theological, metaphysical, aesthetic, and ethical values and their enunciation, in myriad forms, to the ideas and practices of education.

Developing *tawhid* as an ontological first principle of education may be realized, for example, with specific reference to the role knowledge plays in reinforcing this ideal. In his acclaimed study of Islamic civilization, the orientalist Franz Rosenthall (2006) argues that

> '*ilm* [knowledge] is one of those concepts that have dominated Islam and given Muslim civilization . . . its distinctive shape and complexion. In fact, there is no other concept that has been operative as a determinant of Muslim civilization in all its aspects to the same extent as '*ilm* (2).

The Qur'anic revelatory story begins, for example, with knowledge as a means of approaching and understanding the Divine. The first command given to Muhammad via the Angel Gabriel, to "read," or recite The Word, attests to the fashioning of subsequent conceptualizations of the religion's priority toward this idea. Similarly, according to the prophetic oral traditions (*hadith*), it is related that a person who "follows a path for acquiring knowledge, God will make easy the passage for Paradise for him" and the counsel to "seek knowledge from the cradle to the grave." Knowledge, then represents the first means of forging a relationship between 'God and man' in the reality of *tawhid*. However, exactly how this *tawhidic* idea translates into education in lieu of its aims and purposes is to consider the 'object' of learning, namely, the human being and in particular the role of the Prophet of Islam in that process. It is here that the life of Muhammad stands as an essential feature in the discussions of Islamic education. From the religion's initial and surreptitious preaching in 7th century Meccan society to the birth of its higher learning institutions (*madrasa* pl. *madaris*) in the tenth, Muhammad represents the 'perfected human' (*al-Insan al-Kamil*) and stands as a paragon for the community. This 'perfection' is understood in terms of his example (*sunnah*) and comportment (*adab*) to worldly affairs, as well as his earthly ministry, epitomizing the balance (*mizan*) necessary for a reflective and fulfilled religious life expressed in the sanctifying of a *tawhidic* vision of reality. Considering the extent to which one may know and emulate him, the contemporary educational thinker al-Attas argues that the ends of Islamic education can be partly understood as a fidelitous imitation of "producing men and women [who] resemble him as near as possible" (Cook 2011, xxvii). If *tawhid* is the *telos* of learning, the life of Muhammad personifies the human potential of accent to the Divine through living this reality.

Finally, alongside *tawhid*, *'ilm*, and *sunnah* the educationalist wishing to decipher Islamic education will have to venture into 'how' the Muslim conceives the world and the rest of creation. As instantiated souls, humankind's capacity for 'knowing' the world in Islamic thought is primarily represented in a cosmological view wherein the heart (*qalb*) stands as the seat of cognition and is affiliated with intuition, faith, conscience, meaning, and knowledge (Sachiko and Chittick 2006; Webb 2010). Reason (*'aql*), on the other hand, is accorded the ability to comprehend empirical realities and create abstractions thereof. This dichotomy of 'heart' and 'mind' (a division that stands in tandem to other faith traditions) are positioned on either side of a complex being whose complimentary faculties come to apprehend the Divine yet, however, do not translate into a reductive 'faith versus reason' or flesh vs spirit dichotomy as it may in other faith traditions (Goody 2003). Considered together, this depiction of human faculties serves to illumine *tawhid*, *'ilm*, and *sunnah* as principles guiding education. Moreover, they cohere toward a broad vision through which the contemporary educationalist may begin to interpret, when classical Islamic scholarship argues, for example, that education is to "know the meaning of obedience and service [to God]" (al-Ghazali in Cook 2011, xv).

ISLAMIC EDUCATION IN PRACTICE: BETWEEN UNITY AND DIVERSITY

Apart from purely religious considerations, the educationalist studying Islamic education and its historical practices will note the conspicuous absence of a distinct subject matter per se of formal pedagogy (*'ilm al-tarbiyya*). He will instead likely come across historical works entitled *Rules of Conduct for Teachers and Students* (*adab al-ʿalim wa-l-mutaʿallim*) or philosophical treaties dealing with household management through which advice is offered on how best to instruct the young (Swain 2013). These occurrences may be read as blind spots in Islamic pedagogy yet can alternatively be viewed as providing insights into the status and nature of premodern education as a 'whole' process (engaged in ideas of learning and the good life), which could not be separated as a distinctive discipline due to its ontological dependency upon *tawhid*. Arguably, the scholarship, institutions, guilds, and educational discourses that the premodern Islamic world inhabited were part of what the renowned orientalist Montgomery Watt (2010) has perspicuously referred to as an 'integrated society' incorporated by a common human ethic. Whereas this world of meaning, from which we are pushed out by time and context (or the *aletheia* of a past world, in Heideggerian terms), it is nonetheless an important start for understanding historical and contemporary practices of education and the complexities existing within them.

However, as with the *tawhidic* principle of Islamic education, its pedagogic diversity may be understood as gravitating toward certain ideals. In particular, the 'whole' or 'integrated' status of learning guiding historical practices is discernible in a familiar pedagogic language of *tarbiyya, ta'dib,* and *ta'lim. Tarbiyya* (to grow, increase) is, for example, identified with individual personal and moral development; *ta'dib* (to be disciplined, cultured) infers the special development and awareness of the student, and *ta'lim*, (to know, perceive, discern) suggests the formalizing of knowledge acquisition and transmission (Cook 2010; Halstead 2004). As one segues through these stages, which are not limited to cognitive capabilities, they portend the forging of a moral being and intend to bequeath the individual's consciousness with the realization of a state of *ubudiyyah* (dependency on God) through refining his nature and to act ultimately in the prophetic manner, with probity and fidelity, as God's custodian on earth. A consequence of this pedagogic circle, returning to a God-centered view (*tawhid*), is an inherent comity that is set at the heart of Islamic education, as evidenced by its unitary notion of disciplines and sciences (Rahman 2008), allowing us to speak, in theoretical terms at least, of Islamic education as a process *in toto*. It is not dissimilar in this sense with the modern 'liberal' ideal in European education which similarly wishes to nurture, in myriad ways, personal traits and intellectual sensibilities of consilience, balance, and unity (Bloom 1995; Wilson 1999).

Such diversity is also present in Islamic 'institutional' practice of education, which, again, can be said to bear certain elective affinities (in so far as Islamic art or poetry can be said to do the same) that, although differentiated, form a patterned language of variegated expression. The eminent orientalist scholar George Makdisi (1970), for example, commenting on higher educational differences between Christian and Islamic institutions summates their divergences as:

> Centralization in medieval European cities, and decentralization in those of medieval Islam—such was the situation in the institutions of

> learning on both sides of the Mediterranean. Paris was a city with one university; Baghdad, on the other hand, had a great number of institutions of learning. In Paris organized faculties were brought into a single system resting on a hierarchical basis; in Baghdad, one leading scholar (and others of subordinate positions) taught in one of the many institutions, each institution independent of the other, with its own charter, and its own endowment . . . Here we have another essential difference between the two institutional systems: hierarchical and organized in medieval Europe, individualistic and personalized in medieval Islam.
> (Makdisi 1970, 259)

Although the sharp binary of this generalizing account has more recently been called into question (Geelhaar 2011), it presents an important means to acclimatize the educationalist when wishing to learn about Islamic education, its history, and practices. We therefore see that despite the lack of *magisterium* religious councils and centralization in the Islamic faith, its education, which may be mystifyingly diverse for some, bears 'theological' markers in lieu of its *tawhidic* worldview and 'pedagogical' overtures via its leaning toward the trivium of *tarbiyya, ta'dib,* and *ta'lim.* The interests of this book, and the chapter contributions in particular, take a similar starting point, namely, to embrace educational diversity (of meaning and practice) so as to mirror these realities and by extension not isolate itself from the literature, but rather create a rapprochement with it instead.

THE STATE OF THE 'FIELD'

Tracing the academic study of Islamic education poses problems not dissimilar to those identified earlier with its initial definition. Due to the diversity that such education exhibits, plotting a 'field' evidently becomes problematic with regard to its varied topography or its disciplinary themes. To this end, we may locate a number of 'research streams' derived from different academic approaches that suggest, albeit imperfectly, trajectories for the study of Islamic education including, but not limited to, 'classical' orientalist scholarship, 'historical' case studies, and 'contemporary-social' approaches.

The first draws upon a large body of literature focused on specific texts and manuals of education dealing with works on formal instruction of pupils, curricula disputes, classification of knowledge, etc. Reference to 'orientalist' here, infers the study and commentary on the classical (middle ages and late medieval) 'orient,' namely, the near and far east, and is characterized by a tendency toward translations and commentaries on key texts. Important contributions include Dodge's (2011) descriptions of medieval curricula, Makdisi (1995) on the formative period of higher learning institutions, as well the practice and organizing of learning (Endress, 2006; Morris 2002). Other important translation works by von Grunebaum and Abel (2003), Schacht (1964) and Zurayk (1968) have provided vital stimulus for understanding the ideas and practices of Islamic learning and pedagogy to the Western academic world.

The 'historical' study of Islamic education has equally produced important contributions, and although one may draw parallels to the aforementioned orientalist output, the specific concentration may here be identified with case studies from the classical to the modern era, which explore and highlight certain key areas of academic interest. These extend to general historical accounts of educational history (Eickelman 1978; Lowry 2004), geographically specific studies of the Indian subcontinent (Metcalf 1978; Zaman 2008), the Ottoman world (Evered 2012), medieval institutions and pedagogy (Berkey 1992), etc. Finally, the amorphous 'contemporary-social' bracketing of research explores a plethora of interests from Muslim participation in modern secular education (Cheruvallil-Contractor and Scott Baumann 2015; Modood 2006), to growing Islamic institutions in non-Muslim majority countries (Bruinessen and Allievi 2011; Shahin, 2003), to conceiving traditional Islamic ideas of learning in the 21st century (Wan Dawud 1989), as well as the use of critical theory in the development of new ideas of education (Waghid 2011). Such issues are tackled through utilizing religious discourses, as well as adopting modern social theory, as a means of expanding upon classical debates. In the case of the former, theorists such as Husain and Ashraf (1982), al-Attas (1979), and Nasr (2012), among others, remain cautious of modernity's intellectual and social norms, which have sought, in their estimation, to recalibrate education away from 'God-centered' ends toward secular and material ones. Alternatively, in the case of the latter, the use of social science and critical theory is also employed to understand and engage with the contemporary intellectual milieu. This research repertoire can aptly be defined by Waghid's (2011) work, for example, which comments on the need for intellectual resurgence in debates of Islamic education and points to social theory (specifically the work of Jacques Derrida) which can help direct learning in *madaris* toward a richer conception of social care and 'responsibility' in the 21st century.

The present book, in appreciating this collage of intellectual interests surrounding Islamic education, attempts to position itself both 'within' and 'outside' the literature. With regard to the former, it sits well within the present literature and is, for example, 'orientalist' in the manner that it appreciates the importance of classical works/ideas on theology and pedagogy as enunciating values motivating Islamic learning, 'historical' with reference to accumulated practices of education and seeking their relevancy today, whereas it is 'contemporary' in that it engages with the unique challenges (both social and philosophical) facing Islamic education. Though not promulgating any one form of Islamic education, it is also 'outside' of these debates seeing itself as part of an evolving discourse of practice that cannot be limited to academic debates alone and thus converges upon faith and liturgical life.

'PHILOSOPHY' OF ISLAMIC EDUCATION

As with the caveats of studying 'Islamic education' mentioned earlier, the researcher investigating premodern literature on Islamic education is also unlikely to find works on 'philosophy of education' (*Falsafa at tarbiya al Islamiya* for example). As a subdiscipline of educational studies, its intellectual lineage is drawn from the works of Noddings (2011), Peters (2010), and Pring (2005), all of whom have been interested in the broader questions of what, how, and why we educate. Presenting a formal definition, Noddings (2011) argues, "philosophers of education study the problems of education from a philosophical perspective. To do this, they need to know something about several of the standard branches of philosophy . . . This is a formidable task" (xiv). However, falling short of the demands of such a definition, it has diversified into a myriad of concerns spreading outside the field of academic philosophy. Within the discourse of Islamic education, a starting point for philosophical questions has been to understand what Shahed Ali argues are "the source of any system of education . . . [and which can] be traced to its philosophy of life and . . . [which] is organically connected with the ethical and moral values that spring from that philosophy (cited in Cook 2010, xxviii)." However, there is also a potential confrontation between 'philosophy' and education within an Islamic context, as highlighted by Halstead (2004) when he suggests that in

> the case of 'philosophy,' as we have seen, some Muslims took the foreign word into the Arabic language . . . to render the alien concept compatible with Islamic teaching. In the case of 'education,' on the other hand, the problem is not that the word does not exist in Arabic, but that the central meaning of the term in Arabic does not correspond very closely with the central meaning of 'education' as expounded by liberal philosophers of education in the west.
>
> (519)

This portends the problem of anachronistically applying terms such as 'philosophy of education' to historical thinking on Islamic education, leaving the contemporary literature contentious of philosophical inquiry made relevant to Islam (Panjwani 2004; Waghid 2011; Wan Daud 1989). For example, Nasr (2012) encourages the ability of Islamic philosophical thought to orientate itself to education, which he claims would enliven ideas of the

> arts [and] beauty; correctly filling the wells of the emotions, not letting them die or being indifferent to them; our moral sense; our mental faculties, and everything else; and above all, of course, our faith and need for God, for religion, which should permeate the whole of education. This effort at the integration of the philosophy of education . . . is extremely important.
>
> (20)

Philosophy, for such thinkers, stands as a lens within which we may speculate on questions dealing with the purpose of education, how it conceives relations between God and man, what is known, and whether there are limits to formal reasoning. Such questions make a distinction between 'philosophy of Islamic education,' which incorporates such ideas and infers the interests of the larger subfield of the philosophy of education, and 'Islamic educational philosophy,' which denotes a narrower focus limited to questions of pedagogy and practice. The present book takes as its inspiration the former, in that 'being philosophical' refers to articulating and confronting perennial questions in education with reference to theological, historic, and sociological explanatory systems. If being philosophical is an 'activity,' then the presentation and progression of the chapters are designed not to articulate any one idea of Islamic education, nor to necessarily instruct the reader in 'how to be' philosophical, but rather stand as an 'aid' for philosophical thought via consideration of the varied contexts of Islamic education.

STRUCTURE AND PURPOSE OF THE BOOK

Amongst the emerging education paradoxes of our times is that as the 21st century ushers in ever new and triumphalist discourses for universal schooling, they are increasingly accompanied by sustained and sweeping critiques of modern education (Baker 2015). In the wake of this turbidity, the voice of dissident and novel educational approaches have come to be heard. It is within this educational climate that the present volume stands, exploring Islamic education as a means to engage with contemporary practice and discourse. Its task, as with the question of being 'philosophical,' is not to provide definitive statements regarding the unresolved intellectual inquires in the field of educational studies, rather it is to be a propaedeutic text on Islamic educational thought and act as a means for further investigative work appealing to educational theorists, academics, and practitioners alike. The flow of the book reflects this desire and is broadly divided into a 'theological-historic' emphasis wherein an understanding is offered pertaining to the ideas that frame Islamic education, whereas the second 'sociological-contemporary' deals with debates and practices centered on issues relating to present concerns. These emphases are divided to form the four thematic sections of the book.

This first of these sections, 'Theology and the Idea of Islamic Education,' lays a framework for broadly understanding the religious, specifically theological, impetuses and discourses shaping Islamic ideas of education. Seyyed Hossein Nasr's introductory chapter provides generous initial parameters for the discussion of education and couples personal reflection with experience, to foreground the importance of 'philosophy.' In doing so, he also provides ways of thinking about learning via a vertical axis in which humankind recognizes as well as fulfills their ontological dependency upon God. Tim Winter expands upon these ideas with a theological investigation of reason (*'aql*) and rationality within Islamic thought as well as how, contra contemporary divides between reason-faith,

> Islam departed from the classical European insistence on a dichotomy between body and mind. Real rationalism, that is to say, reverence for the miracle of *'aql*, must include a belief in innate knowledge, because the experiences of the senses are inadequate in explaining how we have come to know certain things.
>
> (p.35)

The last chapter in this section provides an account of Islamic philosophy as a broader epistemological treatment of the relationship between man, creation, and God. Highlighting three prominent medieval thinkers (al-Ghazali, Shuhawardi, and Ibn Arabi) David Burrell's investigation discusses how these relationships were intellectually mapped as well as their subsequent implications for conceiving knowledge and the enterprise of education.

Section two on 'Positioning Knowledge between the Student and Teacher' builds upon the themes of ontology and epistemology by converging discussion on the pedagogic process. The principle 'teacher-student' relations, and matters related to curricula are approached in lieu of the sacred role of knowledge and spiritual development within Islamic education. Abdullah Trevathan's chapter begins the section with a discussion of education as a means toward 'spirituality' and the difficulties with attempting to broach such a discourse in a secular age. Centering the discussion on spiritual sincerity (*ikhlās*), which is "designed to awaken students to the possibility of choice and to thereby transcend the self within the context of the Prophetic way. (p.68)," he argues this can create an environment of "integrity and straightforwardness permeating the school ethos (p.64)." The remaining chapters continue this focus via specific historical references in which education, as spiritual alleviation, becomes lived in practice. Sebastian Günther's chapter importantly identifies key medieval pedagogic texts and manuals that feature the diverse and subtle pedagogic treatment of the student-teacher relation. Günther impresses upon the reader that, despite their variety "the common link between these educational theories . . . is the great importance [they] assign to ethics in all aspects of teaching and learning" (p.90). Often marginalized in the study of intellectual history, descriptions of these texts suggest their axial relevance to Islamic attitudes toward learning and life. Omar Qureshi furthers these observations with a detailed summary of 'disciplinarity' and Islamic education. Considering al-Farabi, al-Kindi, Ṭāshkubrī-Zādah, and al-Ghazali, among others, Qureshi explicates and takes the reader through the complex world of the classification of 'sciences' (encompassing all forms of knowledge) and the way Muslim thinkers have historically attempted to create 'harmony and order' to the disciplines of formal learning. The final chapter of this section moves from descriptions of the intellectual architecture to the differing ways education has been institutionally organized. Talal Al-Azem does so through descriptions of elementary (*maktab*) to higher level university (*madrasa*) learning and their polyvalent apparatus for harnessing education toward a moral and social ethic, melding disparate organizations into discernible systems of pedagogy. Through these historical reflections, Al-Azem reminds us that

> however different their social structures and political contexts, and however unique their nascent intellectual directions, these new institutions, such as the Ottoman *ilmiye*, ultimately extended the metaphysical architecture and moral parameters of Islamicate society and culture.
>
> (p.121)

The penultimate section, 'Schools, Universities and Pedagogies,' aims to address some of the key contemporaneous matters facing Islamic education with reference to Muslim communities living outside Muslim-majority countries, particularly in Europe and North America. The first of these chapters by Shaikh Abdul Mabud places into historical context the importance, and frequently neglected relevancy of the 1977 World Conference on Muslim Education which, being the first of its kind, would come to shape much of the agenda on Islamic education in the West. Amongst the key intellectual contributions from the gathering came from Naquib al-Attas and his 'Islamization of knowledge' thesis, which critiqued Western concepts of knowledge (premised on Enlightenment and secular ideas of the human being) and made a plea for a renewed understanding of epistemology through the vista of an Islamic worldview placing God at its center. Nadeem Memon, focuses on the rise of Muslim schools in the West in lieu of these discourses. Commenting on progressive changes, he suggests that

> [e]arly Islamic schools in the 1980s and 1990s were inclusive by default, because there was often only one school to choose from, and it was associated with the local mosque, which also was likely the sole mosque in the city. Today many major cities have multiple schools to choose from, some of which are privately initiated and administered. As a result, religious orientations and generational differences are beginning to more authentically shape and reshape definitions of Islamic education.
>
> (p.157)

Moving toward higher education, Omar Qargha case studies Zaytuna College, America's first Muslim Liberal Arts College, and how its curricula, mission statement, and pedagogy attempt to forge traditional Islamic values and educational legacies with intellectual life in 21st century America. The final chapter of the section questions the normative assumptions of pedagogy through an elaborative exegesis of the famous 'Hadith Gabriel' narrative from the life of Muhammad by Steffen Stelzer, who presents a thought experiment and novel methodology to explore the idea of 'stories,' not just to inform *about* religious belief, but as an instrument for *teaching* religion. This distinction is made as the author explains the *hadith* and presents a unique pedagogical incident often overlooked by educational thinkers. With reference to classical exegesis and contemporary literary theory, Stelzer offers subtle and unexpected shifts in formal pedagogic assumptions that arise from the *hadith* that will make practitioners and theorists question the traditional role of teacher and student.

The final section of the book on 'Contemporary Debates' casts the analytic net still further to engage with present philosophical concerns. Susan Douglass and Ann El-Moslimany explore this intention with an exposition of the seeming conflicts that lay between Islamic education and democratic values in the United States. Through case studies of Muslim teacher experiences, they find that an exploration of democratic education and the ideas imparted therein emerge not as timeless sets of beliefs and ideas, but are rather an ongoing discussion in the quest for justice, peace, and coexistence. These form, argue the authors, new paths for understanding the growth and capability of Islamic education in the United States. Sarfaroz Niyozov's chapter builds upon this argument through the concept of 'pluralism' and Islamic education in Canada. Pluralistic education stands as a means "not just [of] tolerance, but *the active seeking of understanding across lines of difference* (p.203, emphasis in original)." As a common globalizing ideal in education, the challenge of understanding the 'other' presents new questions for traditional ideas of Islamic learning. Niyozov investigates these concerns and seeks answers within Muslim communities and their own emerging understandings of education that may cope and contribute to notions of pluralism and citizenship in the 21st century. The problem of contextualization and educational methods is apparent in the work of Yusef Waghid and Nuraan Davids, whose chapter traces the idea of 'Islamization of knowledge' around the world through schools and intellectuals who have refined and attempted to implement the original thesis of al-Attas. Suggesting that the hitherto lack of successful implementation of such ideas has been due to political rather than educational inertia, they make a strong case for a new 'imaginary of democratic citizenship' in which Muslim-majority countries take "into account the rights and dignity of all—whether majority or minority groups— . . . [toward] the greatest potential of transforming not only patriarchal constructions, but in ensuring an Islamized curriculum, which is politically, socially, and culturally inclusive" (p.234). In the final chapter of the book, Farah Ahmed and Ibrahim Lawson suggest that an internal conversation within the religion is required to achieve answers toward Waghid and Davids' inquiry. Questioning the limits of critical thinking in Islamic education, they remind us that a popular pluralism comes in a variety of guises and that there is the need to review understandings of 'critical thinking' in Islamic education in today's discourses. Arguing that a vibrant presence of critical inquiry can emerge from Islamic education, the authors suggest that "criticality is increasingly important for Muslim students in that the Islamic worldview is under constant challenge and without engaging with personal beliefs critically, young Muslims will struggle to make sense of their place in a fast changing world" (p.249).

The editors of this volume owe a substantial debt of gratitude to the contributors for their efforts, thoughts, and support in bringing this work to fruition. It is their unique collaboration that gives this work its special hue and offerings to the field of education. As a microcosm of Islamic education itself, the range and interests of the chapters will, we hope, open and encourage discussion beyond the immediacy of its religious origins to a new generation of scholars, students, and practitioners in thinking about the ways we conceive and practice education.

BIBLIOGRAPHY

Ashraf, S. A. 1982. 'Islamic principles and methods in the teaching of literature.' in *Philosophy, Literature and Fine Arts,* S. H. Nasr (Ed.), pp. 22–40. London: Hodder & Stoughton.

al-Attas, S. M. N. 1979. *Aims and Objectives of Islamic Education.* London: Arnold Overseas.

Baker, P. D. 2015. *The Schooled Society: The Educational Transformation of Global Culture.* Stanford University Press.

Berkey, J. 1992. *The Transmission of Knowledge in Medieval Cairo: A Social History of Islamic Education.* Princeton University Press.

Bloom, H. 1995. *The Western Canon.* New York: Riverhead Books.

van Bruinessen, M. and Allievi, S. 2011. *Producing Islamic Knowledge: Transmission and Dissemination in Western Europe.* Abingdon: Routledge.

Bryfman, D. (Ed.). 2014. *Experience and Jewish Education.* Los Angeles: Torah aura Productions.

Cheruvallil-Contractor, S. and Scott Baumann, A. 2015. *Islamic Education in Britain: New Pluralist Paradigms.* London: Bloomsbury Academic.

Cook, J. B. 2010. *Classical Foundations of Islamic Educational Thought.* Utah: Brigham Young University Press.

Dodge, B. 1961. *Al-Azhar, a Millennium of Muslim Learning.* Washington D.C: The Middle East Institute. And, 2011 ed. Whitefish: Literary Licensing, LLC.

Eickelman, F. D. 1978. The Art of Memory: Islamic Education and Its Social Reproduction, *Comparative Studies in Society and History* 20(4), pp. 485–516.

Endress, G. (Ed.) 2006. *Organizing Knowledge: Encyclopaedic Activities in the Pre-Eighteenth Century Islamic World.* Leiden: Brill.

Evered, E. 2012. *Empire and Education Under the Ottomans: Politics, Reform and Resistance from the Tanzimat to the Young Turks.* New York: I. B. Tauris.
Goody, J. 2003. *Islam in Europe.* Cambridge: Polity Press.
von Grunebaum, E. G. and Abel, M. T. 2003. (trans.) *Instruction of the Student: The Method of Learning.* Chicago: Starlatch Press.
Halstead, J. M. (2004). An Islamic Concept of Education, *Comparative Education* 40(1), pp. 517–529.
Hefner W. R. and Zaman, Q. M. (Ed.) 2007. *Schooling Islam: The Culture and Politics of Modern Muslim Education.* Princeton University Press.
Geelhaar, T. 2011. 'Did the Medieval West Receive a "Complete Model" of Education from Classical Islam? Reconsidering George Makdisi and His Thesis' in *Cultural Transfers in Dispute: Representations in Asia, Europe and the Arab World since the Middle Ages,* J. Feuchter, F. Hoffmann, and B. Yun (Eds.), pp. 61–83. Frankfurt: Campus Verlag GmbH.
Lowry, E. J. 2004. *Law and Education in Medieval Islam: Studies in Memory of George Makdisi.* Chippenham: E. J. W. Gibb Memorial Trust.
Makdisi, G. 1995. 'Baghdad, Bologna, and Scholasticism' in *Centres of Learning: Learning and Location in PreModern Europe and the Near East,* Jan Willem Drijvers & Alasdair A. MacDonald (Eds.), pp. 141–157. Leiden: E.J. Brill.
Makdisi, G. 1970. Madrasa and University in the Middle Ages, *Studia Islamica,* 32, pp. 255–264.
Metcalf, B. 1978. The Madrasa at Deoband: A Model for Religious Education in Modern India, *Modern Asian Studies,* 12(1), pp. 111–134.
Modood, T., Triandafyllidou, A. and Zapata-Barrero, R. 2006. *Multiculturalism, Muslims and Citizenship: A European Approach.* London: Routledge.
Morris, R. J. (Ed. and trans). 2002. *The Master and the Disciple: An Early Islamic Spiritual Dialogue on Conversion Kitab al-ʿalim wa'l-ghulam.* London: I.B.Tauris.
Murata, S. and Chittick, C. W. 2006. *Vision of Islam.* London: I.B.Tauris.
Nasr, H. S. 2012. Islamic Pedagogy: An Interview, *Islam and Science,* 10(1), pp. 7–24.
Noddings, N. 2011. *Philosophy of Education.* Boulder: Westview Press.
Panjwani, F. 2004. The "Islamic" in Islamic Education: Assessing the Discourse. *Contemporary Issues in Comparative Education,* 7(1), pp. 19–29.
Peters, S. R. 2010. *The Concept of Education.* London: Routledge.
Piderit J. J. and Morey, M. M. 2012. *Teaching the Tradition: Catholic Themes in Academic Disciplines.* Oxford: Oxford University Press.
Pring, R. 2005. *Philosophy of Education.* London: Continuum.
Schacht, J. 1964. An early Murciʾite treatise: The Kitāb al-ʿĀlim wa-l-mutaʿallim [Abū Ḥanīfa/al-Samarqandī]. *Oriens,* 17, pp. 96–117.
Shahin, A. 2013. *New Directions in Islamic Education: Pedagogy and Identity Formation.* Leicester: Kube Publishing Ltd.
Rahman, S., Street, T., and Tahiri, H. 2008. *The Unity of Science in the Arabic Tradition: Science, Logic, Epistemology and their Interactions.* Basel: Springer.
Rosenthal, F. 2006. *Knowledge Triumphant: The Concept of Knowledge in Medieval Islam.* Leiden: Brill.
Watt, M., W. 2010. *Islam and the Integration of Society.* Abingdon: Routledge.
Webb, H. 2010. *The Medieval Heart.* New Haven: Yale University Press.
Waghid, Y. 2011. *Conceptions of Islamic Education: Pedagogical Framings.* Oxford: Peter Lang Publishing Inc.

Wan Daud, W. M. N. 1989. *The Concept of Knowledge in Islam: And Its Implications for Education in a Developing*. London: Continuum International Publishing.
Wilson, O. E. 1999. *Consilience: The Unity of Knowledge*. London: Abacus.
Zurayk, K. C. 1968. (trans.) *The Refinement of Character*. Beirut: The American University of Beirut.

Part I

Theology and the Idea of Islamic Education

1 Philosophical Considerations of Islamic Education—Past and Future

Interview with Seyyed Hossein Nasr

Seyyed Hossein Nasr

This chapter is a transcript of an interview with Professor Seyyed Hossein Nasr conducted in January 2014 (The George Washington University, USA) for the purpose of this volume. Professor Nasr is an internationally renowned scholar in the field of Islamic Studies and has written extensively on the philosophy of Islamic education and the 'Islamization of Knowledge.' In order to draw out further reflections from his extensive work, this interview centers upon his educational reflections and thoughts for the field. The following transcript is an edited version of the interview conducted by Omar Qargha, a contributor to this volume.

PRINCIPLES OF ISLAMIC EDUCATION

1) *Considering your research and experiences in Islamic education over the past half century, academically and as a practitioner, could you comment initially on whether there are motivating principles (or a logos) which one may identify signifying Islamic education?*

If you mean rethinking this question in light of the principles of education, then a caveat should be asserted concerning the fact that there exists (by the principle of necessity and not accidentally) divergent ways through which one can understand Islamic education. This is manifest, for example, in the ways curricula, disciplines, and academic structures are apparently different from one another in Persia, Turkey, or Malaysia, etc. However, there are also, and often more importantly, convergent ways in which these ostensible differences become secondary to what may be thought of as a continuing theme or 'pattern' to Islamic education. This is essential to remember considering the manner in which the destructive influences of modern life have ruptured and often destroyed premodern Islamic ideas of knowledge, the sacred, identity, and life. That we can still speak of a functioning and vibrant idea of Islamic education in the 21st century is itself remarkable. Whatever may be said of the differences in the practice of Islamic education in various countries, there is a unifying inheritance, which remains consistently 'Islamic.'

Islam has never encouraged nor itself created a monoculture as well as no formal *magisterium* or religious councils controlling religious learning. The history of the *madrasa* system seems emblematic of this process of decentralization, wherein the principles of learning and teaching remained decidedly universal despite local differences. When it comes to studying the details of Islamic educational systems, one discovers that learning, while being based on universal Islamic principles, was tailored to the particular culture and social conditions of that part of the Islamic world in which an educational institution functioned. This diversity was not an historical peculiarity but something encouraged by Muslim societies, a fact that is often forgotten today. Subsequently, when we think about Islamic education, we must think of 'diversity within unity.'

There are local differences in various aspects of Islamic civilization, for example, between a Moroccan mosque and one in Lahore or somewhere farther east. However, there are also certain principles and forms that are universal and shared between them from vegetal designs, arabesques, vaulting, and geometric patterns, etc., to their shared concepts of space. There were also local conditions, be they related to climate or culture, that though these mosques do not look identical they bear close family resemblance to one another. The result of this is that someone from Scandinavia, for example, who has had no previous contact with the Islamic world, seeing a Moroccan mosque and then a Persian or Indian one, would notice that they are from the same civilization; he could discern the unity and certain profound similarities but at the same time their local differences. Although these examples demonstrate 'unity in diversity' within Islamic architecture, for Islamic education, the same can be said in that it follows a similar historical and cultural trajectory. It would be useful for the emerging academic field of comparative Islamic educational studies to be perceptive of this way of looking at things. Returning to your question, one may say that this is how we might understand the *logos* for Islamic education, with the *logos* referring to the principles that created so many Islamic educational institutions under very diverse conditions.

As for the *madrasa* system, certain disciplines and subjects were taught universally in them, such as the Quran, the Arabic language, *Ḥadīth* (Prophetic sayings and teachings), *fiqh* (law), *kalām* (theology), historical aspects of the *sīrah* (Prophetic biography), etc. Other aspects of the curricula were not uniform, as we see, for example, by taking the curriculum of al-Azhar University in the Fāṭimid period and comparing it to the Niẓāmiyya schools in the Seljuq era. It is very interesting to note that there are many common elements between them, but they also had a number of differing features as well. In general, one can observe, despite some local differences, the universal presence of a distinct philosophy of education related to the principles of Islamic learning (underpinned by knowing God) and subsequently a system for the transmission of knowledge and teacher-student relations, all of which have held remarkably intact as a living tradition till today, at least in certain places in the Islamic world.

REVIVING 'AUTHENTIC' ISLAMIC EDUCATION

> 2) *With the associated problems of colonization and secular modernity still prominent within Muslim-majority countries, could you comment on how specifically these countries (as well as elsewhere in the world) one may begin to revive authentic conceptions of Islamic education rooted in historical and spiritual traditions.*

It is accurate to say that in the Islamic world, Western influences have come to dominate more and more of the educational and intellectual landscape in nearly every sphere since the 19th century, except for some of the *madrasas*. It is for this reason that the *madrasa* is a good starting point for our discussion. Their exemptions from the modernizing processes in the Islamic world were perhaps due in some places to geographical isolation or the fact that they were excluded from modernized segments of society. However, as they exist today, they do not provide (on the whole) sustainable models of retaining institutional identities for Islamic education. As a consequence of historical processes, the subjects taught there, by which I mean their formal curriculum, have become increasingly limited. This fact is also true, as far as Islamic subjects are concerned, of those *madrasas* that were more openly influenced by modernistic ideas. In a *madrasa* in Egypt a thousand years ago, for example, you would have studied mathematics, but even as recently as three centuries ago such subjects began to be excluded from the curricula. There was a shriveling in many areas of the curriculum even before the advent of European modernism and colonial contact. Yet, this process was not uniform throughout the Islamic world. There are of course variations and in some places, such as the Indian subcontinent, 'traditional' education, which was of course religious, survived in more recognizable ways as related to traditional scholarly models, for example, the Farangi Mahal with its intellectual heritage going back to 11th-century Baghdad and the Niẓāmiyya Schools.

With the arrival of modernizing trends, however, and the colonial context, many of the academic 'Islamic' disciplines were either neglected or recast in terms often alien to their origins. The problem was further exacerbated by the elite education of indigenous colonized classes along Western models, which further marginalized classical pedagogic models. The stark difference between religious and nonreligious secular learning remains evident till this day in such countries as Iran, Pakistan and Egypt, wherein almost 90% of the children of the elite classes attend Western schools. The significance of these trends, amidst the preponderance of secular thinking based on secular rationalism, which can be observed around the Islamic world, is problematic to the extent that they restrict or reject other 'forms of knowing' and 'ways of being' in the world and cause an indoctrination of the Muslim intelligentsia.

To help create more balance in Islamic educational institutions and provide alternatives to these often globalizing and monopolistic modernist tendencies, we must revisit the idea of the classical *madrasa* and what it has stood for traditionally, namely, as an institution standing at the apotheosis of authentic Islamic intellectual inquiry in the Islamic world. Yes, we are facing a major crisis. Within the context of existing conditions, I believe that there are some practical steps that can be taken. Firstly, to strengthen the *madrasa* system wherever it continues to exist, which does not simply mean to start merely teaching physics or other natural sciences in them i.e., to turn them into modern secular universities where one can gain a degree in dentistry with a faculty of religious studies on the side, as we see, for example, as what happened to al-Azhar (Egypt) during the past half century. The *madrasa* presents an exciting meeting point between different worlds of understanding/knowing and has a reality far from the negative clichés that many are ascribed to it today. However, any revivification of the *madrasa* system must be authentic and faithful to Islamic traditions of learning and the sanctity of the process of Islamic education itself.

There are examples in the modern Islamic world of such attempts but with varying degrees of success. For example, the Qarawiyyin in Morocco, among the Islamic world's oldest and most prominent centers of learning, has been co-opted into the theological faculty of the University of Rabat and has become a Divinity School in the modern sense. At the al-Azhar, there have been attempts, unsuccessful for the most part, from the point of view of Islamic education, to modernize the curriculum by adding new faculties such as engineering. Such piecemeal attempts are not what I am alluding to, for they only demonstrate further an incapacity to think imaginatively about the ways Muslims can educate and nurture minds holistically and in conformity with an Islamic perspective.

There is a very important point to add here. There has been a movement in some Islamic countries to extend the *madrasa* system, especially, for example, in Afghanistan after the Soviet invasion ended. Saudi Arabia established new *madrasas* there and also in Pakistan with far-reaching political consequences. Some of these efforts have proven to be very problematic with the creation of institutions that are not traditional Islamic *madrasas* but represent an extremist understanding of Islam and are closed to intellectual and spiritual dimensions of the religion. They are creating a kind of narrow exclusivism at best and hatred and violence at worst, both of which have not solved the deep-rooted educational problems of those respective countries. The result has been the rise of the Taliban, which colloquially in Persian means students of a *madrasa*. We need something more profound than what has occurred in recent years there.

There is another important factor involved in order to revive these traditional systems of learning namely, political will. In Turkey, under Kamal Ataturk, political will existed but for other purposes when after 1924 modern *madrasas* were created under government supervision so that they could be controlled by the state. However, these efforts failed to a large extent to create well-rounded inclusive individuals able to engage their faith with consideration of the challenges of the modern world (although there have been some exceptions). Let us also consider other Muslim countries such as Iran, Egypt, parts of Muslim India, Pakistan and Tunisia, for example, where the demand for a revival of an authentic *madrasa* system can be carried out in authentic ways if there is the political will combined with a cultural wisdom ensuring that institutions created do not become insular and irrelevant to the contemporary world.

Secondly, and in parallel with this effort, there is the possibility to create from scratch small centers of learning, not of the size of a large *madrasa* with ten thousand students, but small units of Islamic education operating at an intellectually advanced level and incorporating some nontraditional subjects that could be integrated into an Islamic system through the so-called 'Islamization' of knowledge. The concept of Islamization of knowledge is something that many, including myself, have been speaking about for fifty years and has involved so far mostly rhetoric with little actually being done as far as creating integrated Islamic educational systems are concerned. However, there are now attempts to implement here and there such ideas including in the US and in Iran; for example, where there is a major movement to Islamize the humanities taught in universities; yet even there one does not, as yet, see many concrete results on a large scale. When we organized the 1977 World Congress on Muslim Education in Makkah, the goal was to create an Islamic integrated system of knowledge of academic disciplines. Thereafter, some Islamic universities were created which have become 'Islamic' only in name. Their features resemble Islamic education in the sense that they have law and theological faculties based on Islamic ideas and models, but you can also study in these institutions mathematics, physics, engineering, etc., that are not at all integrated into an Islamic philosophy of science and learning and are completely secular. These universities do provide an Islamic ambience for learning but in terms of intellectually integrating and providing new ways to conceive knowledge Islamically, little has been achieved.

Let me return to the small units about which I was speaking. I will give you an example of what I have in mind. In 1973, we established the Iranian Academy of Philosophy, which was autonomous from governmental interference. We had created it not only to study Islamic but also Western philosophy from the perspective of Islam. That institution has been active for some fifty years and is still one of the most important philosophical institutes in Iran today, even in comparison with places like Qom and has done much to revive the Islamic intellectual tradition.

I believe that, in the present situation, small units of learning can achieve wonders. In relation to this idea, I can perhaps also say a word about education in Pakistan. I would often visit the country in the 1960s and '70s and see, among many scholars and authorities, the Education Minister, Ishtiaq Husain Quraishi. We spoke together about preserving quality in education when there was so much pressure to accept more and more students.

I offered him the advice to start a few small institutions with twenty to fifty students, trying to train them at a high level in traditional Islamic subjects, especially the Quran and *Ḥadīth*, law, logic, philosophical theology, and philosophy proper, but also have them learn Western subjects from an Islamic point of view with the goal that the students would later act as cultural bridges. Unfortunately, my advice was not followed except in a couple of cases. Instead, the large and often alien systems we have today continued to flourish there and elsewhere, eating into the bones and sinews of the culture in Pakistan and other Islamic countries. What we have in much of the Islamic world today then could be comparable to a situation in which 90% of all affluent children in Texas would be studying at Islamic schools. This is merely jest but shows where the Islamic world is right now.

3) These smaller institutions you have mentioned, do you foresee them as subject-specific or supplementing other educational entities?

I believe that they should be relatively subject-specific especially at the beginning (perhaps like the older *Ecoles* in France). We have a couple of good examples, such as the School of Art and Architecture established in Jordan on the model of the Prince of Wales School of Art and Architecture located in London and established by Prince Charles, based on traditional principles. I was also consulted in the founding of this latter important institution. This is the kind of school that is subject-specific but within a universal, traditional perspective and is what I have in mind. It trains a small number of people in traditional and authentic forms of Islamic art and architecture and refrains from doing much else in order to preserve their intellectual concentration. Gradually as they grow, such institutions can be brought together to create an Islamic college or university which can then offer degrees in several subjects. This brings to mind an important point, namely that a tradition of learning can be revived only when it is authentic and faithful to past practices and is not insular or inflexible in the world it inhabits. As such, rethinking pedagogical elements should include an educational ambience and such matters as the relationship between students and teacher, even the place of where they sit (typically on the ground) when possible. In the Iranian Academy of Philosophy, we all sat on the ground when I taught, which was a deliberate attempt to restore an element of traditional pedagogy.

These institutions could also operate at earlier education levels. I know that there have been a few successful schools, for example, in Iran, achieving the kind of goals we have mentioned by focusing on the humanities at precollege levels. However, I would suggest that for now we concentrate most of all at the higher end, on students who may then become university, high school, or elementary schoolteachers themselves or teachers of the teachers of such groups.

4) How does one begin to bring about a rapprochement between classic Islamic pedagogic perspectives and those developed through contemporary social sciences?

I do not think that it is even necessary to do such a thing in most cases. Firstly, perspectives developed through the Western social sciences are not harmonious even in relation to each other. Rather, there are many different perspectives in the West at war with one another. There is not a homogenous Western philosophy of education, for example, except in the common goal of having a secular outlook of the world, generally. Secondly, the goal for Islamic education should be to develop something organic that is Islamic while benefiting from the experiences of the West and other parts of the world including India, China, etc., and to know that being 'Islamic' means also to benefit judiciously on the basis of Islamic principles from other traditions in the world.

COMPATIBILITY OF WESTERN NOTIONS OF EDUCATION WITH ISLAMIC EDUCATION

> *5) Turning now to comparisons between Islamic and predominantly Western ideas of education: Do you feel the exhortation of 'selfhood' as defined within the Western liberal educational canon can be compatible with notions of selfhood that Islamic education seeks to inculcate?*

This is difficult to say. Perhaps if we were to consider the idea of the "self" within the diversity of modern 'Western' liberal education firstly as a misnomer it would be a start. As for Islamic education, it seeks to deliver us from our *nafs*, or lower self, and not simply educate the self. If we were to consider the diversity of modern 'Western' liberal education, we would first of all realize that 'liberal' in its current meaning is a misnomer. The term goes back to the *artes liberales* in Latin. In the premodern Christian West, and in association with the *trivium* and the *quadrivium*, education was seen as part of a universal religious training of mind and soul with which the *artes liberales* was concerned. This view became, however, secularized from the Renaissance onward and from the 18th century, the soul and mind of Western man came to be viewed in mainstream education as operating mostly independent of God, i.e., in the secularity of the self. This Western perspective is therefore not one that can be entertained by Islamic education, although there are elements in Islamic education that may correspond to an authentic Western liberal arts education. Traditionally this type of education was referred to in Islam as *adab*. The Western *trivium* especially has correspondences to what was taught in traditional Islamic *adab* education. Therefore, within historical Islamic conceptions of education, there is a correspondence to the medieval Western liberal arts, but the content of subjects were not the same and this becomes particularly evident for modern Western education, which moved so far away from its own medieval past.

Secular education in the modern West nurtures the creation of "Promethean man" with independent rational faculties and so on, whereby the spiritual aspects and facilities are almost entirely neglected, such elements as building a relation to God or cultivating means of access to the higher levels of consciousness.

6) Do you perceive a difference in the role of the teacher in Islamic education from that of the teacher in modern educational institutions, such as high schools and universities in Western contexts?

There are two very important matters to consider. First of all, in Islamic education, there is a great esteem and reverence for the teacher, as there is in other traditional civilizations, be they Buddhist or Hindu, etc., whereas school teaching is one of the least well-paid positions in modern society and there is little respect for the teaching profession. Teachers have direct and very human relations with their students, like a parent, and Islamic society perceived the essentiality of this relation for an all-round spiritual and intellectual education that is not founded merely on formal mental instruction. Today, only in certain preparatory or boarding schools in the West do you have the same kind of relationship, where a lot of time is made for students inside and outside of the classroom to interact with their teachers, whereas in most high schools and universities this is lost almost entirely.

Secondly, in the Islamic world, the teacher was expected to be not only learned in his subject but also to embody certain moral and ethical norms, and this was not seen as being divorced from his role as an instructor, i.e. knowledge and ethics were bound together in the pedagogic role model. A person who became a teacher was highly respected in Islamic society to the extent that according to a Prophetic tradition (*ḥadīth*) that, after the prophets, it is the teachers and scholars who are the most important members of a society. For example, there is the famous saying by the cousin of the Prophet of Islam ʿAlī, who said, "Whosoever has taught me a single word, I have become his slave." A related point concerns the status of knowledge in the West, which, having become increasingly secularized, has divorced ethics and spirituality from learning and in the educational sense become progressively utility oriented. In Islam, knowledge is considered a sacred 'light' and those involved in the process of transmitting knowledge have always been seen as transmitting a Divine gift and thus performing a religious act and duty. This is the reason why early schools in the Islamic world (as well as in Christian Europe) developed in or near places of worship, as most teachers were also religious scholars and, in the Medieval West, priests.

ISLAMIC EDUCATION IN THE 21ST CENTURY

7) What may an Islamic education look like in a globalized 21st century world?

Let me start by saying that I do not take the idea of the 'global village' very seriously. People often speak about this metaphor as being of great importance. Yet it seems to me that we cannot speak quite seriously about it until the diversity of cultures ebbs or when the cultures of New York City and Cairo become similar, for example. I believe in the value and the genuineness of all traditional cultures that have survived over the centuries, making them all precious. Thus I am against the homogenization of them. The scenario itself of a global village is not to be taken very seriously in my consideration. Yes, the process of homogenization is afoot, but it is not the only reality. In fact, it is against such trends that de-Westernization is taking place in many places. Mass media, which makes communication much easier on a certain level, also presents challenges to authentic communication on a deeper level.

If we want to see changes of the kind mentioned earlier, there must be a return to the principles and norms of Islamic learning and the application of them to our present-day conditions. Now, such an undertaking will take time, intellectual effort, and of course Divine Mercy and Succor. It also engenders an important yet forgotten element of the educational experience, namely, the cultivation of noble character (*adab*). As for your question, 'What would it look like,' I would say that there would be a certain amount of continuity with that which had existed previously in the traditional Islamic world and was then eclipsed to a large extent by the tumultuous events of the 19th century. Along with the revivification of the models of learning that have existed, there would also need to be the teaching of new subjects based, as much as possible, on a religious framework. For example, when Euclid's work on geometry was translated into Arabic, Muslims studied it and wrote about and 'Islamized' it so that there was a level of continuity but also a modification on the level of philosophical understanding of geometry that took place to conform it to what we call an 'Islamic perspective.'

Whether such institutions look like the Nizamiyya or the Azhar is uncertain, but with new subjects added from Western models, these new educational units will have little to do with so-called Islamic universities, which are often divorced from authentic Islamic intellectual traditions except in the fields of law and theology. A field that is easier to start with, outside the purely religious disciplines, is the humanities and to some extent the social sciences, all of which are easier to integrate into an Islamic perspective than let us say quantum mechanics. Without the intellectual effort to both absorb and reject critically various forms of modern knowledge on the basis of an Islamic philosophy and praxis of education, it is not therefore possible to create an authentic Islamic educational system that is both Islamic and contemporary.

2 Education as 'Drawing-Out'
The Forms of Islamic Reason

Tim Winter

From a theologian's perspective, the word 'education' is likely to trigger a parsing of the disputes over its etymology: Does the Latin *e* (or *ex*) *duco* primarily suggest a process of inculcation from without or, rather, as the literal sense requires, a 'drawing-out' from within? Is the Muslim educator's task mainly one of supplying information guided by theocentric propositions or one of nurturing and cultivating a virtuous form of life and a religious awareness that inhere already in *homo religiosus*? Evidently both will be variously involved in any Muslim pedagogic process; but locating the balance between educational input and introspective discovery will not be a straightforward task. In addressing this question, this essay will offer some reflections on the significance of *ʿaql*, often translated as 'intellect' or 'reason,' in the religion's guiding assumptions about the nature of mental and moral uplift. This will allow us to entertain the question of whether Islam ought to be seen by its educational theorists as preeminently a religion of reason or of inspiration. On this issue hang significant implications for pedagogy and curriculum design in the modern context.

Muslim theologians and educationalists have often wished to champion the revelation as a supreme advocate of reason, seen as an objective canon and method that enlightens an otherwise ignorant (*jāhil*) human self. God's word, as speech (*nuṭq*), is said to be the very ground and guarantor of logic (*manṭiq*), and the Book presents itself as a series of arguments accessible to the mind. This theme has been ratcheted up in modern-Muslim discussions about education as these have emerged from 19th- and 20th-century apologetics—more or less anti-Christian and anti-Western—which were concerned to present the scripture as a quintessential appeal to man's *ʿaql*.

> Read through a Biblical concordance [says Rashīd Riḍā, d.1935], and you will never find the word 'intellect' [*ʿaql*], or any synonym for this human faculty which raises human beings above the entire animal kingdom, whether it be 'insight' [*lubb*] or 'intelligence' [*nuhā*]. This is because this category is never mentioned in either the Old or the New Testament, since it is not a basis for the understanding of religion and its arguments and lessons; neither is the Bible's religious discourse

> rationally oriented or based on reason. Similarly absent are the words 'thinking' [*tafakkur*], 'contemplation' [*tadabbur*], and looking at the world, all of which are among the greatest functions of the intellect. By contrast, the intellect is referred to approximately fifty times by name in the Noble Qur'ān; the phrase 'people of insight' [*ulu'l-albāb*], which is to say, 'people of intellect,' appears more than ten times, while 'people of discernment' [*ulu'l-nuhā*] is also to be found, once, at the end of Sūra Ṭāhā. Furthermore, these Qur'ānic references mostly apply to God's signs [*āyāt*], and to the fact that those who are addressed by them, who understand them and receive guidance through them, are the intelligent [*'uqalā'*]. Most of these verses pertain to the physical universe, which point to God's knowledge, will, wisdom, and compassion.
>
> (Riḍā 1985, 195)

Such polemics were reactive against a European belief in 'Oriental unreason,' which imperial discourses were propounding as the explanation for the East's status as a mass of unknowing ripe for Western uplift and discipline. Ernest Rénan (d. 1892 AD), riding the warhorse of European triumphalism, influentially attacked Islam as a kind of militant Judaism, describing it as an irrational legalism, which rejected the spirit of reason and needed to be fought without mercy.[1] It was this atmosphere of fierce polemic that sharpened the characteristic modern-Muslim apologist's retort that Islam is, in fact, quintessentially reasonable, a view that among some believers also drew strength from the rising polemic against Sufism. Ali Bulaç has documented the recurrence of this Islam = rationality trope as perhaps the most characteristic apologetic motif in 20th-century Islam, in Turkey and elsewhere.[2] In the Western milieu, many converts to Islam also claim that they are attracted to what they regard as the religion's clear, rationally accessible teachings, said to be unobscured by elaborate mysteries.[3] But it is not only insiders who wish to take this view. Non-Muslim academic accounts, which have largely left Rénan behind, today frequently draw attention to the central role that reason and logic play in Islamic theology.[4] Oliver Leaman, for instance, has claimed that "whereas Judaism is strongly linked with ethnicity, and Christianity with a leap of faith, Islam has successfully grown, by contrast with these religions, by stressing its rationality and evidentiality."[5] Josef van Ess, author of the greatest history of Islamic theology ever to have appeared in a European language, concludes in rather similar terms: "Christianity speaks of the 'mysteries' of faith; Islam has nothing like that. For Saint Paul, reason belongs to the realm of the 'flesh,' for Muslims, reason, *'aql*, has always been the chief faculty granted human beings by God."[6]

Virtually all these attempts, Muslim and non-Muslim, to portray Islam as the reasonable religion par excellence have sought to root themselves in the Qur'ānic text. "The Qur'ān does indeed," says Leaman, "display an unusual commitment to argument and logic in its self-explanation,"[7] and a systematic exposition of this has been offered by Rosalind Gwynne.[8] Such characterizations of Qur'ānic religion as implicitly hospitable to dialectical processes and a natural theology are now widely current in the academic study of Islam.

The equation is not uncontested, however. Contrasting sharply with this model of essential Islamic rationality and reasonableness, we note the increasingly salient modern fundamentalist tendencies, emanating frequently from Saudi Arabia and tracing their ancestry back to Ibn Taymīya's (d. 1328 AD) inventive reading of scripture, which rejected systematic dialectics and was markedly skeptical about reason's formal claims in matters of religion. Such thinkers held that all-important truth, which is to say, truth that saves, is necessarily explicit in the Book, from which "We have omitted nothing" (6:38). Scripture is 'clear' (*mubīn*), and God has not burdened humanity with the requirement to evolve elaborate metaphysical interpretations either of His evidences in nature or in the specific revelation of the Qur'ān. Those who do so are guilty of underestimating both the clarity of the Book and the benign intentions of a God who wishes all to be saved, including those incapable of following a syllogism.[9]

Both advocates and minimizers of reason source their positions in scripture. Who is normative? One way of answering might be to look further back in history, beyond the modern apologetics, which are so transparently reactive to a colonial history, and note the very prevalent favoring of 'reason,' rather than a Taymīyan literalism, in premodern *madrasa* curricula, which based education on sciences of *naẓar*, formal theology and legal theory sustained by a firm logical armature. To support this, one can easily document the notable thinness of support for Ibn Taymīya's Ḥanbalite fideism, and the centrality of sophisticated philosophical theology in the medieval curricula (the manuals of Jurjānī, Ījī, Nasafī, and Taftāzānī and their later epitomes, and then the commentaries that these generated). The community's scholars largely welcomed the logic-based theologies, which, definitively schematized by Rāzī, believed that they traced their roots back to early Islam's need to deploy some form of dialectic against schismatics and vindicated themselves through reference to God's own debating techniques in scripture. *Kalām*, particularly in its later expressions, presented itself as a fiercely inductive and rationalistic discipline, according to some more so even than Islamic philosophy (*falsafa*).[10] A standard *kalām* text such as Taftāzānī's (d. 1390 AD) *Sharḥ al-ʿAqā'id* devotes three quarters of its length to systematic metaphysics (*ilāhiyyāt*), with the remainder dedicated to such issues of prophecy and the afterlife as can only be demonstrated through revelation. Such was Islam's classical norm. Yet the recent, post-postcolonial repristination of a Taymīyan discourse rooted in a particular view of the intentions of scripture and the wisdom of the ordinary believer cannot be dismissed so easily as un-Qur'ānic. An arbitration is required, and this must begin with a scrutiny of the texts themselves.

The Qur'ān is, like most prophetic deliverances, a staccato, ecstatic collocation of insights, promises, and forebodings. Famously, but not uniquely (one thinks of the Psalms, for instance), it feels little need to respect conventional notions of thematic sequence.[11] Despite Gwynne's typology of divine debating techniques, most Muslims experience it not as a set of integrated cumulative arguments, but as a dithyramb that affectively transforms the soul. The text does contain arguments but remains manifestly dissimilar to the kind of systematic manual normal in the *madrasa* universe. Its frequent difficulty has also made it an unpromising text for literalists, and even they were often caught up in the mystical tide that represented the major alternative to the epistemology of *kalām*. Until recent times, literalist piety typically found its outlet not in purely formalist religion, but in forms of Sufism, typically in its normative Junaydī garb.

It is easy to see how this happened. Much of the scripture's power appears to lie in aurality and in our human receptivity to the Ineffable's mantic voice. Its language and imagery are anagogical, not linear; it educates through the divine presence actualized in God's uncreated speech.[12] Qur'ānic cantillation, the Islamic art (that is to say, mediator of the sacred) par excellence, thus appears as a purely nonrational mode of education, of 'drawing-out.'

Here is Isabelle Eberhardt, visiting an Algiers mosque:

> The place was cool and dark as I went in, and a handful of oil lamps were the only source of light. A feeling of ancient Islam, tranquil and mysterious.
>
> Stood for a long time near the *mihrab*. Somewhere far behind us, a clear, fresh, high voice went up, a dreamlike voice that took turns with that of the elderly imam standing in the *mihrab* where he recited the *fatiha* with his quavering voice.
>
> Standing next to each other, we all prayed as we listened to the exhilarating yet solemn exchange between those two voices. The one in front of us sounded old and hoarse, but gradually grew louder till it was strong and powerful, while the other one seemed to come from somewhere high up in the mosque's dark reaches as it sang triumphantly in regular intervals of its unshakeable, radiant faith in Allah and his Prophet . . . I felt almost in ecstasy, my chest tightening and my heart soaring up toward the heavenly regions that the second voice seemed to be coming from in a tone of melancholy joy, utterly convinced and at peace.
>
> Oh, to lie upon the rugs of some silent mosque, far from the mindless noise of city life, and, eyes closed, the soul's gaze turned heavenwards, listen to Islam's song forever!
>
> (Eberhardt 2002, 55–6)

This is the Qur'ān educating through presence and 'healing' (17:82), as a balm for hearts injured by doubts and sinful desires. The scripture seems to imply that our tragedy is an ignorant alienation from the Real, the sole source of wholeness and appropriate behavior, and that only heaven can send down the rain that revives the spirit. The Book does not seem to be saving, or 'drawing-out,' through formal analogies and static inference; it does not deny such things, but it insists on an epistemology of 'descending upon your heart' (2:97), for its author declares himself incomparable and unreachable by the faculties of perception (6:104). It is no coincidence that Islam showed a historic hospitality to Platonism, regretted deeply by modernist champions of a presumed Averroist rationalism but noted in detail by Henry Corbin and others; and this is to be attributed not only to the Platonic habit of resolving all diversity to the completely unitive Source—so congenial to Islam's rejection of a triune or other differentiation within the Godhead—but also to the sense that, as in the *Timaeus*, the One is manifest aesthetically and, particularly, musically, in the ground of creation. Ion, in the early dialogue with Socrates, acknowledges that as a singer of poems he is an instrument played upon by a supernatural power. And the Prophet Muḥammad, like him, is an Aeolian harp: the wind 'plays' him, while his mortal personhood contributes nothing; the Voice which 'draws out' is therefore the pure sound and presence of the Unseen. God's education of him takes place so far from the schoolroom that he is 'unlettered.' The Qur'ān, described in a hadith as "a woodwind pipe from the kin of David,"[13] is in this rather Platonic sense understood as the voice of the divine substrate of creation; it is the true music of the spheres.[14] The ascent to the One, therefore, is not through the logic-chopping powers of our 'dingy clay,' but through acquiring a true and loving ear that can properly hear this music. True learning is, as Suhrawardī put it, an escape from the city of reason to the wilderness where God can be found.[15] This is education not by the accumulation of premises and proofs, but through the deepening of our ontological consciousness.

Perhaps, some souls have imagined, this is the lesson of the Qur'ānic prologue to history where the Devil, Iblīs, falls from grace. God has commanded the angelic orders to prostrate themselves before Adam, the newly created, sleepy creature, and they do so, "except Iblīs," who protests, "You have created me of fire, and him of clay" (7:12). Hence this proud worshiper of God Alone, who uses logic to defy God's own command, is cast out to become the calamity of the world.[16] Meditating upon this story, some Sufis have taken it as a condign warning against a presumptuous, vainglorious reliance upon reason and so against the first sin, which originated in a syllogism. God's command, for His lovers, is enough; His beauty makes all argument irrelevant. Here is Rūmī:

> O master, (you must avoid) the analogy drawn by the low senses in regard to the Revelation which is illimitable.
>
> If your sensuous ear is fit for (understanding) the letter (of the Revelation), know that your ear that receives the unseen (meaning) is deaf.
>
> The first person who produced these paltry analogies in the presence of the Lights of God was Iblis.

He said, "Beyond doubt fire is superior to earth: I am of fire, and he (Adam) is of dingy earth."

(Nicholson 1926, 184–5)

For this hugely influential reading of the Qur'ān (and Rūmī remains unchallenged as Islam's greatest poet), love is the Burāq, the miraculous winged beast that helps us ascend to true knowledge. Reason, the steed of the formal theologians, is a noble part of God's creation, but is desperately slow and limited.

> Intelligence is (like) swimming in the seas: he (the swimmer) is not saved: he is drowned at the end of the business.
>
> Leave off swimming, let pride and enmity go; this is not the Oxus or a (lesser) river, it is an ocean;
>
> And, moreover, (it is) the deep Ocean without refuge: it sweeps away the seven seas like straw.
>
> Love is as a ship for the elect: seldom is calamity (the result); for the most part it is deliverance.
>
> Sell intelligence and buy bewilderment: intelligence is opinion, while bewilderment is (immediate) vision.
>
> Sacrifice your understanding in the presence of Muṣṭafā (Muḥammad): say, "*Ḥasbiya 'llāh*, for God sufficeth me."
>
> (Nicholson, 1926, 349–50)[17]

Muslims have thus found themselves dispersed over a very wide epistemological spectrum. The Qur'ān is open to so many receptions that Ibn Rushd, the iconic Arab 'rationalist,' can use its verses as exemplary cases of rational induction,[18] and modern-Muslim rationalists like Fazlur Rahman can and do use it to dispel mystical fancies. The *madrasa* curricula have been overwhelmingly dialectical, not inspirational.[19] But the fact of the 'uncreated' Qur'ān's origin in the empyrean has made it also the religion's theophany of theophanies, a fully mystic fact, whose very shape or sound inspires an ecstasy that seems to 'draw out' God more reliably than any logical inference ever could.

The Qur'ān thus seems to be the authentic root of two disciplines whose mutual relations are controversial: formal systematic theology (*kalām*) and Sufism (*taṣawwuf*). Sufism was typically absent from the scholastic curriculum, which historically gave pride of place to *kalām*. Formal theological texts defined orthodoxy; yet they seem to have been less influential upon the minds of most Muslims than the emotional Sufism of the likes of Rūmī, whose pessimism about *naẓar* is so salient. Formal education was concentrated in the *madrasa*, which coexisted in complex ways with the Sufi lodge, scene of a very different pedagogy, which far from being marginal was often much more attuned to the concerns of popular piety. The masses' desire both for direct access to the holy and for a commonsensical reading of the plain meaning of scripture ensured the ongoing popularity of Sufism for many centuries.

Thinkers such as Ghazālī, who are normative in Sunnism, spoke of *kalām* as a valid discipline within its own, essentially apologetic and even therapeutic space, as a useful tool to wield against formalistic errors, notably those of Avicennist philosophers and the Muʿtazila. As though to refute those who characterized Muslim theology as denying the rationality of God, he insisted that the formal rules of logic have an objective validity that must characterize the divine power and acts.[20] As the shape of his own career implied, however, he regarded inner experience, or what he calls 'tasting' (*dhawq*), as superior; although it can never challenge the truths drawn out by theology; rather, it supplies a more authentic proof for them.

Before the modern decay of the old bifurcation, processes of synthetic renewal, which often drew in individuals acclaimed as the 'renewers' (*mujaddidūn*) of their centuries, furnished a key dynamic for Islamic religion and history. Tendencies perceived as erroneous or even heretical were often understood as the result of an imbalance toward one type of epistemology at the expense of the other, when *madrasa* or Sufi lodge evolved excessively at each other's expense, damaging the proper counterpoint between the two. Ghazālī (d. 1111 AD) is remembered as the most obvious and successful case of a polemicist who reinvigorated the synthesis and the symbiosis. Other claimants might include Ibn ʿArabī (d .1240 AD), ʿAbd al-Raḥman Jāmī (d. 1486 AD),[21] Ibn Kemāl (d. 1534 AD), Shāh Walī Allāh al-Dihlawī (d. 1762 AD), and Sait Nursi (d. 1960 AD). Sachiko Murata and William Chittick have reflected extensively on this inner Islamic metabolism of a complexly symbiotic dual epistemology, identifying *kalām* with the principle of drawing out inferences about God as dissimilarity (*tanzīh*), and Sufism with the principle of experiencing God as similarity (*tashbīh*), the dyadic categorization of divine predicates as Names of Rigor and Names of Beauty was perhaps the most familiar outcome.[22] These two inexorable consequences of the postulate of monotheism run like twin constants through Muslim religious history. Each was usually allocated in its own realm, form of discourse, and even, on occasion, ritual expression and structured authority.

This fairly stable modus vivendi was progressively eroded in the modern period, when synthetic theologies were challenged by modernists and fundamentalists, both of whom, for different reasons, had become uneasy with mysticism and *kalām* and who conceived a 'post-civilizational' piety in which antinomies and parallel discourses were experienced and suppressed as destabilizing principles. Where once a cynicism about rationalizing theology expressed itself in mysticism, as with some of the most illustrious Ḥanbalī authors,[23] more recent forms of this cynicism have often combined themselves with the rejection of Sufism as well. Under post-traditional conditions, presided over by modernizing and centralizing ministries of education, the old binary model of Islamic education may today be described as shattered. The dominant state religious curricula, generally aiming to promote a quietist civic faith, have not filled the gap left by the great *madrasa* institutions of the past; still less have they compensated for the spiritual and aesthetic loss entailed by the closure of initiatic institutions, such as the Sufi lodges and the craft guilds. This is, we may surmise, one reason for the evidently shallow and vehement tenor of much Islamist activist discourse in our generation. The state schools have transmitted a vague but emotive sense of Muslim belonging, but have not easily inculcated compassion, aesthetics, or wisdom or the deep dialectical reasons for adherence.[24] Deprived of access to a serious theological education, but having no access to the Sufi illuminationism, which was its traditional counterpoint, Muslim pupils and students increasingly incline either to secular lifestyles or to nonmystical readings of Ibn Taymīya.[25]

To suggest how some form of authentically Muslim education might evolve or recuperate given the collapse of the old binary arrangement, it may prove helpful to focus on the early period when this visible bifurcation hardly existed. Before the 3rd century, it was not customary to record inner experiences and 'unveilings,' and it is therefore not always easy to discern how these interacted with other registers of religious discourse, or transformed the whole. However it is likely that a close integration was normal. This was certainly the case with regard to the balance between 'reason and revelation,' which, again, do not seem to have been experienced as dichotomous principles in the first two centuries.[26] The Muʿtazilite theologians who emerged toward the end of this period seem to have been the first to have proposed such a tension (*ʿaql* in tension with *naql*, or tradition), and although the theologians finally decided against Muʿtazilism on the grounds of its tendency to expand human freedom in a way that radically curtailed the power of God, the polarity that the Muʿtazilites had identified remained a theme, proving its durability in several autonomously Sunni contexts.

Prior to this perhaps inevitable bifurcation (which at its extremes led to an arid transcendentalism—Zamakhsharī laughs at the Sufis because they love God[27] —or to apparent Ismaili resurrections of ancient 'Eastern' theories of divine incarnation), *fiqh*, 'understanding,' seems to have meant an integrated experience of body, mind, and soul. In the apostolic period, *ʿaql*, a word that later evolved in contentious ways, essentially denoted *fiqh* itself. This, certainly, was the insight of Muḥāsibī, taken up in Ghazālī's project of reintegration.[28] For the first Muslims, knowledge was not obtained by formally alternate and perhaps complementary routes. Truth was given in the *vestigia dei* evident in nature, which mystically activated the 'heart,' a process facilitated and given a discursive outcome by the special revelation in scripture. *ʿAql*, or *fiqh*, were not solitary principles or methods; rather every evolution that they implied into areas of recondite logical theory was the consequence of an originally unitive epistemology, to which the Qur'ān, in its sonic and discursive totality, provided the key. The Prophet's own mysticism, exemplified in vital episodes of his life, such as the Ascension (*miʿrāj*), was not a kind of affective rapture disconnected from the fields of *ʿaql* or *fiqh*, but was simply one of its dramatic expressions and outcomes.

In primal Islam, the word *ʿaql* thus inhabited a supple, comprehensive semantic field. A hadith displays a principle that later underlay juridical definitions of human accountability (*taklīf*): "The Pen does not record the works of three [types of] people: one sleeping until he awakes, the one who is mentally unsound until he regains his sanity (*ḥattā yaʿqil*), and the child before he attains maturity" (ibn Ḥanbal, AH 1313. pp. 104). In a similar hadith we read:

> Four [human types shall be excused] on the Day of Resurrection: a deaf man who could hear nothing, a stupid person [*aḥmaq*], a senile man, and someone who died in the period [*fatra*] between the decline of one religion and the arrival of the next.
>
> (ibn Ḥanbal, AH 1313. pp. 24)

Here the prophetic voice explains that consciousness is what defines our status as human beings. *ʿAql* is what makes us human and distinguishes us from other orders of creation for which there will be no eschatological judgment.

In other hadiths, a more abstract portrayal of the mind is suggested.

> When God created the *ʿaql*, he commanded it to come—and it came. Then He commanded it to move away—and it moved away. Then he declared: "I have created nothing nobler than you. It is through you that I take, and through you that I give."[29]

Such examples could be multiplied. It is clear that the new religion valued reason and intelligence highly, albeit in a versatile and intuitive way that implied a broader definition than the usual contemporary understanding of 'mind,' a principle of consciousness that is reductively presumed to have a purely neurological basis. The starting point was the corpus of 'God's arguments,' as Gwynne describes the Qur'ān's own reasoning, which allowed the mood of primal Islam to maintain a high regard for the mind (indeed, some of the first Christians who observed Islam had argued for the new religion's inferiority because of its emphasis on reason and its apparent disinterest in mystery).[30]

The need to filter the proliferating hadith canon with systematic tools not only of textual authentication but also of analogical methods of inferring laws ensured that intellectual precision was expected of scholars (excepting, sometimes, those Ḥanbalites who preferred the anthologizing of huge quantities of often doubtful material). The generation of an expert elite was a necessary consequence not only of the evolution of Islam's response to new intellectual threats, but of the inherent complexity and massive bulk of the founding texts themselves. The nature of those texts made Islam an infertile context for exoteric fundamentalism; again, literalism tended to lead the community toward Sufism, rather than to a simpleminded exoterism.

The early material cited earlier does not refer to the intellect in anything like a scholastic way, although it came to be cited by those who evolved such definitions. Instead, it denotes a general humanistic sense that our integrity is maintained by rational deliberation, a principle that underlies axioms of piety, such as the careful formulation of intentions, self-scrutiny, and the exclusion of emotion and egotism from the exegesis of scripture. *ʿAql*, therefore, incorporates centrally the principle of self-knowledge and self-control (the word *ʿaql* originally signified 'restraint,' the 'hobbling of a beast'); and this placed Islam firmly in the camp of the ancients who began all philosophy with the Delphic 'know thyself.' The discipline of Sufism emerged in part to provide formal mechanisms for the restraint of the 'beast' of the ego, and Ghazālī saw clearly how necessary this was for the performance of any objective theory choice in *naẓar*.[31] Primal Islam had launched an integrative human project that united bodily functions (through consciously practiced and assessed purity laws and rituals) with social relations, political and economic life, formal worship, and the gifts of the spirit. As Ghazālī reminded his generation, the purpose of every form of the revealed law was to uplift humanity by the remembrance of God; and this 'reminder' (*dhikr*) required a consciousness that was seen to be inseparable from reason.

For Ghazālī, and therefore for normative Sunni Muslims, the disciplined mind is, in a sense, identical to the *sunna*, the Prophetic precedent. *Fiqh*, including—and even especially—its practical regulatory aspects, *is* intelligence, not just a mechanism of physical and societal order. Here Islam departed from the classical European insistence on a dichotomy between body and mind. Real rationalism, that is to say, reverence for the miracle of *ʿaql*, must include a belief in innate knowledge, because the experiences of the senses are inadequate in explaining how we have come to know certain things. There are certain truths, such as the arithmetical, which we experience as intuitive and as rooted in an innate knowledge. Ethical knowledge also seems to be a priori:[32] it is 'drawn-out,' proceeding from *ʿaql* as understood as the wise perceptions of the human totality (*kamāl*), including the corporeal (cf. what Merleau-Ponty calls the 'body-subject'). True reason is therefore a knowledge by recollection (*dhikr*); and we have seen that this calls the *Timaeus* to mind. What we know, where it matters, is what we have managed to remember, which is why the Founder is 'only a reminder' (88:21), whereas the Qur'ān too is 'a reminder; and whoever wishes, will remember' (84:54). To achieve this 'remembering,' and therefore to account for the apparent mystery of our a priori knowledge of axioms and ethics,[33] we are required to exist in a harmonious balance that incorporates body, intellect, and soul into a single human subject, an *omnium*, *al-insān al-kāmil*. Only such a being, dialectically regulated by *kalām* and emotionally disciplined by Sufism, is capable of true reason, of *ʿaql*, and thus of being 'drawn-out.'

The classical Sunni consensus, as it evolved new disciplines to cope with the intellectual and societal challenges facing a post-Arabian *umma*, was concerned to restore the well-being of this human subject, conserving the primal unitive Islamic self by means of a complex armature of defense mechanisms that protected the community and the individual believer from an array of philosophical and social hazards. Only those scholars' Ghazālī styles the *ḥashwiyya*, the 'stuffing-men,' claimed that Islam and its primal vision could be adequately protected without the ulema's evolved intellectual and spiritual systems. As we have seen, the community consistently rejected the *ḥashwiyya* tendency: Islam was to be a religion of intellectual and spiritual sophistication, not a naïve and vulnerable fundamentalism. The Islamic self was to be a synergy of body (regulated by *fiqh*), intellect (burnished by *kalām*), and spirit (deepened by Sufism); and in the normative Ghazālian vision, it was this harmony that would manifest and conserve the pristine integrality of the Islamic subject.

CONCLUSION: SOME CONTEMPORARY IMPLICATIONS

The modern-Muslim ministries of education, whose determination to emulate Western models has generated the kind of alienated psyche that seems so easily to support both secularity and fundamentalism, might find grounds for sobering reflection in more recent discussions that have evolved in the Western world. Contemplating the apparently fragmented contemporary self, secular philosophers have been exploring a range of remedies. Some have emphasized the importance of recovering an embodied wisdom as a basis for knowledge, and certain feminist thinkers such as Irigaray have placed this at the center of their epistemology.[34] Others have advocated a secular retrieval of ancient spiritual techniques of meditation or ritual.[35] Such moves are driven by a sense that the post-Enlightenment subject is in crisis and by a fear that the end result of the contemporary disaggregation of the body-mind-spirit composite may be a vehement reaction against one or a combination of these three principles (many substantial forms of youth culture now imply this imbalance). Secularity, which did much to trigger this disaggregation, is thereby further reinforced.

Whether such an unraveling of *ʿaql* is to prevail in Muslim societies as well may depend on the fortunes not only of Westernizing agendas but also of the current wave of *ḥashwiyya* zeal and certain other unmistakable signs of Muslim cultural decline and pedagogic failure. If it is the case that an implicit tension between body, mind, and spirit provided a *point d'appui* for secularist tendencies that ultimately allowed the collapse of Christian commitment in Europe and the fragmentation of the Western self,[36] then it is necessary to acknowledge that through modern influences, the same fissiparous tendency is shaping some of the most significant of contemporary Islamic societies. The modern turn away from *kalām* and Sufism, and from the texts of the great synthetic renewals that reintegrated Islam's various disciplines, has produced a fragmented and impoverished Muslim intellectuality and spiritual habitus, which, one may foretell, will not long resist the same disenchanting tendencies that have caused the atrophy of European Christianity and the prevalence of what Charles Taylor calls the 'felt flatness' of modernity.[37]

The most conspicuous reaction to this threat, which manifests currently in the fundamentalist, Taymīyan turn toward an empowering of the individual believer in the making of deep choices about law, doctrine, and politics, together with the discrediting of the earlier Sunni consensus, is likely to serve the same unintended outcomes that the Reformation's claims for the individual conscience's relationship to scripture did in Europe.[38] A Protestant turn to the individual, and a revolt against continuity and inherited cumulative consensus, has clearly begun. Educationalists anxious to avoid a secular flattening of the culture of Muslim students, while remaining alert to the no less flattening consequences of fundamentalism, will have to draw on the wisdom of Islam's ideal of an integrated human self, which balances inculcation with 'drawing-out,' and respect the viability of the ancient settlement about 'reason and inspiration.' The authority of the classical consensus will, in some fashion, have to be maintained.

Given the history of fundamentalisms, the Taymīyan turn is liable to prove divisive and self-defeating and seems unlikely to restore the primal social and ideational unity that it vaunts. Yet the alternative is no longer readily at hand. Muslim educational institutions inserted into the late-modern world, in which governments seek to dictate unified curricula while society disaggregates into irreconcilable epistemes, can no longer draw on the historically recurrent Muslim pattern of a *madrasa*-lodge bifurcation, which we have described in this essay. Destroyed both by secular national regimes and by the new fundamentalism, that metabolism is now not only irretrievable but is largely forgotten. Recognizing this, Muslim education must beware of a futile nostalgia as it theorizes its strategy of *ressourcement*. As Taylor warns:

> The process of disenchantment is irreversible. The aspiration to reenchant [. . .] points to a different process, which may indeed reproduce features analogous to the enchanted world, but does not in any simple sense restore it.
>
> (Taylor 2001, 287)

However the ongoing imposition of mid-20th-century Western models also looks like a fruitless nostalgia, which may only intensify the current destabilization of Muslim identity and aggravate the ungovernability of Islamic societies. New types of institutions and curricula need to retrieve what can be retrieved of the old religious wisdom enshrined in rigorously rational theologies and in spiritual inspirationalism and ethics, if there is to be any prospect for the retrieval of the integrality of the civilization's reading of its scripture. There should be a chaste awareness, however, that the older complementarity of disciplines and institutions may no longer be appropriate or feasible.

NOTES

1 "At the present time, the essential precondition for the spread of European civilization is the destruction of the Semitic thing par excellence . . . the destruction of Islam . . . Islam is the most complete negation of Europe: Islam is fanaticism . . . The future, sirs, is therefore Europe's, and Europe's alone . . . Here is eternal war, the war which will end only when the last son of Ishmael dies in misery, or is banished through terror to the depths of the desert." (Ernest Rénan, *De la part des peuples sémitiques dans l'histoire de la civilisation*, discours d'ouverture du cours de langue hébraique, chaldaïque et syriaque au College de France [Paris: Michel Lévy, 1862], 27–8.)

2 Ali Bulaç, *Din ve Modernizm* (Istanbul: Endülüs, 1990); an example of the genre in translation is Hilmi Ziya Ülken (the Turkish translator of Spinoza and Rousseau), *Islam Düşüncesi* (Istanbul: Istanbul Üniversitesi Edebiyat Fakültesi, 1947); French translation by Gauthier Dubois, Max Bilen, and Hilmi Ülken, *Pensée de l'Islam* (Istanbul: Fakülteler Matbaası, 1953).

3 Anne-Sophie Roald, *New Muslims in the European Context: The Experience of Scandinavian Converts* (Leiden: E.J. Brill, 2004), 116–26.

4 An older school, associated with the pupils of Leo Strauss, still sometimes maintain the idea of an Islamic 'orthodoxy' that fought against Hellenistic 'rationalism'; but the works of Dimitri Gutas, Robert Wisnovsky, and Peter Adamson have largely discredited this thesis.

5 Oliver Leaman, 'Arguments and the Qur'ān,' 55–67 of Leaman (ed.) *An Encyclopedia of the Qur'ān* (London: Routledge, 2005), see p. 55.

6 Josef van Ess, *The Flowering of Muslim Theology* (Cambridge MA: Harvard University Press, 2006), 153–4.

7 Leaman, 65. See also J. Waardenburg, 'Faith and Reason in the Argumentation of the Qur'ān,' in *Perennitas: Studi in Onore di Angelo Brelich* (Rome: Edizioni dell'Ateneo, 1980), 619–33.

8 Rosalind Ward Gwynne, *Logic, Rhetoric and Legal Reasoning in the Qur'ān* (London and New York: RoutledgeCurzon, 2004), 203: "Reasoning and argument are so integral to the content of the Qur'ān and so inseparable from its structure that they in many ways shaped the very consciousness of Qur'ānic scholars."

9 See Racha el Omari, 'Ibn Taymiyya's "Theology of the Sunna" and His Polemics with the Ash'arites,' pp. 101–122 of Yossef Rapoport and Shahab Ahmed (eds.), *Ibn Taymiyya and His Times* (Oxford: Oxford University Press, 2010). See also Ovamir Anjum, *Politics, Law, and Community in Islamic Thought: The Taymiyyan Moment* (Cambridge: Cambridge University Press, 2012). Anjum's theory, which he finds in Ibn Taymīya, is essentially that Muslim unity can be restored and political stability buttressed if logically supported theologies and legal systems are set aside, together with the clerisy that transmits them, so that the believing masses are allowed to trust their natural disposition (*fiṭra*), selecting scholars, rulers, and movements accordingly. It remains to be seen whether the aftermath of the 'Arab Spring' will vindicate this Taymīyan optimism, rather than the cautiousness of the traditional ulema.

10 For a justification of this claim, see Eric Ormsby, *Ghazālī: the Revival of Islam* (Oxford: Oneworld, 2008), 47. Ormsby points out that Ghazālī's refutation of the Arab philosophers was based on rationality and a *kalām* approach: "as a science of dialectic, relying on argument and counter-argument, theology possessed an inbuilt mechanism for correcting itself."

11 Although there is no shortage of theories that propose one, such as the *na·m* thesis of Amin Ahsan Islahi; see the appreciative summary in Neal Robinson, *Discovering the Qur'ān: A Contemporary Approach to a Veiled Text* (London: SCM, 1996), 271–283.

12 For the anagogic Qur'an, see Louis Massignon, tr. Benjamin Clark, *Essay on the Origins of the Technical Language of Islamic Mysticism* (Notre Dame: University of Notre Dame Press, 1997), 94–8.

13 Bukhārī, Faḍā'il al-Qur'ān, 31.

14 For the experience of the scripture as a preeminently mystical event, see Jean-Michel Hirt, *Le Voyageur nocturne: Lire à l'infini le Coran* (Paris: Bayard, 2010).

15 John Renard, *Seven Doors to Islam* (Berkeley and London: University of California Press, 1996), 233.

16 Hirt, 41–50.

17 "*Ḥasbiya 'llāh*" is "God sufficeth me" (Qur'ān 9:129).

18 Gwynne, 26.

19 It is evident that this is a generalization; note, in particular, the importance of Sa'dī, Ḥāfiẓ, and Rūmī in the *madrasa* culture of South Asia.

20 Taneli Kukkonen, 'Possible Worlds in the *Tahāfut al-Falāsifa*: Al-Ghazālī on Creation and Contingency,' *Journal of the History of Philosophy* 38 (2000), 479–502.

21 For an illuminating example in translation, see Nicholas Heer (tr.), *The Precious Pearl: al-Jāmī's al-Durra al-Fākhira, Together with His Glosses and the Commentary of 'Abd al-Ghafūr al-Lārī* (Albany: State University of New York Press, 1979).

22 Sachiko Murata and William C. Chittick, *The Vision of Islam* (London and New York: I.B. Tauris, 1994), 251–3.

23 Ḥanbalism was unusually productive of Sufi literature: as in the cases of 'Abd Allāh Anṣārī, Rashīd al-Din Maybudī (perhaps a Shāfi'ī, but Ḥanbalī in many things), and 'Abd al-Qādir al-Jīlānī. This was recorded notably in Ibn al-Qayyim's *Madārij al-Sālikīn*. Similarly, the even more literalistic and anti-rationalizing Ẓāhirī school of doctrine and jurisprudence converged in significant and not coincidental ways with the mysticism of Ibn 'Arabī.

24 Compare, for example, Tunisian society, deeply divided between secularists and Taymīyan fundamentalists, the result, in part, of the imposition of a deeply modern and positivistic educational system (Driss Abbassi *Quand la Tunisie s'invente: entre Orient et Occident, des imaginaires politiques* [Paris: Éditions Autrement, 2009], 67–76), and the situation in Senegal, in which the Sufi orders continued to be active in mass education in the modern period, apparently limiting both tendencies (Cheikh Anta Babou, *Fighting the Greater Jihad: Amadu Bamba and the Founding of the Muridiyya of Senegal, 1853–1913* [Athens OH: Ohio University Press, 2007], 79–85).

25 It scarily needs adding that Ibn Taymīya was not an adversary of Sufism in all its manifestations; it is safer to consider him a stern censor of certain practices that in his day were often associated with it. This sets him in the wider context of Sufi self-criticism. See Daphna Ephrat, 'Purifying Sufism: Observations on the Marginalization and Exclusion of Undesirable and Rejected Elements in the Earlier Middle Period (late fourth/tenth to mid-seventh/thirteenth centuries,' *Al-Qantara* 35 (2014), 255–76.

26 "[T]here is no doubt that in the ancient Muslim attitude reason and revelation or reason and Shari'a were not distinct." Fazlur Rahman, *Islam* (London: Weidenfeld and Nicholson, 1966), 104.
27 Zamakhsharī's *Kashshāf*, to Qur'ān 3:31.
28 Al-Ḥārith al-Muḥāsibī (ed. Ḥusayn al-Quwwatlī), *al-ʿAql wa-fahm al-Qur'ān* (2nd edition, n.p.: Dār al-Kindī and Dār al-Fikr, 1398/1978); Abū Ḥāmid al-Ghazālī, *Ihyā' ʿUlūm al-Dīn* (Jeddah: Dār al-Minhāj, second revised edition 1434/2013), I, 305–327 (K. al-ʿilm, bāb 7).
29 Ṣalāḥ al-Dīn al-Munajjid, *al-Islām wa'l-ʿaql ʿalā aw' al-Qur'ān al-Karīm wa'l-ḥadīth al-nabawī* (Beirut: Dār al-Kitāb al-Jadīd, 1976), 40: the hadith is classified as 'good' (*jayyid*); see al-Murtaḍā al-Zabīdī, *Itḥāf al-sādat al-muttaqīn bi-sharḥ Iḥyā' ʿulūm al-dīn* (Cairo: al-Maymaniyya 1311), I, 455.
30 Sidney H. Griffith, 'Comparative Religion in the Apologetics of the First Christian Arabic Theologians,' in *Proceedings of the Patristic, Medieval and Renaissance Conference* 4 (1979), 63–87.
31 Ghazālī, 6, 656 (Dhamm al-ghurūr, Bayān aṣnāf al-mughtarrīn, ṣinf 1).
32 This is not disputed by Ashʿarism, which merely seeks to deny that such knowledge is itself sufficient to render us morally accountable.
33 And perhaps, if Chomsky is right, our knowledge of a universal general grammar.
34 Luce Irigaray, tr. Carolyn Burke, and Gillian C. Gill, *An Ethics of Sexual Difference* (London: Athlone Press, 1993).
35 See the essays in Clare Carlisle and Jonardon Ganeri, *Philosophy as Therapeia* (Cambridge: Cambridge University Press, 2010).
36 The great exponent of this view among European Muslim theologians was undoubtedly the late Tage Lindbom; see, for instance, his *Myth of Democracy* (Grand Rapids: Eerdmans, 1996), a book that has had considerable influence on current European Islamic self-understanding.
37 Charles Taylor, *A Secular Age* (Cambridge MA and London: Harvard University Press, 2007), 307.
38 Brad S. Gregory, *The Unintended Reformation: How a Religious Revolution Secularized Society* (Cambridge MA: Harvard University Press, 2012).

BIBLIOGRAPHY

Abbassi, D. 2009. *Quand la Tunisie s'invente: entre Orient et Occident, des imaginaires politiques*. Paris: Éditions Autrement.

al-Dīn al-Munajjid, S. D. 1976. *al-Islām wa'l-ʿaql ʿalā aw' al-Qur'ān al-Karīm wa'l-ḥadīth al-nabawī*. Beirut: Dār al-Kitāb al-Jadīd.

Anjum, O. 2012. *Politics, Law and Community in Islamic Thought: The Taymiyyan Moment*. Cambridge: Cambridge University Press.

Babou, A. C. 2007. *Fighting the Greater Jihad: Amadu Bamba and the Founding of the Muridiyya of Senegal, 1853–1913*. Athens OH: Ohio University Press.

Bulaç, A. 1947. *Din ve Modernizm* (Istanbul: Endülüs, 1990); an example of the genre in translation is Hilmi Ziya Ülken (the Turkish translator of Spinoza and Rousseau), *Islam Düşüncesi* (Istanbul: Istanbul Üniversitesi Edebiyat Fakültesi, 1947).

Carlisle, C. and Ganeri, J. 2010. *Philosophy as Therapeia*. Cambridge: Cambridge University Press.

Dubois, G., Bilen, M. and Ülken, H. 1953. *Pensée de l'Islam*. Istanbul: Fakülteler Matbaası.

Eberhardt, I. 2002. *The Diaries of Isabelle Eberhardt*, ed. and tr. Elizabeth Kershaw. Chichester: Summersdale.

Ephrat, D. 2014. 'Purifying Sufism: Observations on the Marginalization and Exclusion of Undesirable and Rejected Elements in the Earlier Middle Period (late fourth/tenth to mid-seventh/thirteenth centuries,' *Al-Qantara* 35, pp. 255–7.

van Ess, J. 2006. *The Flowering of Muslim Theology.* Cambridge MA: Harvard University Press.

al-Ghazālī, H. 2013. *Ihyā' 'Ulūm al-Dīn.* (2nd revised edition) (1434). Jeddah: Dār al-Minhāj.

Gregory, S. B. 2012. *The Unintended Reformation: How a Religious Rrevolution Secularised Society.* Cambridge MA: Harvard University Press.

Griffith, H. S. 1979. 'Comparative Religion in the Apologetics of the First Christian Arabic Theologians,' in *Proceedings of the Patristic, Medieval and Renaissance Conference* 4, pp. 63–87.

Gwynne, W. R. 2004. *Logic, Rhetoric and Legal Reasoning in the Qur'ān.* London and New York: Routledge Curzon.

ibn Ḥanbal, (AH1313). *A. al-Musnad.* Cairo: al-Maymaniyya,

Haleem, A. 2008. *The Quran.* Oxford: Oxford University Press.

Heer, N. 1979. (trans.) *The Precious Pearl: al-Jāmī's al-Durra al-Fākhira, Together With His Glosses and the Commentary of 'Abd al-Ghafūr al-Lārī.* Albany: State University of New York Press.

Hirt, J. 2010. *Le Voyageur nocturne: Lire à l'infini le Coran.* Paris: Bayard.

Irigaray, L. 1993. *An Ethics of Sexual Difference* (tr. Carolyn Burke and Gillian C. Gill). London: Athlone Press.

Kukkonen, T. 2000. 'Possible Worlds in the Tahāfut al-Falāsifa: Al-Ghazālī on Creation and Contingency,' *Journal of the History of Philosophy* 38, pp. 479–502.

Leaman, O. 2005. 'Arguments and the Qur'ān,' pp. 55–67 of O. Leaman (ed.) *An Encyclopedia of the Qur'ān.* London: Routledge.

Lindbom, T. 1996. *Myth of Democracy.* Grand Rapids: Eerdmans.

Massignon, L. 1997. (tr. Benjamin Clark) *Essay on the Origins of the Technical Language of Islamic Mysticism.* Notre Dame: University of Notre Dame Press.

al-Muḥāsibī, H. 1978. (ed. Ḥusayn al-Quwwatlī), *al-'Aql wa-fahm al-Qur'ān* (2nd edition) (1398), Dār al-Kindī and Dār al-Fikr.

Murata, S. and Chittick, C. W. 1994. *The Vision of Islam.* London and New York: I.B. Tauris,

al-Murtaḍā al-Zabīdī. 1311. *Itḥāf al-sādat al-muttaqīn bi-sharḥ Iḥyā' 'ulūm al-dīn.* Cairo: al-Maymaniyya.

Nicholson, A. R. 1926. (trans.) Jalāl al-Dīn Rūmī, *Mathnawī.* London: E.J.W. Gibb Memorial Trust.

el Omari, R. 2010. 'Ibn Taymiyya's "Theology of the Sunna" and His Polemics with the Ash'arites,' pp. 101–122 of Yossef Rapoport and Shahab Ahmed (eds.), *Ibn Taymiyya and His Times.* Oxford: Oxford University Press.

Ormsby, E. 2008. *Ghazālī: The Revival of Islam.* Oxford: Oneworld.

Rahman, F. 1966. *Islam.* London: Weidenfeld and Nicholson.

Rénan, E. 1862. *De la part des peuples sémitiques dans l'histoire de la civilisation*, discours d'ouverture du cours de langue hébraique, chaldaïque et syriaque au College de France, Paris: Michel Lévy.

Renard, J. 1996. *Seven Doors to Islam.* Berkeley and London: University of California Press.

Riḍā, R. 1985. *al-Waḥy al-Muḥammadī*. Cairo: al-Manār.

Roald, A. 2004. *New Muslims in the European Context: The Experience of Scandinavian Converts*. Leiden: E.J. Brill.

Robinson, N. 1996. *Discovering the Qur'ān: A Contemporary Approach to a Veiled Text*. London: SCM.

Taylor, C. 2011. *Dilemmas and Connections: Selected Essays*. Cambridge MA: Harvard University Press.

Taylor, C. 2007. *A Secular Age*. Cambridge MA and London: Harvard University Press.

Waardenburg, J. 1980. 'Faith and Reason in the Argumentation of the Qur'ān,' pp. 619–636 of *Perennitas: Studi in Onore di Angelo Brelich*. Rome: Edizioni dell'Ateneo.

3 Islamic Philosophical Traditions

Knowledge and Man's Path to a Creator*

David B. Burrell

For a volume on the 'Philosophy of Islamic Education,' a discussion of how Islam deals with the question of 'knowledge' and its relation to man's understanding of God and nature forms an important area of inquiry. This is not least because education stands as a means, knowingly or otherwise, to respond (via curricula) or reconcile (via its aims) to these perennial questions. Whether attempting to construct philosophical systems of learning, defining Islamic philosophy of education, or commenting on the role philosophy plays in such education, how Islamic thinkers have engaged and provided answers to the question of a meeting between 'man-cosmos-God' remains an essential part of an Islamic pedagogy. Our aim in this chapter is primarily to explicate the development of Islamic philosophy and its most notable medieval contributions regarding this question. In doing so, it is hoped that we may develop an understanding of how their ideas construct an overarching ontological vista for Islamic education.

However, before such a discussion may take place, there is a need to consider what we mean by 'Islamic Philosophy' and its historical context. The editors of a Cambridge publication offer a rationale for their title—*Cambridge Companion to Arabic Philosophy*—by coupling 'Arabic' with 'Islamic' (Adamson and Taylor 2005). Yet whereas Arabic served the Islamic intellectual world, much as Latin did the medieval Christian world, the fact remains that Arabs today account for but 20% of Muslims, and a considerable portion of the Islamic, intellectual tradition, has been forged and transmitted in other languages notably Persian, Urdu, and Turkish. Indeed, key intellectual figures in Islam have themselves been Persian, sometimes composing in both Arabic and their native Farsi, as their itineraries will display. So 'Islamic' offers a more comprehensive cultural descriptor, whereas we may reserve the adjective 'Muslim' in this narrative for the faith-component of Islam (equally one could, in an analogous manner, employ the term 'Arabic' ethnically or culturally.) It is that tradition

* A version of this article is originally published in *Islamochristiana* (PISAI, Rome) as "Islamic Philosophical Theology and the West," Burrell, David B. *Islamochristiana* 33 (2007) 75–90.

that this chapter shall attempt to capture by presenting a brief history of Islamic philosophical thought through its ongoing attempt to understand the Qur'anic revelation (via conversations with rational strategies inherited from the Greeks and Persians) with an emphasis on understanding the complex and contentious ways in which Creator and His creation relate to one another. Specific emphasis is given to the arguably unique ways in which reason and supra-rationality have come to dominate these debates. Relying on three prominent thinkers in this regard, namely, al-Ghazali (d. 1111 AD), Suhrawardi (d. 1191 AD), and ibn-al-Arabi (d. 1240 AD) to explore these issues, it is hoped to shed light on the ways in which 'reason' has been used as a means (often in a limited sense) to comprehend the world.

THE BEGINNINGS OF ISLAMIC PHILOSOPHY

The story of Islamic philosophy begins with the spectacular overtaking of the hinterlands of the Byzantine Empire in the 7th century by disciplined and motivated bands from the Arabian Peninsula, who before long sought to assimilate the high culture of that empire. Utilizing the offices of Syriac translators, they made key Hellenic philosophical texts available in Arabic, facilitating the emergence of thinkers such as al-Kindi, al-Farabi, ibn Sina (Avicenna), and ibn Rushd (Averroes) (Walzer 1970). As the equivalent Latin names illustrate, these philosophers—called *falasifa* in Arabic—inspired cognate Christian medieval thinkers, with the Latinate equivalent (of ibn Rushd) naming an entire way of thinking, for example, in terms of the designation 'Latin Averroism.' The import of this East-West cultural exchange in the 11th through 13th centuries proved especially significant for the West, whereas the movement in the Islamic world itself was soon to lose its vitality. In the 11th century, the brilliant theologian and thinker, al-Ghazali (Algazel), levied an attack on 'the philosophers,' which subsequently curtailed their influence in Islamic culture. That dispute, with ibn Rushd's stalwart retort, is displayed in two documents: al-Ghazali's "Deconstruction of the Philosophers" and ibn Rushd's "Deconstruction of the Deconstruction," which itself contains the entire text of al-Ghazali (Ghazali 2000, ibn Rush 1954). Whereas ibn Rushd represents *philosophy* unadulterated by *faith*, al-Ghazali's critique based on faith effectively curtails any mediating use of reason to elaborate the Islamic intellectual tradition. Yet a recent study by Avital Wohlman, hardly favorable to al-Ghazali as a philosopher, effectively replaces a 'rationalist' ibn Sina (the target of al-Ghazali's initial critique) with a thoroughly Islamic thinker (Wohlman 2010). The conversation between 'faith and reason' and the role philosophical inquiry plays therein informs much of the subsequent debates in Islamic philosophical history and it is here, within this classical period, that we begin our intellectual profiles.

AL-GHAZALI AND PHILOSOPHICAL DISCOURSE[1]

Considering the 'faith versus reason' debates alluded to earlier, we may trace al-Ghazali's specific contribution to philosophical discourse and the role 'knowledge' plays in his intellectual system by way of a central text, the book of *Faith in Divine Unity and Trust in Divine Providence* (*Kitab al-tawhid wa'l-tawakkul*) of the *Ihya' 'Ulum al-Din* (*Revivifying Religious Sciences*). Together with *al-iqtisad al-i'ttiqad* (*Preserving the Faith*), the effect of these works was to qualify al-Ghazali as a Muslim theologian in the full medieval meaning of that term and not in the merely descriptive sense extended to those adept at *kalām* or the dialectical defense of faith. That is, al-Ghazali was intent on using human reason, as he found it elaborated in the important philosopher ibn Sina and others, to lead Muslim faithful to a deeper penetration of the mysteries of their revealed religion, central among them being the free creation of the universe by the one God (Burrell 1993). As the works of the philosophers themselves were not always helpful to him in their native state, he set out to 'purify' them of their pretensions, to offer an accessibility of truth that was not independent of, and superior to, that of divine revelation, the Qur'an. Hence his need to understand the philosophers thoroughly is embodied in the work "The Intentions of the Philosophers" (*Maqasid al-falasifa*), itself conceived as an extended introduction to his *Deconstruction of the Philosophers* (*Tahafut al-falasifa*) (Ghazali 2000). The negative tone of this latter work, together with its detailed refutation by Averroes (ibn Rushd, 1954, *Tahafut al-Tahafut*) left the impression that al-Ghazali should never be ranked with 'the philosophers' but always left with 'the theologians' as a defender of *kalām* orthodoxy in the face of reasonable inquiry. It is precisely that stereotype that Wohlman's work and others' challenges and deconstructs the historical image that al-Ghazali partly helped to create for himself.

ROLE OF KNOWLEDGE IN GHAZALI'S UNDERSTANDING OF NATURE

The "*Book of Faith in Divine Unity* (tawhid) *and Trust in Divine Providence* (tawakkul)" is Book 35 in Ghazali's (d. 1111 AD) masterwork, the *Ihya' 'Ulum al-Din* (Ghazali 2000), which is intent upon a clear understanding of matters religious, yet one which continues to give primacy to 'practice,' i.e., faith being rooted in trust and expressed through pious acts of worship. Commenting on the vicissitudes of knowledge, he argues that

> Certain[ity in] knowledge is that in which the thing known reveals itself without leaving any room for doubt or any possibility of error or illusion, nor can the heart allow such a possibility. One must be

> protected from error, and should be so bound to certainty that any attempt, for example, to transform a stone into gold or a stick into a serpent would not raise doubts or engender contrary probabilities. I know very well that ten is more than three. If anyone tries to dissuade me by saying, "No three is more than ten," and wants to prove it by changing in front of me this stick into a serpent, even if I saw him changing it, still this fact would engender no doubt about my knowledge. Certainly, I would be astonished at such a power, but would not doubt my knowledge.
>
> (Ali 2007, 409)

The pretensions of the philosophers, for Ghazali, to understand the mysteries of "the heavens and the earth and all that is between them" (Quran, 15:85), proceeding by conceptual argument alone, must be exposed as just that, namely, pretension in the face of the central assertion that the universe was *freely* created by the one sovereign God. Yet reason, which they are at pains to elaborate, is an indispensable tool in directing our minds and our hearts to understand how to think and live as a consequence of free creation. Such is Ghazali's intent. For *tawhid* or "faith in divine unity," sounds the distinctive note of Islam that grounds every Muslims belief in the *shahada*: "There is no god but God." Yet what interests Ghazali is the implications of the community's *faith* in divine unity. What Ghazali's wishes to assert is that everything comes from God so that "there is no agent but God" and justifies this by way of showing how *tawakkul*—trust in divine providence—is grounded in *tawhid*, as anchored in faith and *state* (of being) in *knowledge*. In doing so, he is insistent that

> there is no agent but God the Most High: of all that exists in creation-sustenance given or withheld, life or death, riches or poverty, and everything else that can be named, the sole one who initiated and originated it all is God Most High. And when this has been made clear to you, you will not see anything else, so that your fear will be of Him, your hope in Him, your trust in Him, and your security with Him, for He is the sole agent without any other. Everything else is in His service, for not even the smallest atom in the worlds of heaven and earth is independent of Him for its movement. If the gates of mystical insight were opened to you, this would be clear to you with a clarity more perfect than ordinary vision.
>
> (al-Ghazali 2000, 15–16)

If Ghazali tends to rely on "mystical insight" in places where philosophers would prefer conceptual schemes, he is merely suggesting that certain domains quite outstrip human conceptualizing. Yet more significant, however, is that everything he says about practice can be carried out quite independently of such "mystical insight," as indeed it must be for the vast majority of the faithful.

al-Ghazali is of great historical importance not merely in his bringing the purely rationalizing elements of philosophical inquiry with those of the mystical ' "supra" rational' but also that any program of education worthy of the nomenclature 'Islamic' must accept, if not root, itself within such knowledge. As he was among the greatest of Islamic thinkers, we can say to a degree that his position 'won' not only in terms of orthodox belief concerning the omnipotence of God but also with regard to the arguments of the philosophers. It is the twin elements of human inquiry in attempting to discern the corporal world and an explicit realization that it subsequently mystifies us that stand as hallmarks that would come to define Islamic orthodox thought. Hence the importance of al-Ghazali as a *doctor of theology*, in the post-classical age (post-14th-century AD) of Islamic thought, helped to define a lasting narrative within which education and specifically the rational sciences were to be perceived.

SUHRAWARDI'S *PHILOSOPHY OF ILLUMINATION*

Despite notorious difficulties in presenting and interpreting Suhrawardi's (d. 1191 AD) philosophical *opus*, we can plausibly present him as the figure initiating a distinctive phase in post-Ghazalian Islamic philosophical thought. His early and tragic demise at thirty-seven, at the behest of Saladin for a complex of strategic political reasons, hardly allowed time for a mature development of his thought, although his oeuvre remains considerable. John Walbridge (2005, 203) divides his work into four categories: (1) juvenilia; (2) mystical works, notably a number of allegories, (3) works expounding the principles of the Peripatetics according to their methods, and (4) *The Philosophy of Illumination* (Suhrawardi 1999). The greater part of his extensive work has yet to be published and only the last one is translated, but his influence and ability to weave through a diverse number of sources from figures such as Plato qualify him as an important figure for discussion.

Emphasizing *seeing*, his celebrated "knowledge by presence" attempts to move beyond the *subject/object* structure of knowing, endemic to Plato, and led him to argue that essences could only be known through direct acquaintance. The vision intimated in *The Philosophy of Illumination* introduced an epistemological ascent, the pinnacle of which being the 'Light of Lights' which the author explicates as

> the ruling Agent despite all intermediaries, the cause of their activity, the Origin of every emanation, the absolute Creator, without intermediary.

> There is no effect which does not contain Its effect, although It may allow the relation of activity to be shared with another.
>
> (114)

The metaphor of *light* provides Suhrawardi with a manifestly epistemological tool, yet it also helps to express the pervasiveness of the Creator's primary causality, for "you will find nothing that has an effect both near and far save light" (130). Drawing from both Plato and Aristotle, created things are ordered by "desire [which] bears the perceptive essences to the Light of Lights; that which is greater in its desire is more attracted and climbs higher toward the world of the All-Highest Light" (145). Indeed, the culminating passages of the book are full of Qur'anic terminology, showing that what can be learned of the mystical quest can be found in the celestial prototype of the Qur'an. For Suhrawardi, this composition is hoped to lead readers to the consummation of Islamic philosophy, namely, "to turn with all your being to God our Lord, the Light of Lights." For

> he who studies [this book] will learn that what escaped the Ancients and the Moderns God has been entrusted to my tongue. One wondrous day the Holy Spirit blew it into my heart in a single instant, though its writing took many months due to the interruption of journeys.
>
> (162)

Attaining this goal means employing rigorous conceptual arguments, of course, yet much more as well:

> give it only to one well versed in the methods of the Peripatetics, a lover of the light of God. Let him meditate for forty days, abstaining from meat, taking little food, concentrating upon the contemplation of the light of God, most Mighty and Glorious, and upon he who holds the authority to teach the Book shall command.
>
> (162)

This 'eclectic' philosophical approach is considered both through 'intellect and intuition' and sees knowledge on a scale from intuitive, observational, and, finally, to illumination. For the educationalist, Suhrawardi's approach presents an important way in which the student evolves through this epistemic journey in knowing and what Nowrozi (2012) argues is "very prominent in the history of Islamic education and philosophy (282)." We see here, as with Ghazali, the need for reason to stand at a revered distance to the superordinate spiritual elements of human discovery in that they bear an "attitude toward[s] knowledge . . . that [shows] pedagogy [and its] reflection on different levels of knowledge, namely sensory, mystical, and illuminated knowledge, and also reflection on ultimate goals of education" (283).

With reference to how this educational approach is intimated by a teacher/spiritual guide requires one to

1 Settle the educational process on the basis of the learner's nature, so he should know the learner's characteristics.
2 Organize educational opportunities in the manner that the student will be able to learn by doing certain activities.
3 Consider this problem that how to give the learners more and more experiences (teacher illuminated experiences) and how to help them in doing the activities (291).

Suhrawardi was conscious of leading others along a path of understanding knowledge as ending in a 'liberating light' as he himself had been illuminated. In this exposition, there is no competition between conceptual methods and intuitive realization, except when the first refuses to give way to the latter, what emerges is then a transcendent goal and Islam's recognition of knowledge as a means to order the world in light of the relationship between Creator and creation.

IBN AL-ARABI: THE "RATIONALIZING MYSTIC"

A contemporary of al-Suhrawardi's, the life and work of the 13th-century Andalusian scholar and saint ibn al-Arabi (d. 1148 AD) continues to be among the most studied and controversial figures in Islamic intellectual history. Sajjad Rizvi adopts the descriptor "rationalizing mystic" from Philip Merlan's reference to show how "later Neoplatonists, [tried to convey an] absolute transparency between the knower, the known, and knowledge itself" in such a cognitive relation to the Creator God. Indeed, what specifies this cognitive manner of relating to the Creator, as articulated in "illuminationist [*ishraqi*] philosophy, is its integration of spiritual practice into the pursuit of wisdom (Rizvi 2005, 227)." What is sought here is a way of articulating the relation between creator and creatures, parallel to that between *existence* and *existents*. For ibn al-Arabi, the category of knowledge open to individuals of spiritual clarity, are whom he calls

> "the Folk of Allah," [and] consider knowledge to be a gift (*wahb*). For them this gift has not been suddenly withheld with the death of the Prophet . . . It is given as long as the Giver exists. When the recipients of this knowledge work, they work on themselves for the pleasure of the Giver. And with their explanation and understanding they return only what is already written and said. That is, they return the meaning of the Holy Quran and the Sayings of the Prophet.
>
> (41)

Ibn al-Arabi uses Qur'anic language to intimate this idea with specific reference to the verse, "He originates and brings back" (85:13). Whereas this verse had been understood to refer to "God's bringing people back at the resurrection," ibn al-Arabi offers a more metaphysical reading linked to the idea that

> there is no existent thing to which the Real gives existence without finishing with giving it existence. Then that existent thing considers God and sees that He has come back to giving existence to another entity. So it continues perpetually and endlessly.
>
> (Chittick 1998, 65–66)

However difficult it may be for contemporary philosophers to follow such a hybrid inquiry, especially those who cannot avail themselves of a faith tradition of 'free creation,' they could nevertheless be assisted by William Chittick (1992, 1998) and Salman Bashier (1998) to move beyond the stereotype of ibn al-Arabi as a 'monist' that is, one who dissolves the distinction of 'creatures' from 'Creator.' For the precise function of the intermediary space between earthly life and existence after the final judgment is to highlight the relation *between* Creator and creatures, which, however paradoxical it may be for us to formulate, remains a *relation*, even though comparing it to an ordinary relation between creatures effectively elides creation itself. The idea of an intermediary space forging a special connectivity is also represented in his ideas of dreams and visions. However, such ideas pose problems for the modern reader; as Izutsu (1970) explains, these are due to a tendency

> to consider all kinds of creative inspirations, whether religious, philosophic, or artistic, as something purely subjective. For ibn 'Arabi, however, the authentic inspirations (including veridical dreams) are of a preeminently objective nature. They do have an objective basis; that is to say, they subsist in their own peculiar ontological dimension. That ontological dimension is the "world of images." The latter, in ibn al-'Arabi's conception, is an intermediate or intermediary world existing between the purely spiritual, purely immaterial world and the universe of things perceptible to the senses. It is a mid-zone between heaven and earth, the supra sensory world of the archetypal idea-images, in which all prophetic inspirations, theophanic visions, and symbolic events have their own objective ground. The "creative imagination" is a special organ of a spiritual energy which perceives, and at the same time confers concrete existence upon, the particular realities subsisting in this ontological dimension.
>
> (434)

For ibn al-Arabi, the human being represents an incredible capability for apprehending Divine truths, something that the rest of creation is incapable.

However, in order to do so, he reminds us again, one must understand the proper order of human potential to reach such heights. This is what he refers to as courtesy (*adab*) of knowing and explicates this account by reference to those who know God by reason as well as supra-rationally. In a longer and poetical description, he equates rationality with a 'scale' whereby abstractions and measurements of the world are forged, just as our previous thinkers mentioned earlier, into 'other' ways of knowing. He continues that

> Since there is no agent but God, while the jurist and theologian comes to the Divine Presence with his scale to weigh God, not recognizing that God gave him those scales only to weigh with them *for* God, not to weigh God Himself, he is deprived of courtesy. And he who lacks courtesy is punished by ignorance of the God-given knowledge of opening [depths in understanding the Divine]. Hence he will not be upon insight in his affair.
>
> If he should have an ample rational faculty, he will know from whence he is stricken. Among them are those who enter in and leave their scale at the door. Once they come back out, they take it along to weigh with it for God's sake. This is the best state of those who enter upon God with the rational faculty. However, the heart of such a person is attached to what he left behind, since in his soul he will return to it. Hence he is deprived of the sought-for-Truth to the extent that his mind is attached to what he has left behind, because of the regard he pays to it.
>
> Even better than this person is the state of him who smashes his scale. If it is made from wood, he burns it, and if it is something that melts he melts it. Or he freezes it, so it ceases being a scale. If its substance remain, she does not care. But this is exceedingly rare. I have not found that anyone has done it, though we can suppose it, and it is not impossible that God should strengthen one of His servants until he does something like this.
>
> (cited in 50)

The importance of ibn al-Arabi's understanding of knowledge and God is made clear here, as well as his rapprochement with the aforementioned thinkers. On this reading, what makes ibn al-Arabi so radical is not an heretical denial of "the distinction" between the 'One' and 'all-that-is,' but rather a thoroughgoing attempt to keep that distinction from being so trivialized that the One ceases to be "the One" or "the Real" or becomes "the biggest thing around" (Burrell 2001).

EDUCATIONAL THOUGHT TODAY AND CLASSICAL PHILOSOPHICAL

The debates offered by premodern thinkers on the distinctions and arguments regarding 'Creator-creator' and humankind's relation to nature are embedded in larger theological and philosophical discussions. As such, their relevancy for contemporary educational debates may seem ponderous and antiquated. However, for the educationalist, as practitioner or theoretician, these arguments lay important elemental structures and, in particular, harness ways in which students learn to comport themselves within the world of created things. Whereas modern education has a tendency toward fissuring the student between a great many divisions and purists, talk of interconnectedness (physical and metaphysical) tends to become increasingly irrelevant. This is what Harris (2012) calls the 'uncommon' foundations of the university community, where discourses of unity (as in a premodern worldview) are dislocated to propitiate democratic and open debates by advocating *difference*. Harris argues that such an approach maintains the universalizing elements of the university community i.e., cohesion through discordance. Within this structural climate where there is a tendency toward centralization of meaning, there are unintended consequences, such as what the educationalist Smelser (2013) has called the "structural accretions" of education; namely, the "incorporation of new functions over time without, however, shedding existing ones or splitting into separate organizations" (13).

Alternatively, it is important to note that within both Muslim and Christian traditions, the turn toward 'practices' (spiritual-contemplative acts) serves to move philosophical discussions of the Creator-creation beyond rationalized formulations, especially when the very structure of the formulas display that they will not suffice. In this regard, the classicist Pierre Hadot (1993, 2002) reminds us that the tradition of ancient philosophy has done the same. As a long-time translator of Plotinus, he argues that the very effort of translating (itself a spiritual exercise) alerted him to the difference between a modern and a classical conception of the virtues required to "do philosophy." Indeed, modern philosophy seldom alludes to "intellectual virtues" and contends itself rather with "propositional attitudes," yet when one presses these *attitudes*, something like virtue can in fact emerge. That is to say, modernity's account of what philosophy (and by extension the philosophy of Islamic education today) is and how one engages in it may well prove inadequate to the activity itself, which could also explain why philosophy continues to criticize itself and not merely its findings. The focus of contemporary philosophers such as Stephen Toulmin and Alasdair MacIntyre on 'practice' can help us see how Hadot's ideas on ancient philosophy are far more pertinent than a historical exercise. It was his own engagement with Plotinus's intellectual journey that taught Hadot the need for spiritual exercises to follow his mentor. Indeed, the master/disciple relationship, and all that it portends, offers a useful way of characterizing the exercises relevant to attaining this metaphysical standpoint. Whereas there can be no absolute demonstration of these matters, we are nonetheless led to realize that we cannot understand created things, within an Islamic discourse, properly without a sustained attempt to grasp the internal link they have with a Creator in their very forms of existence. Yet whereas this mode of inquiry exceeds the bounds of philosophical inquiry as normally practiced by Islamic philosophers, such as ibn Sina, it is arguable that they too realized that an authentically philosophical search must move into these more esoteric arenas (Burrell 2003, 196–208). This chapter has attempted to show some of the areas and key figures whose important contributions have provided means to think about these matters. Although the debates will continue to form the backdrop, in one way or another, of Islamic philosophical inquiry, it remains important to review their arguments for an idea of 'Islamic' education. Although such education (whether historical or otherwise) may not ostensibly interact with such quandaries, the study of Islamic pedagogical systems cannot be divorced from them and the often implicit ways in which education provides its own negotiations for the question of relating 'Creator and creation' to one another.

NOTE

1 This section adapts from the Introduction to Ghazali 2000 with permission of the publisher.

BIBLIOGRAPHY

Adamson, Peter and Taylor, Richard. 2005. *Cambridge Companion to Arabic Philosophy*. Cambridge: Cambridge University Press.

Al-Ghazali, Abu Hamid. 2000. *Al-Ghazali on Faith in Divine Unity and Trust in Divine Providence*. Translation of Book. 35 of *Ihya' 'Ulum ad-Din* by David Burrell. Louisville, KY: Fons Vitae.

Ali, I, Zain. 2007. "Al-Ghazālī and Schopenhauer on Knowledge and Suffering." *Philosophy East and West* 57: 409–419.

Bashier, Salman. 2004. *ibn al-'Arabi's Barzakh: Concept of the Limit and the Relationship between God and the World*. Albany: State University of New York Press.

Burrell, David. 1993. *Freedom and Creation in Three Traditions*. Notre Dame IN: University of Notre Dame Press.

Burrell, David. 2001. "Creation, Metaphysics, and Ethics." *Faith and Philosophy* 18: 204–221.

Burrell, David. 2003. "Avicenna." In *A Companion to Philosophy in the Middles Ages*, edited by Jorge J. E. Gracia and Timothy B. Noone, 196–208. Oxford: Blackwell.

Chittick, William. 1992. *Faith and Practice in Islam*. Albany: State University of New York Press.

Chittick, William. 1998. *Self-Disclosure of God: Principles of ibn al-Arabi's Cosmology*. Albany: State University of New York Press.

Hadot, Pierre. 1993. *Exercises spirituels et philosophie antique* [3ème éd]. Paris: Gallimard.

Hadot, Pierre. 2002. *What Is Ancient Philosophy?* Cambridge MA: Belknap Press of Harvard University, translation of *Qu'est-ce que la philosophie*. Paris: Gallimard, 1995.

Harris, Suzy. 2012. "The University's Uncommon Community." *Journal of Philosophy of Education*, 46: 236–51.

Izutsu, Toshihiko. 1970. "Book Review: Creative Imagination in the Sufism of ibn 'Arabi, by Henry Corbin." *Philosophy East and West* 20: 433–435.

Nowrozi, A. Reza., Ardakani, Hashemi, H. S. and Shiri, S. Ali. 2012. "Suhrawardi's Epistemological Point of View and its Educational Outcomes." *Religious* Education 107: 281–294.

Rizvi, Sajjad. 2005. "Mysticism and philosophy." In *Cambridge Companion to Arabic Philosophy*, edited by Peter Adamson and Richard Taylor, 224–246. Cambridge: Cambridge University Press.

ibn Rushd. 1954. *Tahafut al-Tahafut*: Tr. Simon van den Bergh. Cambridge: Cambridge University Press.

Smelser, J., Neil. 2013. *Dynamics of the Contemporary: University Growth, Accretion, and Conflict.* Berkeley: University of California Press.

Suhrawardi, Shihab al-Din. 1999. *The Philosophy of Illumination*. Eds. and trans. J. Walbridge and H. Ziai. Provo UT: Brigham Young University Press.

Walbridge, John. 2005. "Suhrawardi and Illuminationism." In *Cambridge Companion to Arabic Philosophy*, edited by Peter Adamson and Richard Taylor, 201–223. Cambridge: Cambridge University Press.

Walzer, Richard. 1970. *Greek into Arabic: Essays on Islamic Philosophy.* Columbia SC: University of South Carolina Press.

Wohlman, Avital. 2010. *Counterpoint between Common Sense and Philosophy in Islam.* London Routledge; trans. of *Contrepoint entre le sens commun et la philosophie en Islam: Al-Ghazali et Averroes*. Paris: Editions du Cerf, 2008.

Part II

Positioning Knowledge between the Student and Teacher

4 Spirituality in Muslim Education

Abdullah Trevathan

This work sets out to examine the question of spirituality in Muslim schools with specific reference to those schools that aspire to modern forms of education. Such schools may generally be found in Europe, North American, and Australia, and in some cases, are publicly funded, (i.e., Britain, Holland, and Belgium). There are an increasing number of private schools offering Islamic education in the Muslim homelands that fall under this category, as well as some public education offered in some Muslim countries that could be included in the discussion that follows. Ultimately, what is presented here cannot solely be limited to the realm of schooling, for education is simply a microcosm of the society in which it is placed.

The work presented here begins with an initial discussion concerning the difficulties of defining spirituality and the educational implications thereof. Nonetheless, an attempt is made to articulate some general indications of the term, including some deliberations around the relationship between mysticism, spirituality, and religious traditions. Building upon this, an inquiry is undertaken to explore the effectiveness of spiritual development within the context of a modern educational framework. It is argued that despite obvious superficial differences, religious and secular schools do not essentially diverge, as both are based on modern managerial systems and methodologies and therefore similar issues can effect spiritual development in both types of school settings. Furthermore, the extent to which an alleged reification process within the Muslim world has resulted in an eclipsing of the spiritual and mystical is looked into and whether the result has been a reduction of Islam to a socio-political ideology and its spirituality to a moral code. The possible effects this might have on education are also delved into.

One contention made here is that Muslim educationalists need to venture out of current educational models to create a pedagogy that is more inherently reflective of classical Muslim thought and culture, including approaches to the spiritual. In attempting to exemplify this, it is proposed that the 'spiritual education' tag should be dropped and more focus given to some parallel concepts in the Arabic language that encompasses the spiritual. The alternative concepts of *adab*, *akhlāq ihsān*, and *ikhlās* are presented, weighed up, and compared with the latter eventually being decided upon as both more practicable and a requisite to the other concepts. A short review of the ethos, ambience, and context in which *ikhlās* might be taught is given, followed by a practical example of a class wherein such an approach might be used based upon an amalgamation of actual classroom experiences followed by a brief analysis at the end.

In summary, this work ultimately sets out to stimulate further thought into the question of spiritual education within Muslim education. In pursuit of this, it addresses the question of whether spiritual development is compatible with modern education systems and whether such questions are pertinent to Muslim spiritual education. What alternatives for spiritual development are there for Muslim schools and how can these be realized?

AN INDICATION OF THE SPIRITUAL

Can we accept, as Wittgenstein suggests (2009), that some words may be understood in a general sense without demanding absolute definitions? This seems particularly appropriate in relation to the elusive term *spiritual*, which nevertheless possesses some consensus as to what is indicated, i.e., something beyond material, ordinary experience. From a classical (*naqli*) Muslim perspective, *tawfid* is the conscious attitude of not over questioning nor analyzing the enigmatic, aptly summed up in the Qur'an: 'Say: The Spirit is from the matters of my Lord!' (17:85). Within Muslim spirituality, such things are termed as *sirr*, literally 'secret,' not in the sense of keeping confidences but by dint of being indescribable. The spiritual can vaguely be defined as something that brings about a penetrating awareness or an acute sense of a force majeure. These may manifest during occasions of extraordinary beauty or momentous events or even within ordinary daily experience, although viscerally experienced as remarkable. It may come about through intense emotions of awe, veneration, gratitude, or selflessness but does not usually appear to be the result of extreme religious fervor. The spiritual might also hold forth out of personal vulnerability or existential unveilings of the self. The Arabic word for spirituality is *ruhaniyya*, related to wind or breath, ungraspable yet with evident effects. Its advent and departure are unbidden and unpredictable and termed as *ahwāl* (states; sing; *hāl*), "something that descends from God into a man's heart, without his being able to repel it when it comes, or to attract it when it goes, by his own effort" (Al-Hujwīrī 2000, 181).

Despite the deep affinity between the spiritual and the religious, Stephen Gould (1999) believed that contemporary religion is frequently lived and expressed in terms that are fundamentally contradictory to its spiritual roots. Nor can any discussion of religion and spirituality take place without mention of mysticism, something perhaps not as fantastical as many imagine. As Wittgenstein said, "It is not *how* things are in the world that is mystical but *that* it exists" (2002, 88). Mysticism can be popularly understood as referring to unexplainable phenomena such as bilocation, extrasensory perception, visions, and healing by touch, which are popular misconceptions and tend to obscure an inherent earthiness that is characteristic of the mystics (Abbas 1993; de Waal 2001, 45). Whereas Bertrand Russell (2007) understood it as the antithesis of rationality in stating that a mystic could not also be a rational individual, Heidegger expressed the view that genuine mystics could be "astoundingly clear" and expound views characterized by "extreme sharpness and depth of though" (1996, 39). In analyzing the work of Orhan Pamuk and Abdolkarim Soroush, Heyking depicts them as intellectually engaging with mysticism, "not as an escape . . . but as a means of recapturing a more authentic experience of reality characterized by existential openness" (2006, 73).

There seems to be some initial mystical event at the heart of every major world religion, as Steindl-Rast would have it, "There is no religious doctrine that could not ultimately be traced back to its roots in mystical experience" (1989, 11). This is certainly the case with Islam, evident from the Prophet's revelatory experience in the Cave of Hira and the *mihraj* (the heavenly ascent) to the less mentioned yet strongly affirmed *hadiths* depicting events of a profoundly otherworldly nature. This would seem to necessitate an a priori existential choice before each believer to either accept or reject the *mystical* experiences of the Prophet. Despite the rationalist tendencies of Muslim modernists and reformers to perceive mysticism as something imported from other religions (El-Fadl 2001), there can be no overlooking of validated narrated events in the Prophet's life that can only be described as mystical. These include conversing with animals, trees moving through the earth toward him or crying at his departure as depicted in the famed *Ash-Shifa of Qadi 'Iyad* (1991) and other hadith collections widely accepted by *ulama* (scholars) of varying positions. It is interesting to postulate possible explanations to these inexplicable occurrences from different theological quarters; a Muslim modernist perspective might excuse these as hagiographic exaggerations. From the esoteric perspective, they would be perhaps seen as symbolic and mythical, whereas from the classical Muslim perspective, such things are left unquestioned in what has been referred to previously as *tawfid*.

Historical evidence clearly demonstrates the eventual reification of all religions and an ensuing conflict with the mystical and spiritual. "The same plot is acted out repeatedly on the stage of history: every religion seems to begin with mysticism and end up in politics" (Steindl-Rast 1989, 11). Into this mix we can throw Cantwell Smith's theory of the 'mundane process' (1991), the global historical shift from the sacred to the worldly, manifesting specifically within the Muslim context as a move from an intrinsically numinous phenomena to an ideology of socio-political defiance (Armstrong 2000; Esposito 2010; Nasr 1990; Winkel 1997). This has to be contrasted with accounts of classical Muslim society (Abbas 1993; Cornell 1996; 1998, Chodkiewisz 1993), which as Cantwell Smith contends show that,

" . . . over the course of the centuries there has been a demonstrable drift from the personalist, vivid and open sort of interpretation toward the other, closed and reified view that today is common" (1991, 110).

SPIRITUAL DEVELOPMENT IN EDUCATION

Since the early '90s, there has been a burgeoning move toward addressing children's spirituality within mainstream education provoking an ongoing controversy. Is spirituality only appropriate within religious schools or can it be extended to secular education (Hay and Nye 2006; Hyde 2007)? Such debates pertain again to defining spirituality, with some insisting that it relates to the self in relation to others (Moriarty 2011). Others perceive it as the link between the individual and the Divine (Fisher 2010), whereas still others comprehend it as a form of self-transcendence (Hay and Nye 2006). Nevertheless, despite these disputations, there is a consensus that spirituality can be identified by its characteristics and attributes (Best 1995; McCrery 1994).

Whatever the arguments are, fundamental incongruities remain, for it is questionable whether spiritual education, whether in secular or religious settings, is compatible with contemporary education. Schuerkens speaks of the "global discourse of management" (2014, 2), readily apparent in state administrations, corporations, leisure industries, labor unions, schools, education, religious institutions, and catering industries resulting in "a world controlled by managers" in a discourse "so widespread that it seems difficult to escape its grip" (ibid). Ritzer's theory of McDonaldization indicates the same, so that like squared watermelons, knowledge must be packaged to fit the demands of a target-based education. As Ritzer would have it, we move "from rationalized educational systems to rationalized work places, from rationalized recreational settings to rationalized homes" (Ritzer 1996, 21). There is also the phenomena of "a growing commercialization of 'religion' in the form of 'spirituality' as it is found in education, health-care, counseling, business training, management theory and marketing" (Carrette and King 2005, x), all of which seems fundamentally opposed to the spiritual.

With the outcome-based framework of contemporary education, the spiritual is tampered with, as with the watermelons, to enable assessment processes. Although describing another subject area, Cohen, Manion, and Morrison state, "Physical Fitness, for example, is not directly measurable until it has been operationally defined" (2007, 286). The fact that all subjects are measured by the same yardstick as the more 'calculative' subjects can be seen in "outcomes based approaches, with their emphasis on observed competencies, have impacted (. . .) not only on literacy and numeracy, but on religious education as well" (Hyde 2004, 118). Hyde's research in Australian Catholic schools was intended to provide "something tangible for teachers in recognizing when their students may be expressing their spirituality" for "they need to know how they might consciously plan experiences to achieve this aim within an outcomes-based culture" (Hyde 2004, 118). Whereas Buchanan and Hyde may claim that good spiritual education lies in setting up classroom environments wherein children learn to be more inwardly reflective (2008, 313), how 'plannable' and assessable can the spiritual be? As the mystic Ibn Ataillah said, "He who wishes that there appear, at a given moment, other than what God has manifested in it, has not left ignorance behind at all!" (1984, 36). Despite these arguments against, one must applaud the attempts to foster spiritual development within adverse circumstances, acknowledging that there are partial ways to get around the ethos of educational management systems to foster something beyond behavioral or outcome-based targets. But such endeavors are restricted as the 'subversion' is more than likely limited to the quality of the relationships established by individual teachers within a class.

For obvious reasons, one might expect more of the spiritual education provided in religious schools, whereas in fact such schools differ very little from the mainstream in meeting the managerial demands of contemporary education. In addition, many people confuse moral education with spiritual education. The similarity with mainstream education is not surprising when one considers that such schools, despite religious trappings, have adopted the same paradigms of mainstream education based upon utilitarian values stemming directly from the Enlightenment and the Industrial Revolution (Lawson and Silver 2013). In Britain, faith schools have the same National Curriculum and are accountable to the same educational authorities—how different can they be? Surely the marked differences in how the world is perceived from secular and religious perspectives should result in hugely contrasting educational philosophies and practices.

SPIRITUAL DEVELOPMENT IN MUSLIM EDUCATION

As we have seen, there seems to be some human need to perpetually quantify, codify, and systematize, and Muslim communities provide no exception to that rule. This can be seen from the 11th-century *Dars al Nizami* (educational system) reforms up to and including the contemporary modernist claim of Islam as a system of life.

> The explicit notion that life should be or can be ordered according to a system, even an ideal one, and that it is the business of Islam to provide such a system seems to be a modern idea (and perhaps a rather questionable one).
>
> (Cantwell-Smith 1991, 117)

This does not negate the Muslim claim of Islam simultaneously bearing upon all aspects of life nor dividing the sacred from the profane. Nevertheless, there is an increasingly common impression of Islam as a delineated systematic reality, which seems irreconcilable with the dynamic flow of the spiritual, whereas educational management systems would clearly be more compatible with this.

The written aims and objectives of most educational projects and endeavors carried out by Muslim communities make mention of the spiritual, usually expressed in terms of it constituting an essential element of the education offered (Al Attas, 1979; Ashraf, 1985; Rauf 1988). However, it is seldom very clear exactly what Muslim spirituality consists of, nor how this is translated into the classroom, which reflects a similar debate in the mainstream that took place between Marples (2006) and Best (2008). Yet for the purposes of this work, it will be assumed that there is something that can be termed spiritual and as Soroush asserts, "Islam also has a spiritual side. I think it is so powerful and so important that it has to be reintroduced in modern times" (quoted in Leezenberg 2007, 2). Nonetheless, many Muslim schools seem to link spirituality to the performance of *salat* (communal prayer) rendering it "a spirituality that is clearly referenced to religion" (Rossiter 2010a, 7). Whereas ritual may play a key role in developing spirituality, it is less effective and meaningful if limited only to this. Spiritual values must extend into dispositional values and the ethos of a school. But what are these values and how might they be realized?

With the spiritual now arrogated by educational management culture to be 'operationally defined,' it is suggested here that the term should now be abandoned in regard to contemporary Muslim education. Notwithstanding, there can be no negation of spirituality or mysticism as integral elements of 'Muslimness.' Despite foregoing these terms, certain aspects of both should be retained to support an education that provides ineffable modes of thinking counteracting the reduction of everything to the predominant calculative thinking of our time (Heidegger 2003, 105–106). This is not to deny the unique role of rationality in human affairs. The critique presented earlier focuses on static rationalism as opposed to more dynamic and creative rationality, yet recognizing neither as adequate in all instances of human experience.

ADAB, *AKHLĀQ*, *IHSĀN*, AND *IKHLĀS*

> Actions are lifeless forms (*suwar qa'ima*), but the presence of an inner reality of sincerity (*sirr al-ikhlās*) within them is what endows them with life-giving Spirit.
>
> (Ibn 'Atā'illah 1984, 25)

Two essential aims of any Muslim educational venture must be to foster awareness of the Divine presence in every moment and to know that even without this awareness, Allah is ceaselessly aware of each individual. This is based on the Prophet's definition of *ihsān*: "It is to worship Allah as though you see Him, and though you do not see Him, know that He sees you" (Sahih Bukhari 1997, 47: 1). It follows from this that one should remember God as much as possible; in turn, suggesting that *ihsān* could adequately replace the spiritual term. However, in doing so, we might be delving into something that ultimately proves counterproductive. Whereas *Islam* may be taught as skills and knowledge and *iman* can also develop through knowledge (*ilm kasbi*), yet *ihsān* cannot be obtained either through taught knowledge or skills (*ilm wahbi*) in any modern educational sense. It might be preferable to turn toward the more tangible aspect of refining character (*akhlāq*) based on the Prophetic claim, "I came for nothing but to perfect character" (Musnad Ahmad Ibn Hanbal: 8595). This concept is closely associated to yet another contender, the concept of *adab*, defining a profound spiritual courtesy with others, the self, objects, and the Divine and encompassing a spontaneous generosity in thought and action, although it is often mistakenly minimized in translation to having good manners. In a sociological study of *adab* within Egyptian and Sudanese society (although something that will be reflected throughout the Muslim world), Fabós relates that *adab* is reflected in those whose "homes and their kitchens are always open, that whatever possessions they have should be shared and given to guests" and feel "they ought to freely share their time and money with people in need, relegating their own needs or interests to secondary importance" (2008, 98). But unfortunately *adab* does not lend itself to educational settings and is something that evolves naturally and cannot be codified or theorized upon.

Nevertheless, a prerequisite for *adab* and the other suggested alternatives would have to be *ikhlās*. A word frequently translated as *sincerity* but argued here as being more appropriately related to the concept of *authenticity* as depicted in the following:

> more strenuous (. . .) than "sincerity," a more exigent conception of the self and of what being true to it consists in, a wider reference to the universe and man's place in it and a less acceptant and genial view of the social circumstances of life.
>
> (Trilling 1972, 11)

Trilling's definition seems to accord more readily with the sense of import conveyed by *ikhlās* in Arabic. Personal authenticity as an educational aim involves a process of coming to self-integrity and an awareness of personal choice and responsibility. It can be a movement from mindless conformity to mindful autonomy, yet not necessitating any rejection of tradition. *Ikhlās* entails a process toward inward integrity mirrored naturally in outward action rooted in an authentically determined historical praxis (Islam) situated in the 'now' and as such is precursorial to either *adab*, *akhlāq*, *or ihsān* referred to earlier.

Inauthenticity is an integral part of the human condition, resulting from personal choice with an ensuing loss of the self, compliant and acceptable to others wherein "Everyone is the other and no one is himself" as Heidegger says (1996, 120). Fortunately, an inauthentic life can be overcome and the self regained, a sense conveyed by the German word for authenticity, *eigentlich* meaning 'own self.' Authenticity is the retrieving of one's true self or the wresting of one's identity from the inclinations of the many or the world generally.

Ibn 'Arabi bases much of his thought on the *hadith*, "He who knows himself knows his Lord" (quoted by Chittick 1989, 312), which he establishes as one of the main objectives of the mystic path. Kierkegaard states, "The human being is spirit. But what is spirit? Spirit is the self. But what is the self? The self is a relation which relates itself to its own self" (2004, 43). In simpler terms, this implies that the self consists of that which recognizes itself as a self and a self in relation to others. Kierkegaard understood selfhood as consisting of the process of coming to the perception of one as a genuine individual and the awakening search for this is the most important human undertaking possible, an imperative. Eliade perceived human authenticity as laying within a nondualist 'Real,' beyond all definition and limitations, an Ultimate Reality which lays at the core of what is considered the sacred (1979, 28, 139–145). Human existence is essentially a striving for authenticity, chiefly consisting of the search for liberation from the limitations of the temporal and spatial (1979, 10). Bearing all of this in mind, Welch defines the mystics as those who are "clarifiers of what it means to be human" (1996, 123).

IN PRACTICE

How can this regaining of the self play out as spiritual education within Muslim schools? *Ikhlās* can be perceived as a summoning of the singular and the unique, insofar that it refers to the singularity or uniqueness of each person and each moment. As such, in any educational setting, the term *ikhlās* should not become codified in establishing achievement targets but indicate an ambience of *muhasaba* (self-reckoning), integrity, and straightforwardness permeating the school ethos. Dualistic judgments of authenticity and inauthenticity are to be avoided, for inauthenticity must be good-humoredly accepted as part of the human condition, although the cost of maintaining it should be made clear. Equally, when authenticity occurs, it should be acknowledged yet not overly aggrandized.

Some indication of how *ikhlās* would play out practically in a class is needed, and it is thought best to provide an imaginary classroom scenario consisting of an amalgamation of real classroom experiences blended together followed by a brief analysis. Hence this imaginary class takes place within a thinking skills lesson made up of a group of fifteen seventeen-year-olds.

During some exploratory discussion, the subject of divorce emerges spontaneously and it is soon revealed that the majority of the students in the class have divorced parents. The teacher responds to this by revealing that not only is she divorced but she also has divorced parents, and upon sharing this, a tangible and heightened shift in the class energy is evident. The discussion moves onto the nature of marital relationships and the how and why of marriage breakdown. There is a sentiment of anger apparent when students concur on the irresponsibility of parents in getting married and having children if they were not fully committed. As the conversation moves on in this vein, the teacher asks how old their parents were when they married, and although some of them do not know, others reckoned it to be in their early twenties. The teacher goes on to point out that only a few years separate them from their parents' age when they married and the students are asked to imagine their parents in their early twenties. This is met with a moment of silence as the students take this in. Surely people are allowed to make mistakes, the teacher points out, and surely in the class there must be people who had already had the experience of 'falling in love' where one felt able to devote their whole life to another. Do these feelings remain constant? One of the students responds by saying that feelings do change and can actually shift to rage against the same person. Why would their parents be any different, the teacher suggests. Students laugh, some self-consciously, and there is general agreement that feelings can be deceptive. One student mentions that her parents' broken relationship had made her very wary of any possible relationship in the future. From there the subject of absent parents arises and there seems to be universal agreement from those students who undergo this that such parents are remiss and do not seem to care. Many of them had stopped communicating with the absent parent and only begrudgingly met them when necessary; i.e., so as to obtain money, which they saw as their right. While explaining that she found her father a fascinating man yet very distant, one student becomes visibly upset and tearful. She had refused to communicate with him for over a year and complained that he never tried to contact her during that time. Her outbreak and the frank revelation ratchets up yet another shift in the atmosphere. In response, another student, normally irreverently disruptive, points out with deliberate kindness that she was doing the same as her father in not communicating and one of them had to break the cycle. This brings forth a series of observations concerning the validity of this type of emotional retribution with the majority seeing the absent parent deserving of this treatment. One student puts forward the idea that there is no blame—the breakdown of the relationship between the parents is a matter between them, which brings about general agreement—what is important is to maintain ties with both parents and keep judgments to a minimum. Whereas the satisfaction of retribution might be gained, the teacher points out, the hurt of no relationship with the absent parent remains. There is a general consensus that someone has to break the cycle of not being in communication with an absent parent and any type of disagreement with anyone resulting in no contact. One has to be honest with oneself about whether one wishes contact and if so, admit it and approach the other. Someone else admits that one has to be ready to be hurt, for the parent may not respond despite the special effort.

In the final phase of the class, the teacher puts forward some relevant Qur'anic verses, *hadith*, and applications of *fiqh* interpretations depicting the Prophetic view on the questions of divorce and redressing grievances and maintaining the ties of kinship. Applying individual examples of relation breakdowns just provided by the students, students were asked what they thought the Prophet would recommend. Inevitably, in each case, it was acknowledged that brokering peace with the estranged person would have been the recommendation. The status of parents and holding them in some esteem was broached. The teacher suggested that it was important to not foment situations wherein parental reactions would cause one to lose respect. Despite their faults, they are the very first men and women that one encounters. If relations with them are not sound, then how will future relations with other men and women be as life proceeds?

A BRIEF POST ANALYSIS

There is a distinct psychological element inherent in the session, which should not be equated with some new age spiritualization of psychology. Nor is there anything untoward in this, as Frankl says:

> Yet responsibility and freedom comprise the spiritual domain of man. Contemporary man, however, has become weary of all that is spiritual and this weariness is perhaps the essence of that nihilism which has so often been mentioned and so rarely been defined. It will have to be countered by collective psychotherapy.
>
> (Frankl 1986, xxiv)

Within the lesson, the matter of divorce arises extemporaneously, indicating that content is directed throughout by the students. It is important to start from where the students are rather than impose theoretical ideas outside of any immediate experience. An eventual expansion of ideas beyond those yet related to the existent situation may be applied later. Had this been a planned learning activity to deal with divorce or relations with parents, the results would have been very different. In order for such opportunities to arise in class, a climate and culture needs to be established that would have to be part of a whole school attitudinal approach. The teacher's skill lies in vigilantly waiting for something to emerge, allowing for opportunities to impartially identify inauthenticity and demonstrate the possibility of authenticity. This involves having the confidence to proceed without the assurance of knowing where it will end. Interjections are made only when necessary and a constant nonjudgmental demeanor is maintained. Students feel respected and are disarmed by a teacher's straightforward sharing of his or her own vulnerabilities, and there is an increased likelihood of students opening up more about themselves than usual. This could be seen in the fact that students' social images were momentarily shed and they spoke poignantly from within and were responded to in equal terms. When such moments arise, there is a marked change in the class atmosphere; students behave differently, authentically manifesting emotions such as tearfulness. Such encounters mark them out as significant, arguably even sacred, and are both memorable and meaningful, possibly spilling over into other areas of their lives.

During the class, individual and group inauthenticities are identified, although in and of themselves, not specifically by the teacher. These inauthenticities are acknowledged by some and maintained by others. Some recognized that they had tricked themselves into attitudes that were damaging (inauthenticity) and came to realize that they bore some responsibility for the state of affairs with the absent parent (authenticity). In the final phase of the class, there was application of Qur'anic and Prophetic perspectives and the *usul* (guiding principles) to some of the ideas arrived at during the class. These may not have been as extensive as one would like, due to the impromptu nature of the class and not all teachers being able to link reference easily and therefore a follow-up to the class might look into these further but always in reference to what had been discussed. It is of utmost importance that these are not presented as rule-based truths but as flexible principals (*al-qawa'id*).

Authenticity evolves from individual conviction and living up to the ideals of the self often associated with a breaking with custom: "the issue of authenticity cannot arise in traditional society" (Lee 1997, 16). Although this may apply in some situations, nevertheless, an automatic rejection of tradition as part of an authentic move is a popular misconception, and there is no tangible reason why classical Islam cannot be lived out authentically by free choice.

Leading on from this, what is proposed must be distinguished from what Frankfurt (2005) identifies as antirealists who, when it "makes no sense to try to be true to the facts, he must therefore try instead to be true to himself" (2005, 67) rejects objective reality to replace it with self-constructed 'truths.' As Frankfurt rightly suggests, how can an individual validate him or herself objectively if he or she only uses subjective criteria? "Facts about ourselves are not peculiarly solid and resistant to sceptical dissolution. Our natures are, indeed, elusively insubstantial and notoriously less stable and less inherent than the natures of other things" (ibid). The pursuit of *ikhlās* suggested in this work is diametrically opposite from the voguish attempt to justify the biddings of the self.

CONCLUSION

One Prophetic aim was seemingly to create extraordinary people able to transcend the ordinary limitations of human thought and behavior. This calls for a different way of thinking, a spiritual and religious thinking that should be markedly different from global management thinking and is something that should and could be addressed at an educational level.

The spiritual development proposed here through the auspices of *ikhlās* is designed to awaken students to the possibility of choice and to thereby transcend the self within the context of the Prophetic way. No claim is made here of this being the only device to bring about a much-needed change in Muslim education for much more needs to be done. Such changes need to occur initially within a paradigm shift in the thinking of Muslim educationalists and then filter down to the level of the classroom. As such, the practical classroom example afforded earlier is more for theoretical use than the practical.

It has been argued that Islam is primarily a spiritual phenomenon, seen in the initial events in the Cave of Hira despite the Muslim community having undergone a profound move away from this over the last fifty to seventy years to a globalized, political ideology. It has been suggested that the mystical events of the Prophet's life be given more import than is currently the case to present a different way of thinking. Simply put, a case has been presented that education has come to be dominated by modern management systems, that this by necessity is at odds with any spiritual development, and that the antidote to the rationalism of our times lies within the spiritual and mystical.

Whether Muslim schools utilizing a modern pedagogy, employing the notion of *ikhlās*, would be effective remains an open question. Yet there is no question that it is time for a markedly different type of education to evolve out of the unique perspective of Islam, which could evolve out of an increasing interest in returning to the classical and spiritual. Nor need this be a xenophobic type of reaction, but rather allow greater active participation, as opposed to the present passive interaction, in contributing to the educational debate globally. Even if in disagreement, it is hoped that there were some ideas presented earlier that may stimulate further thought and action with Muslim educational circles.

BIBLIOGRAPHY

Abbas, Claude. 1993. *Quest for the Red Sulphur—The Life of In al-'Arabia*. Translated by Peter Kingsley. Cambridge: Islamic Texts Society.

al-Attas, Syed Muhammad al-Naquib. 1979. "Preliminary Thoughts on the Nature of Knowledge and the Definition of the Aims of Education" in *Aims and Objectives of Islamic Education,* Edited by Syed Muhammad al-Naquib al-Attas, 19–47. Aylesbury: Hodder & Stoughton.

Al-Hujwīrī, Ali ibn-Uthman. 2000. *Kashf al-Majūb—(The Revelation of the Unveiled) An Early Persian Treastise on Sufism*. Translated by Reynold Alleyne Nicholson. London: Gibb Memorial Series.

Armstrong, Karen. 2000. *The Battle for God*. London: Harper.

Ashraf. Syed Ali. 1985. *New Horizons in Muslim Education*. Cambridge: Hodder & Stoughton.

Best, Ron. 2008. "In defence of the concept of 'spiritual education': A reply to Roger Marples," *International Journal of Children's Spirituality*, 13 (4): November: 321–329. Taylor & Francis.

Best, Ron. 1995. *Education, Spirituality, and the Whole Child*, edited by Ron Best. New York: Cassell.

Brown, Daniel. 1996. *Rethinking Tradition in Modern Islamic Thought*. Cambridge: Cambridge University Press.

Bruinessen, Martin van & Julia Day Howell. 2007. *Sufism and the "Modern" in Islam*. London and New York: I.B. Tauris.

Cantwell Smith, Wilfrid. 1981. *On Understanding Islam—Selected Studies*. The Hague: Mouton Publishers.

Cantwell Smith, Wilfrid.1991. *The Meaning and End of Religion*. Minneapolis, Fortress Press.

Chittick, William. 1989. *The Sufi Path of Knowledge—Ibn 'Arabi's Metaphysics of the Imagination*. Albany, New York: SUNY Press.

Chittick, William. 2005. *Ibn Al-'Arabi—Heir to the Prophets*. Oxford: Oneworld.

Chodkiewicz, Michel. 1993. *An Ocean without Shore, the Book, and the Law*. Translated by David Streight. Albany, New York: SUNY Press.

Cohen, Louis, Lawrence Manion & Keith Morrison. 2007. *Research Methods in Education*, Abingdon: Routledge.

Cornell, Vincent. 1996. *The Way of Abu Madyan: Doctrinal and Poetic Works of Abu Madyan Shu'ayb ibn al Husayn al-Ansari*. Cambridge: Islamic Text Society.

Cornell, Vincent. 1998. *Realm of the Saint: Power and Authority in Moroccan Sufism*. Austin: University of Texas.

Cornell, Vincent. 2004. "Practical Sufism: An Akbarian Foundation for a Liberal Theology of Difference." *Journal of the Muhyiddin Ibn 'Arabi Society* 36: 59–84.

De Waal, Esther. 2001. *Seeking God*. Collegeville, Minnesota: Liturgical Press.

El Fadl, Khalid Abou. 2001. "Islam and the Theology of Power." *Middle East Research and Information Project* 31 (Winter): 28–33.

Eliade, Mircea. 1979. *The Two and the One*. Translated by J. M Cohen, Chicago: University of Chicago Press.

Mircea. 1998. *Myth and Reality*. Long Grove, Illinois: Waveland Press.

Eliade, Mircea.1991. *The Myth of the Eternal Return Or, Cosmos and History*, Princeton, New Jersey: Princeton University Press.

Esposito, John L. 2010. *The Future of Islam*. Oxford: Oxford University Press.

Fabós, Anita. 2008. *Brothers or Others—Propriety and Gender for Muslim Arab Sudanese in Egypt*. Oxford and New York: Berghahn Books.

Frankfurt, Harry Gordon. 2005. *On Bullshit*. Princeton, New Jersey: Princeton University Press.

Frankl, Viktor. 1986. *The Doctor and the Soul—From Psychotherapy to Logotherapy*. New York: Vintage.

Gould, Stephen Jay. 1999. *Rock of Ages—Science and Religion in the fullness of Life*. London: Jonathan Cape.

Hay, David & Rebecca Nye. 2006. *The Spirit of the Child*. London: Jessica Kingsley Publishers.

Heidegger, Martin. 1996. *The Principle of Reason*. Translated by Reginald Storrs Lilly. Bloomington, Indianapolis: Indiana University Press.

Heidegger, Martin. 2003. *The End of Philosophy*. Translated by Joan Stambuagh. Chicago: University of Chicago.

Heidegger M. (1982). *The Question of Technology and Other Essays*. New York: Harper and Row.

Hyde, Brendan. 2005. Integrating awareness: A characteristic of children's spirituality in Australian Catholic primary schools. *Journal of Religious Education* 53 (4): 54–62.

Hyde, Brendan. 2006. "Nurturing the Spirit in Primary Religious Education Classrooms." In *International Handbook of the Religious, Moral and Spiritual Dimensions in Education,* Edited by Marian de Souza, Gloria Durka, Kathleen Engebretson, Robert Jackson & Andrew McGrady. 1179–1192. Dordrecht: Springer.

Hyde, Brendan. 2007. "A Pedagogy of Spirit." In *Religious Education in Early Childhood: A Reader,* Edited by J. Grajczonek & M. Ryan. 18–31. Brisbane: Lumino Press.

Hyde, Brendan. 2008. "The identification of four characteristics of children's spirituality in Australian Catholic primary schools." *International Journal of Children's Spirituality* 13 (2): 117–127.

Ibn 'Atā'illāh, Taj ad-Din. 1978. *Sufi Aphorisms—Kitāb al-Hikam.* Translated by Victor Danner. Leiden: Brill.

Kierkegaard, Søren, 2004. *Sickness Unto Death*. Translated by Alastair Hannay. London: Penguin.

Lawson, John, and Harold Silver. 2013. *A Social History of Education in England.* Abingdon: Routledge.

Lee, Robert D. 1997. *Overcoming Tradition and Modernity: The Search for Islamic Authenticity*. Boulder: Westview Press.

Leezenberg, Michiel. 2007. "Interview Soroush: Enlightenment & Philosophy in Islam." *International Institute for the Study of Islam in the Modern World.* Review 20, Autumn 2007, University of Leiden. Accessed January 1, 2015. http://www.scribd.com/doc/38105739/An-Interveiw-with-Abdolkarim-Soroush-by-Michiel-Leezenberg-Enlightenment-and-Philosophy-in-Islam.

Lings, Martin. 1993. *A Sufi Saint of the Twentieth Century: Shaikh Ahmad al-Alawi, His Spirtual Heritage and Legacy.* Cambridge: Islamic Texts Society.

Marples, Roger. 2006. "Against (the use of the term) 'spiritual education.' " *International Journal of Children's Spirituality* 11 (2): 293–306.

McCreery, Elaine. 1994. "Toward an understanding of the notion of the spiritual in education." *Early Child Development and Care* 100 (1): 93–99.

Moriarty, Micheline Wyn. 2011. "A conceptualization of children's spirituality arising out of recent research." *International Journal of Children's Spirituality* 16 (3): 271–285.

Nasr, Seyyed Hussein. 1990. *Traditional Islam in the Modern World.* London: Kegan Paul International.

Qadi 'Iyad ibn Musa al-Yasubi. 1991. *Muhammad, Messenger of Allah, Ash-Shifa of Qadi 'Iyad.* Translated by Aisha Abdurahman Bewley. Granada: Madinah Press.

Rauf, S. M. A. 1988. *Mawdudi on Education*. Karachi: Islamic Research Academy.

Rossiter, Graham. 2010a. "A case for a 'big picture' re-orientation of K–12 Australian Catholic school religious education in the light of contemporary spirituality." *Journal of Religious Education* 58 (3): 5–18.

Rossiter, Graham. 2010b. "Religious education and the changing landscape of spirituality: Through the lens of change in cultural meanings." *Journal of Religious Education* 58 (2): 25–36.

Russell, Bertrand. 2007. *Mysticism and Logic*. Nottingham: Spokesman Books.

Steindl-Rast, Br. David. 1989. *The Mystical Core of Organized Religion*. ReVision 12 (1): 11–14. Accessed March 15, 2015. http://csp.org/experience/docs/steindl mystical.html.

Trilling, Lionel. 1972. *Sincerity and Authenticity*. Oxford: Oxford University Press.

Welch, John. 1996. *The Carmelite Way—An Ancient Path for Today*. Mahwah, New Jersey: Paulist Press.

Wittgenstein, Ludwig. 2002. *Tractatus Logico-Philosophicus*. London: Routledge.

Wittgenstein, Ludwig. 2009. *Philosophical Investigations*. Translated by Gertrude Elizabeth Margaret Anscombe, Peter Michael Stephen Hacker and Joachim Schulte, Hoboken: Wiley-Blackwell.

Winkel, Eric.1997. *Islam and the Living Law—The Ibn Arabi Approach*. Karachi: Oxford University Press.

5 "Your Educational Achievements Shall Not Stop Your Efforts to Seek Beyond"

Principles of Teaching and Learning in Classical Arabic Writings[1]

Sebastian Günther

Scholarly discussions on theoretical and practical issues in teaching and learning are essential components in a large variety of Arabic writings from the classical period of Islam, covering the time between the 8th and the 15th century CE.[2] Muslim scholars addressing pedagogical and didactic issues included philosophers, theologians, jurists, hadith scholars, littérateurs, and natural scientists. They came from various backgrounds and scholarly disciplines, each with his own theological and juridical stance, ethnic origin, or geographical affiliation. Although many of these intellectuals taught, none of them were exclusively specialized in education or its theories.

Generally speaking, classical Arabic texts devoted to issues in Islamic education are characterized by their fundamental grounding in principles expressed in the Quran and the prophetic tradition (*ḥadīth*). No less important, however, is that a great number of these educational considerations are deeply shaped by paradigms of the ancient Greek *paideia* ('rearing,' 'education'), as well as elements of ancient Arabian and Persian culture, which Muslim scholars had creatively adapted to their educational views and further developed, mostly during the 9th and 10th centuries. It should be noted, however, that whereas educational thought in antiquity was almost exclusively philosophical in nature, in Islam it was to a great extent informed and shaped by religion. In addition, Islamic education in medieval times correlated—partly in mutually beneficial exchanges—with medieval Jewish and Christian views and practices of learning significant to the world of Islam at the time.

Among Arabic texts explicitly dealing with Islamic education, the genre called *ādāb al-ʿālim wa-l-mutaʿallim* ("Rules of Conduct for Teachers and Students") stands out. This category of Arabic works, both short treatises and larger compendia, explains and analyses—in an erudite and often literary manner—the objectives, ideals, and methods of teaching and learning, including the ways in which teachers and students act and behave, their (moral) characteristics, and their relationships with one another in the educational process. This included didactic issues such as the organization and content of learning and the curriculum, as well as the means and methods of imparting and absorbing knowledge. Therefore, the *ādāb al-ʿālim wa-l-mutaʿallim* literature is rightly called 'pedagogical,' even though there was no scholarly discipline in premodern Islam expressly known as *ʿilm al-tarbiya*, 'pedagogy.'[3]

On these premises, this chapter offers insights into certain Arabic pedagogical writings from the classical period of Islam, which, due to their scholarly originality and/or special authoritative character, are true landmarks in the history of Islam's educational thought. Whereas these classical texts provide us with valuable information on the early beginnings and the dynamic advancement of educational theory and curriculum development in Islam, they also demonstrate that certain problems encountered in medieval times continue to concern us today.

ABŪ ḤANĪFA AND AL-SAMARQANDĪ: CRITICAL THINKING PROMOTES LEARNING

The earliest treatise in Islam with an explicit pedagogical approach is the *Kitāb al-ʿālim wa-l-mutaʿallim* ("The Book of the One Who Knows and the One Who Wants to Know"). This work has traditionally been ascribed to the Kufan jurist and theologian Abū Ḥanīfa al-Nuʿmān ibn Thābit (d. 148/767 AD), eponym of the largest of the four Sunni schools of law. However, the person who actually drafted this, one of the most popular among Hanafi's works, was Abū Muqātil al-Samarqandī (d. 208/823 AD), who apparently was one of Abū Ḥanīfa's students. Not much is known about Abū Muqātil al-Samarqandī. The sources indicate, however, that he was a pious and almost ascetic scholar. While he seems not to have been particularly reliable as a transmitter of prophetic traditions, he was well recognized among his peers as a specialist in the field of Islamic jurisprudence.[4]

Basically, the *Kitāb al-ʿālim wa-l-mutaʿallim* consists of the *quaestiones* a disciple asks his master, and the *responsa* the master offers to his student. In this regard, this early Arabic manual is very close to the genre of Socratic dialogue, as the following passages demonstrate:

> THE MASTER STATED: *What a great decision of yours to search for what is of benefit to you. Know that actions follow knowledge like the body parts comply with the eyesight. Therefore, learning knowledge with little action is better than ignorance with much action . . . . This is why God stated [in the Quran]: "Say, 'How can those who know be equal to those who do not know?' Only those who have understanding will take heed."*
>
> (Q 39:9, tr. Abdel Haleem)
>
> THE DISCIPLEDI REPLIED: *You have motivated me to seek knowledge even more! . . . So instruct me about the proofs against*

them (i.e., people who would advise learners to follow the tradition without any thoughts of their own).

[THE MASTER STATED:] I saw people saying, "Do not engage yourself with these arguments, for the Companions of the Messenger of God—peace be upon him and grant him salvation—did not engage themselves in anything related to these matters. Perhaps, what was sufficient for them should also be sufficient for you." But these people only increased my sadness. I have come to see them like someone telling a man who is drowning in a huge, water-rich river and seeking a ford to cross, "Stay where you are and, by no means attempt to find a ford!"

THE MASTER—MAY HE REST IN PEACE—SAID [FURTHERMORE]: [By now,] I think you understand not only some of the deficiencies of these people, but also the proof against them [and their arguments]. However, if they tell you, "Should not suffice you what had sufficed the Companions of the Prophet?"—peace be upon him and grant him salvation—, then respond to them, "It certainly should, had I been in their rank and position. But I have not witnessed what they witnessed. [Moreover,] we [today] have to deal with people who vilify us and permit that our blood is shed. Therefore, we will not make progress, if we do not know who amongst us is right and who is wrong. [Hence, we must use our own minds and understanding in order to assess matters and make decisions.]"

(Abū Ḥanīfa/al-Samarqandī 1964, 9)

The treatise's overall thematic focus is on Islamic "creeds and advice concerning the way a student asks a question and how a teacher responds," as the great Ottoman historian and geographer Ḥajjī Khalīfa (d. 1067/1657 AD) observed.[5] In addition to a number of dogmatic instructions, this book offers important pedagogical advice: It promotes the question-and-answer pattern as a key method of active learning, stresses the need for making creative use of the intellect and of reasoning even in religious matters, highlights the importance of always identifying 'true' and 'false' by cognitive investigation; and emphasizes the obligation of those striving for knowledge to concentrate on the essence of things.

AL-JĀḤIẒ: AN OPEN MIND MAKES KNOWLEDGE ACQUISITION VIRTUOUS

Perhaps the earliest literary-philosophical essay dedicated to 'the teachers' was composed by ʿAmr ibn Baḥr al-Jāḥiẓ, the celebrated philosophical theologian. Al-Jāḥiẓ was born in about 160/776 in Basra and died there in 255/868–9. He was probably of Ethiopian origin and received his sobriquet due to an ocular malformation (al-Jāḥiẓ means 'the pop-eyed'). From an early age, al-Jāḥiẓ dedicated himself to learning. He took a special interest in the works of the ancient Greek philosophers, especially Aristotle, available in Arabic because of the great translation movement under Caliph al-Ma᾽mūn (r. 813–833), and participated frequently in the intellectual discussions that took place in the literary salons of the upper class.

The working conditions and often unfair treatment of professional teachers that al-Jāḥiẓ witnessed may have prompted him to compose a *Kitāb al-Mu῾allimīn* ("The Book of the Teachers") in which he not only defends but champions schoolteachers by stressing their superiority over all other types of educators and tutors.[6] He also expressed clear pedagogical advice in this treatise: He highlights the importance of instructing students in the techniques of logical argumentation and deduction, as well as in good written expression; advocates the reading of books for the purpose of instruction, as it is said to promote creative thinking; advises teachers to organize schooling in a way that takes the mental abilities of the students into due account; and states that students always need to be treated with special care and kindness.

Remarkably, in stark contrast to the majority opinion of traditional medieval Muslim scholarship, al-Jāḥiẓ questions both the supremacy of memorization in Islamic learning and the view that only firmly established knowledge should be transmitted. Such an approach, al-Jāḥiẓ observes, would make "the mind disregard distinction" and prevent learners from reaching conclusions on their own. Yet, as a dialectical intellectual, al-Jāḥiẓ expresses his criticism in balanced words when he states:

> *The leading sages, masters of the art of deductive reasoning and [independent] thinking, were averse to excellence in memorization, because of [one's] dependence on it and [its rendering] the mind negligent of rational judgment . . . .*
>
> *[They were averse to memorization] because a student engaged in memorizing is only an imitator, whereas deductive reasoning brings the student to deliberate certainty and great confidence.*
>
> *The true proposition and the praiseworthy judgment is that, when [a student] learns only by memorization, this harms his deductive reasoning. But conversely, when he uses only deductive reasoning, this harms his learning by memorization—even if memorization has a more honorable rank than [deductive reasoning]. So, when he neglects rational reflection, ideas do not come quickly to him, and when he neglects memorization, [such ideas] do not stick in his mind or remain long in his heart. [Although] the nature of memorization is different to that of deductive reasoning, both are concerned with and support the same thing: to free the mind and [make the student] desire only one thing [that is, learning]. By means of these two [approaches] (i.e., freeing the mind and desiring only to learn), perfection comes to be and virtue appears.*
>
> (Günther 2005b, 122)

As for the curriculum, al-Jāḥiẓ lists compulsory disciplines in the following order: writing, arithmetic, law, the pillars of religion, the Quran, grammar, prosody, and poetry. Optional topics of instruction would include polo, archery, horsemanship, and music, as well as chess and other games. Interestingly, al-Jāḥiẓ makes another significant point regarding education in stressing the fundamental impact that writing has had on human civilization. Writing and recording, along with calculation, he calls 'the pillars' on which the present and the future of civilization and "the welfare of this world" rest. Writing and calculation are God-given, as are the teachers themselves, for God "made them available to us." (Günther 2005b, 144).

IBN SAḤNŪN: MODESTY AND PASSION ARE INDISPENSABLE IN TEACHING

The first real handbook for Muslim teachers was compiled in the 3rd/9th century by Muḥammad ibn Saḥnūn al-Tanūkhī, a Maliki jurist, hadith scholar, historian, and biographer from a region in what today is Tunisia. Ibn Saḥnūn was born in 202/817 in Kairouan, a city that, at the beginning of the 3rd/9th century, was a nucleus of the Maliki school of law in the western lands of Islam. Ibn Saḥnūn was of Arab descent. After his father's death, Ibn Saḥnūn became chief judge of the Malikites in the Maghreb. He died in Kairouan in 256/870 at the age of only fifty-four. Ibn Saḥnūn was a prolific scholar and is reported to have written nearly two hundred books and treatises, but only three texts have been preserved.

Ibn Saḥnūn's best-known work is his treatise *Ādāb al-muʿallimīn* ("Rules of Conduct for Teachers").[7] In this book, he offers legal and practical advice for elementary schoolteachers regarding such issues as hiring and paying teachers, organization of teaching units and curriculum, working with students in class, permissibility of punishment, classroom equipment and teaching materials, examination, and graduation (Günther 2006, 369–71). More specifically, Ibn Saḥnūn stresses the following:

- Modesty, patience, and a passion for working with children are indispensable qualifications for teachers.
- A classroom atmosphere, which motivates pupils to learn and challenges their minds, makes teaching more effective and generally facilitates learning.
- Teamwork should be encouraged, along with fair competition among pupils, because both help advance character formation and intellectual development in children.

Ibn Saḥnūn also advises against teaching the Quran to the children of Christians. This seems to indicate that Muslim and Christian children were attending classes together in Ibn Saḥnūn's day. It also suggests that the author took the Quranic injunction "There is no compulsion in matters of faith" (Q 2:256) to mean that faith is a matter of individual concern and commitment and not something to be enforced. Furthermore, quoting his famous father, Saḥnūn states:

> *The teacher must be committed to working hard. He must devote himself to the pupils, . . . because he is a salaried employee; he cannot leave his work [for no reason].*
>
> *[Also, the teacher] must schedule a fixed time to review [the children's knowledge] of the Quran, such as Thursdays or Wednesday evenings. Yet, he must give them a day off on Fridays. This has been the practice since there have been teachers, and they have never been criticized for that.*
>
> (Günther 2005a, 105–108)

The curriculum that Ibn Saḥnūn outlines is to a degree representative of medieval Islamic elementary schooling (beginning at six or seven years of age). It includes obligatory teaching subjects such as the precise articulation and memorization of the Quran, or parts of it; the duties of worship; reading and writing; and good manners, because these are obligations toward God. It also recommended instructing pupils in the basics of the Arabic language and grammar, good handwriting, mathematics, poetry (as long as the verses are morally decent), proverbs, and speeches, as well as Arab history.

AL-FĀRĀBĪ: A COMPREHENSIVE EDUCATION LEADS TO HUMAN PERFECTION

Abū Naṣr al-Fārābī (d. 339/950 AD) is considered the most important political philosopher in classical Islam and probably the first truly eminent Muslim logician. Interestingly, he was also a noted metaphysician and a brilliant musical theorist. Born in Turkestan, he lived most of his life in Baghdad, Iraq, and, for a short period, in Aleppo, Syria. Al-Fārābī studied with the leading philosophers and logicians of his day, including certain prominent scholars in the Baghdad school of Christian Aristotelians. Al-Fārābī died in Damascus at the age of eighty years or more.

Concerning al-Fārābī's principal views on learning, it is important to note that he assigns ethics a key role in education, asserting that both the intention and conduct of learning need to be virtuous. Thus, for al-Fārābī, a perfect human being (*insān kāmil*) is

> *the one who has obtained theoretical virtue—thus completing his intellectual knowledge—and has acquired practical moral virtues—thus becoming perfect in his moral behavior. Only when these theoretical*

> *and moral virtues support effective power, do they become anchored in the souls of individual members of the community who come to assume the responsibility of political leadership.*
>
> ('Al-Fārābī 1993, 355)

Al-Fārābī further maintains that, whereas every human possesses certain inborn aptitudes or natural abilities on which an education must be built, teachers are still responsible for bringing out the best in their students, regardless of whether a student is slow in learning or intelligent. Yet a student's excellence deserves support under all circumstances. In a similar vein, al-Fārābī suggests that students ought to cherish and honor their teacher, but not to the extent that they prefer their teacher's opinion to the truth. With this in mind, al-Fārābī specifically recommends:

> *As for the teacher's measured approach (qiyās) [to instructing students], he should be neither too controlling nor too humble. Too much dominance drives the student to hate his teacher. [However,] if the student sees too much humility in his teacher, this leads him to belittle him and become slothful towards him and his teaching.*
>
> (Günther 2010, 18)

In his *Iḥṣā' al-'ulūm* ("The Enumeration of the Sciences"), al-Fārābī makes a strong case for an integrated curriculum, covering both the 'indigenous' and the 'foreign' branches of knowledge (i.e., the religious subjects based on the Quran and its interpretation on the one hand, and the subjects based on Greek philosophy and other, more secular disciplines on the other) (Günther 2006, 373–376). This inclusive approach to education was adopted and developed further by Muslim sages, such as Ibn Sīnā (d. 428/1037 AD) and the Brethren of Purity (in the second half of the 4th/10th century). It influenced the studies of the philosophers (and the physicians) who largely followed this curriculum in their informal study and discussion circles. It did not, however, become established in formalized higher education in Islam.[8]

JA'FAR IBN MANṢŪR AL-YAMAN: TRUE SPIRITUAL KNOWLEDGE IS ATTAINABLE

Another early educational manual was written by the mid-4th/10th century Isma'ili author Ja'far ibn Manṣūr al-Yaman. Very little is known about his life. Ibn Manṣūr al-Yaman was born in about 218/883 into a devout and learned Shi'i family. His father, Ibn Hawshab, of Kufan background, had converted from Twelver Shi'ism to Isma'ilism before moving to Yemen, where he became the leader and cofounder of the Yemeni Isma'ili community. Ja'far ibn Manṣūr al-Yaman, the son, actively worked for the Isma'ili community and wrote books on Shi'i theology and doctrine. It is this scholarly work, which earned him, from early Fatimid times onward, high prestige among Yemeni Isma'ilis as a teacher of Isma'ili scriptural interpretation (*ta'wīl*).[9]

In his *Kitāb al-'Ālim wa-l-ghulām* ("The Master and the Disciple"), Ibn Manṣur al-Yaman offers a full-scale narrated dramatic dialogue of spiritual initiation. Relating the quest for and the gradual realization of spiritual knowledge, the author artfully instructs in both "the proper behaviour of those who are seeking the truth (*ādāb al-ṭālibīn*) and the 'ways of proceeding'—through appropriate action, teaching and belief—of 'the righteous,' of those who are spiritually receptive, prepared and suited for those ways (*madhāhib al-ṣāliḥīn*)" (Morris 2002, 3).

Among Ibn Manṣūr al-Yaman's many pieces of pedagogical advice, two stand out: The first is the message that each intellectually qualified person may aspire to—and can eventually attain—the highest degree of true spiritual knowledge, and this may achieve insight provided he or she observes a certain degree of inner discipline, makes spiritual intention his or her guide, and accepts that divine grace and support is an essential prerequisite of spiritual learning. Second, everything that he or she learns needs to be put into practice so that both the individual and the community may benefit. The following extract of a dialogue between a disciple and his master illustrates this approach to spiritual education:

> *[DISCIPLE:] . . . Can that lofty level of mystical knowledge and perfection be reached by following the trail of the levels that are below it?*
>
> *[MASTER:] . . . That level can only be attained through the most excellent and meritorious action. However, if you perform the actions appropriate to this level and strive for it in the proper way, with the most sincere certainty and a pure, attentive heart, then you can hope to reach as much of it as was reached by "the friends of God, the chosen and purified ones, the very best."*
>
> (Q 38:47)

> *[DISCIPLE:] And who . . . would even aspire to attain such a spiritual level through which "God has raised up"* (Q 2:253). *His friends?*
>
> *[MASTER:] . . . The creatures only come close to God through their spiritual mindfulness and appropriate actions. . . . As for that knowledge 'through which God raised up'* (Q 12:76; 58:11). *His friends, you are now at the beginning of that. So if you put that knowledge into action, you can reach its culmination. For it is only right for God to help you reach the attainments of "the pure and righteous"* (e.g., Q 2:130, 21:105) *among them, and "He will not treat you unjustly"* (e.g., Q 9:70) *in respect to anything which He bestowed on them."*
>
> (Morris 2002, 10)

Ibn Manṣūr al-Yaman does not offer a specific curriculum. He does, however, provide a number of principles and characteristics of successful learning and teaching, for example:

- Learning is a gradual process, leading from the lower to the higher levels of knowledge, and from the simpler to the more complex kind of understanding. Thus ignorance (as an infant) is no stigma. On the contrary, it is a God-given "sign pointing toward knowledge."
- Teaching, in order to be virtuous and true, requires: (a) trust on the part of the teacher that all knowledge eventually comes from one source, God, the first and highest Teacher and (b) the insight that ethics are of utmost importance in education. Indeed, instructors will reach true merit only if they do "the deeds of kindness . . . of what is truly good" (Morris 2002, 73–74).
- Learning is equal to belief in God. Indeed, "the full attainment of knowledge and the furthest extent of (your intellectual) power," is the best way to obey God and perform right actions wholeheartedly (Morris 2002, 109).

MISKAWAYH: STRUCTURED AND ETHICAL LEARNING REINFORCES EDUCATION

Abū ʿAlī Aḥmad ibn Miskawayh is one of the most original medieval Muslim thinkers. He was interested in a wide array of scholarly disciplines, ranging from philosophy to history, literature, medicine, psychology, and chemistry. Above all, however, his scholarly reputation rests on his influential work on philosophical ethics, *Tahdhīb al-akhlāq wa-taṭhīr al-aʿrāq* ("The Refinement of Character Traits and Purification of Dispositions")—for which he is considered the "father of Islamic ethics" among modern scholarship.[10]

Miskawayh, of Persian origin, was born in 320/932 in the city of Rayy, near Teheran. He died in 421/1030 in Isfahan. Even in his youth, Miskawayh took part in teaching sessions in Baghdad held by renowned thinkers of his time, where he familiarized himself with the ancient Greek sciences, especially logic and medicine. Next to scholars of his own faith, he also studied with Jewish and Christian scholars, including Yaḥyā ibn ʿAdī (d. 974 AD), a noted Syriac-Orthodox philosopher, theologian, and translator of Greek sources (from their Syriac versions) into Arabic. In later years, Miskawayh was appointed treasurer and librarian in the large libraries of Buyid rulers, a position that enabled him to continue his intensive study of the Arabic translations of the works of Plato, Aristotle, and other Greek authors. He drew inspiration in particular, as he said himself, from the *Kitāb Fī tadbīr al-manzil* ("The Book of Household Management"), the Arabic translation of *Oikonomikos,* a work written in Greek by the little known author Bryson.[11]

Although Miskawayh composed his famous *The Refinement of Character Traits* "especially for lovers of philosophy rather than for laymen" (Miskawayh 65), and in spite of the fact that this work is expressly on ethics rather than learning as such, this manual is a particularly rich source of scholarly advice on Islamic education in the narrow sense of the word as well.

The vital implications of *The Refinement* for education are already clear in Miskawayh's introduction, in which the author explains that the purpose of the volume is to provide the reader with guidance for "the acquisition of a noble character, i.e., a character which imparts to us a nobility that is essential and real, not one that is accidental, unstable, and unreal," and "by which all our actions issuing therefrom may be performed by us easily, without any constraint or difficulty" (Miskawayh 5). The means to accomplish this goal is, according to Miskawayh, an 'art' (or 'science,' *ṣināʿa*), that is, the "the art of character training which is concerned with the betterment of the actions of humans as human beings; this is the most excellent of the arts" (Miskawayh 33). The best way to reach this aim is through a didactic, "organized, gradual process of instruction" (*tartīb taʿlīmī*). The principal ethical aspect of this idea is stressed again in his maintaining that, although one can—and should—'learn' how to refine one's character, the ultimate state to which a person can aspire is that of 'spontaneous' performance, where good acts are performed without prior thinking or deliberation.[12]

In this regard, Miskawayh draws once again on an ancient Greek idea according to which the 'aim' or 'end' (*ghāya*) of an act may influence—and even define—the 'principle' or 'beginning' (*mabdaʾ*) of an undertaking. Accordingly, the objective of an act may come to characterize the action itself: If the objective of a deed is virtuous, the action that leads to it may—or would necessarily—acquire the quality of being virtuous. Translated into an educational context, this means that, if the aim of learning is virtuous, learning as such is a virtuous activity as well. Miskawayh writes in this regard:

> *. . . we must observe the 'principle' which plays the role of the 'end,' so that, having observed the 'end,' one can come down gradually, by way of analysis, to the physical things, and then start from the bottom and proceed, by way of synthesis, until one reaches again the 'end' which had been observed before.*
>
> (Miskawayh 1994, 64)

Generally, learning is seen as a life-long process and as something that requires more modesty and humility than any other activity, as Miskawayh states:

> *Should the one who is seeking to preserve this health [of the soul] become unique and eminent in knowledge, then let not his pride in what*

> *he has achieved cause him to cease to seek beyond, for knowledge has no limit, and above every man of knowledge there is One who knows.*
> (Miskawayh 1994, 60)

Some of Miskawayh's more specific educational recommendations include the following advice:

- Only those of virtuous morals should be engaged in the education of the young.
- If reprimand is unavoidable, it should never be too explicit verbally nor excessive physically, as this leads to the opposite of the intended effect: The student might become accustomed to penalization, become ill mannered, and unresponsive.
- Instruction needs to take the intellectual and physical capabilities of the young into due account. "Some of them are more responsive to the 'art' [of learning and character formation], and others less" (Miskawayh 1994, 31, 32, 49, 52).
- Miskawayh's educational ideas significantly influenced the concepts of learning held by principal Muslim scholars of later times, in particular the highly influential Sunni theologian and mystic Abū Ḥāmid al-Ghazālī (d. 505/1111 AD) and the eminent Shiʿi philosopher-vizier Naṣīr al-Dīn al-Tūsī (d. 672/1274 AD).
- Likewise it is notable that, although Miskawayh speaks in his *Refinement of the Character* only of the education of boys and male youth, his pedagogical advice appears to convey ideas, which one could call humanistic, if they are understood in the context of modern societies, which express gender-unspecific, universal values and ethics.

AL-GHAZĀLĪ: CLEANSING THE HEART IS THE BEGINNING OF HUMAN GROWTH

Abū Ḥāmid al-Ghazālī is known today as the most important philosophical theologian of Islam. In addition, he was a noted jurist, mystic, and an influential religious reformer. He was born in 445/1056 in the district of Tus, near Mashhad, in northeast Iran. He died there in 505/1111.

Al-Ghazālī pursued much of his education and higher studies in Nishapur, Iran, and Baghdad, Iraq. In 484/1091, at the age of thirty-three, he accepted the head teaching position at the newly founded Niẓāmiyya College, the most famous institution of higher learning in Baghdad and the entire Muslim world in the 4th/11th century. He occupied this position for several years before suddenly giving it up in 488/1095 on the pretext of going on pilgrimage. During this journey to Mecca and Medina, which lasted three years, he stayed for some time in Damascus and Jerusalem. In Hebron, at the grave of Abraham, he vowed no longer to serve any state authority. He only briefly returned to Baghdad to teach again, before leaving for Khorasan, where he spent the rest of his life.

In addition to the far-reaching impact that al-Ghazālī has had on Islamic religious thought, he can also be seen as the principal architect of classical Islamic education. He accepted Greek logic as a neutral means of learning and recommended that students of religion-related subjects, including theology and jurisprudence, learn to understand and apply it. Al-Ghazālī's wealth of experience in teaching is reflected in his many treatises on the role of knowledge in the educational process, and of teaching and learning as activities in providing, acquiring, and deepening the understanding of certain subject matters. For al-Ghazālī, all who "seek God through knowledge, no matter what kind" are embarking on a blessed journey. Therefore, it is important for him to offer assistance to both those beginning their educational voyage and those who guide others on the path of learning. Along these lines, al-Ghazālī has the following important advice for students:

> *O Disciple, advice is easy—what is difficult is accepting it. . . . This is particularly so for whoever is the student of conventional knowledge, who is occupied with gratifying his ego and with worldly exploits, for he supposes that his knowledge alone will be his salvation and that his deliverance is in it, and that he can do without deeds . . . as the Messenger of God—God bless him and give him peace—said, "The man most severely punished on the Day of Resurrection is a scholar whom God did not benefit by his knowledge."*
>
> (Al-Ghazālī 2005, 6)

With this kind of counsel, al-Ghazālī begins his famous treatise *Ayyuhā l-walad* ("O Disciple"), which is probably one of his last and most appealing works. While reflecting in this book upon his own life, he uses a spiritual-mystical literary framework to address a mature student and to provide him with specific educational and ethical advice. These recommendations concern, above all, two aspects: the urge to fear God and the encouragement to acquire knowledge and to better oneself. This is the way, al-Ghazālī advocates, to live a meaningful and virtuous life in this world and to earn an eternal life in paradise in the next.

In what is perhaps al-Ghazālī's most important book, *Iḥyā᾽ ʿulūm al-dīn* (*The Revivification of the Religious Sciences*), the author first advises learners:

- Begin the educational voyage by cleansing the soul of bad morals and reprehensible qualities so as to put oneself in a state worthy of receiving knowledge;
- Devote all of one's physical and mental abilities to learning, and study with focus and concentration;
- Show no arrogance toward a subject or a teacher;

- Achieve a firm grasp of one discipline, beginning with the most important items of knowledge first, before moving on to a new subject; and
- Aspire to spiritual perfection rather than worldly fame and fortune.

As for the curriculum, al-Ghazālī highlights the supremacy of the religious sciences vis-à-vis the secular disciplines in the context of Islamic learning. According to al-Ghazālī, religious instruction comprises both 'religious practice' and the 'sacred sciences' (*shar'iyya*). The former, which al-Ghazālī equates with "the knowledge of the conditions of the heart," is a discipline that does not require analytical study, i.e., learning "through scrutiny, investigation, and research." Rather, it suffices to believe and to confess sincerely and without hesitation. The 'sacred sciences,' on the other hand, are devoted to the knowledge acquired from the prophets and incorporate the following:

- Fundamental topics of learning such as the Quran, the authoritative custom and precedence of the Prophet (*sunna*), the consensus (*ijmā'*) of the Muslim community, and the traditions relating to the companions of the Prophet (*āthār al-ṣaḥāba*), and such topics as:
- The derived disciplines, which deal with the systematic elaboration of canonical Islamic law and with ethics;
- Preparatory disciplines, such as linguistics and syntax, as these are tools necessary for the understanding of the Holy Scripture and the prophetic traditions;
- Supplementary disciplines, such as the variant readings of the Quran; and
- The history of the revelation and the biographies of virtuous people and transmitters of prophetic traditions are complementary study topics.

Finally, there are the 'secular sciences' (*ghayr shar'iyya*) consisting of:

1. Praiseworthy disciplines such as medicine, arithmetic, and astronomy. These sciences are indispensable for the welfare of society;
2. Blameworthy disciplines, such as magic, talismanic science, juggling, trickery, and the like; and
3. Permissible disciplines subordinate to philosophy. These include geometry and arithmetic; logic, which studies the manner of proofs and conditions; metaphysics, which investigates the being of God and His attributes; and physics, which investigates different substances of the natural world, their properties, transformations, and changes.

Finally, as al-Ghazālī also says, although jurisprudence is related to religion, it deals predominantly with the affairs of this world, which is merely "the preparation for the hereafter," and which is the reason why legal study and practice are restricted to the affairs of the here and now.

AL-ZARNŪJĪ: PROPER STUDY METHOD ENSURES LEARNING SUCCESS

Burhān al-Dīn al-Zarnūjī was a scholar who modeled his own educational views very closely on the examples of al-Ghazālī. Very little is known about al-Zarnūjī's biography. He was born and apparently lived much of his active life in Zarnuj, a town in the present Turkistan, where he flourished in the late 6th/12th and early 7th/13th century. He died in Bukhara, in what today is Uzbekistan.[13] Al-Zarnūjī appears to have been a philosophically inclined theologian and an expert on Islamic jurisprudence, belonging to the Hanafi School of Law. Moreover, his honorary name, Burhān al-Dīn ('Proof of Religion'), indicates that within his lifetime, his peers already held him in high esteem as a particularly learned religious scholar.

Al-Zarnūjī's *Taʿlīm al-mutaʿallim ṭarīq at-taʿallum* ("Instructing the Learner in the Method of Learning") is a pedagogical manual that was particularly widely read and already famous in medieval times, as the many manuscript copies of this work preserved in Oriental libraries suggest. The author was prompted to write this treatise because, as he himself states in the opening paragraph of his manual:

> *I observed in our day many students of learning striving to attain knowledge but failing to do so and are thus barred from its utility and fruition. This is because they have missed the [proper] methods [of learning] and have abandoned its conditions. Anyone who misses this way goes astray and, therefore, does not reach [its] objective, however modest or glorious.*
>
> *It is my desire here to elucidate the proven methods of study that I myself had either read about in books or heard from my learned wise teachers. It is my hope that those sincerely interested in this matter would pray for my deliverance and redemption on the Day of Judgment.*
>
> (Al-Zarnūjī 2003, 1)

Al-Zarnūjī stresses, "the joys of knowledge, learning, and insight are a sufficient incentive for the intelligent" so that they would not need any further motivation or stimulus to acquire knowledge and to learn. As for the techniques and the course of studying, he emphasizes:

> *Our elders stated that it is necessary that the length of study for the beginner be an amount in which he can retain in his memory after two repetitions. Every day he should increase [the measure of] his recall by one word, so that even if the duration and quantity of his study become large, it would [still] remain possible for him to recall [his lessons by repeating them] twice. He would thus increase [his capacity] gently and gradually. . . .*

> *[Also,] it is necessary to begin [studying] with matters that are more readily understood. . . . [Therefore,] the right procedure is what our elders practiced. They chose to begin with a few subjects of broad content because these are more readily understood and retained [before proceeding to busy themselves with more detailed topics]. . . .*
>
> *It is important that the student exert himself strenuously to understand what he is offered by the teacher, applying intelligence, reflection, and much repetition. For if reading is limited but repetition and reflection are extensive, then [the student] will attain a firm grasp and understanding [of all material taught].*
>
> (Al-Zarnūjī 2003, 25–26)

Like several of his scholarly predecessors, al-Zarnūjī does not give a full-scale curriculum. However, he does name certain disciplines that hold special importance for religious learning and certain others that involve dangers for pious learners. Thus jurisprudence is singled out as a particularly beneficial field of study, for the knowledge of one's rights and duties "is the best guide to piety and the fear of God, and it is the straightest path to the ultimate goal"; that is, the reward of eternal bliss in paradise. The study of astronomy is discouraged with the qualification that one is permitted to learn just enough of it to enable the person to determine the direction (*qibla*) and the times (*mīqāt*) of prayer. Furthermore, dealing with medicine is permitted because "it deals with accidental causes. Therefore, its study is allowed, as is [the study] of other worldly necessities." Generally, one ought to choose those branches of learning that are beneficial and needed for one's current life and future. More specifically, however, one must always give preference to 'established traditions' over 'new things,' so as to "beware of becoming engrossed in those disputes which come about after one has cut loose from the traditional authorities" (Al-Zarnūjī 2003, 3–5 and 9).

IBN JAMĀʿA: BOOKS ARE INDISPENSABLE IN EDUCATION

Another scholar of principal importance in the development of pedagogical thought in classical Islam was Badr al-Dīn Abū ʿAbdallāh Muḥammad ibn Ibrāhīm ibn Jamāʿa, a distinguished scholar and Shafiʿi Chief Judge in Cairo and Damascus.

Ibn Jamāʿa was born in 639/1241 in the North Syrian city of Hama, where he received the primary and first levels of his higher education in the traditional religious disciplines. Later, he traveled to Aleppo, Damascus, Alexandria, and Jerusalem to continue his education. Thanks to his academic standing and friendship with Mamluk rulers and governmental administrators, he was granted several prestigious juridical and academic appointments at institutions in Egypt and Syria, many of which included teaching responsibilities. Ibn Jamāʿa died in 733/1333 in Cairo.

Ibn Jamāʿa is probably best known today for his pedagogical handbook *Tadhkirat al-sāmiʿ wa-l-mutakallim fī ādāb al-ʿālim wa-l-mutaʿallim* ("The Memorandum for the Listener and the Speaker [in Teaching Sessions] Concerning the Rules of Behavior for the Learned and the Learner").[14] It is a systematic outline of views on traditional higher learning, with a certain emphasis on the prophetic tradition and jurisprudence. Issues in elementary education are mentioned only "in some isolated instances such as the incidental admonitions for students to sit before their professors as children do before the teacher of the Qurʾān," as F. Rosenthal observed (Rosenthal 2007, 296).

Throughout this treatise, Ibn Jamāʿa stresses two points of principle importance to his educational thought: One is the central role, which he assigns to the Quran, and the prophetic tradition as primary sources of knowledge and learning. Another relates to his strong promotion of books as indispensable tools in the educational process. Whereas the first point had already become a very characteristic feature of classical Islamic education, the second is noteworthy despite the fact that Ibn Jamāʿa wrote it at a time when the written word was already firmly established as a tool of learning throughout the Islamic Empire. Nevertheless, the author feels it necessary to emphasize the special usefulness of books for all kinds of scholarly pursuit.

Furthermore, students are expressly instructed as follows:

1. To be sincere in their desire to learn;
2. To devote the time of youth entirely to the pursuit of knowledge;
3. To divide the nights and days so as to learn most effectively: Scheduling memorization in the early morning, research at dawn, writing around midday, and study and discussion in the evening is most advisable; and
4. Not least important, a teacher is central to a student's learning, to the extent that students should be denied access to sources that might contradict a teacher's position (Ibn Jamāʿa 1991, 49–57; Rosenthal 1947, 7–19).

Apart from the highly ethical and pious tenor of Ibn Jamāʿa's manual, the similarity of his educational views and statements with those offered by his famous predecessor, al-Ghazālī, is striking. It is, therefore, not surprising that Ibn Jamāʿa's handbook was a great source of inspiration for many later generations of Muslim scholars writing on education. A notable example in this regard is ʿAbd al-Bāsiṭ ibn Mūsā al-ʿAlmawī (d. 981/1573 AD), who, in his *Muʿīd fī adab al-mufīd wa-l-mustafīd* ("The Tutor Concerning the Etiquette of the Provider and the Acquirer [of Knowledge]"), repeated much of Ibn Jamāʿa's ideas, some of them verbatim.[15]

These classical Muslim thinkers significantly contributed to the foundations on which Islamic educational thought in the centuries to come would grow and prosper. At the same time, it must be stressed that the pedagogical writings reviewed here provide but a glimpse of the richness of the educational literature, which evolved during the classical period of Islam. Many works by other Muslim scholars with specific pedagogical interests could be added to this list, such as the *Kitāb Ādāb al-murīdīn* ("Rules of Conduct for Novices"), a guidebook on mystic-spiritual growth, by Abū l-Najīb al-Suhrawardī (d. 632/1168 AD); *Adab al-imlāʾ wa-l-istimlāʾ* ("The Codex of Dictating and Taking Notes from Dictation"), a work on the rules of written text transmission, by ʿAbd al-Karīm al-Samʿānī (d. 562/1166–67 AD); the *Kitāb Ādāb al-mutaʿallimīn* ("Rules of Conduct for Students") by the Shiʿite author Naṣīr al-Dīn al-Ṭūsī (d. 672/1274 AD), or the historian, jurist, and sociologist Ibn Khaldūn (d. 808/1406 AD), whose *Muqaddima* ("Prolegomena") deals extensively—often in discrete chapters or special expositions—with key issues in the theory and practice of Islamic learning, to mention just a few particularly original examples.[16]

CONCLUSIONS

Although each of the texts reviewed in this chapter is distinct and needs to be appreciated on its own scholarly terms and historical conditions, a number of aspects that link these works are striking, as they appear to represent major characteristics common to pedagogical thought in classical Islam:

1. More than one of our authors emphasizes, as did Socrates, Plato, and Aristotle before them, the importance of teacher assistance in student learning. Thus they highlight the usefulness of the so-called 'maieutic method' in recalling and bringing out in students knowledge that they "already knew."[17] Principals of this kind of instruction clearly indicated in the texts we surveyed include the power of observation (to deepen and expand knowledge) and personal experience (in problem solving), for example. Basically, however, it is the interaction between teacher and student through reflective dialogue and the teaching through question and answer, which guides the student to reach deeper insight and eventually enables him to learn, as Abū Ḥanīfa/al-Samarqandī, Ibn Saḥnūn, and al-Zarnūjī suggest. These scholars highlight, in the context of learning, the advantages of inductively discovering contextual relationships and conclusions. Then the role of the teachers in this regard is specifically addressed by al-Jāḥiẓ in his recommendation that teachers should not oversee and control learning too strictly. Flexible and student-responsive supervision would generally ensure that students learn to form their own opinions in the process of education and also may develop a critical approach toward the materials they use in learning.
2 Thoughtful structuring is particularly conducive to successful instruction. This includes careful planning in general, as well as a well-designed

presentation of the teaching content more specifically, which takes the learner progressively from basic topics to the more complex, as Ibn Jamā'a suggests. This manner of teaching enables learners to familiarize themselves systematically with the contents of learning, as Miskawayh, al-Ghazālī, and al-Zarnūjī state. Likewise, connecting new topics to knowledge that students already possess, and the idea of learning through observation and imitation (of the teacher), are major principles of education in Islamic learning. This manner of progressive education is particularly effective not only for students individually or in groups but also for large groups of people or even nations. When seen in this perspective, it is not surprising that the sociologist and historian Ibn Khaldūn, in particular, emphasizes this insight. [18]

3. A caring and respectful attitude toward pupils and students is key in Islamic education. This idea is underscored on more than one occasion by almost all the medieval Muslim scholars surveyed here. Al-Jāḥiẓ, al-Fārābī, and Ibn Jamā'a recommend paying close attention to the individual intellectual capabilities of the learners, as these are, in their views, essential preconditions for a person to make progress in learning. The emotional dimensions of instruction, in turn, are crucial parts of Ibn Manṣūr al-Yaman's and al-Ghazālī's deliberations. In addition, several Muslim scholars identify motivation, as known already in antiquity,[19] as particularly stimulating to learning.
4. To learners, a great deal of principal advice is offered. Al-Fārābī and Miskawayh, for example, stress that students should begin—and continue—learning with an open mind. Al-Zarnūjī speaks about the need for students to work with focus and determination. Ibn Jamā'a explicates that the students' polite, punctual, and respectful behavior as well as their alertness in class significantly facilitate learning.
5. Most of the medieval Muslim authors looked at here regard memorizing and a close reliance on the written tradition as important measures toward gaining scholarly proficiency. This view seems to relegate the practical application of acquired knowledge to a position of secondary importance—especially, as Ibn Saḥnūn and al-Zarnūjī state, when rote memorization is given priority. In contrast, al-Jāḥiẓ and Ibn Manṣūr al-Yaman are more balanced in their views. They see memorization, repetition, and reading (new) books as components inseparably interconnected with each other and, thus, as particularly helpful in making learning into a creative and sustainable process. This way of knowledge acquisition would ultimately lead students to new insights and a sound application of information they acquired. The fact that a genuine and, perhaps, practical interest on the part of the students in what they learn substantially promotes learning success seems to be indicated in what Ibn Manṣūr al-Yaman writes.
6. Finally, and no less importantly, in the classical time of Islam it seems that, even within a more strictly religion-based framework, a good

and comprehensive education is based on the acquisition of both secular and religious expertise. Obviously, whether the secular or the religious constituents of learning are stressed significantly differs in the educational theories of the Muslim scholars discussed here. At the same time, all our classical scholars determine that the secular and the religious aspects of Islamic education are inseparably connected. This general quality of classical Islamic educational thought expresses itself in a rich and quite dynamic spectrum of educational theories. Here the rationalist theologian and man of letters al-Jāḥiẓ and the logician and philosopher al-Fārābī seem to represent the one, more secular-oriented end of the spectrum, as they stress the centrality of the mind, as well as reasoning and creative thinking for learning. The other, much more strongly religion-oriented educational approach is epitomized by the theologian and mystic al-Ghazālī, the legal scholars al-Zarnūjī and Ibn Jamāʿa, as well as several other pedagogically interested scholars of later time who famously put the Quran, the prophetic tradition, and spiritual experience at the very heart of the Islamic education. The common link between these educational theories, however, is the great importance that their representatives assign to ethics in all aspects of teaching and learning. Ethics, as Miskawayh highlights, thus appear as a central and defining component in the search of classical Muslims for human perfection and happiness, if not in this world, then in the next.

NOTES

1 The quotation in the title refers to a statement by the early 4th/11th century scholar Miskawayh, which he included in his work on Islamic ethics, Constantine K. Zurayk, trans., *The Refinement of Character* Beirut: The American University of Beirut, 160. The relevant passage is cited in full on pp. 81–2 of the present chapter. All translations from the Arabic are my own, unless indicated otherwise. Dates are given according to both the Islamic calendar and the Gregorian, thus "Hijiri date/common era date".

2 For the use of the term 'classical' in the context of Islam's intellectual history, see Tarif Khalidi, *Arabic Historical Thought in the Classical Period* (Cambridge: Cambridge University Press, 1994), xi; Sebastian Günther, ed., *Ideas, Images, and Methods of Portrayal: Insights into Classical Arabic Literature and Islam* (Leiden: Brill, 2005), xvii–xx; and Thomas Bauer, *Die Kultur der Ambiguität: Eine andere Geschichte des Islams* (Berlin: Verlag der Weltreligionen, 2011), 14.

3 A similar connotation is commonly conveyed by the Arabic term *tarbiya* (from *rabbā*, 'to let grow,' 'to raise,' and 'to educate'). It expresses the meaning of 'education' in its general sense, denoting the act, process, and result of imparting and acquiring knowledge, values and skills. Other terms used in premodern times to convey the concept of education are *taʿlīm* and *taʿallum* ('teaching and learning'), *tadrīs* ('[more advanced] instruction'), as well as *taʾdīb* ('tutoring, educating'), leading to *adab* ('cultural and intellectual refinement, education'); cf. Sebastian Günther, "Education," in *Encyclopaedia of Islam*, third edition, forthcoming.

4 Cf. Joseph Schacht, "An early Murciʾite treatise: The Kitāb al-ʿĀlim wa-l-mutaʿallim," *Oriens* 17 (1964): 96–117; Josef van Ess, *Theologie und Gesellschaft im 2. und 3. Jahrhundert Hidschra: Eine Geschichte des religiösen Denkens im frühen Islam*, 6 vols. (Berlin: De Gruyter, 1991–1997), esp. i: 183–214; Ulrich Rudolph, *Al-Māturīdī and the Development of Sunnī Theology in Samarqand* (Leiden: Brill, 2014), 44–53.

5 According to Schacht, "An early Murciʾite treatise," 97.

6 Ed. in Ibrahim Geries, ed., *Kitabān li-l-Jāḥiẓ: Kitāb al-Muʿallimīn wa-Kitāb fī l-radd ʿalā l-mushabbiha* (Tel Aviv: Tel Aviv University, 1980), 57–87.

7 Ed. Muḥammad al-ʿArūsī al-Maṭwī, [repr.] in ʿAbd al-Raḥmān Uthmān Ḥijāzī, *Al-Madhhab al-tarbawī ʿinda Ibn Saḥnūn* (Beirut: Muʾassasat al-Risāla), 1406/1986, 111–128.

8 Charles M. Stanton, *Higher Learning in Islam: The Classical Period: A.D. 700–1300* (Savage, Maryland: Rowman and Littlefield, 1990), 84; David C. Reisman, "Al-Farabi and the Philosophical Curriculum," in *The Cambridge Companion to Arabic Philosophy*, ed. Peter Adamson and Richard C. Taylor (Cambridge: Cambridge University Press, 2011), 52–71.

9 Ed. in James R. Morris, ed. and trans., *The Master and the Disciple: An Early Islamic Spiritual Dialogue on Conversion Kitāb al-ʿĀlim wa'l-ghulām* (London: I.B.Tauris, 2002), esp. 22–27.

10 Ed. Qusṭanṭīn Zurayq (Beirut: al-Jāmiʿa al-Amīrikīya), 1966. For an English translation, see n. 1.

11 Bryson was apparently a Neopythagorean who lived in the 1st century CE. His *Oikonomikos* is lost today in Greek, but extant in an Arabic translation from about 900 CE, as well as in Latin and Hebrew translations. It was used by a range of ancient authors and became the standard work of its time on the topic in the Islamic tradition. Cf. Simon Swain, *Economy, Family, and Society from Rome to Islam: A Critical Edition, English Translation, and Study of Bryson's Management of the Estate* (Cambridge: Cambridge University Press, 2013).

12 Nadia Gamal al-Din, "Miskawayh (A.H. 320–421/A.D. 932–1030)," *Prospects: The Quarterly Review of Comparative Education* 24.1–2 (1994): 131–152, esp. 137–145 and *passim* [repr. in Zaghloul Morsy, ed., *Thinkers on Education*, 4 vols. (UNESCO 1994, 1995, 1997)].

13 Al-Zarnūjī's death dates occasionally given in the secondary literature range from 620/1223 to 640/1242–3. However, all of them seem to be based on speculation (cf. Martin Plessner and Jonathan P. Berkey, "al-Zarnūdjī," in *Encyclopaedia of Islam*, Second Edition, ed. Peri Bearman (Leiden, Brill), vol. xi, 462.

14 Ed. Hyderabad: Dāʾirat al-Maʿārif al-Uthmāniyya, 1353/[1934]); Noor M. Ghifari, trans., *Ibn Jamāʿah* (sic), *The Memoir of the Listener and the Speaker in the Training of Teacher and Student* (Islamabad: Pakistan Hijra Council, 1991).

15 For more on this topic, see the detailed study by Rosenthal, *Technique*, 7–24.

16 See also the rich collection of studies by Joseph E. Lowry et al., eds., *Law and Education in Medieval Islam: Studies in Memory of George Makdisi* (Chippenham: E.J.W. Gibb Memorial Trust, 2004).

17 Maieutic relates to Greek *maieutikos* (from *maieuesthai*, 'to act as midwife'). It conveys the image of the teacher assisting the student to bring out and to fruition knowledge he already has, as a midwife helps the infant to see the world. It may be noted here as well that Plato explicitly suggested that teachers should guide the students in a way that enables them to think consistently with supporting evidence, instead of 'infusing' knowledge into them; cf. his *The Republic*, Book VII ("students cannot learn . . . unless they have a director").

18 For the question of tying new information to what the students have already learned, see R.C. Clark and R.E. Mayer, *e-Learning and the Science of Instruction: Proven*

Guidelines for Consumers and Designers of Multimedia Learning (San Francisco: Pfeiffer), 2011.

19 Aristotle, for example, in his *De Anima* III, chapter 10, saw motivation as "the real or the apparent good" of some anticipated consequence of "what is to come" (be it pleasant or painful); that is, as something that makes it a force and stimulus also in learning.

BIBLIOGRAPHY

'Ammār al-Tālbī, Al-Fārābī. 1993. *Perspectives: Revue trimestrielle d'éducation comparée* (Paris, UNESCO), vol. XXIII, 387–377.

Bauer, T. 2011. *Die Kultur der Ambiguität: Eine andere Geschichte des Islams*. Berlin: Verlag der Weltreligionen.

Clark, C. R. and Mayer, E. R. 2011. *e-Learning and the Science of Instruction: Proven Guidelines for Consumers and Designers of Multimedia Learning*. San Francisco: Pfeiffer.

van Ess, J. 1991–1997. *Theologie und Gesellschaft im 2. und 3. Jahrhundert Hidschra: Eine Geschichte des religiösen Denkens im frühen Islam*, 6 vols. Berlin: De Gruyter.

Gamal al-Din, N. 1994. "Miskawayh (A.H. 320–421/A.D. 932–1030)" *Prospects: The Quarterly Review of Comparative Education* 24(1–2): 131–152.

Geries, I. 1980. *Kitabān li-l-Jāḥiẓ: Kitāb al-Mu'allimīn wa-Kitāb fī l-radd 'alā l-mushabbiha*. Tel Aviv: Tel Aviv University.

Ghifari, M. N. 1991. trans., Ibn Jamā'ah (sic), *The Memoir of the Listener and the Speaker in the Training of Teacher and Student*. Islamabad: Pakistan Hijra Council.

Günther, S. 2005a."Advice for teachers: The 9th century Muslim scholars Ibn Saḥnūn and al-Jāḥiẓ on pedagogy and didactics," in Günther, *Ideas, Images, and Methods of Portrayal: Insights into Classical Arabic Literature and Islam* (Islamic History and Civilization). 79–116. Leiden: Brill.

Günther, S. (ed.) 2005b. *Ideas, Images, and Methods of Portrayal: Insights into Classical Arabic Literature and Islam*. Leiden: Brill.

Günther, S. forthcoming. "Education," in Kate Fleet, et al., eds., *Encyclopaedia of Islam*, third edition.

Günther, S. 2006. "Be Masters in That You Teach and Continue to Learn: Medieval Muslim Thinkers on Educational Theory," *Comparative Education Review* 50(3): 367–388.

Günther, S. 2010. "The Principles of Instruction are the Grounds of our Knowledge: Al-Fārābī's (d. 950) Philosophical and al-Ghazālī's (d. 1111) Spiritual Approaches to Learning," in Osama Abi-Mershed, ed., *Trajectories of Education in the Arab World: Legacies and Challenges*. 15–34. London: Routledge.

von Grunebaum, E. G. and Abel, M. T. 2003. (trans). *Al-Ghazālī, Letter to a Disciple, Bilingual English-Arabic Edition, Translated with an Introduction and Note*. Chicago: Starlatch Press.

von Grunebaum. E. G. and Abel, M. T. 2003. (trans.) *Instruction of the Student: The Method of Learning*. Chicago: Starlatch Press.

Haleem, A. 2008. *The Quran*. Oxford: Oxford University Press.

Ḥijāzī, U. and Abd, R. 1986. *Al-Madhhab al-tarbawī ʿinda Ibn-Saḥnūn, in (ed.) Muḥammad al-ʿArūsī al-Maṭwī, [repr.].* Beirut: Muʾassasat al-Risāla.

Khalidi. T. 1994. *Arabic Historical Thought in the Classical Period.* Cambridge: Cambridge University Press.

Lowry, E. J. 2004. *Law and Education in Medieval Islam: Studies in Memory of George Makdisi.* Chippenham: E. J. W. Gibb Memorial Trust.

Mayer, T. 2005. *Al-Ghazālī, Letter to a Disciple, Bilingual English-Arabic Edition, Translated with an Introduction and Notes.* Cambridge: Islamic Texts Society.

Morris, R. J. (ed. and trans) 2002. *The Master and the Disciple: An Early Islamic Spiritual Dialogue on Conversion Kitab al-ʿalim wa'l-ghulam.* London: I.B.Tauris.

Morsy, Z. (ed.) 1995. *Thinkers on Education*, Vol. 3. Paris UNESCO.

Plessner, M. and Berkey, P. J. "al-Zarnūdjī," in *Encyclopaedia of Islam* Second Edition (vol. xi) ed. Peri Bearman. 462–463. Leiden: Brill.

David C. Reisman, "Al-Farabi and the philosophical curriculum," in *The Cambridge Companion to Arabic Philosophy,* ed. Peter Adamson and Richard C. Taylor. 22–27. Cambridge: Cambridge University Press.

Rosenthal, F. 1947. *Technique. The Technique and Approach of Muslim Scholarship. Pontificium Institutum Biblicum.* Rome: Pontificium Institutum Biblicum.

Rosenthal, F. 2007. *Knowledge Triumphant: The Concept of Knowledge in Medieval Islam.* Leiden: Brill.

Rudolph, U. 2014. *Al-Māturīdī and the Development of Sunnī Theology in Samarqand.* Leiden: Brill.

Schacht, J.1964. An early Murciʾite treatise: The Kitāb al-ʿĀlim wa-l-mutaʿallim [Abū Ḥanīfa/al-Samarqandī]. *Oriens* 17: 96–117.

Stanton, M. C. 2011. *Higher Learning in Islam: The Classical Period: A.D. 700–1300.* Savage, Maryland: Rowman and Littlefield, 1990, 84.

Swain, S. 2013. *Economy, Family, and Society from Rome to Islam: A Critical Edition, English Translation, and Study of Bryson's Management of the Estate.* Cambridge: Cambridge University Press.

Zurayk, K. C. (trans.) 1968. *The Refinement of Character* Beirut: The American University of Beirut.

6 Disciplinarity and Islamic Education

Omar Anwar Qureshi

Charles Taylor identifies disengaged reason as being a central component of the modern self. Contrary to a Platonic understanding of reason where a meaningful order exists in the cosmos and in the soul that serves as a source for the highest good for reason to discover and conform to, disengaged reason "is no longer defined in terms of a vision of order in the cosmos" (Taylor 1989, 20). This disengagement allows reason to look at the world from an 'autonomous' viewpoint, leading to the abandonment of all 'horizons' or frameworks "within which we know where we stand, and what meanings things have for us" (Taylor 1989, 29), thus rendering any inquiry to be independent of an overarching *telos*, or a comprehensive conception of the good life.

The impact of disengaged reason can be observed in various notions of the purpose of educational institutions, the purpose of acquiring knowledge, and the conception of knowledge. Alasdair MacIntyre notes that, "each academic discipline is treated as autonomous and self-defining . . . And in order to excel in any one particular discipline, one need in general know little or nothing about any of the others" (MacIntyre 2009, 15–16). The current state of the modern university is such that the integrating of these autonomous disciplines and relating them to one another is not seen as a task that is important to undertake. In religious educational institutions, however, it was either theology or philosophy that served as the framework that facilitated the integrating and interrelating of the disciplines of knowledge and was the overarching independent science under which any inquiry to understanding reality was made. MacIntyre argues,

> theology would be taught both for its own sake and as a key to that overall understanding. And it would be the central task of philosophy in such a university to inquire into the nature of the relationship between theology and the secular disciplines.
>
> (MacIntyre 2009, 17)

Thus inquiry within each discipline would take place as part of a larger overall understanding of reality and the relationship of each discipline to the other, construed within 'horizons,' developed within a theological or philosophical perspective. In the secular university, the dislodging of theology has resulted in the emergence of autonomous disciplines of knowledge with little disregard of how the deliverables of each science relates to each other and to a larger understanding of reality. Likewise, the purpose of inquiry is rendered a vacuum left to the individual scientists to determine for themselves without references to a 'horizon.'

In this chapter, we intend to investigate the way sciences have been variously conceived in Islamic intellectual history and explore the disciplines and the different ways they were classified in the Islamic tradition. It will be shown that the Islamic understanding of knowledge is that it is one, and all the various sciences contribute toward understanding the same reality. Consequently, there must be coherency between all the sciences, which was achieved through the universal science of Kalām theology, thus rendering the notion of reason in the Islamic tradition as being is embedded in a cosmos that is hierarchical. The central role of Kalām theology along with the universal/particular hierarchical relationship of the sciences provides Islamic educational efforts in the West with an alternative framework thus avoiding the fragmentation trajectory of the disciplines and inquiry besetting secular institutions of education and curricula.

HOW TO CLASSIFY A SCIENCE: THE SUBJECT MATTER

The concern for knowledge has been present since the first Muslim community. The Prophet of Islam on numerous occasions provided guidance on acquiring knowledge and the types that a Muslim is required to learn. God spoke to His Prophet, encouraging him and the rest of his community saying, "O Prophet, do not rush to recite before the revelation is fully complete but say, 'My Lord, increase me in knowledge!'" (20:114). This prayer is not to be understood as a desire to increase in all types of knowledge, as the Qur'ān reminds us that not all knowledge is beneficial. Referring to sorcery that the two angels Harut and Marut taught, the Qur'ān says about the people who learned sorcery that, "they learned what harmed them, not what benefited them" (2:102). The Prophet Muhammad is reported to have prayed, "O God, I seek your protection from knowledge that does not bring benefit" (ibn al-Ḥajjāj 1991, 2088). From the early days of Islam, one encounters the idea that knowledge is a typological concept and not all that is knowable should be pursued.

Yet one also finds that there is knowledge that God has made an obligation on all believers to pursue. Thus the categories of obligatory and nonobligatory knowledge represent another classification scheme that was present in the early community. The Prophet Muhammad said, "Acquiring knowledge is an obligation upon every Muslim" (al-Suyūṭī 1988). The exact type of knowledge referred to in the statement of the Prophet has been widely discussed by Muslim scholars and will be explored in this chapter. Similarly, other types of knowledge are praiseworthy depending on the purpose and amount of time an individual spends acquiring them. The Prophet Muhammad remarked when hearing an individual being praised for his expertise in the science of genealogy, "Knowledge of it does not benefit while ignorance of it does not bring harm" (al-ʻAsqalānī 2002, 4:173). Yet on another occasion we hear the Prophet telling his companions, "Know your lineages to maintain your ties of kinship" (al-Tirmidhī 1990, 4:351). What is understood from these statements is that genealogy is a science that could be beneficial if studied for correct purposes, such as maintaining ties of kinship, whereas if studied for taking boastful pride in one's ancestors then it would not be beneficial. Thus purpose plays a significant role in determining whether acquiring knowledge is a praiseworthy act or not.

In the search for understanding which knowledge is praiseworthy, obligatory, beneficial, and harmful, Muslim scholars have generated a rich literature exploring these and other related issues to knowledge and its acquisition. This led to the development of what is known as 'the ten foundations of every science' (*al-mabādīʾ al-ʻasharah*) or its alternative form, 'the eight foundations of every science' (*al-ruʾūs al-thamānīyah*). They have served as the introduction to virtually all teaching manuals in each discipline up until our own time. Each foundation provides the student studying a particular science with the necessary information about the science to ensure its proper conception and application. The ten principles are:

1. The definition of the science (*al-ḥadd*);
2. Its subject matter (*al-mawḍūʻ*);
3. The goods that serve as the end of the science (*al-ghāyah*);
4. Its merits (*al-faḍl*);
5. Its relation to other sciences or its classification (*al-nisab*);
6. The founder of the science (*al-wāḍiʻ*);
7. The name of the science (*al-ism*);
8. Its sources (*al-istimdād*);
9. The legal ruling of learning the science (*ḥukm al-shāriʻ*); and
10. The questions investigated in the science (*al-masāʾil*).

The eight foundations comprise most of the same with some variations: the sources of a science, its legal ruling, and its definition do not appear in the eight foundations. The foundations are intended to guide the student and are not detrimental to acquiring a science if all the foundations are not covered (al-Tahānawī n.d., 1:13). It is clear that the correct understanding of the relationship of the science (*al-nisab*) to other sciences was a major focus when teaching.

What concerns us here in our examination of the classification of the sciences are the definition (*al-ḥadd*), the good that the science aims at (*al-ghāyah*), the questions investigated in the science (*al-masāʾil*), and the subject matter (*al-mawḍū'*), as these all relate to how Muslim scholars have differentiated the sciences from one another. What is intended by definition here is the logical definition of a science, which is composed of the science's genus (*al-jins*) and differentia (*al-faṣl*). This provides the student with an understanding of what separates one science from another. Although, according to Muslim theologians and philosophers, this is not what differentiates one science from another. The definition separates one science from another only in terms of how it is conceived in the mind (*bī ḥasab al-mafhūm*) of a student not the science itself (al-Taftāzānī 1989, 1:167).

The aims of a science are those goods that its practitioner aims to achieve. They relate to an Aristotelian notion of the final cause of an act that Muslim theologians have appropriated, which is central to their understanding of the enterprise of knowledge. Every act must have goods that it aims to secure, and these goods serve as the final end of the entire act providing that act with a purpose or *telos*. Ibn al-Akfānī (d. 749/1348 AD) explains that the *telos*, "is always antecedent [to the act] in thought and consequent [to the act] in obtainment" (Ibn al-Akfānī 1994, 47). Some acts have goods that serve to achieve other higher goods and hence there is a hierarchy of goods. Al-Mar'ashi (d. 1145/1732 AD) states in his *Tartīb al-'ulūm* or *The Hierarchy of the Sciences*,

> Know that each of the mentioned [sciences] possesses a good (*fā'īdah*) and this good has another good [for which it serves] until [one achieves] success by obtaining happiness in the two abodes. In the *Sharḥ al-Mawāqif* [it states], "the good [aimed at] in the science of theology is the obtainment of happiness in the two abodes. This is the ultimate purpose and the highest good (*ghāyat-l-ghāyāt*)." I say: the religious sciences are more likely than the ancillary sciences to bring about this happiness. Know that any benefit that results from an act is termed a good (*fā'idah*) from the perspective of it resulting from that act. It is termed an end (*al-ghāyah*) because it (the good) occurs at the end and the completion of the act. It is termed an aim (*gharaḍ*) because the agent undertakes the act to obtain it (the good).
>
> (Sajiqli-zādah 1998, 85–86)

Identifying the goods of a science serves to orient the student toward the correct motivation for studying and application of the science and not to acquire it or apply it in a manner not aligned with its purpose thereby resulting in the good of the science not being acquired. Every science will have immediate goods that are practical and applied to bring about benefit and happiness in this life. These immediate goods are ultimately meant to obtain eternal happiness in the life after death as well.

Whereas some scholars have maintained that it is the goods and the aims of a science that separate it from another, al-Taftāzānī states that, "the agreed upon position of theologians (*al-qawm*) is that the differentiation of the sciences in themselves is based on the differentiation of subject matters" (al-Taftāzānī 1989, 1:167). It is the subject matter that is what unites the various questions investigated in the science (*al-masā'il*) and thus separates one science from another. The aims of the science may differentiate a science, yet it is only the subject matter that brings together questions investigated in a science considering no other factor but the questions themselves, for a science may have multiple aims. Quṭb al-Dīn al-Rāzī explains,

> The subject matter of each science is the essential properties (*al-'awāriḍ al-dhātīyyah*) of the object which the science investigates. As in case of the human body for the science of medicine, for the various states of the human body such as health and illness are investigated in the science of medicine, similar is the case of speech for grammar, for [grammar] investigates the qualities of speech in terms of being inflected or uninflected.
>
> (al-Rāzī 2007, 152)

The *al-'awāriḍ al-dhātīyyah* are nonessential properties that a thing possesses by virtue of its species, such as the property of laughing when predicated of a human being. Muslim logicians classify properties into a species-specific property (*al-'araḍ al-khāṣṣ*) and a general property (*al-'araḍ al-'āmm*) that is to be found in other species within a genus. An example of an accident would be 'movement' in humans, horses, dogs, and other animals that is not found only in one species. The subject matter of a science investigates only properties that are specific to the species to which the object belongs and for this reason served as the basis for classifying sciences.

EARLY CLASSIFICATION WORKS

In the *falsafa* tradition, there is the work on the sciences by al-Kindī (d. 870 AD) who attempted to arrange the works of Aristotle and addressed how they should be studied by the student. Al-Farābī's (d. 339/950 AD) *Ihsā' al-'ulūm* or the *Classification of the Sciences* is a highly influential early exposition on the classification of the sciences among Muslim philosophers. He composed this work so a person can, "compare sciences in order to know which one is superior and most beneficial"; additionally, based on this classification, one will be able to, "uncover the one who claims to have expertise in sciences and is not as he claims" (al- Farābī 1996). In al-Farābī's classification scheme, there are five major divisions of the sciences, which he classifies based on the subject matter (*mawḍū'*) of each science.

Al-Farābī's framework for classification is based on an Aristotelian understanding of the theoretical and practical sciences. The theoretical sciences (*al-'ulūm al-naẓarīyyah*) concern that which should be known for its own sake, whereas the practical sciences (*al-'ulūm al-'amaliyyah*) concern human conduct. Although al-Farābī does not mention this division in *Ihsā' al-'ulūm*, he does mention it in his other works. Additionally, one can clearly observe the fivefold division in this book fitting into this pattern. The first three sciences, the science of language, logic, and mathematics, are considered theoretical sciences, whereas the natural and political sciences fall under the category of practical sciences. The first of the five major divisions are the sciences of language (*'ilm al-lisān*), of which the subject matter is the preservation of the words that signify meaning from whatever nation the words may be from and the preservation of the rules related to those words. The science of language has seven subdivisions: the science of simple words, the science of compound words, rules related to simple words, rules related to compound words, rules related to correct writing, and rules related to composing poetry.

Second al-Farābī follows the section on the science of language with the science of logic (*'ilm al-mantiq*). The science of language preserves a person's speech from error, whereas the science of logic preserves a person from making errors in thought. Al-Farābī expands on the relationship between grammar and logic, where grammar provides rules relating to utterances of a particular people and logic provides us with rules related to utterances of all people. The subject matters of logic and grammar "are intelligibles (*ma'qulāt*) that words signify, and words in so far as they signify intelligibles." The third division of the sciences are the mathematical sciences (*'ilm al-ta'ālīm*), which have seven subdivisions: arithmetic (*'ilm al-'adad*), geometry (*'ilm al-handasa*), optics (*'ilm al-manāẓir*), astronomy (*'ilm al-nujūm*), music (*'ilm al-musīqī*), technology and weights (*'ilm al-athqāl*), and mechanics (*'ilm al-hiyal*). The fourth division are the natural sciences (*'ilm al-ṭabi'ī*) whose subject matter is objects in the natural world and the qualities that compose them. These objects include natural objects such in the heavens and earth, plants, animals, and objects that are manufactured such as glasses, swords, and beds. Metaphysics (*'ilm al-ilahī*) comes under this division, whose subject matter is existents and their accidents. First principles that serve as the foundation of the other sciences and existents that are neither bodies (*ajsām*) nor inhere in bodies that include the soul, the active intellect, and God.

The last major division of the sciences is political science (*'ilm al-madanī*), which has as its matter the types of acts, law, and ethics. Political science concerns itself with identifying the aims of actions and what happiness (*sa'ādah*) entails, political leadership, and what makes up the virtuous city (*al-madinah al-fāḍilah*). The science of law (*'ilm al-fiqh*) and theology (*'ilm al-kalām*) both fall under this division as well. Law's subject matter are those rulings of the Sacred Law (*sharī'ah*) that have not been explicitly stated. The science of law provides the jurist the ability to derive rulings in accordance with the intentions of the Lawgiver from the Sacred Law. Theology has mainly a defensive function whose role is to provide one with skills to defend religious doctrine.

The works of two Ottoman writers have held influential and representational positions in the Sunni Muslim world. Aḥmad ibn Muṣṭafā's (d. 968/1560–1 AD), known as Ṭāshkubrī-Zādah, *Miftāḥ al-sa'ādah wa-miṣbāḥ al-siyādah fī mawḍū'āt al-'ulūm* (*The Keys to Happiness and the Lamp of Leadership: Concerning the Subject Matters of the Sciences*) and Muhammad ibn Abu Bakr al-Mar'ashī's (d. 1145/1732 AD) work *Tartīb al-'ulūm*. Students in Ṭāshkubrī-Zādah's time would carve out their own path of study and not achieve their objectives. He advises students to rely on the counsel of their instructor to develop a curriculum for them to follow in their studies. He reasons that the adept, in this case, the instructor, is of more experience than the novice and more aware of his students' natures and potentials. At the same time, many students were either bewildered by the abundance of sciences to learn or thought of themselves having reached the pinnacles of knowledge and stopped learning. Consequently, Ṭāshkubrī-Zādah composed *Miftāḥ al-sa'ādah* to outline and clarify the path of learning for those eager to study. Additionally, he wanted to demonstrate to those who assume they have acquired all there is to know that a number of sciences still exist that remain to be acquired.

Ṭāshkubrī-Zādah arranges all of the sciences according to an ontological framework of existent entities. He states, "Know that things are predicated with existence in four ways: existence in written form (*al-kitābah*), existence in spoken form (*'ibārah*), mental existence (*al-'adhhan*), and concrete existence (*al-'a'yān*)." (Ṭāshkubrī-Zādah 1985, 1:54). This can be explained by taking a car as an example. When we say that a particular car exists, we can intend by the term existence four possible levels in that when I write the word 'car' it signifies the spoken word 'car,' which signifies the car I am conceiving in my mind. The car that exists in my mind ultimately is derived from the existence of the car outside the mind in the world, which I observe through my senses. Thus any object's existence is recognized at the level of its concrete existence outside the mind, its written existence, its spoken existence, and its existence in the mind.

> It should not be hidden [to anyone] that concrete existence is the real actual existence [of an object], whereas there is a debate on whether mental existence (*al-wujūd al-dhihnī*) is real or metaphorical. Regarding the first two [levels of existence], their existence is [to be considered] conclusively metaphorical.
>
> (Ṭāshkubrī-Zādah 1985, 1:54)

Ṭāshkubrī-Zādah takes as his framework for classification the various ways an object can exist. Every science will be investigating an object. All sciences can be reduced to a study of a particular object at one of its level of existence according to this scheme.

Prior to exploring how this maps on to the sciences, there are other equally important classifications that Ṭāshkubrī-Zādah brings to his discussion of the sciences. When looking at the source of knowledge, a science can either be a religious science (*al-'ilm al-shar'ī*) or a rational science (*al-'ilm al-ḥikamī*). A religious science is one that can only be known by means of a prophet or divine revelation. Al- Ghazālī's discussion of this dichotomy is fairly similar to Ṭāshkubrī-Zādah's and most likely the source of this classification. Al- Ghazālī's clarifies the distinction between religious sciences and nonreligious sciences (*al-'ulūm ghayr al-shar'ī*) in the following passage,

> What I intend by the religious [sciences] (*shar'īyyah*) are those sciences gained from the prophets (God's blessings and peace be upon them!) that the intellect [unaided] does not arrive at such as the Reckoning (*al-ḥisab*), nor does sense experience (*al-tajribah*) such as medicine, nor does transmitted knowledge (*al-samā'*) such as the [science] of language.
> (al-Ghazālī, 1998, 1:41–42)

So it is not that the religious sciences are irrational or contrary to reason. Rather, this classification indicates that the intellect cannot independently arrive at the religious sciences and that there must be a source outside of the intellect that affirms that which the intellect concludes to be rationally possible.

The remaining considerations Ṭāshkubrī-Zādah brings to the discussion are the propaedeutic sciences (*al-'ulūm al-'ālīyyah*), which are concerned with the sciences that fall under the first three levels of existence: written, spoken, and mental. The propaedeutic sciences are those sciences that serve as tools to obtaining sciences that are sought intrinsically. Ṭāshkubrī-Zādah further explains *al-al-'ilm al-ḥikamī* as those sciences that are arrived at by sole means of the intellect. Based on this division of *shar'ī* and non-*shar'*ī, objects at the level of concrete existence may be studied according to these two approaches. The sciences that come under the division of concrete existence may either be practical (*'amalī*) or theoretical (*naẓarī*). Based on Ṭāshkubrī-Zādah explanation, we find much that is similar to Aristotle's classification. The practical sciences "are not sought for their own sake, but for a purpose other than itself. The theoretical sciences are sought for their own sake." Each division, practical and theoretical, can be studied based on Islamic principles and will then be considered religious (*shar'ī*). If they are approached on purely rational principles and means, excluding religious teachings as serving the foundations of inquiry, then those same sciences are considered rational (*ghayr al-shar'ī*). In this sense, the object of inquiry and the subject matter of the science is the same. It is the approach and framework adopted by the inquirer that determines whether the science is religious or rational. This is what differentiates the science of theology from philosophy and metaphysics.

In total then, there are seven major divisions in Ṭāshkubrī-Zādah's classification of sciences. In terms of the structure of the book and the presentation of each major division of the sciences, Ṭāshkubrī-Zādah based his classification on the level of existence and the subject matter and name of each science. Each major division is called *al-doḥah*, which is an Arabic term referring to a great tree with wide-spreading branches; fitting imagery for how he conceives the many sciences as branching out from one major source. Each major subdivision has foundational sciences (*usūl*) and derived sciences (*furū'*), which he identifies in his discussion of each of the major divisions. Starting with the order mentioned by Ṭāshkubrī-Zādah the seven major divisions of the sciences are:

1. Sciences of the written word (*al-'ulūm al-khattīyyah*).
2. Sciences of the spoken word (*al-'ulūm tata'alluq bi-l-alfāẓ*).
3. Sciences that investigate mental entities or secondary intelligibles (*al-'ulūm al-bāḥitha 'an mā fī al-'aẓhan min al-ma'qūlāt al-thānīyyah*).
4. Sciences dealing with concrete existents—the theoretical sciences (*al-ḥikmah al-naẓarīyyah*).
5. Practical philosophy (*al-ḥikmah al-'amalīyyah*).
6. The religious sciences (*al-'ulūm al-shar'īyyah*).
7. The sciences of inward states (*al-'ulūm al-bāṭin*).

Here we see the four ontological levels of an existent correspond to the major division of the sciences. The first division corresponds to an object's existence in written form and concerns sciences such as handwriting, penmanship, dictation, writing instruments, the order of letters, and rules of script. The second division corresponds to an object's existence in spoken form and concerns sciences such as the correct pronunciation of letters, lexicography, etymology, philosophy of language (*'ilm al-waḍ'*), morphology (*'ilm al-ṣarf*), grammar, prosody, rhetoric (*'ilm al-bayān*), and history. The third division corresponds to an object's mental existence. The sciences in this category are logic, dialectics (*'ilm al-jadal*) disputation (*'ilm al-naẓar*), and science of juristic disagreement (*'ilm al-khilaf*).

The fourth division is concerned with the theoretical sciences and has as its subject matter concrete existents. Ṭāshkubrī-Zādah places metaphysics (*al-al-'ilm al-ilahī*), the mathematical sciences (*al-al-'ilm al-riyāḍī*), and the natural sciences (*al-'ilm al-ṭabi'ī*) in this division, which serve as the division's three foundational sciences from which many other sciences are derived. Metaphysics

> is a science where existents (*al-mawjūdat*) in so far as they are existents are investigated. Its subject-matter is being qua being (*al-mawjūd min haythu huwa*). The aim of the science is the acquiring of true beliefs (*al-i'tiqādat*) and correct conceptions in order to obtain everlasting happiness and continual supremacy.
>
> (Ṭāshkubrī-Zādah 1985, 1:289)

The sciences in this division are theoretical and their subject matter may be investigated in two different ways. Based on these approaches adopted in the investigation, these sciences may be considered philosophical or religious. In this division are those sciences that may either be studied

> based solely on opinion (*mujarrad al-ra'y*) and the dictates of reason (*muqtaḍa al-'aql*). These are the philosophical sciences or theoretical philosophy (*al-'ulūm al-ḥikamiyya*) which investigate the states of external existents as much as humanly possible. Investigations that take place based on the principles of religion (*al-shar'*) admitting premises derived from prophets constitute the science of the principles of religion (*usūl al-dīn*) . . . We have placed the rational sciences prior to Kalām theology because the rational sciences were codified prior to Kalām theology (*'ilm al-kalām*) and because it is more fitting that Kalām theology be placed in the second part of this treatise.
>
> (Ṭāshkubrī-Zādah 1985, 1:287)

This passage provides a significant insight into the way all of the sciences are to be considered and how each science relates to another. What is it about these approaches that Ṭāshkubrī-Zādah sees as the determining factor or factors that changes the quality of the sciences? It would seem that what differentiates the approaches are the first principles and assumptions that inform the study of the sciences. The term used by Ṭāshkubrī-Zādah to refer to these principles and assumptions is *qawā'id al-shar'* or the principles of revealed religion. The *qawā'id* are composed of laws of rational thought, ontological categories, theological positions, and religious doctrines. These principles form the framework for which the study of the natural world is carried out. They are termed religious principles because they are taken, in addition to the intellect, from religion as well. If the first principles and conceptual framework adopted for the study of these sciences is taken from religion, then the sciences would be called, according to Ṭāshkubrī-Zādah sciences of the foundations of religion. On the other hand, the term 'philosophical sciences' refers to the study of these sciences based on a framework not derived from religion, but solely based on the dictates of reason. Under the science of metaphysics are the sciences of the human soul, angelology, the resurrection, signs of prophethood, heresiography, and the science of the classification of the sciences.

The subject matter of the natural sciences (*al-'ilm al-ṭabi'ī*) is the natural body in so far as it undergoes change. There derivative sciences that come under the natural sciences are ten: medicine, equestrian science (*'ilm al-bayṭara*) and the ostring arts (*'ilm al-bayzara*), physiognomy (*'ilm al-firāsah*), science of dream interpretation, astrology (*'ilm aḥkām al-nujūm*), the occult arts (*'ilm al-siḥr*), science of theurgy (*'ilm al-ṭilasmāt*), and the sciences of phantasmagoria (*'ilm al-sīmiyā'*), alchemy (*al-'ilm al-kīmiyā'*), and agriculture (*'ilm al- filāḥa*). The sciences of botany, zoology, agriculture, mineralogy (*'ilm al-ma'ādin*), geology (*'ilm al-jawāhir*), atmospheric science (*'ilm al-kawn wa al-fasād*), and science of the rainbow (*'ilm qaws qazih*) are also categorized under the natural sciences.

Ṭāshkubrī-Zādah developed his classification scheme in the following manner: A body can either be simple, composite, or bodies more general than the two. Simple bodies are either celestial (*falakī*), which astrology studies, or elemental (*'unsurī*), which the science of theurgy studies. Composite bodies either do not possess a temperament, which the science of phantasmagoria studies, or do possess a temperament. These composite bodies either do not possess a soul, which alchemy studies, or they do. They may possess a soul that does not perceive, which the science of agriculture studies, or the soul may perceive. Souls that perceive are either those that can reason completely or not. It is only human beings that possess souls that are able to reason completely. Souls that cannot reason, such as other animals, are studied in the equestrian and ostring sciences and the other derivative sciences with the same subject matter. The science of medicine, physiognomy, dream interpretation all relate to the human being. Bodies that are more general than being simple or composite are the subject matter of the occult arts.

Ibn Khaldun observed that, "human social organization is something necessary." The philosophers expressed this fact by saying, "Man is 'political' by nature." That is, he cannot do without the social organization for which the philosophers use the technical term "town" (*polis*) (Ibn Khaldūn 1967, 1:98). The necessity of practical philosophy arises because, humans, being naturally social animals, are inclined to acquire what is in their interests and resist what harms them. This leads to social unrest as one person will attempt to acquire what another person possesses. Divine wisdom dictates that laws that are universal in nature are set in place whereby cities and nations may organize themselves around in a just manner that leads to the creation of the science of practical philosophy. Practical philosophy (*al-ḥikmah al-ʿamalīyyah*) makes up the fifth division and is composed of the science of ethics (*ʿilm al-akhlāq*), household management (*tadbīr al-manzil*), and politics (*ʿilm al-siyāsa*), with the aim of developing modes of conduct that ensure that justice is achieved in the individual, home, city, and other modes of human organization. The science of the proper conduct of kings (*'ilm ādāb al-mulūk*), the proper conduct of viziers (*'ilm ādāb al-wuzarāʾ*), sciences relating to market regulation and supervision (*'ilm al-iḥtisāb*), and military science (*'ilm qawad al-ʿasākir wa-l juyūsh*) are derivative sciences of this division.

The sixth division Ṭāshkubrī-Zādah dedicates to the religious sciences (*'ulūm al-sharʿīyyah*), also called *'ilm al-nawāmīs* emphasizing the fact that these sciences are only known by revelation to a prophet through the intermediation of an angel (*nāmūs*) not independently by the intellect, an understanding echoing al-Ghazālī's understanding as we will see later. Ṭāshkubrī-Zādah identifies seven sciences that constitute the principal sciences of the Sacred Law (*usūl al-sharīʿah*). This schema is reasoned as follows: The religious sciences either relate to transmission (*al-naqal*) of religious knowledge, apprehension of it, probative evidence of it, or deriving rulings from what it is. The science of the variant readings of the Qurʾān (*'ilm al-qirāʾāt)* and the science of *ḥadīth* transmission (*'ilm riwāya al-ḥadīth)* constitute the first category.

The second category is constituted by the sciences of Qur'ānic exegesis (*'ilm al-tafsīr*) and content analysis of *ḥadīth* (*'ilm dirāya al-ḥadīth)*. The science of theology (*'ilm usūl al-dīn*) is concerned with providing probative evidence of religious doctrine, whereas legal theory (*'ilm usūl al-fiqh*) provides probative evidence for acts from a legal perspective, and lastly, the science of jurisprudence *('ilm al-fiqh)* is concerned with deriving legal rulings from the sources of the Sacred Law. Numerous other derivative sciences fall under these seven principle sciences, such as the science of dialectics and disputation *('ilm al-jadal wa-l munāẓara)*, science of issuing legal responsa *('ilm al-fatwā)*, and the science of assessing *ḥadīth* transmitters ('ilm al-jarh wa-l ta'dīl).

The seventh and final division of the sciences, termed *'ulūm al-bāṭin*, all concern themselves with the inner dimensions of the human being. A human being, explains Ṭāshkubrī-Zādah, is constituted of entities originating from two different realms: a corporeal body, which is native to the sensory realm known as the 'realm of bodies' (*'ālam al- 'ajsām*) and a subtle spirit, which is native to an extrasensory realm known as the 'realm of dominion' or 'sovereignty' (*'ālam al-malakūt*). The subtle spirit, which is the rational soul (*al-nafs al-nāṭiqah*), obtains knowledge in two possible ways: either via the intermediation of the senses, which is termed acquired knowledge (*al-'ilm al-ḥuṣūlī*), or directly without the intermediation of the senses and is termed presential knowledge (*al-'ilm al-ḥudūrī*). Ṭāshkubrī-Zādah furthers explains that,

> the means to acquired knowledge are reflection (*al-fikr*) and reasoning (*al-naẓar*) about sense objects, while the means to acquire presential knowledge is the purification of the soul from worldly preoccupations, for the soul is like a mirror, and sensible preoccupations cause it to rust. Once a person polishes the mirror of these preoccupations, knowledges engrave themselves on the mirror instantaneously, without need to acquire knowledge by means of the senses.
>
> (Ṭāshkubrī-Zādah 1985, 3:6–7)

The subject matter of the *'ulūm al-bāṭin* is the means of purification of the soul. Ṭāshkubrī-Zādah's conception of the *'ulūm al-bāṭin* follows al-Ghazālī's structure of his *Iḥyāḥ' 'ulūm al-dīn* almost identically. There are four principal divisions that make up *'ulūm al-bāṭin*: acts of worship, the norms of daily life, the destructive vices, and the salvific virtues. These sciences are termed *'ilm al-mu'āmalah* because they focus on the method of purification, whereas the knowledge that is obtained at the end of the purification process, *'ilm al-mukāshafah* is not discussed.

KALĀM THEOLOGY (*'ILM AL-KALĀM*): A NEW ROLE FOR THE UNIVERSAL SCIENCE

The *qawā'id al-shar'* form the horizon for any discipline of knowledge and consequently allow us to consider the relationship between the various disciplines of knowledge. We find that it is Kalām theology as a science that comprises the *qawā'id al-shar'*. Consequently, Kalām theology occupies the highest rank among all the rational and religious sciences in the Islamic tradition. We will further explore the place and role of theology (*'ilm al-kalām*) among all the sciences in the Islamic tradition and the implications of this for Islamic educational institutions in the West.

"The good aimed at (*al-ghāyah*) in Kalām theology," al-Taftāzānī states, "is for faith and assent to the rulings of the Sacred Law to become certain and firm such that it is not shaken by the misgivings of the followers of falsehood (*mubṭilīn*)" (al-Taftāzānī 1989, 1:175). This is certainly not the only purpose for the science of Kalām theology, as theologians identify many other purposes. The strengthening of faith and the ability to reply to and withstand the responses of the skeptics are the more salient purposes identified by theologians. In the *Iḥyā'*, al-Ghazālī sees theology as primarily having a defensive role, a science to be used by a few and in a limited manner. Theology is not in itself a blameworthy science as "knowledge is never intrinsically blameworthy" (al-Ghazālī 1998, 1:62) according to al-Ghazālī. It is only in the harm that results from the science that is blameworthy. The harms must be weighed against the benefits of the science in order to arrive at a conclusion about the science. According to al-Ghazālī, the science of theology, depending on the person, may result in the lack of certainty in the average believer, creating new misgivings and possibly causing the heretic to be more resolute in his innovative theology. Al-Ghazālī concludes his discussion on the benefits and harms of theology by identifying the one good of theology, stating, "In fact, the one good of the science of theology is safeguarding the creed of the common person that we have explained and protecting it from the misgivings of heretics brought about by various dialectics (*al-jadal*)" (al-Ghazālī 1998, 1:173).

Al-Ghazālī's begins his discussion on the rank of the science of legal theory (*uṣul al-fiqh*) and its relation to other sciences, setting up a classification of the sciences different than the one in the *Iḥyā'* and his other works. The sciences, in general, are classified as rational (*'aqlīyyah*) or religious (*dīnīyyah*). This classification is based on whether or not a science can be known without the aid of revelation or the science can only be known through revelation. The rational sciences include medicine, arithmetic (*al-ḥisāb*), and geometry (*al-handasa*), whereas the religious sciences include Kalām theology (*al-kalām*), jurisprudence and its theory, the science of prophetic traditions (*'ilm al-ḥadīth*), and the science related to the state of the heart and ridding it of blameworthy character traits.

The two categories of rational and religious sciences can each be further classified into universal (*kullī*) and particular (*juz'ī*). It is this classification that is not seen elsewhere in al-Ghazālī's writings. He does not further expand on the rational sciences, but he does expand on the religious sciences. The only science that is a universal religious science is Kalām theology. All of the other religious sciences such as jurisprudence and legal theory are particular religious sciences. This specific classification scheme is observed in the writings of al-Farābī prior to al-Ghazālī, where al-Farābī, in his "On the Aims of Metaphysics" (*Maqāla fī aghrāḍ mā ba'da l-ṭabī'a*), also classifies the sciences into universal and particular. There are many aspects of an object that may be investigated. "Particular sciences are those whose subject-matters are some existents or some imaginary objects, and whose investigation regards specifically the accidents that are proper to them" (Bertolacci 2006, 67). These aspects can be reduced to one that is common to all existents, and this is what the universal science investigates. Al-Farābī explains that the

> Universal science, on the other hand, investigates the thing that is common to all existents (like existence and oneness), its species and attributes, the things which are not proper accidents of any of the subject matters of the particular sciences (such as priority and posteriority, potency and act, perfect and deficient, and similar things) and the common Principle of all existents, namely the thing that ought to be called by the name of God—may His glory be exalted.
>
> (Bertolacci 2006, 68)

This universal science al-Farābī which calls metaphysics investigates existence, its species, and attributes.

How is Kalām theology the only universal religious science? The answer to this question, according to al-Ghazālī, is that Kalām theology serves as the foundation of the particular religions sciences. Al-Ghazālī, states "The theologian investigates the most general of all things—existent entities (*al-mawjūd*)." The theologian studies existents qua existents, which is similar to al-Farābī's understanding of the subject matter of metaphysics. In a lengthy passage, al-Ghazālī elaborates how the theologian investigates existent entities stating,

> [He] categorizes existent entities, firstly, into eternal and temporal entities. Temporal entities are [further] categorized into substance and accident. He then classifies an accident into an accident for which life is a pre-requisite, such as knowledge, will, power, speech, hearing, listening, and sight, and an accident which does not require life such as color, odor, and taste. He categorizes the substance into an animal, a plant, or a mineral and he clarifies that they differ by types or accidents. Next, the theologian investigates the Eternal Existent and explains that the Eternal Existent is neither multiple nor can [it] be categorized according to the categories of accidents. Rather, it is necessary [that] the Eternal Existent be one and different from temporal entities by attributes that are necessary of Him, attributes that are impossible of Him, and qualities that are possible of Him, being neither necessary nor impossible. The theologian differentiates what is possible, necessary, and impossible of the Eternal Existent. Next the theologian explains that the principle

> of action is possible of Him, and [the bringing into existence] of the universe is of His possible acts and because it is possible, it requires an agent [to bring it into existence]. [He further explains] that sending messengers (*al-rusul*) is also of the possible acts of the Eternal Existent and that He has the power to carry out this act, and [He] makes known the truthfulness of them by means of evidentiary miracles and this act [does in fact] takes place. It is at this point, the discussion of the theologian ends and the capacity of the intellect has reached its limit. In fact, the intellect demonstrates the truthfulness of the prophet and then steps back and accepts all that it receives from the prophet: what he conveys regarding God, the Last Day, and those matters which the intellect cannot independently arrive at nor does it conclude their impossibility. For the Sacred Law does not impart that which is contrary to the intellect, however, the Sacred Law does impart that which the intellect cannot arrive at independently. For example, the intellect cannot [independently] determine that acts of obedience are the cause of happiness in the Hereafter, and that acts of disobedience are the cause of misery. At the same time, the intellect does not conclude it being impossible either. The intellect also concludes that truthfulness is a necessary [attribute] of a person which miracles have established his truthfulness. Therefore, when a Messenger imparts [knowledge] of Him, the intellect concludes it as being true in line with this way [of reasoning]. All of this is the subject matter of Kalām theology.
>
> From this [explanation] you come to know that the theologian begins his investigation with the most general of all things—which is the existent entity and then gradually descends in his investigation to the particulars in the manner we have mentioned. He establishes the foundations of all the religious sciences: the Qur'ān, the Sunnah, and the truthfulness of the Messenger. The Qur'ānic exegete will then investigate one particular from a specific aspect of all what the theologian investigates, which is the Qur'ān, and investigate its meanings. The *ḥadīth* scholar will investigate one particular from a specific aspect, the Sunnah, and investigate its ways of authentication. The jurist (*faqīh*) will investigate one particular from a specific aspect, namely the action of the legally responsible person. He will investigate its relationship to the statement of the Lawgiver on whether the act is obligatory, forbidden, or permissible.
>
> (al-Ghazālī n.d., 1:5–6)

Kalām theology establishes truths and premises that serve as givens in the particular religious sciences. In this way it serves as "the foundations of all the religious sciences" and is considered the universal science. Each religious science takes, as its subject matter, one particular and investigates it from a certain aspect and take as givens conclusions established in Kalām theology. So the jurist will not investigate that the Qur'ān is the word of God or the veracity of the Prophet Muḥammad's claim to prophethood but will assume them as a true premise and investigate the Qur'ān and the Sunnah to derive legal rulings. It is in this sense that Kalām theology is a universal science by being logically prior to the religious science by establishing premises that are later used as givens in all the particular religious sciences and thus taking the place as the highest-ranking science.[1] In other words, the particular religious sciences are all predicated on premises whose truth value Kalām theology, whereas the particular religious sciences merely assume them as being true. Practitioners of particular religious sciences do not have to necessarily be theologians to practice their science. Rather, they take what the theologian has established by merely accepting the authority of the theologian (*taqlīd*), the role of the theologian being to establish the foundations of all the religious sciences. By providing the foundational premises of the religious sciences, Kalām theology thus informs all the other religious sciences. Additionally, it integrates the sciences and provides a basis for relating one science to another hierarchically (al-Ghazālī n.d., 1:7).

Al-Ghazālī stated that Kalām theology serves as the universal science for religious sciences, and his discussion demonstrated how this is so. Additionally, he claimed that the rational sciences also have a universal science, which he did not elaborate on in this work. I will attempt to identify the universal rational science that al-Ghazālī posits. He lists medicine, arithmetic (*al-ḥisāb*) and geometry (*al-handasa*) as examples of rational sciences. These sciences have concrete existents as its subject matter according to Ṭāshkubrī-Zādah and include other sciences, such as chemistry, anatomy, pharmacy, surgery as well as other physical sciences. All of these sciences, being classified as rational by al-Ghazālī and Ṭāshkubrī-Zādah provide knowledge that can be obtained without the aid of revelation from God through prophets. This does not entail that the subject matters of these sciences are studied independent of any framework or universal science that informs how the deliverables of the sciences are to be understood. As we have seen, these sciences can be studied based solely on the dictates of reason or on principles provided by revealed religion (*qawāʿid al-sharʿ*).

What separates the science of metaphysics (*al-ʿilm al-ilahī*) from Kalām theology is not the subject matter, but presuppositions, the *qawāʿid al-sharʿ* or what al-Taftāzānī terms the *qānūn al-islam*, that inform the investigations. Al-Taftāzānī explains the *qānūn al-islam* as being constituted of,

> the good way termed religion (*al-dīn*) and creed (*al-millah*), and the definitively established principles from the Qur'ān, Sunnah, and the consensus of scholars such as [the doctrine of] one entity bringing into existence multiple entities, an angel descending from heaven, the cosmos being preceded by non-existence and ceasing to exist after existing, and other doctrines [that form the] principles that are taken as definitive in Islam and not in philosophy.

Metaphysical and theological propositions that a Muslim presupposes when carrying out investigations in the rational and religious sciences constitute these *qānūn*. They are those doctrines that are definitively established as constituting the religion of Islam and are delivered by the science of Kalām theology.

The fragmentation of the disciplines resulting in each discipline being an autonomous entity, as MacIntyre described, has resulted in numerous attempts to relate the disciplines to one another due to the lack of relevancy and meaning to students when learning discipline-specific content. Muslim scholars would agree with MacIntyre's and Taylor's assessment that this situation has resulted from absences of a horizon. Kalām theology serves a vital role to avoid this trajectory in Muslim educational efforts in the context of secular political arrangements by serving as the universal science that forms the horizon based on which goods, which includes knowledge, can be arranged based on each good's relationship to another.

NOTE

1 For a reconciliation of al-Ghazālī's two views of Kalām theology, see Treiger, Alexander. "Al-Ghazālī's Classifications of the Sciences and Descriptions of the Highest Theoretical Science." *Dîvân: Disiplinlerarası Çalısmalar Dergisi* 16 (2011): 1–32.

BIBLIOGRAPHY

Bertolacci, Amos. 2006. *The Reception of Aristotle's 'Metaphysics' in Avicenna's Kitāb al-Shifā': A Milestone of Western Metaphysical Thought*. Leiden: Brill.

al-Fārābī, Muḥammad Ibn Muḥammad AbūNaṣr. 1996. *Iḥṣāḥ' al-'ulūm* edited by ʿAlī Bū Malḥam. Beirut: Dār wa Maktaba al-Hilāl.

al-Ghazālī, Abū Ḥāmid Muḥammad. 1998. *Iḥyā' 'Ulūm al-Dīn*. Aleppo: Dār al-Waʿī al-ʿArabī.

———. n.d. *al-Mustaṣfā min 'Ilm al-Uṣūl*. 2 vols. Beirut: Dār al-ʿUlūm al-Ḥadīthīyyah

Ibn al-Akfānī, Muḥammad ibn Ibrāhīm. 1994. *Irshād al-Qāṣid ilā Asnā al-Maqāṣid* edited by Muḥammad 'Awwāḥmah and Hasan 'Ibajiī. Jeddah: Dār al-Qibla lil-Thaqāfah al-Islāḥmīyah.

Ibn Hajar al-ʿAsqalānī, Ahmad ibn ʿAlī. 2002. *Lisān al-Mīzān* edited by 'Abd al-Fattāh Abū Ghuddah. Beirut: Dār al-Bashāʾir al-Islāmīyyah.

Ibn al-Ḥajjāj, Muslim. 1991. *Ṣaḥīḥ Muslim*. Edited by Fūʾad ʿAbd al-Bāqī. 5 vols. Beirut: Dār al-Fikr.

Ibn Khaldūn, 'Abd al-Raḥmān Ibn Muḥammad. 1967. *The Muqaddimah: An Introduction to History*. Trans. Franz Rosenthal: 3 Vols. Princeton, NJ: Princeton University Press.

Macintyre, Alasdair. 2009. *God, Philosophy, Universities: A Selective History of the Catholic Philosophical Tradition*. Maryland: Rowman & Littlefield Publishing Group, Inc.

al-Rāzī, Quṭb al-Dīn Maḥmūd b. Muḥammad. 2007. "Taḥrīr al-Qawāḥ'id al-Manṭiqiyya Sharḥ Matn al-Shamsiyya," in *Shurūḥ al-Shamsiyya: Majmū' al-Ḥawāshin Wa Ta'līqāt*. Qum: Madin.

Sajiqli Zādah, Muhammad ibn Abī Bakr al-Mar'ashi. 1988. *Tartīb al-'Ulūm*. Beirut: Dar al-Bashā'ir al-Islāmīyyah.

al-Taftāzānī, Mas'ūd ibn 'Umar. 1989. *Sharḥ al-Maqāṣid* edited by 'Abd al-Raḥmān 'Umayrah. Beirut: 'Ālam al-Kutub.

al-Tahānawī, Muḥammad A'lā ibn 'Alī. n.d. 1998. *Kashshāf Iṣṭilāḥāt al-Funūn*. Beirut: Dār al-Ṣadr.

Ṭāshkubrī-Zādah, Aḥmad ibn Muṣṭafā. 1985. *Kitāb Miftāḥ al-Sa'ādah wa-Miṣbaḥ al-Siyādah fī Mawḍu'āt al-'Ulūm*. 3 vols. Beirut: Dār al-Kutub al-Ilmīyyah.

Taylor, Charles. 1989. *Sources of the Self: The Making of the Modern Identity*. Cambridge, Mass: Harvard University Press.

al-Tirmidhī, Muḥammad ibn 'Īsa, Aḥmad. 1990. *al-Jāmi' al-Ṣaḥīḥ: Wa-Huwa Sunan al-Tirmidhī*. Edited by Muḥammad Shākir. 5 vols. Beirut: Dār Iḥyā' al-Turāth al-'Arabī.

al-Suyūṭī, Jalāl al-Dīn 'Abd al-Raḥmān ibn Abī Bakr. 1988. *Juz' Fīhi Ṭuruq Ḥadīth Ṭalab al-'Ilm Farīḍah 'Alā Kulli Muslim*. Edited by 'Alī ḥasan 'Alī 'Abd al-Ḥamīd. Amman, Jordan: Dār 'Ammār.

7 The Transmission of *Adab*

Educational Ideals and their Institutional Manifestations

Talal Al-Azem[1]

Any attempt to organize a body of knowledge demands these efforts be preserved, transmitted, and cultivated. This is notably true in the case of the historical Muslim community. Early on, the Muslims inaugurated extensive oral and written learned traditions to transmit the text of the Prophet's revelation, to safeguard his memory, and to organize and make intelligible the practices of the Prophet and of the earliest Muslims to their own rapidly changing times. Increased contact with non-Muslims who proudly possessed ancient scholarly traditions of their own—and whose descendants sometimes became Muslim scholars themselves—only quickened this process. Learned Muslims took on this task in numerous ways: they developed forms of textual criticism; articulated and debated a range of speculative, mystical, and moral theologies; cultivated rational and ancillary disciplines that served as aids to their scholarship; and investigated, translated, and supported a broad range of sciences, from the natural and experimental to the metaphysical and religious. Society, in turn, supported these endeavors materially: first by patronizing scholars directly, and eventually by founding and endowing specialized academies of learning.

From the earliest centuries, one kind of knowledge was identified as both a condition and an end of the educational enterprise; namely, the transmission and inculcation of *adab* in the person of learning—where 'adab' denotes propriety of comportment, of attitude, and of conduct. The present essay explores how the institutions of learning which arose in the Muslim world institutionalized this notion of *adab*, and how Muslim educators and educationalists sought to operationalize it in the craft of teaching. Though different institutions and ritualized practices of learning existed from the earliest days of the nascent Muslim community,[2] this chapter shall focus on institutionalized education in the so-called 'late medieval period' of the eleventh to the sixteenth centuries: the period in which a number of the Muslim world's most recognizable institutions of learning developed and spread, such as the *madrasa*, or college, and the *khānaqāh*, or Sufi hospice. The appearance of these institutions reconfigured much of the sociology of knowledge in the Muslim world: institutionalization brought in its wake the professionalization of learning, more formalized educational practices, and an expanded internationalization of the resulting scholarship.[3]

Practical manuals on the art of educating and learning had been written for centuries and had long offered pedagogical and moral advice to teachers and students alike. However, in the age of guilds of law (*madhhab*s), of mystical orders, of colleges, and of hospices, educationalists adapted this genre to their new socio-intellectual settings. They sought to reign in what they saw as the deleterious effects of professionalization and institutionalization by impressing upon their scholarly readership a correct attitude toward the craft of education and by outlining the proper conduct (*adab*) of teachers and of students befitting the new educational spaces created by the endowed college.

By assessing the types of learned institutions and their practices, we will better understand how they served to transmit what medieval scholars deemed the cardinal virtue resulting from any mode of education—namely, proper comportment, attitude, and conduct (*adab*)—and what this might tell us about the nature of an Islamic education.

MODES OF EDUCATING AND THEIR INSTITUTIONAL MANIFESTATIONS

Survey the classical literature treating education in the Muslim world and you quickly discover that a discreet set of terms emerges: *taʿlīm*, *tadrīs*, *taʾdīb*, and *tarbiya*. While related and often used in close proximity—at times almost interchangeably—each normally conveys a distinct meaning in the context of the institutions and practices of learning, and each reflects a nuance of educational objective. A brief review of the vocabulary of education can provide us with a window into the ways in which Muslims thought about learning and its objectives, allowing us to sketch the relationship between the types of learning and the types of educational institutions.

The first two terms mentioned signal the transfer of positivized forms of knowledge. *Taʿlīm* denotes instruction, most commonly in a formal teacher-student relationship. The '*muʿallim*,' or instructor, is one who has been commissioned to systematically develop a student's understanding of a specific subject.[4] The second, *tadrīs*, is the delivery of a lecture, or *dars*, and represents a ritualized dimension of formal knowledge transmission.[5] On the other hand, the latter two terms—*taʾdīb* and *tarbiya*—denote the educative formation, or reformation, of the internal dimensions of the person: *taʾdīb* conveys the inculcation of virtues, of moral disciplines, and of the manners of proper conduct (*adab*) and, in the context of learning, was most closely associated with primary education.[6] *Tarbiya*—to rear, to nurture, and to train—reflects the educative process that transforms the person over time, causing them to mature from a state of juvenility to maturity. Both denote a principled, programmatic approach to character formation.[7]

As the disciplines and institutions of learning came to be distinguished over time, each of these terms came to be associated with particular branches of learning and often with a different institutional setting. Law, theology, medicine, Qur'anic studies, philosophy, Prophetic traditions, mysticism, and language—each professed its own accentuated mode of knowledge and unique educational objective. *Tadrīs*, for example, comes to be used almost exclusively for the teaching of law; in many settings, *mudarris* (he who delivers the '*dars*,' or lesson) and *faqīh* (jurist) came to serve as exchangeable terms for the professor of law (*fiqh*). *Tarbiya*, on the other hand, was intimately associated with the spiritual disciplines of Sufism, where the *shaykh al-tarbiya* (the training master) was often juxtaposed with the *shaykh al-taʿlīm* (the instructing master): The former provided personal spiritual guidance over a lifetime of personal change, whereas the latter was a teacher who exposited the technical vocabulary and doctrines of Sufism as found in Sufi literature.[8] Initiation was usually a prerequisite of both, and indeed the two forms of Sufi instruction often resided within the same *shaykh*. Nonetheless, the objectives, and thus the craft and qualifications of each, were fundamentally different: the 16th-century Egyptian jurist and mystic ʿAbd al-Wahhāb al-Shaʿrānī wrote and taught some of the most celebrated scholarly manuals of Sufism of any age, uniting the metaphysical and practical traditions, whereas his own spiritual guide, ʿAlī al-Khawwāṣ, was an unlettered master of training.[9]

These various modes of educating that have been discussed—*tarbiya*, *taʿlīm*, *taʾdīb*, and *tadrīs*—were also reflected in different scholarly practices and unique forms of scholarly social organization. For example, the centrality of *adab* in primary education may be perceived in one of the terms used to denote the schoolteacher—*muʾaddib al-aṭfāl* (teachers of *adab* to children)—reflecting that the teacher's principal task was to teach proper conduct and discipline, so much so, that the setting of a primary school (sing. *maktab*, pl. *kuttāb*) might also be referred to as a *majlis al-adab* (a place where one sits to learn proper conduct).[10]

However, nowhere is the relationship of socio-intellectual vision to institutions more clearly illustrated than in the emergence of two, parallel (and deeply related) types of learned institutions in Muslim societies: the self-regulated, social associations of persons of learning, such as the *madhhab* and the *ṭarīqa* and the societally funded, 'brick-and-mortar' architectural sites of learning, such as the *madrasa* and the *khānaqāh*. Whereas many other types of both social associations and built institutions existed, the relationships of the *madhhab* to the *madrasa*, and of the *ṭarīqa* to the *khānaqāh*, serve as an excellent illustration of the determining effect that modes of knowledge had upon the institutional forms they assumed.

Often translated as 'school of law,' the medieval Muslim *madhhab* is better understood as a professional guild: a self-regulating, hierarchical association of jurists serving the needs of society by issuing legal opinions (*fatwa*s), providing trained jurists to serve as judges in the government's judiciary, and delivering legal education.[11] Like many other forms of Muslim learning, legal education began historically in the first native institution of Islam, the mosque. By the 11th-century CE, however, it came to be housed in a new 'purpose-built' institution: the *madrasa*—an endowed college initially founded for the exclusive purpose of delivering the *dars*, or lecture in law.[12] Other specialized colleges soon began to spring up in Damascus, Cairo, and Baghdad, some for hadith, some for Qur'an, and yet others for the study of medicine.[13]

So too did the Sufi *ṭarīqa*, or spiritual order (literally, 'path'), stand to the Sufi hospice or *khānaqāh* (sometimes referred to as the *zāwiya*, or *ribāṭ*). Personal relationships of disciples to spiritual masters was a common feature of earlier periods, but more formal associations of Sufi brotherhoods began to appear by the 5th and 6th centuries of the *hijra* (eleventh and twelfth CE). These orders and brotherhoods developed ritualized processes of initiation, of transmission, and of legitimation alongside bodies of mystical doctrines and renunciant practices. Rulers and other affluent members of society often would found hospices for the better-known Sufi *shaykhs* and their communities of disciples: Thus did Saladin, as well as his Ayyubid descendants, establish dozens of such hospices throughout Egypt and the Levant. Alongside serving as halls of residence for the disciples and hospices for wayfarers, these *khānaqāh*s served as centers of teaching Sufism—as well as other disciplines that the hospice's director thought would aid the Sufi community in its spiritual life, such as the study of the Qur'an—just as the *madrasa*s did for the teaching of law.[14]

In short, those disciplines based upon 'positivist' branches of knowledge (or, in traditional terms, 'outward' [*ẓāhir*] kinds of knowledge) — such as law, *ḥadīth*, and medicine—came to be housed in colleges. For a range of cultural and political reasons, many others, such as philosophy, the precise sciences, and even theology never came to receive the same kind of specialized institutionalization: They generally were not granted purpose-built buildings with endowments. But this should not be understood to mean that the transmission and study of these disciplines did not flourish or that they did not develop certain institutional forms: The library, the private home, the observatory, and the hospital (*bīmāristān*) all were alternative 'centers of learning,' where the study and cultivation of these sciences thrived; and they often developed their own chains of transmission and pedagogic practices.[15] Furthermore, the 14th and 15th centuries witnessed the rise of a new form of institution that tore down many of these barriers: the educational-charitable complex. Starting in Timurid, Iran, and quickly spreading throughout the Mamluk realm into Mecca and throughout Anatolia, many of the different educational institutions listed earlier began to be merged into large complexes. These complexes often supported numerous professorial chairs in law (often across multiple *madhhab*s), Sufi hospices, 'soup kitchens' serving over a thousand poor people a day, teaching hospitals, and training in mathematics and astronomy, as well as primary schools for poor or orphan children (*maktab*s).[16]

Whether the institutions were small, like many of the rural *khānaqāh*s that proliferated after the dissolution of the Mongol Ilkhanate in Iran, or imperial, such as the charitable-complexes with their multiple faculties, what remains constant in most documented cases is the personal relationship of the student to the teacher—what was referred to in various educational and Sufi manuals as *ṣuḥba*, or personal fellowship and apprenticeship. However large the institution and complex, its organizational form, and whatever discipline of education with its attendant mode of learning was pursued (legal, spiritual, medical, etc.), the etiquette and manners of *ṣuḥba* served to govern the manner in which education was experienced.

Despite the intensely personal nature of these associations, it would be a mistake to read their concomitant forms of education as purely informal.[17] Whether the *madhhab*s or the urban *ṭarīqa*s, these institutions usually comprised well-defined rules, regulations for association, limitations on the activities of associates, and processes that ensured that the objectives for which they were established were realized. This was especially the case in the *madrasa*: Students and teachers, as well as assistants and other maintainers of the colleges, were all formally and hierarchically ranked, as evidenced by the procedures and rituals that graduate students (*muntahūn*) were expected to pass before being certified (through an *ijāza* or 'license to teach') and recognized as masters (*shaykh*s) in their own right.[18] Students' abilities to take up posts in the judiciary, the colleges, in the mosques, or in other governmental and civil institutions depended upon this certification—a certification that was issued not by the institution (for it possessed no corporate identity by which to issue legally recognized documents in its own name), but by the masters under whom the students had studied.[19] Whereas the most common such certificate was the *ijāzat al-iftāʾ wa-al-tadrīs* (the license to issue legal opinions and to teach law), licenses were likewise issued for the teaching of medicine and exact sciences in the regular madrasas. There is even evidence that licenses were issued for the *practice* of medicine at the end of medical apprenticeships.[20] The system was formal, but personal. Whether in law, in Sufism, or in medicine, students were expected not only to read the known textbooks of the discipline with a master, but to practice their arts, as apprentices, under the watchful eye of the same or another master until he was satisfied with the student's mastery of the subject and that student was then admitted into the guild of masters himself.

Whereas many political and social factors could and often did influence the appointments that college graduates especially would go on to assume,[21] both the *madhhab* and the *ṭarīqa* were essentially civil institutions of society: The hierarchies of positions and responsibilities internal to any guild were determined and filled by the individuals who comprised the body of these associations. This entailed that the maintaining of internal order and discipline was left to the creative devices of these social institutions' own members. The conditions of appointment and of admission to any given *madrasa* or *khānaqāh* were usually spelled out by the founder in his endowment (*waqf*) deed and were enforceable by law. But it was the masters of these guilds and orders who determined the admission of scholars into the *madhhabs* or of aspirants into the *ṭarīqas*, and who delineated and inculcated the proper attitude and conduct. And it was in the literature of *adab* manuals that these rules were spelled out and adapted for new social circumstances over time.

THE CRAFT OF TEACHING IN A WORLD OF PROFESSIONALIZED EDUCATION

The personal character of teaching was recognized as a keystone of educational practice in the theoretical literature and manuals to students and educators. Indeed, in the eyes of many a premodern Muslim writer, teaching was categorized as that most personal form of creative production: a craft.[22] Arguably, such a categorization has certain consequences for a society's vision of teaching, as all crafts are, by definition, intensely human and personal and are fashioned and pursued in connection with some productive, final end (*ghāya*). In his survey of the crafts, professions, and offices of his age, the 14th-century theologian and jurisprudent Tāj al-Dīn al-Subkī (d. 771/1370 AD) includes no less than twelve chapters on various types of people associated with higher learning. From the professor (*mudarris*) to the graduate student (*muntahī*) to the beginning students of law (*fuqahā'*), Subkī reminds each that the exercise of his craft is first and foremost a means for cultivating his virtues through performance of the craft in good faith and trust and, as such, an avenue for expressing gratitude (*shukr*) to the Divine.[23]

By the age of Subkī, teaching truly had become a craft, both in the productive sense of the word (a *ṣināʿa* or a utilitarian art producing goods required by society), as well as in the professional sense (a *ḥirfa* or a vocation by which one earns ones living). This professionalization had started in the eastern lands in the late 10th century and became increasingly internationalized with the establishment of the first endowed circuit of colleges, the Niẓāmiyya, by the Seljuk vizier Niẓām al-Mulk (d. 485/1092 AD). Long before Subkī sought to remind educators and other professionals as to their responsibilities to God and society, the famous Abū Ḥāmid al-Ghazālī (d. 505/1111 AD)—a contemporary of Niẓām al-Mulk and one of the earliest professors at the latter's Niẓāmiyya of Baghdad—had likewise opened his magnum opus, the *Ihyā' ʿulūm al-dīn* ("The Revivification of Religious Knowledges"), with sharp criticism of the jurists and other increasingly professionalized scholars for their competitiveness over stipends and posts and the concern with prestige and wealth this reflected. The endowment deeds that underwrote the colleges and supported the scholars, and the institutional hierarchies that evolved, were, for morally minded professors, such as Ghazālī and Subkī, at once a source of great good (insofar as they facilitated education), as well as a potential spoiler of the high-mindedness expected from those involved with this most sacred craft.

It is in light of this professionalized and institutionalized context that the important text *Tadhkirat al-sāmiʿ wa-al-mutakallim fī adab al-ʿālim wa-al-mutaʿallim* ("A Memorandum for Students and Lecturers: Rules of Conduct for the Learned and the Learning") of Badr al-Dīn Ibn Jamāʿa (d. 733/1333 AD) must be read. Like Ghazālī before him, and Subkī after, Ibn Jamāʿa was no stranger to the collegiate system of higher learning. A celebrated jurisprudent, theoretician of constitutional law, and chief judge of the highest courts, Ibn Jamāʿa was also a tireless educator, lecturing throughout his life to many students in the numerous colleges of Damascus, Jerusalem, and Cairo. Like the many pieces of educational literature penned before his, Ibn Jamāʿa's *Tadhkira* is replete with practical and moral advice for learners and lecturers alike, including conventional treatments of the virtues of learning and the learned and of the proper conduct (*adab*) of teachers and students. What is unique about the work, however, is how it frames these familiar topics within the context of the now ubiquitous *madrasa* and college culture that had developed in its wake:

> I was moved . . . to apprise the student of what is incumbent upon him, and to present the rules of conduct (*al-adab*) common to both, the rules to be followed in using books, and the rules of behavior for those who live in colleges (*madrasahs*) either as graduates or as students, as such colleges are usually the residences of seekers of learning nowadays.[24]

In some ways, there is no departure: The central concern of the work is still very much *adab*—the proper rules, comportment, and attitude befitting those involved with learning and education—as it had been in the works of earlier scholars such as Ibn Saḥnūn and ʿAbd al-Karīm al-Samʿānī.[25] *Adab* is at the heart of Ibn Jamāʿa's educational manual: It features prominently in the very title of the work, in the introduction, and in four of the five central themes of the work, as reflected in the chapter titles: the *adab* for the teacher toward his own self, with his students, and regards the lessons he delivers; the *adab* of the student toward his own self, with his master and colleagues, and toward the lessons he attends; the *adab* of the scholar toward books; and the *adab* of residing in colleges.

In this fifth and final chapter, Ibn Jamāʿa addresses the proper conduct of those who reside in colleges. This section is unique to his work, there being no equivalent treatment in the important earlier pedagogic text, *Taʿlīm al-mutaʿallim* of Burhān al-Dīn al-Zarnūjī (fl. 620/1223) or in other preceding educational treatises. This is understandable: So prevalent had the colleges become in Syro-Egypt, and so far had professionalization reconfigured the expectations and advantages of a career in learning, that it is not unwarranted for us to speak of the appearance of a 'college culture' by the 1300s. In part, this may be ascribed to the sheer number of colleges that sprung up in the main cities of learning: In the 14th century, Damascus alone could boast of ninety-four colleges, with yet three more being built in the following century. So widespread was the support for education in this city, that Ibn Jubayr (d. 614/1217 AD), in his famous travel log, chastens any student who failed to avail himself of its bounties:

> The facilities provided to foreign students in this town are too great in number to even attempt to count. . . . Any beginning student from the Muslim West (*al-maghrib*) who aspires to a successful career in learning should leave his homeland and set forth at once to these lands for the sake of seeking knowledge. Anyone who does so will find no end to the support he will receive. Most importantly, it will permit him to completely free his mind of any concern for his own livelihood . . .[26]

Many aside from Ibn Jubayr noticed rewards were to be reaped from the institutionalization of learning made possible by college endowments and trusts. In this college culture, the *madrasas* had become the regular place of residence, not only for students arriving from foreign lands but also for graduate students who served as repetitors and assistants and for the professors (as well as their dependents). It was not uncommon for scholars from learned families to be born in *madrasa*s and likewise to die in these very institutions.[27] The residential facilities of the colleges had evolved fully from temporary residences for foreign students (the *masjid-khān* of the pre-11th century) to an expected benefit of a professional career as a scholar.

With nearly one hundred colleges in a city such as Damascus, conflicts of interest could and did arise. Multiple professorial appointments were a routine feature of academic life, but no one professor was meant to receive living quarters at multiple institutions in one city, let alone to profit by subleasing them to others. Likewise were students free to attend lectures in multiple institutions on the condition that they first fulfill the basic curricular, social, and religious obligations stipulated upon them as residents of the college that provided them their room, board, and stipends.[28] Students were ranked, and each class was expected to fully engage in the form of learning appropriate to its level: beginners (*al-ṭālib*) in reading, memorizing, and discussing the basic textbooks; graduates (*al-muntahī*, lit. 'terminal student') in disputations; and those being trained in providing legal opinions (*iftāʾ*) in research. Advanced students also frequently served as repetitors (*muʿīd*) and junior instructors (*mufīd*); but they could only justify receiving stipends if they conscientiously fulfilled their pedagogic duties toward the less advanced students of their own college.[29]

In light of these historical considerations, we may better understand what motivated Ibn Jamāʿa to pen rules such as the following:

1. As far as possible, [the student] should choose for himself a college whose founder was closest to piety and farthest from undesirable innovations so that he can be reasonably sure that the college and its endowment are from a licit source of income and that any stipend received is from untainted funds.
2. The professor at the college . . . should attract pupils, encourage diligent students, dismiss triflers, and act equitably toward researchers. . . . The assistant at the college should give priority to tutoring its students over any others at the regular time specified, especially if he is receiving a stipend for his assistantship, for this is what he has been appointed to do as long as he is assistant. Tutoring others is beyond the call of duty or is a collective duty . . .
3. The student should acquaint himself with the stipulations of the school's endowment so that he can fulfill them. The more he can keep aloof from the school stipend the better . . .
4. If the founder has restricted residence in the school to stipendiaries only, no one else may live there; if anyone else does so, he is being disobedient and unjust. If the founder made no such restriction, there is no harm in it if the resident is worthy. If a non-stipendiary resides in the school, he should be courteous to its people and give them priority over himself in what they need from the school. He should attend the school's teaching, that being the greatest of the religious purposes for which it was built and endowed. . . . If the resident abandons this, he has abandoned the purpose for which his residence was built, and this obviously violates the founder's intent . . .
5. He should not busy himself there with socializing and companionship. . . . The smart student makes the college a way station where he fulfills his object and then leaves. . . . Colleges and their endowments were not established merely for residence and socializing or merely for devotion to prayer and fasting like Sufi hostels. They were established to help people acquire learning, devote themselves to it, and isolate themselves from distractions in the dwellings of their family and kin (Ibn Jamāʿah, *A Memorandum*, 2010. pp.200–3).

The rules of conduct listed by Ibn Jamāʿa and the proper attitudes and responsibilities befitting those engaged in the learned profession as outlined by Subkī were both descriptive (of the actual practices of their day) and prescriptive (by seeking to align teachers' and students' conduct to one befitting sincere gratitude to God, or *shukr*, and the recognized patterns of *adab*). In so doing, Ibn Jamāʿa's fifth chapter meant to bring the new college culture in line with all the ethical and spiritual norms that Muslim educationalists had posited before him and to curtail the abuses arising from the new, potentially destabilizing, effects of professionalization. Not only had the institutionalization of learning redefined the urban landscape of cities such as Nishapur, Baghdad, Damascus, and Cairo, but its attendant professionalization threatened to scramble its moral landscape. In the writings of Ibn Jamāʿa and Subkī, the internal 'moral technologies of the self'—such as Divine gratitude (*shukr*) and proper comportment (*adab*)—were no less important for countering the negative social and intellectual influences of institutionalization and professionalization than the 'external' mechanisms of state inspections of the colleges (*ḥisba*) for abuses of the endowments' stipulations.[30] The books of Sufism, with which the likes of Ibn Jamāʿa and Subkī were well familiar, hammered home the centrality of these two moral virtues and the necessity of acquiring them through personal fellowship (*ṣuḥba*) with those who possess them. In an age in which such scholars would have spent many years in institutions of Sufism, as well as in colleges, it is not surprising to find such devices emphasized in manuals treating the craft and art of education.

CONCLUSION

The founders and patrons of colleges, teaching hospitals, and hospices were societal elites—viziers, members of ruling families, and international traders and merchants.[31] By means of their wealth and the endowments they established, such elites could influence the social and cultural makeup of society by stipulating, in their endowments, conditions for who should receive a professorship or a studentship. The 14th and 15th centuries, for example, saw an influx of Iranian and Anatolian emigrants into Cairo's scholarly landscape, due to Mamluk endowments earmarked for those specific ethnicities.[32]

Nonetheless, and perhaps remarkably, the contents of the teaching, the personal form of education in the colleges, and the moral impact of the educational system upon the fabric of society were not a matter of state policy. From an educational, intellectual, and moral-cultural perspective, the integration of Turkic and other nonlocal peoples into medieval Islamicate society via the *madrasa*s and *ṭarīqa*s serves as evidence that, in the *longue durée*, the institutions of education helped to enculture both newcomers and existing members of society according to the moral vision embodied in *ʿilm* and not according to any centralizing political agenda. Some of those same emigrants, such as Dāwūd al-Qayṣarī (d. 751/1350 AD) from the fledgling Ottoman realm, returned to their homelands to establish their own networks of colleges and to found entire systems of higher education. However different their social structures and political contexts, and however unique their nascent intellectual directions, these new institutions, such as the Ottoman *ilmiye*, ultimately extended the metaphysical architecture and moral parameters of Islamicate society and culture.[33]

Both social and brick-and-mortar institutions of learning socialize those whom they admit into their ranks. The ubiquity of apprenticeship (*ṣuḥba*) and the unrelenting emphasis on proper comportment, attitude, and conduct (*adab*)—across various Islamicate societies, differing social and physical institutions, and diverse disciplines—reflects the centrality of the personal transmission of comportment (*taʾdīb*) to the educational enterprise. The very notion of proper attitude and conduct was central to the educational enterprises that served to inculcate the moral imagination of Islamicate society. *Adab* not only defined scholarly practice, but served to govern the institutions and their social operations and, to protect against the damages resulting from specialisation and professionalisation. In turn, the educational experience perpetuated the theoretical and embodied transmission of *adab*. In the final calculation, this is what kept premodern Muslim traditions of institutional education not merely personal, but profoundly human.

NOTES

1 Faculty of Oriental Studies, University of Oxford. The writing of this chapter was made possible, in part, by the European Research Council under the European Union's Seventh Framework Programme (FP7/2007–2013) / ERC Starting Grant 263557 IMPAcT.

2 For earlier institutions beginning in the prophetic and caliphal eras, and for the genesis of the Muslim college (*madrasa*) out of the mosque and the mosque-inn (*masjid-khān*), see J. Pedersen and G. Makdisi, 'Madrasa: I. The Institution in the Arabic, Persian and Turkish lands,' in C. E. Bosworth, E. van Donzel, B. Lewis and Ch. Pellat (eds.), *Encyclopaedia of Islam*, New Edition (Brill: Leiden, 1980–2004), 5:1123–34. A generalist review of educational institutions is provided in Amjad M. Hussain, *A Social History of Education in the Muslim Word: From the Prophetic Era to Ottoman Times* (London: Ta Ha Publishers, 1432/2011).

3 For a social history of these twin processes, see Joan E. Gilbert, 'Institutionalization of Muslim Scholarship and Professionalization of the *ʿulamāʾ* in Medieval Damascus,' *Studia Islamica* 52 (1980): 105–34.

4 The centrality of the term is apparent in the title of one of the most historically prominent manuals of Muslim education: *Taʿlīm al-mutaʿallim ṭarīq al-taʿallum* of the Central Asian Ḥanafī scholar Burhān al-Dīn al-Zarnūjī (fl. 620/1223). This work was translated as *Instruction of the Student: The Method of Learning* by Gustave E. von Grunebaum and Theodora Mead Abel (Chicago: Starlatch Press, 2003).

5 On the history of the term '*dars*,' and its origins in legal education, see Makdisi, *Rise of Colleges*, 148–52.

6 Questions related to child education and the responsibilities of the 'muʾaddib' (child educator) are the subjects the Shāfiʿī jurist Ibn Ḥajar al-Haytamī's (d. 974/1567 AD) work, *Taḥrīr al-maqāl fī aḥkām wa-ādāb yaḥtāj la-hā muʾaddibū al-aṭfāl*. On this treatise, see Sherman Jackson, 'Discipline and Duty in a Medieval Muslim Elementary School: Ibn Ḥajar Al-Haytami's *Taqrīr al-maqāl*,' in *Law and Education in Medieval Islam* (Chippenham: Gibb Memorial Trust, 2004): 18–32.

7 The terms *tahdhīb* and *riyāḍa* are often also used to denote such programmatic approaches to character formation. See, for example, Shams al-Dīn al-Ramlī's (d. 1004/1596 AD) *Bughyat al-ikhwān fī riyāḍat al-ṣibyān*, a late medieval work

on the rearing of children that contains advice as to how to ensure they mature into adults of virtuous character; and, from the early modern period, *Riyāḍat al-ṣibyān wa-ta'līmuhum wa-ta'dībuhum* of the 19th-century educationalist and Shaykh al-Azhar Shams al-Dīn al-Inbābī (d. 1313/1896 AD), which addresses a number of the terms we have discussed in relation to the educative formation of children. For a theoretical differentiation of some of these terms by a contemporary educationalist, see Syed Muhammad Naguib Al-Attas, *The Concept of Education in Islam* (Kuala Lumpur: International Institute of Islamic Thought and Civilization, 1980).

8 On the distinction between *shaykh al-tarbiya* and *shaykh al-ta'līm*, see Ahmet T. Karamustafa, *Sufism: The Formative Period* (Edinburgh: Edinburgh University Press, 2007), 117. The terms may first have been theorized by the Andalusian mystic of the Shadhili order, Ibn 'Abbād al-Rundī, whose correspondence in which they appear has been translated in *Ibn 'Abbād of Ronda: Letters on the Sufi Path*, trans. John Renard (New York, 1986), 184–94.

9 On Sha'rānī, see Adam Sabra, 'Illiterate Sufis and Learned Artisans: The Circle of 'Abd al-Wahhāb al-Sha'rānī,' in Richard J. McGregor and Adam Sabra (eds.), *Le Développement du Soufisme en Égypte à l'Époque Mamlouke* (Cairo: Institut Français d'Archéologie Orientale, 2006), 153–168.

10 Pedersen and Makdisi, 'Madrasa,' 1123.

11 On the madhhab as legal guild, see George Makdisi, *The Rise of Humanism in Classical Islam and the Christian West: With Special Reference to Scholasticism* (Edinburgh: Edinburgh University Press, 1990), 21–23.

12 The best presentation of the rise of the *madrasa*, and its nature as a college (as opposed to a university), remains George Makdisi's *The Rise of Colleges: Institutions of Learning in Islam and the West* (New York: Columbia University Press, 1981). For a summary, see sv 'madrasa' in *The Encyclopaedia of Islam*, New Edition.

13 See, for example, the late Mamlūk work *Tanbīh al-ṭālib wa-irshād al-dāris* by the Damascene historian, 'Abd al-Qādir al-Nu'aymī (d. 1521 AD) (published as *al-Dāris fī tārīkh al-madāris*, ed. Ja'far al-Ḥasanī [Damascus, Maṭba'at al-Taraqqī, 1948–1951], 127–138), where he lists a number of '*madāris al-ṭibb*,' or medical colleges, in Damascus.

14 On the *khānaqāh* and its educative roles, see Leonor Fernandes, *The Evolution of a Sufi Institution in Mamluk Egypt: The Khanqah* (Berlin: Klaus Shwarz Verlag, 1988); and Th. Emil Homerin, 'Saving Muslim Souls: The Khānaqāh and the Sufi Duty,' in Mamluk Lands', *Mamlūk Studies Review* 3 (1999): 59–83.

15 On the notion of nonprofessionalized institutions of learning in antiquity, the Muslim world, and the medieval West, see Jan Willem Drijvers and A. A. MacDonald, *Centres of Learning: Learning and Location in Pre-Modern Europe and Near East* (Leiden and New York: Brill, 1995).

16 Said Amir Arjomand, 'The Law, Agency, and Policy in Medieval Islamic Society: Development of the Institutions of Learning from the Tenth to the Fifteenth Century,' *Comparative Studies in Society and History* 41 (1999): 263–93.

17 The 'formality' or 'informality' of premodern Muslim education remains a point of contention between contemporary historians. Perhaps the question of what features should serve as markers of 'formalism' for any given culture's system of education is itself dependent upon a number of questions that remain unasked and unanswered. When it comes to educational practices, should the final cause—the larger institutions of social organization to which an educational system attends, such as the nation state or the corporate guild—serve as a differentiator? Is the ascription of formality to a given pedagogic feature relative to the intellectual ends for which the constructed social practices are meant to obtain? While this brief essay is not the place in which to explore such matters, the answers to such questions may eventually help the historiography of Islamic educational institutions move beyond the current impasse.

18 For a robust demonstration of the formal requirements of such authorization, including the writing of a 'doctoral thesis' and an oral examination, see Devin Stewart, 'The Doctorate of Islamic Law in Mamluk Egypt and Syria,' in Joseph E. Lowry, Devin J. Stewart, and Shawkat M. Toorawa (eds.), *Law and Education in Medieval Islam: Studies in Memory of Professor George Makdisi* (Chippenham: Gibb Memorial Trust, 2004): 45–90.

19 On the noncorporate nature of the *madrasa* in contrast with that of the medieval European university, see George Makdisi, 'Madrasa and University in the Middle Ages,' *Studia Islamica* 32 (1970): 255–64.

20 See Mahmood Ibrahim, 'Practice and Reform in Fourteenth-Century Damascene Madrasas,' *Mamlūk Studies Review* 11/1 (2007): 69–83, esp. 70–74.

21 On the political and social considerations and dynamics of the hierarchies inherent in the *madhhabs* and the Sufi brotherhoods, see Roy Mottahedeh, *Loyalty and Leadership in an Early Islamic Society* (Princeton, NJ: Princeton University Press, 1980); Jonathan P. Berkey, *The Transmission of Knowledge in Medieval Cairo* (Princeton, NJ: Princeton University Press, 1992); and Fernandes, *The Evolution of a Sufi Institution.*

22 "The crafts (*ṣanāʾiʿ*)," wrote the 12th-century Abū al-Faḍl Jaʿfar al-Dimashqī (fl. 12th century) in his treatise on the virtues of commerce, "are either academic (*ʿilmiyya*, mental) or vocational (ʿamaliyya, manual)." Abū al-Faḍl Jaʿfar al-Dimashqī, *The Indicator to the Virtues of Commerce = al-Ishārah ilá maḥāsin al-tijārah*, translated by Adi Setia (Kuala Lumpur: IBFIM, 2011).

23 Tāj al-Dīn ʿAbd al-Wahhāb al-Subkī, *Muʿīd al-niʿam wa-mubīd al-niqam*, edited and introduced by David W. Myhrman (London: Luzac, 1908); for a summary of the various educational and learned professions presented by Subkī, see Makdisi, *The Rise of Colleges*, 175–77.

24 Ibn Jamāʿa, *A Memorandum for Listeners and Lecturers: Rules of Conduct for the Learned and the Learning*, transl. by Michael Fishbein in Bradley J. Cook and Fathi H. Malkawi (eds.), Classical Foundations of Islamic Educational Thought (Provo, Utah: Brigham Young University Press, 2010), 157.

25 See Ibn Saḥnūn, *The Book of Rules of Conduct* (*Kitāb Ādāb al-muʿallimīn*), transl. Michael Fishbein in Bradley J. Cook and Fathi H. Malkawi (eds.), *Classical Foundations of Islamic Educational Thought* (Provo, Utah: Brigham Young University Press, 2010), 1–19; and ʿAbd al-Karīm al-Samʿānī, *Adab al-imlāʾ wa-al-istimlāʾ* (The Etiquette of Dictation and Transcription), ed. Max Weisweiler (Leiden: E.J. Brill, 1952).

26 Ibn Jubayr, Riḥlat Ibn Jubayr (Beirut: Dār Ṣādir, 1964), 258.

27 Ibrahim, 'Practice and Reform,' 74.

28 On the myriad uses of colleges in the medieval Muslim world, and one set of reforms that sought to inspect colleges for such abuses and to further formalize the regulation of their spaces in the 14th century, see Ibrahim, 'Practice and Reform,' 78–82.

29 On the roles and expectations placed upon the assistants, such as the *muʿīd* and *mufīd*, see Makdisi, Rise of Colleges, 192–96.

30 On the term 'moral technologies of the self,' and the role of internal mechanisms for social regulation as opposed to those imposed by the state in Islamic thought and Islamicate institutional practice, see Wael B. Hallaq, *The Impossible State: Islam, Politics, and Modernity's Moral Predicament* (New York: Columbia University Press, 2013).

31 Richard T. Mortel 'Madrasas in Mecca during the Medieval Period: A Descriptive Study Based on Literary Sources,' *Bulletin of the School of Oriental and African Studies* 60/2 (1997): 236–52.

32 Leonor Fernandes. 'Mamluk Politics and Education: The Evidence from Two Fourteenth Century Waqfiyya,' *Annales Islamologiques* 23 (1987): 87–98.

33 On the existence of a unifying international Islamicate civilization, tying together culturally a Muslim world that was severely fragmented politically and on the role of learned and Sufi institutions in its establishment therein, see Marshall Hodgson, *The Venture of Islam: Conscience and History in World Civilization, Volume Two: The Expansion of Islam in the Middle Periods* (Chicago and London: University of Chicago Press, 1977). On the history of the early Ottoman ilmiye, see R.C. Repp, *The Müfti of Istanbul: A Study in the Development of the Ottoman Learned Hierarcy* (London: Ithaca Press, 1986); and Ekmeleddin Ihsanoğlu, 'Ottoman Educational and Scholarly-Scientific Institutions,' in Ekmeleddin Ihsanoğlu (ed.), *History of the Ottoman State, Society and Civilization* (Istanbul: IRCICA, 2002), 2:357–515.

BIBLIOGRAPHY

Arjomand, A. S. 1999. 'The Law, Agency, and Policy in Medieval Islamic Society: Development of the Institutions of Learning from the Tenth to the Fifteenth Century.' *Comparative Studies in Society and History* 41: 263–93.

al-Attas, S. M. N. 1980. *The Concept of Education in Islam.* Kuala Lumpur: International Institute of Islamic Thought and Civilization.

Berkey, P. J. 1992. *The Transmission of Knowledge in Medieval Cairo.* Princeton, NJ: Princeton University Press.

al-Dimashqī, Abū al-Faḍl. 2011. *The Indicator to the Virtues of Commerce = al-Ishārah ilā maḥāsin al-tijārah*, trans. Adi Setia. Kuala Lumpur: IBFIM.

Drijvers, W. J. and MacDonald, A. A. (eds.) 1995. *Centres of Learning: Learning and Location in Pre-Modern Europe and Near East.* Leiden and New York: Brill.

Fernandes. L. 1987. 'Mamluk Politics and Education: The Evidence from Two Fourteenth Century Waqfiyya.' *Annales Islamologiques* 23: 87–98.

Fernandes, L. 1999. *The Evolution of a Sufi Institution in Mamluk Egypt: The Khanqah.* Berlin: Klaus Shwarz Verlag.

Gilbert, E. J. 1980. 'Institutionalization of Muslim Scholarship and Professionalization of the *'ulamā'* in Medieval Damascus.' *Studia Islamica* 52: 105–34.

von Grunebaum, E. G. and Abel, M. T. (trans.) 2003. *Instruction of the Student: The Method of Learning.* Chicago: Starlatch Press.

Hallaq, B. W. 2013. *The Impossible State: Islam, Politics, and Modernity's Moral Predicament.* New York: Columbia University Press.

Homerin, E. 1999. 'Saving Muslim Souls: The *Khānaqāh* and the Sufi Duty in Mamluk Lands.' *Mamlūk Studies Review* 3: 59–83.

Hussain, M. A. 2011. *A Social History of Education in the Muslim Word: From the Prophetic Era to Ottoman.* London: Ta Ha Publishers.

Ibn Jamā'a, Badr al-Dīn. 2010. 'A Memorandum for Listeners and Lecturers: Rules of Conduct for the Learned and the Learning.' Transl. Michael Fishbein. In Bradley J. Cook and Fathi H. Malkwawi (eds.), *Classical Foundations of Islamic Thought.* Provo, Utah: Brigham Young University Press. 156–207.

Ibn Jubayr. 1964. *Riḥlat Ibn Jubayr.* Beirut: Dār Ṣādir.

Ibn Saḥnūn. 2010. 'The Book of Rules of Conduct.' Transl. Michael Fishbein. In Bradley J. Cook and Fathi H. Malkawi (eds.), *Classical Foundations of Islamic Educational Thought.* Provo, Utah: Brigham Young University Press. 1–19.

Ibrahim, M. 2007. 'Practice and Reform in Fourteenth-Century Damascene Madrasas.' *Mamlūk Studies Review* 11(1): 69–83.

Ihsanoğlu, E. 2002. 'Ottoman Educational and Scholarly-Scientific Institutions.' In Ekmeleddin Ihsanoğlu (ed.), *History of the Ottoman State, Society and Civilization*. Istanbul: IRCICA. Vol. 2, 361–515.

Jackson, S. 2004. 'Discipline and Duty in a Medieval Muslim Elementary School: Ibn Ḥajar Al-Haytami's *Taqrīr al-maqāl*.' In Joseph Lowry, Devin Stewart, and Shawkat Toorawa (eds.), *Law and Education in Medieval Islam*. Chippenham: Gibb Memorial Trust. 18–32.

Karamustafa, T. A. 2007. *Sufism: The Formative Period*. Edinburgh: Edinburgh University Press.

Makdisi, G. 1990. *The Rise of Humanism in Classical Islam and the Christian West: With Special Reference to Scholasticism*. Edinburgh: Edinburgh University Press.

Mortel, Richard T. 1997. 'Madrasas in Mecca During the Medieval Period: A Descriptive Study Based on Literary Sources.' *Bulletin of the School of Oriental and African Studies* 60/2: 236–52.

Mottahedeh, R. 1980. *Loyalty and Leadership in an Early Islamic Society*. Princeton, NJ: Princeton University Press.

al-Nuʿaymī, ʿAbd al-Qādir. 1948–1951. *Al-Dāris fī tārīkh al-madāris*, ed. Jaʿfar al-Ḥasanī. Damascus: Maṭbaʿat al-Taraqqī. 127–138.

Pedersen, J. and G. Makdisi. 1980–2004. '*Madrasa*: I. The Institution in the Arabic, Persian and Turkish Lands.' In C. E. Bosworth, E. van Donzel, B. Lewis and Ch. Pellat (eds.), *Encyclopaedia of Islam New Addition*. Leiden: Brill. Vol. 5, 1123–1134.

Renard, J. (trans.) 1986. *Ibn ʿAbbād of Ronda: Letters on the Sufi Path*. New York: Paulist Press.

Repp, C. R. 1986. *The Müfti of Istanbul: A Study in the Development of the Ottoman Learned Hierarcy*. London: Ithaca Press.

Sabra, A. 2006. 'Illiterate Sufis and Learned Artisans: The Circle of ʿAbd al-Wahhāb al-Shaʿrānī." In Richard J. McGregor and Adam Sabra (eds.), *Le Développement du Soufisme en Égypte à l'Époque Mamlouk*. Cairo: Institut Français d'Archéologie Orientale. 53–168.

al-Samʿānī, ʿAbd al-Karīm. 1992. *Adab al-imlāʾ wa-al-istimlāʾ* (The Etiquette of Dictation and Transcription), ed. Max Weisweiler. Leiden: E.J. Brill.

Stewart, D. 2004. 'The Doctorate of Islamic Law in Mamluk Egypt and Syria.' In Joseph E. Lowry, Devin J. Stewart, and Shawkat M. Toorawa (eds.), *Law and Education in Medieval Islam: Studies in Memory of Professor George Makdisi*. Chippenham: Gibb Memorial Trust: 45–90.

al-Subkī, Tāj al-Dīn. 1908. *Muʿīd al-niʿam wa-mubīd al-niqam*. Ed. David W. Myhrman. London: Luzac.

Part III

Schools, Universities, and Pedagogies

8 World Conferences on Muslim Education

Shaping the Agenda of Muslim Education in the Future

Shaikh Abdul Mabud

What constitutes an Islamic education at a given time and place has been a subject of debate among Muslim theologians and educationists throughout Islamic history. Despite ongoing debates on the contents and methods of education, as well as the implementation of knowledge acquired to meet the needs of the community, a consensus has historically emerged denoting the purpose of education as to prepare one to attain the pleasure of God through service to Him, humanity, and creation. The organization of the World Conferences on Muslim Education stands as an important contemporary example, informed by such motivations, to rejuvenate Islamic education and to restructure it on the basis of Islamic concepts drawn from the revealed Book of God and the teachings of Prophet Muhammad. The organization of the First World Conference on Muslim Education was a milestone in the history of Muslim education. It was held in Makkah from 31 March to 8 April 1977 and was attended by 123 participants from Saudi Arabia and 184 from the rest of the world (Zubair 1977, 7). No conference on Muslim education of comparable magnitude has since been organized. The organization of the conference was a mammoth task, which produced a comprehensive repertoire of concepts, theories, recommendations, and approaches to Islamic education. Seven more World Conferences on Muslim Education have been held since 1977.

For the Muslim world, much of the 20th century provided a venue for the confrontation of encroaching secular ideologies and political programs on its doorstep. The organizers of the First World Conference similarly found itself tackling such questions and attempting to reconcile Islamic thought to this burgeoning and often alien intellectual milieu. The fundamental question of the conference was then whether "pre-modern notions of Islamic philosophy and religion were adequate to deal with the increasingly invasive secular culture." The prevalent idea was that in order to combat Western secular philosophy, Muslim educationalists needed to incorporate Western science and technology into their programs of education. This grafting exercise was not intended to imitate Western culture, but rather to 'filter' knowledge from the West (and its presuppositions) and yet at the same time remain true to Muslim intellectual and spiritual traditions. However, the rise of high colonialism led to, what Arkoun observes, the gradual acceptance of "Western modernity and its educational and cultural underpinnings [yet] only 'slowly and reluctantly'" (Abu-Rabi' 2003, 1086). This raised another question: whether partial acceptance of the 'Western' mode of secular thought—be it in the field of education (via pedagogic models) or the social sciences or the application of modern ideas on technology and technocracy and their acceptance as part of Islamic approaches to life—is actually possible without a detrimental impact on the Islamic way of life and thinking. A bifurcation, or rather dichotomy, followed in education within many parts of the Muslim world and ultimately led to the separation of the mosque from education and the state, contravening the normative and integrated features of Islamic society, premised on the concept of *tawhid* (unity) as experienced in all aspects of society (Watt 1961).

THE FIRST WORLD CONFERENCE ON MUSLIM EDUCATION

The genesis of the World Conferences on Muslim Education and any serious study of its history must, therefore, seriously consider these historical precedents. Indeed Professor Syed Ali Ashraf in his book *Islamic Education Movement: An Historical Analysis* gives a vivid description of how the idea of such a conference developed into an event of significance in the recent history of Muslim education. He tells us of the event that sparked the idea of holding the First World Conference in the following way:

> When Shaikh Hassan Al-i-Shaikh, the Education Minister of Saudi Arabia, was returning from America, he was interviewed by some British journalists. The report that came out in the British papers was rather sarcastic. Al-i-Shaikh had talked to the journalists of expansion and modernisation of education in Saudi Arabia, and asserted that the country as a whole was so Islamic that this expansion of education would not erode the Islamic sensibility of the pupils. The journalists commented that this was a blinkered attitude produced by a mind not aware of modernisation and still trying to adhere to an outmoded way of life.
>
> It was this comment that prompted me, and my friend Dr. Motiur Rahman to write a letter to King Faisal, saying that unless steps were taken from now on, Saudi Arabia would fall into the same trap that Pakistan had fallen into [. . .].
>
> We therefore wanted to point out the basic conceptual problem to the Saudi Government, and thought that at the very inception of Modern Education and its expansion, they were the right people to organise courses and thus give a lead to the Muslim World.
>
> Our letter was sent in April 1974.
>
> (Ashraf 1990, 5–6)

Professor Ashraf and Dr. Motiur Rahman's letter set the ball rolling, and with a series of meetings and contacts, both private and official, basic principles and guidelines for the First World Conference were worked out. The conference was so called because "this was the first time that Muslim scholars from all over the world could gather together [on this scale] to deliberate on the education of Muslim children in both Muslim majority and Muslim minority countries" (Zubair 1977, 7). The conference was "only a first step in the right direction" (Zubair 1977, 8) and was masterminded by Professor Ashraf, who was also its organizing secretary. A dedicated team of intellectuals, scholars, administrators, and supporters worked relentlessly for three years to bring the conference to fruition.[1] The aims and objectives of the conference were set as follows:

1. To define the principles, aims, and methodology of the Islamic concept of education.
2. To suggest ways and means of realizing the aforementioned principles in practice.
3. To formulate methods of securing mutual understanding and cooperation among Muslim scholars all over the world (Zubair, 1977, 3).

The organizers of the conference could clearly see that the expansion and modernization of education was going to have a serious impact on the lifestyle of the people of Saudi Arabia, affecting certain aspects of their beliefs and practices. They were aware that the Western world itself had an increasing number of internal critiques leveled at mass public education, which seemingly catered to the perpetuation of a working class. It is significant that Professor Ashraf mentions Pakistan in particular in the aforementioned quote, as that country was created in the name of Islam and Islamic values. Maryam Jameelah, a prolific American Muslim writer on Islam and modernity and a defender of Islamic values and culture who spent fifty-one years of her life in Pakistan, echoes the same concern when she argues that " . . . The stress to transform the higher education is understandable. It is the higher education in the Muslim lands that has brought us low and it is where we traded our dignity for trivial and ephemeral things" (Maryam Jameelah 2015). The impact of modernity on Muslim thought and philosophy was so great that Professor Seyyed Hossein Nasr made the following remark: "the attack of the West on the Arab world, aside from its political effects, was also a direct attack against Islam as a religion" (Nasr 1975, 90). Modernity penetrated into the Muslim lands both intellectually and materially and affected the personal, social, and intellectual life of people in direct and often subtle ways.

As a Western-educated Cambridge graduate himself, why Professor Ashraf was so critical of modern education and why he decided to hold World Conferences on the education of Muslims can be answered through his own reflections:

> I criticised the modern education because it is based on a concept of human nature which does not recognise the human spirit and its

> relationship with God and thereby eliminates the possibility of revelations and God-given knowledge and guidance for mankind. It is also based on a worldview that propagates the concept of society producing values and thereby creating a tradition of values and a tradition of evolution of values. This worldview is fundamentally of this world and hence it does not rouse in the pupils' mind the slightest consciousness of life after death. It is difficult to keep religious consciousness alive in the hearts of children when all branches of knowledge are dominated by such a view of life and when teachers are expected not to teach from the religious point of view [. . .] I therefore suggested and the scholars at the First World Conference agreed to recommend that research should be carried out to replace the secularist concepts at the roots of all branches of knowledge by concepts drawn from the Islamic frame of life and values as found in the Qur'an and the Sunnah [Prophetic example].
>
> (Ashraf 1994, xi)

The main concern of the world conference was to devise an education system that is based on the principles enshrined in the Qur'an and Sunnah and to do away with the dichotomies placed upon it through revolutions of colonial and secular thought in its educational philosophies and practices. The major outcomes of the First World Conference were as follows:

(1) All the recommendations of the conference were published as a book entitled *First World Conference on Muslim Education: Conference Book* (King Abdulaziz University 1977) that included the memorandum of the conference, inaugural speeches, list of participants along with the countries they represented, and suggestions for follow-up activities.
(2) A Follow-up Committee was formed to organize more World Conferences.
(3) All the keynote papers and some selected papers along with some additional papers were published as six books under the "Islamic Education Series."[2]
(4) Several educational and research institutions were set up and academic journals launched to promote Islamic education as will be discussed.

LEGACIES OF THE 1977 CONFERENCE: 'ISLAMIZATION' OF KNOWLEDGE AND EDUCATION

Among the most prominent and long-standing legacies of the First World Conference was the development and rise of the concept of Islamization.[3] There is a broad agreement among Muslim scholars about the need for making education Islamic, but they are not unanimous on the definition of

Islamization or the process of Islamization. In the First World Conference, Syed Muhammad Naquib al-Attas spoke of "Islamization of present-day knowledge" and expounded its various aspects with rigor and profundity. For him, the following key concepts form the essential elements of the Islamic education system: the concepts of religion, man, knowledge, wisdom, justice, right action, and the university. These concepts refer to the purpose, scope, content, criteria, deployment, method, and form of implementation. Islamization of present-day knowledge consists of isolating secular elements and key concepts from knowledge and then infusing it "with the Islamic elements and key concepts, which [. . .] imbue the knowledge with the quality of its natural function and purpose and thus make it true knowledge." One cannot hope to Islamize secular knowledge by merely grafting or transplanting into it Islamic sciences and principles for "this method will but produce conflicting results not altogether beneficial nor desirable" (al-Attas 1979, 43–44). In the Second World Conference, he explained the Islamization of contemporary knowledge as "the deliverance of knowledge from its interpretations based on secular ideology; and from meanings and expressions of the secular" (al-Attas 1991, 43).

Isma'il Raji Al-Faruqi's plans of Islamization, as expressed in his *Islamization of Knowledge*, consists of twelve steps, the most important of which are the mastery and critical assessment of both modern and Islamic disciplines, surveying the problems of the Muslim *ummah* (global community), and reconstructing the disciplines in the framework of Islam (al-Faruqi 1982). For al-Faruqi, Islamization is to have mastery of the modern disciplines and then "to integrate the new knowledge into the corpus of the Islamic legacy by eliminating, amending, re-interpreting and adapting its components as the worldview of Islam and its value dictate" (al-Faruqi 1988, 30). Soon after his book was published it created much enthusiasm among Muslims all over the world, but it also met serious criticisms from scholars as being a naïve attempt to lead the *ummah* out of their maladies toward an Islamist agenda or authoritarian control of knowledge. Ilyas Ba-Yunus finds that this work plan does not pay enough attention to reshaping the curriculum, retraining the teachers, parental guidance, analyzing community problems, and seeking solutions, etc. (Ba-Yunus 1988, 26). Faced with such criticisms, social scientists at the International Institute of Islamic Thought revised al-Faruqi's work plan. Through his "Six Discourses," Taha Jabir al-Alwani has clarified certain issues previously proposed and elaborated on the methodological approach to restore a balance between traditional and modern knowledge (al-Alwani 1995, 81–101). On the other hand, Ashraf's Islamization process is to formulate Islamic concepts for all branches of knowledge first and then to evaluate Western concepts in the light of the Islamic concepts (Ashraf 1991, 35–36). Fazlur Rahman holds a different view altogether. He did not want to "get enamoured over making maps and charts of how to go about creating Islamic knowledge" as human beings do not need *'ilm* (knowledge) only (Rahman 1988, 10). Rather, their use of *'aql* (intellect) deserves attention too, so that they may be able to think constructively and positively within their environments. Rahman wished that successive Muslim generations would go beyond analysis and criticism to the discovery of new knowledge and stand as the hallmark of the Islamization processes.

Not all subsequent scholars have agreed with the Islamization plan, and some have since categorically rejected its importance. Ziauddin Sardar, for example, argues that it is difficult to be convinced of the need for Islamizing disciplines and vehemently opposes al-Faruqi's theory of Islamization. Sardar maintains, "Muslims do not need to Islamize disciplines, whatever that means; but to develop their own disciplines based on their own cultural context and geared to solving their own problems" (Sardar 2004, 200). The reason for this position is explicated in the belief that

> Islamizing disciplines already infused with a materialistic metaphysics and western, secularist ethics is tantamount to a cosmetic epistemological face-lift and nothing more. At best, it would perpetuate the dichotomy of secular and Islamic knowledge that you are so keen to transcend.
>
> (Sardar 2004, 201)

Despite the differences of opinions, the pursuit of Islamizing education continues among the scholars in one form or another. Other scholars have argued that the concept of Islamization, in terms of scientific knowledge, is a blunder. As scientific knowledge is universal and culturally neutral, it cannot be 'religionized.' For example, Parvez Hoodbhoy labors the point in his book *Islam and Science* that faith and science are unrelated and vehemently criticizes the Islamization of science program as a whole (Hoodbhoy 1991, 88). Mohammad Abdus Salam, a Nobel laureate in physics, also holds similar views about the international and universal character of science (Hoodbhoy 1991, Foreword). Such views, however, cannot be defended as has been shown by philosophers and historians of science (Kuhn 1996; Ravetz 1996).

In the educational literature, "Islamization of knowledge" and "Islamization of education" have often been used synonymously. Some traditional scholars hold the view that "Islamization of knowledge" is a meaningless concept as knowledge (*'ilm*) by definition is Islamized and the opposite of knowledge is ignorance. This concept assumes that knowledge by itself is sacred and desacralization of knowledge is impossible and nonknowledge cannot be Islamized. The debate then shifts to the definition of the word 'beneficial' as found in the supplication of the Prophet Muhammad, "Oh God, benefit me from that which You taught me, and teach me that which will benefit me" (*Sunan Ibn Majah*). The Qur'an teaches its followers to ask God for all that is beneficial in the following prayer: "Our Lord! Give us in this world that which is good and in the Hereafter that which is good, and save us from the torment of the Fire!" (Qur'an 2:201). The notions of what is good or bad, or what is beneficial and harmful, have been explained in various commentaries of the Qur'an, and we summate these views as knowledge that does not benefit its seekers nor benefits others should not be pursued.

OTHER WORLD CONFERENCES

On the recommendation of the First World Conference, the Organizing Committee was transformed into the Follow-up Committee with Shaikh Ahmad Salah Jamjoom as the chairman, Professor Ashraf as the secretary, and Dr. Ghulam Nabi Saqeb as the assistant secretary. Professor Ashraf planned three other World Conferences, and he recollects in his book *Islamic Education Movement* how Dr. Abdullah Omar Nasseef was a source of constant help not only in organizing these conferences but also for the Muslim educational movement in general; without him much of what was achieved would not have been possible (Ashraf 1990). Professor Ashraf submitted a proposal to hold three other World Conferences and the Follow-up Committee accepted it. Saqeb has observed that, "Professor Ashraf having masterminded the Conference had further ideas as to how follow-up action should proceed" (Saqeb 2000, 45–68).

The Second World Conference on Muslim Education was held in Islamabad, Pakistan, in 1980. It was organized by Quaid-i-Azam University in cooperation with the Ministry of Education, Pakistan, and King Abdulaziz University, Jeddah. This conference concentrated on curriculum designing and suggested some short-term and some long-term policies. The Third World Conference on Muslim Education was held in 1981 in Dhaka, Bangladesh, and was jointly organized by the Institute of Islamic Education and Research, Bangladesh, and King Abdulaziz University. This conference dealt with the development of textbooks for all levels, suggesting both short-term and long-term strategies. The Fourth World Conference on Muslim Education was held in Jakarta, Indonesia, in 1982 and concentrated on teaching methodologies and teacher education courses. The Third and Fourth World Conferences were organized in cooperation with the World Centre for Islamic Education (WCIE). The Fifth World Conference on Muslim Education was organized in 1987 by the Muslim Youth Organization of Egypt. The aims of this conference were to review the achievements and failures of the previous World Conferences and discuss the ways and means of implementing their recommendations. The sixth one—called the Sixth International Conference on Islamic Education—was organized in 1996 by the Association of Muslim Schools of South Africa. This conference was more like a workshop where participants were divided into groups preparing model lesson plans and teaching guidelines and discussing them in plenary sessions. The National Scholars Association Malaysia; the Islamic Academy, Cambridge; and the International Islamic University College Selangor in Kuala Lumpur organized both the Seventh and the Eighth World Conferences in 2009 and 2012, respectively. The names of these two conferences were shortened as World-COME2009 and World-COME2012 respectively, where COME stands for Conference on Muslim Education. The objectives of these conferences were to discuss a wide range of educational issues in the context of globalization and establish networks among researchers all over the world.

LIMITATIONS OF THE WORLD CONFERENCES

Among the limitations of the World Conferences, which may also be considered to be their 'unique strength,' was that they did not take into account the presence of "non-Islamic people living in Muslim majority countries" (Ashraf 1990, 22). This should not be regarded as a matter of indifference to these crucial issues on the part of the organizers, but rather understood as a result of their preoccupation with the first phase of their plan, which was to deal with "something ideal-typical about the Muslim community in isolation, but not the Muslim community in the national or international context" (Ashraf 1990, 22). Before Muslim scholars could begin dialogue with others on matters of education and learning, it was assumed necessary to assert their philosophical position first from which to hold such dialogues. The second phase of the plan consisted in ascertaining what adjustments and modifications were necessary when such an ideal-typical model was applied to other circumstances. The World Centre for Islamic Education was set up to undertake the implementation and diversification of the ideal-typical model, but after it lost its original status, the task relating to the second phase was undertaken by the Islamic Academy[4] through a series of public lectures and seminars at the University of Cambridge. The Islamic Academy organized a dialogue between Christian and Muslim educationalists in September 1989 entitled "Faith as the Basis of Education in a Multi-Faith Multicultural Country." In 1990, it also organized another seminar of the representatives of six religions—Buddhism, Christianity, Hinduism, Islam, Judaism, and Sikhism—on the same topic (The Islamic Academy 1990). The Islamic Academy and the University of Cambridge organized about a dozen other multi-faith seminars on various educational issues. These seminars were organized in the hope that "There will be unity in diversity and both unity and diversity will coexist within the framework of common humanity which recognises the spiritual, intellectual, rational and physical dimensions of human existence" (Ashraf 1994, xiv). 'Unity' was taken to denote a shared set of beliefs in the concept of a Transcendental Reality, the existence of Spirit in each human being that is endowed with eternal values, and the need for some form of divine guidance. The diversity exists at the doctrinal and sociocultural levels, necessitating the knowledge and understanding of each other and learning from each other so that human beings can cooperate and live together in harmony (Qur'an 5:48). The outcomes of such seminars were preparing statements denoting broad areas of agreement that were offered for "further discussion and comment in the hope that this would help forward the important task of framing more satisfactory educational policies" (The Islamic Academy 1990, 7). These statements were distributed to various educational institutions in the United Kingdom and some selected places overseas.

ASSESSMENT OF THE WORLD CONFERENCES

The achievements of these conferences have been discussed in detail separately by several authors (Ashraf 1990; Saqeb 2000; Rafiu 2007; Rafiu 2012; Olawale 2014). It appears that there have been many problems with the implementation of the recommendations of the World Conferences. Some of these problems were born of governmental resistance, as well as diversified views among Muslim scholars about the nature of Islamization, the lack of coordinated activities to produce curricula and textbooks, inadequate teacher training, and the general economic condition of Muslim countries, etc. Ghulam Nabi Saqeb found that unless curricula, textbooks, reading materials, guidance on Islamic concepts of knowledge, and teaching guidelines are available to teachers, "Islamization of education will remain a pie in the sky" (Saqeb 2000, 63). Fazlur Rahman noted that "[. . .] despite a widespread and sometimes deep consciousness of the dichotomy of education, all efforts at a genuine integration have so far been largely unfruitful" (Rahman 1982, 130). Suleman Dangor observed from his experience in South Africa that, "the implementation of the Islamized syllabi was fraught with difficulties" (Dangor 2014, 379). Rafiu Adebayo finds that in Nigeria the major problems of Islamization are the multi-religious nature of the society, government policy on the curriculum development, lack of support from traditional ulema, lack of trained teachers, books, and curriculum (Adebayo 2004). Bradley Cook was right when he said, "problems are legion when it comes to formulating and implementing concrete solutions. Indeed, since 1977, only a few isolated examples of successful Islamized educational systems can be cited" (Cook 1999, 342).

Despite these criticisms, the World Conferences made some significant progress in many areas of education, the greatest of which being the awareness of the importance of Islamization it created among Muslims and non-Muslims all over the world. The impact of these conferences can be seen in the desire for Islamized curricula; the emergence of new Muslim schools, colleges, universities, and other scholarly institutions; educational reforms in existing educational institutions to introduce Islamic concepts; publication of textbooks, workbooks, and reading materials produced in accordance with the religious requirements of Muslim pupils; publication of scholarly journals dealing with Islamic perspectives on educational, theological, and contemporary issues; organization of lectures, seminars, symposia, and conferences to discuss educational issues of Muslims.

The International Islamic University Malaysia (IIUM, est. 1980) and the International Islamic University Islamabad (IIUI, est. 1980) were established following the recommendations of the First World Conference. IIUM is a vibrant center of education and has produced a large number of scholars over the years. It brings out a number of academic journals and regularly holds seminars and conferences on Islam, education, and the Muslim world. In addition to teaching conventional academic disciplines, IIUI also runs specialized centers such as Dawah Academy, Shariah Academy, and Islamic Research Institute that deal with contemporary issues in the global context.

Following a recommendation of the First World Conference, the World Centre for Islamic Education (WCIE) was established in Makkah in 1980 by OIC (Organization of the Islamic Conference) with Professor Ashraf as its director general, but it lost its international character in 1982. Following another recommendation, the Islamic Educational, Scientific and Cultural Organization (ISESCO) was established in Rabat, Morocco, in 1982.

POSSIBLE FUTURES OF MUSLIM EDUCATION

So what is the future of Muslim education? No government of the Muslim world has completely undertaken the implementation of the recommendations of the World Conferences, not even those countries that sponsored the conferences. However, many nongovernment institutions, schools, and colleges around the world have partially implemented many of the recommendations and are still trying to do so. Islamic education is only a part of the total Islamic way of life, and thus the message that Islamic education cannot operate fully unless other areas of life are also 'Islamized' requires rethinking. Conveying the teachings of Islam through rational arguments, intuitive reflection, and noble examples as well as patience, tolerance, and love may go a long way to achieve the goal of Islamization. On the other hand, imparting religious education in a society where religion does not play a significant role is considered to be the predicament of educational thinkers and practitioners alike. Muslim education has become increasingly politicized since '9/11,' and many scholars find the task of Islamization more challenging. Their concern has been to develop an education system that would be acceptable to all. For them, this will be easier to achieve if the 'sharp edges' of Islam could be subjected to critical inquiry, going as far as even distorting the essence of religion. They forget that every curricular subject should be studied in accordance with its own methodology, and religion is no exception. To apply secularist philosophy to the study of a religion is to destroy its autonomy and violate religious educational principles.

Rukhsana Zia has noted that the new forms of Muslim institutions of education that have emerged in postcolonial Muslim societies do not view themselves as acting against the secular government schools but as complementary to them (Zia 2006). Wadad Kadi considers this to be a healthy step that shows the confidence of Muslims "to experiment in collaboration with the non-Muslims, in the process enriching their circles of interest and engaging with the rest of the world in a dialogue, which is useful to all" (Kadi 2006, 324). Sa'eda Buang and Masturah Ismail give examples of such endeavors in Afghanistan and Indonesia where the curriculum framers are trying "to promote ideals of peace and social justice that are inherent in Islam, while being influenced by Western concepts of pluralism and civil society" through reading materials that are culturally relevant and "capitalise on the strengths of both Islamic and Western perspectives on peace and conflict" (Buang and Ismail 2007, 4). Many of the new curricular developments are taking place in response to extremism and terrorism, and further research is required to see whether this approach is going to remove the dichotomy in Muslim education or whether the original problems for which the World Conferences were organized continue to remain. The policy makers should bear in mind that to ignore Islamic religious sensibility and suppress what people consider to be their right can contribute to radicalism in itself.

In lieu of these developments, Muslim scholars have made various suggestions for future directions. Fazlur Rahman suggests that true Islamization is possible only if "Muslims effectively perform the intellectual task of elaborating an Islamic metaphysics on the basis of the Qur'an" (Rahman 1982, 133). It seems that this daunting task has not been accomplished as yet. It is true that from Western secular perspectives, Islamic educational principles are "riddled with difficulties" as there seems to be no philosophical common ground at the fundamental level between the two worldviews, but Mark Halstead is optimistic that there are possibilities for dialogue between Muslims and such European philosophers as Fichte, Hegel, Schopenhauer, and Buber whose thoughts appear to resonate at least to a certain extent with what Muslims consider to be "the fundamental, unchanging principles and essential values of Islam" (Halstead 2004, 527). An exploration of common ground between Muslim and such Western scholars will hopefully open up areas of understanding. Susan Douglass and Munir Shaikh have similarly noted that "both the obligation to be educated, and the moral, intellectual and cultural concepts of an education in the Muslim tradition are not far removed from similar goals and concepts associated with Western traditions and aspects of education" (Douglass and Shaikh 2004, 15). While understanding that there is a strained relationship between Western and Islamic educational theories, one should keep in mind that the former is not monolithic and that there are many Western educationalists who are sympathetic to religion on rational ground. There are also those who recognize cultural diversity as contributing to the enrichment of the society and want to see this diversity to be reflected in the education policy of the country. Muslims have always cooperated with such people.

The future of the Islamization program requires a new generation of scholars who should have greater understanding of the philosophical concepts of the Qur'an and Hadith and who are also well versed in secular thought. They must be able to discern what is authentically Islamic and what is modern, and they must be able to integrate Islamic principles with a particular branch of knowledge, which requires mastery of both the secular and Islamic disciplines. They should have the intellectual vision that is based not on the secular view of existence and knowledge, but on the God-given principles that lie at the heart of every revealed religion. Unless this is done, Muslims will be rotating round the periphery of Islamic education without ever reaching its center. In their response to modernity, they should continue to develop Islamic principles for all disciplines in the light of the fundamental principles of the Qur'an and Sunnah, as accepted at the World Conferences and, for a multi-religious country, place essential Islamic principles in a tradition "that receives universal assent, at least from all the religious traditions of the world" (Ashraf 1989, 2). In doing this, Muslims should be aware of the writings of those Western scholars who have responded to modernity from a traditional perspective (Casewit 2011).

CONCLUSION

The work of the World Conferences has not had a chance to be implemented except in limited ways. History suggests that more conferences are not likely to bear fruit unless they are geared toward the implementation of the resolutions agreed at the World Conferences or any other resolutions adopted afterward to rethink educational systems as 'Islamic.' Practical steps to implement the recommendations adopted at the conferences have been suggested by scholars and educationalists over the last three decades, yet there has been more discussion on their philosophical subtleties and competencies than on their actual implementation, which is needed in order to test how far these recommendations are feasible in practice and what modifications, if any, are necessary. Whether this will come about through a new generation of scholars and practitioners with experience in Islamic educational philosophy, pedagogy, and administration who can critically analyze the current educational landscape in an inclusive way and take steps for the redesigning and restructuring of the educational system is uncertain. In an age increasingly dominated by modernization, secularization, and globalizing tendencies, the path to Islamization is strewn with pitfalls, uncertainties, and even hostilities. What is more clear is that Islamization of knowledge as a means to achieve a holistic purview of education is an ongoing pursuit in the Muslim world in which all stakeholders—government, administrators, scholars, educationalists, parents, and students must play their necessary roles.

NOTES

1 The Organizing Committee consisted of ten people with H. E. Shaikh Ahmad Salah Jamjoom as the chairman, Professor Syed Ali Ashraf and Dr. Abdullah Muhammad Zaid as secretaries, and Dr. Ghulam Nabi Saqeb as the assistant

secretary. The Steering Committee consisted of forty people from various disciplines with H. E. Dr. Muhammad Umar Zubair as the chairman; H. E. Shaikh Ahmad Salah Jamjoom, Dr. Abdullah Omar Nasseef, Dr. Jafar Abdul Rehman Sabbagh, and Dr. Muhammad Ali Hibshi as the vice-chairmen; Professor Syed Ali Ashraf and Dr. Abdullah Muhammad Zaid as secretaries; and Dr. Ghulam Nabi Saqeb as the assistant secretary.

2 The following books in the "Islamic Education Series" were published by London: Hodder and Stoughton and Jeddah: King Abdulaziz University under the general editorship of Syed Ali Ashraf: Syed Sajjad Husain and Syed Ali Ashraf, eds., *Crisis in Muslim Education* (1979); Syed Muhammad Naquib al-Attas, ed., *Aims and Objectives of Islamic Education* (1979); Muhammad Hamid Al-Afendi and Nabi Ahmed Baloch, eds., *Curriculum and Teacher Education* (1980); Isma'il Raji Al-Faruqi and Abdullah Omar Nasseef, eds., *Social and Natural Sciences: The Islamic Perspective* (1981); Mohammad Wasiullah Khan, ed., *Education and Society in the Muslim World* (1981); Seyyed Hossein Nasr, ed., *Philosophy, Literature and Fine Arts* (1982). The book with the proposed title, *Survey of Muslim Education* was never published, although a few years later the Islamic Academy published surveys of Muslim education in some countries.

3 International Institute of Islamic Thought, *Islam: Source and Purpose of Knowledge* (Washington D.C.: International Institute of Islamic Thought, 1988). See also, Suleman E. Dangor, "Islamization and Muslim Independent Schools in South Africa," in *International Handbook of Learning, Teaching and Leading in Faith-based Schools*, eds. Judith D. Chapman, Sue McNamara, Michael J. Reiss and Yusef Waghid (London: Springer, 2014), 376–377; Leif Stenberg, *The Islamization of Science: Four Muslim Positions Developing an Islamic Modernity* (Sweden: Almqvist & Wiskell International, 1996).

4 Founded in Cambridge in 1983 by Professor Ashraf, Shaikh Ahmad Salah Jamjoom, and Dr. Abdullah Omar Nasseef. Professor Ashraf was the first director general of the Islamic Academy, the post he held until his passing away in 1998. The Islamic Academy continues with Dr. Shaikh Abdul Mabud as its director general.

BIBLIOGRAPHY

Abu-Rabi', Ibrahim M. 2003. "The Arab world," In *History of Islamic Philosophy*, ed. Seyyed Hossein Nasr and Oliver Leaman. London and New York: Routledge, 1082–1114.

Adebayo, Rafiu I. 2007. "The Influence of the World Conferences on Muslim Education on Islamic Education in Nigeria." In *Islamic Studies in Contemporary Nigeria, Problems & Prospects*, ed. Lateef M. Adetona. Lagos: Romeo Concepts, 1–34.

Adebayo, Rafiu I. 2012. "A Survey on the Global Success of the Islamization of Knowledge Programme with Particular Reference to Nigeria." *Journal of Al-Tamaddun* 7(1): 91–105.

Adebayo, Rafiu I. 2004. "Islamization of Knowledge: Its Inevitability and Problems of Practicability in Nigeria." *Muslim Education Quarterly* 21(1 and 2): 4–17.

Al-Faruqi, Isma'il Raji. 1982. *Islamization of Knowledge: General Principles and Workplan*. Washington DC: International Institute of Islamic Thought.

Al-Faruqi, Isma'il Raji. 1988. "Islamization of Knowledge: Problems, Principles and Perspective." In *Islam: Source and Purpose of Knowledge*. Washington DC: International Institute of Islamic Thought, 5–63.

al-Alwani, Taha J. 1995. “The Islamization of Knowledge: Yesterday and Today.” *The American Journal of Islamic Social Sciences* 12 (1): 81–101.

al-Attas, Syed M. N. 1979. “Preliminary Thoughts on the Nature of Knowledge and the Definition and Aims of Education.” In *Aims and Objectives of Islamic Education,* ed. Syed M. N. al-Attas. London: Hodder and Stoughton & Jeddah: King Abdulaziz University, 19–47.

al-Attas, Syed M. N. 1991. *The Concept of Education in Islam.* Kuala Lumpur: ISTAC, 1991.

Ashraf, Syed Ali. 1989. “Editorial—The Islamic Frame of Reference: (B) The Intellectual Dimension.” *Muslim Education Quarterly* 7(1): 1–8.

Ashraf, Syed Ali. 1990. *Islamic Education Movement: An Historical Analysis.* Cambridge: The Islamic Academy.

Ashraf, Syed Ali. 1991. “Islamic Education and Evaluation of Past Conferences and Post-Conference Achievements 1977–1989.” In *The Education Conference Papers*, Vol. I, ed. Fathi Malkawi and Hussein Abdul-Fattah. Amman: Islamic Studies and Research Association, 35–36.

Ashraf, Syed Ali. 1994. “Preface.” In *Religion and Education: Islamic and Christian Approaches,* ed. Syed Ali Ashraf and Paul H. Hirst. Cambridge: The Islamic Academy, xi–xiv.

Ba-Yunus, Ilyas. 1988. “Al-Faruqi and Beyond: Future Directions in Islamization of Knowledge.” *The American Journal of Islamic Social Science* 5 (1): 13–28.

Buang, Sa'eda and Ismail, Masturah. 2004. “The Life and Future of Muslim Education.” *Asia Pacific Journal of Education* 27(1): 1–9.

Casewit, Jane. Ed. 2011. *Education in the Light of Tradition.* Bloomington: World Wisdom.

Cook, Bradley J. 1999. “Islamic versus Western Conceptions of Education: Reflections on Egypt.” *International Review of Education* 45 (3 and 4): 339–357.

Dangor, Suleman E. 2014. “Islamization and Muslim Independent Schools in South Africa.” In *International Handbook of Learning, Teaching and Leading in Faith-based Schools,* ed. Judith D. Chapman, Sue McNamara, Michael J. Reiss and Yusef Waghid. London: Springer, 376–377.

Douglass, Susan L. and Shaikh, Munir A. 2007. “Defining Islamic Education: Differentiation and Applications.” *Current Issues in Comparative Education* 7(1): 5–18.

Halstead, Mark. “An Islamic Concept of Education.” *Comparative Education* 40(4): 517–529.

Hoodbhoy, Parvez. 1991. *Islam and Science: Religious Orthodoxy and the Battle for Rationality.* London: Zed Books Ltd.

International Institute of Islamic Thought. 1988. *Islam: Source and Purpose of Knowledge.* Washington DC: International Institute of Islamic Thought.

The Islamic Academy. 1989. *Faith as the Basis of Education in a Multi-faith Multicultural Country: A Discussion Document.* Cambridge: The Islamic Academy.

The Islamic Academy. 1990. *Faith as the Basis of Education in a Multi-faith Multicultural Country: Discussion Document II.* Cambridge: The Islamic Academy.

Jameelah, Maryam. n.d. “The Educational Philosophy and Practice of Syed Muhammad Naquib al-Attas: Book Review.” http://www.allamaiqbal.com/publications/journals/review/oct00/11.htm (accessed June 10, 2015).

Kadi, Wadad. 2006. “Education in Islam—Myths and Truths.” *Comparative Education Review* 50 (3): 311–324.

Kuhn, Thomas S. 1996. *The Structure of Scientific Revolutions*, 3rd ed. Chicago: The University of Chicago Press.
Nasr, Seyyed Hossein. 1975. *Islam and the Plight of Modern Man*. London: Longman.
Olawale, Fahm Abdul Gafar. 2014. "An Assessment of the Islamization of Knowledge Process in Nigeria." *World Journal of Islamic History and Civilization* 4(4):119–124.
Rahman, Fazlur. 1982. *Islam and Modernity: Transformation of an Intellectual Tradition*. Chicago & London: The University of Chicago Press.
Rahman, Fazlur. 1988. "Islamization of Knowledge: A Response." *The American Journal of Islamic Social Science* 5 (1): 3–28.
Ravetz, Jerome R. 1996. *Scientific Knowledge and its Social Problems*, 2nd ed. New Brunswick: Transaction.
Saqeb, Ghulam Nabi. 2000. "Some Reflections on Islamization of Education Since 1977 Makkah Conference: Accomplishments, Failures and Tasks Ahead." *Intellectual Discourse* 8(1): 45–68.
Sardar, Ziauddin. 2004. *Desperately Seeking Paradise: Journeys of a Sceptical Muslim*. London: Granta Books.
Stenberg, Leif. 1996. *The Islamization of Science: Four Muslim Positions Developing an Islamic Modernity*. Sweden: Almqvist & Wiskell International.
Watt, Montgomery. 1961. *Islam and the Integration of Society*. Oxford: Routledge.
Zia, Rukhsana. (Ed.). 2006. *Globalization, Modernization and Education in Muslim Countries*. New York: Nova Science, 2006.
Zubair, Muhammad Umar. 1977. "Foreword." In *First World Conference on Muslim Education: Conference Book*. Jeddah and Makkah: King Abdulaziz University.

9 Diverse Communities, Divergent Aspirations? Islamic Schooling in the West

Nadeem A. Memon

Contemporary K–12 Islamic schools exist in a difficult space. On the one hand they are inheritors of a rich tradition of teaching and learning from classical Muslim societies that they aspire to emulate. On the other hand they are subject to the negative sentiments leveled against current-day madrassas where teaching and learning are considered to be overly dogmatic and rely on rote learning. Full-time K–12 Islamic schools, also referred to as Muslim schools, are a distinct and growing segment of educational institutions among Western Muslim communities. They serve as an alternative to public secular schools for parents who want their children to receive an academically rigorous education in the core curriculum while being educated in a learning environment that nurtures a strong sense of religious identity. Islamic schools are most readily comparable to Jewish day schools or Christian private schools in this sense. These schools arose in Western societies in reaction to mass public secular schools in the 19th and 20th centuries. Although religious schools historically preceded secular public schools, the current iteration of a Jewish, Christian, or Islamic day school is far more structurally aligned with a secular public school than the opposite. Given that these schools are often state accredited or ministry approved and designed to prepare students for university entrance, their school curricula, grade structure, classroom layout, policies and procedures, and the day-to-day schedule mirrors that of the average elementary or secondary school in Canada, Australia, the United States, or the United Kingdom.

The ways in which these schools address the religious aspect of their mission also varies greatly. In an article by Jon Levisohn (2008) on curriculum integration in American Jewish schools, he outlines eight potential ways that Jewish Studies can be approached. Similarly, although there may be 287 state-accredited Islamic schools in the United States (ISLA, 2015) and 156 in the United Kingdom (AMS-UK, 2015), for example, they share structural commonalities and pedagogical distinctions. This chapter will delve into the distinctions and divergences within K–12 Islamic schools. To unpack distinctions in educational aspirations, this chapter begins by establishing a categorization of Muslim communities to provide a framework for analysis. The second part of this chapter then distinguishes between types of Islamic schools.

UNDERSTANDING THE 'MUSLIM' MINDSET

Religious communities are pluralistic. This may seem to be an unnecessary statement, but both insiders and outsiders commonly gloss over their significant diversity. The framing of this chapter around 'Western' schools is similarly a generalization on the part of the author. However, I have made a conscious choice to generalize one identity factor in order to unpack another. Therefore, to delve into the conceptions of Islamic schooling, I consciously set aside the distinct Western contexts in which these schools have evolved in order to focus the analysis on the specific representations of religious education that each school holds. To analyze contemporary Islamic schools, I then begin by unpacking Muslim pluralism.

Muslim communities are united by two essential and interdependent religious sources: God's word in the Qur'an and God's messenger, the Prophet Muhammad. Yet aside from these foundational elements, there exists great plurality in how Muslim communities live Islam and is what Robert Hefner refers to as the "porous pluralism" of Muslim communities that must be acknowledged as a matter worthy of investigation so as to engage diversity and not become consumed by attempts to rationalize the superiority of one over the other (Hefner 2014, 132). Theologically, as in any faith tradition, there is variance in how Islamic beliefs and practices are interpreted. Fundamental differences in religious beliefs have created sects such as the Sunni, Shi'a (Ithna Ashari), Ismaili, and even arguably less globally known communities such as the Nation of Islam in the United States. Within and across sectarian differences, however, there exists a layer of interpretation and emphasis that I will refer to as 'orientations,' which refers to the orientations of communities who agree on the foundational beliefs of a particular sect or faction yet differ on what the practice of those beliefs ought to emphasize. Orientations such as Salafiyyah, Sufism, Ikhwan al Muslimeen, Tabligh Jamaat, Jamaat-i-Islami, Wahabism, represent how Islam can be approached in ways that are as distinct as political to apolitical, social outreach based versus inward spiritually focused, and locally active to globally concerned. These distinctions are what Nasr (2010) categorizes as being on a spectrum between 'Traditional Islam,' 'Islamic Modernism' and 'Islamic Fundamentalism.' First, Traditional Islam refers to an orientation that relies on the Islamic sciences such as jurisprudence, theology, spirituality, philosophy, and art, which are all rooted in the canonical sources of Islam. Essential to Traditional Islam is a reliance on scholarship that is vehemently opposed by Islamic Modernism. A modernist orientation would insist on exercising independent reasoning in order to interpret religious texts striving to find harmony between humanism and rationalism (Rahnema 2005, xlv). Fundamentalism is a reaction to the diminished supremacy of Muslim empires and a call for a return to fundamental beliefs and practices void of non-Islamic influences, as well as being considered 'revivalist' and emphasizing political advocacy.

Second, outside of theology and orientations, Muslim communities also differ culturally, racially, ethnically, and generationally (Kaya 2007, 30). Muslim communities in the United States, for example, have their origins in three types: indigenous, immigrant, and converts. The presence of African American Muslims who were brought to America during the slave trade are indigenous to the United States and undoubtedly prior to immigrant Muslims who primarily came from the Middle East and South Asia. By the time immigrants arrived in significant numbers in the latter half of the 20th century, the cultural and ethnic diversity of American Muslim communities was tremendously broad. Similarly, the diversity of Muslims who have converted to Islam, including African, White, and Hispanic Americans, have equally contributed to the diverse experiences that represent American Islam. Cultural, ethnic, and racial differences are critical to understanding the diversity among Muslim communities because global cultures and experiences have informed the way Islam has been historically practiced (Abd-Allah 2004). Lastly, in attempting to unpack Muslim diversity, we must consider generational differences. The experience of a fourth-generation Lebanese American is far different from that of a first-generation Somali American. The experience of a first-generation Somali American differs tremendously from that of an indigenous African American Muslim. Generational differences add another level of complexity in understanding the Muslim mindset, their level of engagement with their local context, socioeconomic access, and how they engage with their local communities.

These four categories are by no means mutually exclusive; rather, the categories should be considered as concentric circles to reflect the dynamic overlap and complexity that exists within each. People's orientations change over time, and for many Muslims, their orientations are not even pronounced or defined, but rather becoming or implicit—if not influenced by the orientations of their parents, communities, religious leaders, or context. Similarly, cultures and generations are far from clear-cut categories, because we live in an age of hybrid cultures and cross-generational experiences. This attempt to identify categories of Muslim perspectives provides a framework for thinking about the differences and distinctions in Islamic schooling. Sectarian differences are often more easily identifiable. The theological divide between Sunni and Shi'a communities is so clearly pronounced that the average Muslim is able to distinguish between schools based on a school's mission and vision. But beyond sectarian differences, the ways that schools are informed by orientational, cultural, and generational differences is far less clear. These latter three categories are also critical because they inform the educational philosophy, structure, curriculum, and aspirations of an Islamic school. Ibrahim Kalin's approach to acknowledging differences in Muslim communities is useful in analyzing the distinctions and diversities of Islamic schools. Kalin distinguishes between 'uniformity' and 'unity.' He states, "While uniformity denotes a state of bland sameness and oppressive homogeneity, unity points to what connects diverse things. . . . Just as unity does not mean uniformity, plurality does not mean division and chaos" (Kalin 2011, 473). We can apply the framework to a sample set of Islamic schools without intending to promote one type or model of school over another or assuming that Islamic schooling ought to be uniform. Rather, we can recognize that the richness of the burgeoning field of contemporary Islamic schools is a rich diversity of interpretation of what Islamic education is and can be.

COMMON ASPIRATIONS: SCHOOL MISSION AND VISION STATEMENTS

Most Islamic schools have common aspirations. Review of ten Islamic school websites reveals common sentiments about nurturing a strong religious identity, the importance of character building, civic responsibility and national identity, and the need for a learning environment that reinforces all of these elements were prevalent themes. These elements may further be summarized in three common areas that arise across most schools: Identity, Responsibility, and Excellence.

Identity refers to the emphasis on nurturing religious values along with national values of the school's regional context. In many of the schools reviewed, explicit mention of the country of residence is made. Parents want to ensure that sending their children to an Islamic school will not isolate them from the socio-political rhythm of the country. For example, Calgary Islamic School, based in Alberta, Canada, states on their website, "Our aim is to raise students who demonstrate impeccable Islamic character along with advanced academic skills and *exemplary citizenship*" (CIS 2015). Most schools, if not all that were reviewed, make it a point to mention the necessity of teaching Islam in a way that makes it 'real' and 'relevant' to the lived experience of students. Essential to making Islam relevant is for students to understand that they are Muslim in their religious identity and also citizens of a particular nation whose values are part of a student's shared identity. The motto at the Australian Islamic College of Sydney (AICS), for instance is, "Seek Knowledge and serve thy Nation" which is intended to promote "both their spiritual and intellectual development while developing a *distinctive Australian identity*" (AICS 2015).

An essential part of this shared identity is the importance of civic 'responsibility' through community service and being involved in the local community around their school. Al Fatih Academy, located in Virginia, USA, espouses a mission to "cultivate and nurture a thriving *American Muslim identity* that balances religious, academic and cultural knowledge and imparts the importance of *civic involvement and charitable work*" (Al-Fatih 2015, emphasis in original). W. D. Mohammed High School, located in Georgia, USA, the flagship school of the Clara Muhammad Schools consortium, similarly states that they "strive to develop a cooperative partnership among students, family and community in creating a dynamic, prosperous, G'd conscious community of enlightened leaders and effective *global citizens*" (W. D. Mohammed High 2015, emphasis in original). None of the schools reviewed espouse a mission or vision that is isolationist, separatist, or that aspires to keep their students apart from the communities they live in. Some schools do use language such as "protect students from" and "safe learning environment," but that generally refers to social influences that are deemed un-Islamic and this sentiment is less emphasized than it was in the early Islamic schools of the 1980s and 1990s (Memon 2009). The more common aspiration of Islamic schools post 9/11 is a stance to integrate, contribute, and create positive interrelationships with the community around them.

In terms of excellence, parents want to ensure that their children adopt Islamic values and a strong religious identity yet not at the expense of academic success. Islamic schools are supported by the growing Muslim middle class whose socioeconomic status allows them to invest in relatively higher private school fees and also brings expectations of ensuring their children will be academically competitive upon graduation (Keyworth 2009). On the AICS website, for instance, the school is promoted as the preferred school of choice for parents because "Families deem the secure *Islamic environment coupled with academic excellence* as paramount to their children's well-being" (AICS 2015, emphasis in original). Similarly, Averroes Institute (AI), based in California, USA, positions themselves as a school that "is dedicated to developing *well-informed, academic, responsible and compassionate young adults*" (Averroes 2015, emphasis in original). In some countries of Europe, as well as Canada, some religious schools qualify to receive government funding, but this is not the case at all in the United States.

Aside from the general common aspirations of Islamic schools outlined earlier there are certainly exceptions. Some schools espouse a more focused, charter school–like vision that emphasizes a particular element from the common ones listed. For example, Al Fatih Academy's website has a far more explicit emphasis on the importance of civic engagement and responsibility than other schools, and Sakinah Circle, based in Alberta, Canada, makes a more concerted effort to set itself apart with a Qur'anic worldview influencing the school curriculum and ethos. The subsequent sections will delve more deeply in how distinctions exist within such common aspirations.

ORIENTATIONAL FRAMES: NUANCED DEFINITIONS OF ISLAMIC EDUCATION

It is important to acknowledge that despite commonalities expressed in the previous section, there are nuanced definitions, and in some cases, significant distinctions that inform Islamic schools. Cultures, generations, religious foundations, and interpretations or orientations play a significant role here in what is actually emphasized or de-emphasized in schools. Orientations are rarely as explicit as sectarian differences might be. Sectarian differences are easily recognizable because schools of particular sects are often housed in mosques or communities of that sect. Shi'a schools are often found located in Shi'a mosques or Ismaili weekend schools are often associated with an Ismaili Jamatkhana. Similarly, many Sunni schools are affiliated with a local mosque. A growing number of schools today are privately owned, and their mission statements include particular references and terminology to their vision, values, or curriculum emphasis that illustrates the school's orientation. Sahin (2013) emphasizes that education is a value-laden process informed by its sociocultural context and core Islamic values. He argues that, "If this theological dimension is disregarded or naively taken for granted, the 'Islamic' in the expression will function as an ideological heuristic that inaccurately leads to a monolithic and dogmatic conception of education in Islam" (Sahin 2013, 178). From the ten schools reviewed, four orientational frames emerged that are influenced by theological interpretations.

Qur'an and Sunnah or Islamic Tradition

Among orientational differences is the emphasis in some Muslim communities on the Qur'an and Sunnah as the only or primarily credible sources for human guidance. Using Nasr's (2010) terms, these are 'modernist' communities. Other communities, often traditionalist communities, rely on a broader canon of religious texts that include the Qur'an and Sunnah as primary texts along with the centuries of Islamic scholarship that have analyzed and interpreted the Qur'an and Sunnah. The term often employed to identify the latter emphasis is a reliance on the 'Islamic tradition.' This distinction has significant implications for Islamic schooling in the design of the Islamic Studies curriculum.

Deenway Foundation, based in the United Kingdom, for example, states that they strive to provide "meaningful teaching and learning experiences" by "promoting a classical liberal arts education faithful to the Islamic tradition." That section of the website continues by stating that the foundation's "ethos is rooted in the classical Islamic tradition but we are non-partisan" (Deenway 2015). It is rare to find a school that explicitly articulates an orientational leaning on their website. However, in an age where individuals, as opposed to mosque-based community initiatives, are establishing schools, such identifiers are becoming more common. Deenway's explicit reference to the "classical Islamic tradition" demarcates a line between traditionalist and modernist communities. Schools such as Deenway Foundation emphasize the former by designing an Islamic Studies curriculum that teaches the sciences of Arabic grammar and morphology (*sarf* and *nahw*), logic (*mantiq*), law (*fiqh*), belief (*aqida*), and spiritual excellence (*ihsan*)—topics that are not commonly emphasized in modernist-oriented Islamic schools.

In an attempt to disassociate themselves from the realities and complexities of orientational differences, most Islamic schools seek to unify their school communities with an emphasis on the two primary religious sources, the Qur'an and Sunnah. Such an emphasis is not commonly mentioned on school websites or in school policies yet is quite common in practice. When school issues arise where there are differences of opinion such as the use of musical instruments, permissible forms of art, or mixed-gender classrooms as examples, school administrators and teachers commonly will say they rely on the Qur'an and Sunnah to determine the school's position on these matters. Teachers and students are then encouraged to study the Qur'an and Sunnah regarding such matters to use independent reasoning and interpret religious texts, what Nasr (2010) refers to as a modernist orientation.

These distinct orientations influence the entire ethos of an Islamic school but in particular the Islamic Studies curriculum. Schools with a modernist orientation in many ways make the Qur'an their curriculum or, in other words, rely more heavily on primary religious texts. Schools with a traditionalist orientation place their emphasis on secondary canon texts that represent classical scholarship of interpretation of the primary texts.

Community Engagement or Spiritual Development

A second orientational distinction between schools is an emphasis on community engagement and its balance with individual spiritual development. Schools do not solely emphasize community engagement or spiritual development but, based on a school's orientation, often do emphasize one over the other, which is evident in their formal or informal curriculum. Take for instance Olive Grove School, a school that is owned and operated by the Muslim Association of Canada (MAC). MAC is a "religious, educational, social, charitable and non-profit organization" that operates in Canada. The organization provides services such as community programs, schools, and community centers (or mosques) across major Canadian cities such as Toronto, Ottawa, Montreal, and Edmonton. A primary tenet of MAC is to serve both Muslim communities in Canada and also the wider communities, regardless of faith or culture, where Muslims reside. The emphasis on wider community engagement and responsibility can be traced to the orientational roots of the organization that also influences the programs and extracurricular initiatives in their schools. On the MAC website, the organization associates itself with the revivalist movement commonly known globally as the Muslim Brotherhood. The roots of MAC "can be traced to the vigorous intellectual revivalist effort that took hold in Muslim societies starting in the early twentieth century" (MAC 2015) with a

> revival aimed at reconciling faith with the challenges of modernity and providing a clear articulation of balance and moderation in

> understanding Islam. In the Arab world, this revival culminated in the writings of the late Imam Hassan al-Banna and the movement of the Society of Muslim Brothers (commonly known as the Muslim Brotherhood). Al-Banna's core messages of constructive engagement in society, focus on personal and communal empowerment, and organizational development had a deep impact on much of the Muslim world.
>
> (MAC 2015)

The ethic of community engagement espoused by al-Banna's writings and championed by the Muslim Brotherhood globally is also evident in the educational philosophy of Olive Grove School. Olive Grove, for instance, offers student leadership programs, community service initiatives, and parent education programs that are far more embedded into the school ethos than in other schools. For instance, the school's 'EnrichIt! Program' is a cornerstone extracurricular school offering that is featured on the school website (OGS 2015). It reflects commitment to high-level academic learning with community building as an essential element of the school's offerings. Juxtaposed in relation to the community engagement approach is a personal spiritual development approach. Schools such as Averroes promote a curriculum that places significant emphasis on spiritual excellence, which is commonly associated with a traditionalist orientation. For example, in their foundational Sacred Studies (Islamic Studies) course entitled Awareness of Oneself, students "spend extensive time studying the heart at its potential states along with the effects of these states on a person's spiritual and physical world" (Averroes 2015). A second course entitled Islamic Spirituality "delves into the psychological diseases and cures of the heart." The course prepares students for adulthood with the mature and sensitive realities of envy, arrogance, ostentation, and lust (as a few examples) that challenge human experiences and relationships. Other courses in the Averroes curriculum include: Awareness of Society—addressing contemporary social issues in relation to Prophetic wisdom; a course on Ethics related to serving others, war, business, and environmental ethics; Comparative Religions where students gain an appreciation of other faith traditions; Philosophy of a Believing Person that addresses topics such as ethics, metaphysics, epistemology, and logic. The Averroes curriculum is highly reflective of a traditionalist approach that emphasizes the inward nature of religiosity over the outward, service-oriented leanings of a modernist orientation at Olive Grove. Although neither of the school's makes their orientation explicit, the aspects of Islam that are emphasized through their formal and informal curriculum provide insights.

DISTINCT APPROACHES: ACHIEVEMENT AND PHILOSOPHY

The primary audience of school websites is arguably the parents of students. Analyzing school websites and the type of information provided highlights the interests of the parents and what the schools' founders seek to develop in the community. Some schools place a greater emphasis on school events and achievements, whereas others focus on articulating a distinct philosophy of education. For some parents, knowing that an Islamic school is going to foster a religious identity without forfeiting academic achievement is a critical determinant in selecting the right school. For other parents, knowing that a school has deeply distinguished itself from the norms of the secular public schooling experience is more important. When analyzing the select school websites, it became evident that schools either attract parents through an articulation of a well-developed philosophy or by promoting their academic achievements and showcasing that their school's learning environment is conducive to academic achievement.

Olive Grove School represents the type of Islamic school most second- and third-generation parents want. The school is housed in a purpose-built school building with a playground, field, gymnasium, library, office, and all of the structural elements that would remind a Muslim parent of their own secular public school experience growing up in Canada. The website has no explicit mention of a mission, or vision, or philosophy of what makes the school unique, what defines Islamic education, or what distinguishes the school's approach to Islamic education from any other Islamic school. Unlike other school websites, Olive Grove emphasizes achievement. A separate page on the website is dedicated to the school's achievements, a separate page for their enrichment program, and a page on their character education program. The school motto is "Turning student potential into achievement," and the types of achievements and activities listed on the website such as tree planting or raising funds for cancer research, sports competitions such as dragon boating, and religious competitions such as Qur'an or math competitions provide enough fodder for parents to know achievement is a primary focus.

In the absence of a well-articulated school philosophy, school websites provide parents with a sense of comfort in the school's approach. The Islamic Foundation School based in Illinois, USA, for instance, although very similar in structure and objectives to most other schools, such as Olive Grove and AICS, established the Malcolm X Library at the school. Although all schools have libraries, IFS felt that naming the library after one of the most influential American Muslims of the 20th century would serve as a reminder of the values and legacy he left behind. Students in lower grades visit the library twice a week to gain research skills and are "guided to be effective and ethical users of information" (IFS 2015). Malcolm X, as a person who was largely self-educated while in prison, represents life-long reading and embodies one who read, spoke, and lived life with an informed Muslim perspective. The library hopes to nurture these values and serves as a good example of a school promoting academic achievement while fostering an American Muslim identity—something highly important to the demographic of Muslim parents supporting Islamic schools in America post 9/11.

Fewer schools have a written philosophy statement that articulates the purpose and vision of their school. Deenway, Sakinah Circle, and Al Fatih Academy do have such statements. Common to these three schools is that each was established through a group of concerned parents, not through a mosque-based community that serves a wider and more diverse demographic segment of the Muslim community. These schools seem more interested in attracting parents who align with and aspire toward the shared philosophy of the founders. For example, Al Fatih's philosophy is to foster "a commitment to community involvement, a sense of heightened social responsibility, respect for cultural diversity, and understanding of what it means to be an American citizen and a global citizen" (Al Fatih 2015). The vision of Al Fatih from the outset has been to foster a deep sense of civic engagement that exceeds the common school-event approach. Al Fatih integrates civic engagement into the formal and informal curriculum of the school from the literature read in English classes to the problems students solve in mathematics. Being located relatively close to the U.S. capital, Al Fatih has used this proximity as an integral way to reinforce a sense of American Muslim identity in students. Students discuss politics, are encouraged to be conversant in current affairs, and take initiatives to make positive local change in their community.

Both Deenway and Sakinah Circle articulate philosophies of holistic child development where the spiritual, emotional, social, and cognitive needs of students are fostered. There is less emphasis on academic achievement and competition and more emphasis on the learning experiences that the school aims to provide. For instance, Sakinah Circle's mission is "to provide guidance and an environment that recognizes the learner's *fitrah* (innate nature), nurtures *taqwa* (God consciousness), and cultivates learners who strive to become *khulafah* (vicegerents of Allah)" (Sakinah Circle 2015). In principle, most Islamic schools would agree with such a mission statement; yet to achieve this mission, Sakinah Circle has remapped the school curriculum to be based on themes that ignite spiritual awareness. Similar to the transdisciplinary-themes-based approach of the International Baccalaureate curriculum framework, Sakinah Circle has developed a curriculum around foundational themes that consistently encourage students to read the signs (*ayah*) of Allah around them and reflect on the relationship between the world and the universe.

In the case of Deenway, the philosophical statement begins with a description of the school's surroundings being "close to museums, parks, libraries, mosques, civic institutions, and the river Kennet" where children will have access to "meaningful learning experiences inside and outside the school" (Deenway 2015). The statement of philosophy goes on to discuss the school's "beautifully prepared Montessori classrooms" their comprehensive "sacred sports curriculum" that includes archery, Shaolin Kung-Fu, and horseback riding (Deenway 2015). The school aspires to develop students who are

> confident in themselves . . . [have] a life-long attachment to the Qur'an and a strong love for the Messenger of Allah . . . be people of

> righteousness, of forbearance, of gratitude, of charity and compassion, stoic and serious when required, but also able to jest and cultivate joy in themselves and others . . . stewards of the earth, harbingers of peace . . .
> (Deenway 2015)

The philosophy statement emphasizes nurturing individuals in their moral, ethical, spiritual, physical, and intellectual states on the assumption that academic excellence will be an unspoken result if the former is actualized.

It is evident that when a school writes such a philosophy statement, it caters to a particular demographic of the Muslim community—in orientation and generation. In the case of Sakinah Circle and Deenway, centering concepts of spiritual excellence (*ihsan*), spiritual self-awareness, and nurturing a "strong love for the Messenger" leans toward a traditionalist orientation. Deenway's reliance on Montessori principles of child development and Sakinah Circle's remapping of the curriculum based on a Qur'anic worldview also represent an attempt to break away from the norms of conventional public schooling where the overemphasis on cognitive learning is often criticized.

CURRICULUM APPROACH

The conventional curricular approach in most Islamic schools is to teach the mandatory core subjects (English, math, science, social studies) using ministry or state recommended or approved textbooks. The objective of teaching the core curriculum is to match the standards achieved in secular public schools. To this core curriculum, as in most other faith-based schools, a class on religious studies is added to the overall course list. In the case of Islamic schools, the course on Islamic Studies covers foundational topics about beliefs and practices, values and daily etiquette, and biographies of the prophets. Schools that teach Islamic Studies as a single subject often rely on textbooks from a handful of English-medium publishing houses that produce teaching materials for the K–12 market. In addition to Islamic Studies as a single subject, most schools will also include classes either on Arabic language and/or optional classes on Qur'anic memorization.

A rapidly growing approach to Islamic school curriculum is the integrated, interdisciplinary, or holistic approach according to varied models and perspectives as well. These approaches attempt to weave or infuse Islamic values and perspectives across all subjects of the curriculum and not relegate teaching of Islam only to Islamic Studies classes. It is becoming increasingly common for schools to claim that the integrated approach is what they aspire for, but schools are far from actualizing this consistently or in any structured way. Most schools that claim to integrate Islam across the curriculum do so sporadically at best through making connections to Islamic perspectives in areas of common religious debate. Others will integrate Islam through appending to the existing core curriculum, for example, speaking about classical Muslim scientists in classes, adding poetry written by Muslim writers to English classes, or doing research projects on Muslim-majority societies in social studies. Some schools have attempted integration through establishing themes based on Islamic values or perspectives that are then reinforced in each of the core subjects during the same month. Deenway provides an example of what this integration looks like:

> students in upper elementary were studying the Roman Empire in history class; while in Seerah class they were learning about the expedition of Tabuk when news reached the Prophet Muhammad of a potential Roman invasion and the letter the Prophet Muhammad wrote to the Roman emperor Heraclius. And in Qur'an tafseer class students study Surah Rum (Romans).
>
> (Deenway 2015)

Integration in this sense relies on a single topic from the curriculum to make interdisciplinary connections in an authentic way. Sakinah Circle promotes another nuance to the conception of integrated or holistic curriculum. According to their website, "the Alberta Program of Study is taught with a Qur'anic worldview, meaning that we approach all our learning with a Qur'anic lens." The curriculum is structured around broad enduring understandings that are rooted in a Qur'anic worldview through which all other subject-learning outcomes are then mapped. Some of these enduring understandings are 1) Signs and Symbols of Our Creator, 2) Harmony in the Cosmos, 3) We Have a Place in Space and Time, 4) Language is a Divine Gift, 5) All Prophets Brought the Same Essential Message: To Remember God (Sakinah Circle 2015). These enduring understandings or core themes serve as the foundation of the curriculum whereby all other subject content is taught. The distinction between Sakinah and most other schools is that core subject content is integrated into foundational Islamic themes—not vice versa.

MUSLIM TEACHER: A GENERATIONAL DEVELOPMENT

For decades, the primary concern for most parents considering Islamic schooling has been the school's accreditation status. When a school is inspected and accredited by a state or ministry body it represents a particular quality standard. However, in many places, accredited private schools are not required to hire credentialed teachers, especially for elementary classes. As a result, many Islamic schools have become accustomed to hiring teaching staff that are either not formally trained in teaching or internationally certified educators who do not hold the requisite teaching credentials for the particular state/province in which their Islamic school is accredited.

This trend, however, is changing as schools are raising the bar by hiring certified teachers and more avenues are blossoming for teachers from abroad to gain local certification.

However, aside from teacher certification, preparing teachers specifically for teaching in an Islamic school is rarely discussed. Whether the teacher is an observant Muslim, a good person, and a credentialed teacher has certainly been an expectation. But few have acknowledged the disconnect between a teacher being trained in a secular teacher training college to be prepared to teach in a faith-based learning context. Teachers in faith-based learning contexts need the opportunity to consider critical questions such as: What are the stages of a child's spiritual development? At what age should moral issues be introduced and how? How should an educator inspire and reinforce religious etiquette (*adab*) for long-term transformation? How might an educator make religious belief relevant to students' lived experiences? How (and to what extent) should an educator counsel students who are questioning their faith? Such questions are not addressed in conventional teacher preparation programs that lead to government certification.

Aside from the community of Imam Warith Deen Muhammad who established the Muslim Teachers College in the United States in the 1980s to serve teachers of the Clara Muhammad Schools system, no other formal initiative of the like has been established until recently. Deenway initiated the Deenway Teacher Training College (DTTC™), which emphasizes how the "insights of Maria Montessori are perfectly suited to the Islamic tradition" (Deenway 2015). Teachers who successfully complete the program receive an accredited Montessori diploma. Deenway's approach of combining their teacher preparation program with that of a Montessori preparation program is also not uncommon. Schools such as Lote Tree in Toronto, Canada, or River Garden Montessori in Chicago, USA, have a similar approach because of the similarities between the principles of Islamic pedagogy and a Montessori philosophy for early years' education. In the absence of a well-developed teacher preparation program for an Islam-based pedagogical approach, schools such as Lote Tree, River Garden, Deenway, and likely others have relied on articulated contemporary philosophies of education that resonate with Islamic perspectives. The Shakhsiyah Foundation, based in the United Kingdom, acknowledges that most Islamic schools hire separate teachers for Islamic Studies and Arabic versus those for core subjects. But this should not be the case if schools are to truly be holistic in the sense that Islamic values and perspectives are integrated across all subjects. As an article on the Shakhsiyah website states,

> If a child perceives that all other knowledge is taught by their main class teacher and that a special 'ustadh' [teacher] comes in to teach them Islam, they will quickly believe that learning about Islam is only for some 'special' people whilst all other knowledge is for everyone.
> (Shakhsiyah 2015)

To prepare teachers at Shakhsiyah Schools for this responsibility, they have developed the Islamic Teacher Education Course (ITEC). Through a series of workshops, discussions, and assignments, ITEC encourages teachers to think deeply about what education in Islam means, how to teach the National Curriculum from an Islamic perspective and how to approach teaching differently when students are viewed as a moral trust (*amanah*).

Preparing teachers for the Islamic school context is largely a generational development, because as schools have grown over time, parents and teachers alike have begun to raise deeper core questions about the distinctive nature of these schools. Parent supporters of early schools were rightfully concerned about whether an Islamic school could provide an education commensurate of comparable quality to the secular public system. Today, more parent supporters are beginning to ask not how schools are similar to conventional schooling model, but rather how are Islamic schools offering something distinctive that is missing in conventional schools.

CONCLUSION

Analyzing Islamic schooling provides a unique entry point to understanding the Western Muslim diaspora, the communities' diverse paths, aspirations, and ways of articulating their conception of Islam. The categorization presented at the outset of this chapter and then applied to current Islamic schools illustrated common aspirations and yet distinct curricular approaches and pedagogical emphases. As Muslim communities become more established, numbers grow, demographics increasingly diversify, and as a result subgroups have also begun to distinguish themselves. Early Islamic schools in the 1980s and 1990s were inclusive by default, because there was often only one school to choose from, and it was associated with the local mosque, which also was likely the sole mosque in the city. Today many major cities have multiple schools to choose from, some of which are privately initiated and administered. As a result, religious orientations and generational differences are beginning to more authentically shape and reshape definitions of Islamic education. The future challenge for Islamic schools is that community-based schools may try to serve all perspectives but may be in danger of silencing the rich diversity of Muslim orientations and cultural nuances. At the same time, privately established schools articulate a focused philosophy of Islamic education but may benefit only a small group of parent supporters and their children. The hope and potential in the future resides in seeing the benefit of both school approaches. Small schools established with uniquely articulated philosophies should be viewed as hubs of educational innovation, whereas large, well-established schools attract larger segments of parent supporters to the potential of Islamic schooling. Together what outwardly seems as divergent approaches should be viewed as an interdependent alliance that could redefine Islamic schooling in time.

BIBLIOGRAPHY

Abd-Allah, Umar, F. 2004. "Islam and Cultural Imperative." Nawawi Foundation. Accessed January 3, 2015. http://www.nawawi.org/wp-content/uploads/2013/01/Article3.pdf.

Al Fatih Academy, 2015. Accessed April 20. http://www.alfatih.org.

Association of Muslim Schools, 2015. "Frequently Asked Questions." Accessed April 20. http://ams-uk.org/faq/.

Australian Islamic College of Sydney, 2015. Accessed April 20. http://www.aics.nsw.edu.au.

Avorres High School, 2015. Accessed April 20. https://www.averroeshighschool.com.

Calgary Islamic School, 2015. Accessed April 20. http://www.calgaryislamicschool.com.

Deenway, 2015. Accessed April 20. http://www.deenway.org.

Hefner, Robert W. 2014. "Modern Muslims and the Challenge of Plurality." *Springer Science + Business Media* 51: 131–139.

Islamic Foundation School. 2015. Accessed April 20. http://ifsvp.org.

Islamic Schools League of America. "School Search." Accessed April 20. http://theisla.org/page.php/SchoolSearchResults_Map?all_schools=all_schools.

Kalin, Ibrahim. 2011. "Religion, Unity, and Diversity." *Philosophy and Social Criticism* 37(4): 471–478.

Kaya, Ilhan. 2007. "Muslim American Identities and Diversity." *The Journal of Geography* Jan/Feb 106(1): 29–35.

Keyworth, Karen. 2009. "Islamic Schools of America: Data-Based Profiles." In *Educating the Muslims of America*, edited by Yvonee Haddad, Farid Senzai, and Jane Smith, 21–38. New York: Oxford University Press.

Levisohn, Jon, A. 2008. "From Integration of Curricula to the Pedagogy of Integrity." *Journal of Jewish Education* 74(3): 264–294.

Memon, Nadeem. 2009. "From Protest to Praxis: A History of Islamic Schooling in North America." PhD diss., University of Toronto.

Memon, Nadeem. 2011. "What Islamic School Teachers Want: Toward Developing an Islamic Teacher Education Programme." *British Journal of Religious Education* 33(3): 285–298.

Muslim Association of Canada, 2015. Accessed April 20. http://www.macnet.ca/English/Pages/About%20MAC.aspx

Nasr, Seyyed Hossein. 2010. *Islam in the Modern World.* New York: HarperCollins.

Olive Grove School, 2015. Accessed April 20. http://www.olivegroveschool.ca.

Rahnema, Ali, ed. 2005. *Pioneers of Islamic Revival.* London: Zed Books.

Sakinah Circle, 2015. Accessed April 20. http://sakinahcircle.com.

Shakhsiyah Foundation, 2015. Accessed April 20. http://www.isfnet.org.uk.

W.D. Muhammad High School, 2015. Accessed April 20. http://mohammedschools.org.

10 An Olive Tree in the Apple Orchard

Establishing an Islamic College in the United States

Omar Qargha

Modern Western systems of education tie the validity of knowledge to empiricism, rationalism, and subjective constructivism. This is in contrast to classical Islamic systems of education, which tie the validity of knowledge to revelation. Over the last fifty years, Muslim educationalists have tried to synthesize and transform modern advances in knowledge, and its associated educational systems, within an Islamic worldview. The Islamization of Knowledge (IOK) movement is perhaps the most prominent example of this attempt (Al Attas 1979; Nasr 1987). The combination of these two opposing structures continues to pose a tremendous challenge to Islamic education.

This chapter explores how Zaytuna College, a newly formed college in the United States, is dealing with the challenge of negotiating the space between a theistic Islamic worldview and areas of knowledge that are based on secular epistemologies within the structure of a modern university. This chapter tries to shed light on the operational challenges associated with this negotiation. Conceptually, the chapter attempts to contribute to the discourse on Islamization of Knowledge, based on theories of traditionalism and modernism.

The chapter is organized into four major sections. In the first section, Zaytuna College is introduced and contextualized within attempts at alternative epistemologies to positivism and constructivism within the space of higher education in the United States, followed by an overview of outlets for Islamic higher education in the United States. The second section presents the theoretical framework for the chapter, emphasizing the need for understanding the challenge of Islamization of Knowledge within the context of the debate between traditionalism and modernization, and especially the structural effects of modern institutions. The third section presents the case of Zaytuna College and how it is negotiating the challenge of creating an Islamic educational model and forging its identity. The fourth and last section discusses this case study's contribution to the discourse of Islamic philosophy of education and its praxis.

ZAYTUNA COLLEGE

Growing out of a very well-known, community-based program called Zaytuna Institute, Zaytuna College is the most recent and perhaps the most prominent attempt at establishing an independent Muslim college in the United States. With the working motto of "where Islam meets America," the College aims to prepare students who are grounded in the Islamic scholarly tradition and conversant with modern societies. The College identifies itself as rooted in the American liberal arts tradition and offers a bachelor's degree in Islamic Law and Theology as well as a Summer Arabic Intensive Program (HEFCE 2008; Oguntoyinbo 2010).

In 2010, Zaytuna College officially started operations in a rented facility occupying the floor level of a Baptist Seminary college in Berkeley, California. On January 8, 2014, the College acquired its own property atop of 'holy hill' in Berkeley, which is home to a number of seminaries associated with the Graduate Theological Union. A three-member executive team composed of a president, vice president of academic affairs, and vice president of finance and administration make up the leadership for the College. The College is governed by a nine-person board of trustees (seven male, two female) composed of religious scholars, business leaders, technology experts, and medical professionals. The College has fifteen faculty members (ten male, five female), seven of whom serve as full-time faculty. Many of the professors are American converts to Islam. Seven faculty members either hold a doctoral degree or are working toward a PhD. Nine of the fifteen faculty members have either studied in traditional Islamic institutions and/or received *ijaza* (traditional license) to teach Islamic subjects. The *ijazas* cover a variety of Islamic sciences, with the president of the College holding the most extensive number of *ijazas*. The College lists thirty classical Islamic scholars as their "perennial faculty" with the aim to highlight the College's commitment to being connected to foundational scholars who have laid the groundwork for the Islamic intellectual and spiritual sciences. The works of these thirty classical scholars are part of the curriculum for the College.

The student body for Zaytuna College includes both males and females, made up of African American, South Asian, Hispanic, White, Afghan, and Arab origins. All students are American citizens, and the majority of students are non residents of California. Some students come directly from high school, whereas others already have degrees or have changed midway in their academic careers to join Zaytuna.

The experience and struggle of Zaytuna College is taking place within the context of other efforts at offering Islamic higher education specifically, and within the general framework of alternative and other faith-based Colleges in the United States in general. What follows provides the landscape of these two efforts and tries to place Zaytuna College within this overall context.

RELIGION, ALTERNATIVE WORLDVIEWS, AND HIGHER EDUCATION IN THE UNITED STATES

The history of higher education in the United States is intimately tied to faith-based traditions. A large number of private colleges and universities in the United States, including Harvard, Yale, Princeton, and the University of Chicago, started with very clear Christian identities. However, with modernization, the overt merger of religion and higher education became delegitimized, and most of the institutions took on secular identities (Benne 2001; Parker, Beaty, Mencken, & Lyon 2007; Wilshire 1990).

There are many reasons why faith became alienated from public higher education in the United States. However, the primary reason was the shift from an epistemology based on religion and the metaphysical to that of the rational and the scientific. Whereas faith-based approaches rely on the revelation of knowledge through scripture, the rational and scientific paradigm views the source of knowledge in verifiable and observable empirical experiences (Benne 2001; Clitheroe 2010). Some scholars have described this shift as the replacement of faith in traditional religion by that of faith in science, professionalism, and the myth of rationalization (Ramirez 2006; Wilshire 1990). Another reason for the alienation of faith from higher education has been the diversification of administration, faculty, and students to meet government diversity standards within the public university campus in order to be eligible for financial support from the government and many private foundations. In many cases, this diversification has resulted in the weakening of both the original religious identity of the university and religious authority within the university (Dillon 1995; Dovre 2000). Although these changes have resulted in financial prosperity and cultural diversity, the cost has been the loss of religious identity within the institutions (Dovre 2000).

Despite the historical trend of distancing faith from higher education, in recent years there has been an increased interest in religion, spirituality, and alternative models of higher education in the United States. This increased interest, which is observable among incoming students (Schuman 2009), is the result of communities desiring a renewed identity (Bull 1994), and is also influenced by a move toward the legitimacy of more qualitative ways of knowing (Dovre 2000). Faith-based colleges and universities have used varied strategies for restoring and preserving their traditions within higher education.

ISLAMIC HIGHER EDUCATION IN THE UNITED STATES

Two types of Islamic educational outlets exist within higher education in the United States: Islamic Studies programs within established universities and independent Muslim-governed higher education institutions. The origins of what can be considered Islamic Studies in U.S. higher education goes back to the 'Mohmmaden Department' established in 1911 at Hartford Seminary College (Kurzman and Ernest 2012). There has been a noticeable rise in the number of Islamic Studies programs within university departments over the last decade. A survey conducted by the American Academy of Religion in 2000 found that 299 departments offered an Islamic Studies concentration for an undergraduate degree and a more recent study shows that about half of the thirty-four PhD programs in Religious Studies offer a concentration in Islamic Studies (HEFCE 2008). The majority of these programs started with an Orientalist framework and/or Christian theological perspective (Kurzman and Ernst 2009; Nasr 2009). However, in more recent years, Islamic Studies has expanded to overlap with Middle East area studies, the social science disciplines, and especially religious studies within the humanities. The Hartford Seminary's Islamic Chaplaincy Program is a prominent example of this new approach and concentrates on preparing Muslim chaplains for universities, hospitals, and the military. The Ecumenical Theological Seminary in Detroit has followed in the footsteps of Hartford by launching its Urban Ministry Diploma in Muslim Chaplaincy in 2011 (Khoja-Moolji 2011). Although there has been considerable gains made in Islamic Studies in U.S. higher education, the discipline is limited by Supreme Court rulings to "teaching about Islam" as an academic activity outside of the tradition, as opposed to "teaching Islam" from within the tradition for the purpose of inculcating Islamic doctrines and habits appropriate for an Islamic identity (Kruzman and Ernest 2012; Nasr 2009). Because of this limitation, this chapter focuses more on independent Muslim-governed institutions.

The establishment of independent Muslim-governed institutions of higher education has a shorter history in the United States, but there have been very noteworthy attempts to establish such institutions. Three such institutions currently exist in the United States.

Established in 1981, the Chicago-based American Islamic College (AIC) is the oldest Muslim-governed higher education institution in the United States. It began offering classes in 1983, but the Illinois Board of Higher Education (IBHE) pulled its operating license in 2004 due to the organization's failure to meet the IBHE criteria. After reorganization, in April of 2014, the AIC regained degree-granting authority and enrolled the first cohort of BA and MA students in Islamic Studies (American Islamic College 2014). AIC's mission is to contextualize Islamic Studies for the current global environment by focusing on inter-religious and inter-cultural understanding and is believed to be associated with the Fetullah Gulen's Hizmet movement of schools. Currently the College offers a variety of subjects ranging from the Life of Prophet Muhammad (pbuh), Arabic Calligraphy, History of Christian Muslim Relations, Turkish Art, to Economics, Psychology, and Sociology as part of its program. The faculty, adjunct faculty, and visiting instructors at AIC are mainly Muslim scholars. Prior to renewing its degree-giving authority in 2014, AIC offered nondegree programs in art, language, and Islamic Studies (American Islamic College 2014).

The Graduate School of Islamic and Social Sciences (GSISS) in Virginia, which was renamed Cardoba University in 2005, was established in 1997 with the aim of focusing on the "American experience of Islam." GSISS does not have academic accreditation. According to its website, it offers a Master of Islamic Education degree with a focus on preparing students to meet the challenges of the modern world from an Islamic perspective. The curriculum is based on a framework of *ijtihad*, which the school defines as a method to derive legal rulings from the Islamic sources while taking into consideration the circumstances of the Muslim society. The university's approach seems to be based on reliance on the understanding of the Quran and Sunnah and using the social sciences to inform legal rulings related to the Muslim experience in modern times. According to its website, graduates of the university have become imams of mosques, chaplains for the military, universities, and hospitals; and have pursued careers in academia (Cardoba University 2011; Khoja-Moolji 2011). Currently the university's website and phone are both inactive.

Although AIC and GSISS have a longer history, Zaytuna College has attracted the attention of both the media and academia and has been characterized as the "most influential institution shaping American Muslim thought" (Rachel 2009).

ADVANCING THE DISCOURSE ON ISLAMIZATION OF KNOWLEDGE

In order to understand Zaytuna's contribution to the IOK discourse, it is important to frame the discussion around the foundational constructs of traditionalism and modernization. It is hoped that by focusing on these foundational constructs, a more clear understanding of the opportunities and limitations that the Zaytuna model introduces to the discussion on Islamization of Knowledge can be identified.

Islamization of Knowledge is perhaps one of the most well-known contemporary responses of Muslim intellectuals to the challenge of modernization as manifested in education. The IOK movement can be traced back to the early 1960s in the writings of individuals such as Seyyed Hossein Nasr, Syed Naquib al-Attas, and others. The movement gained international attention as the main focus of the First World Conference on Muslim Education in 1977. However, the crystallization of the movement with its aims and current form can be attributed to the writings of Ismail al-Faruqi's publication of *Islamization of Knowledge: General Principles and Work Plan*, which was published by the International Institute of Islamic Thought (IIIT).

The central assertion of the IOK movement is that modern knowledge is biased toward a Western secular perspective, is developed through methodologies that are not in line with an Islamic worldview, and which promote a secular epistemology. The aim of the IOK movement is to synthesize current knowledge from the perspective of an Islamic paradigm. Two primary mechanisms have been used to accomplish this goal. The first has been the attempt to produce university-level textbooks, following a twelve-step work plan; the second has been to open Islamic universities and institutions of learning. The IIIT mentioned earlier, International Islamic University of Islamabad, International Islamic University of Malaysia, and other such institutions are the result of the second strategy.

IOK has been criticized for not producing a true Islamic alternative. The textbook production approach is largely regarded as a failed attempt, and the Islamic universities are critiqued as simply a recreation of the "Western model" of higher education with an Islamic atmosphere. Proponents of Islamization agree on the aims of the movement. The core area of contention is in regard to operationalization of those aims. Nasr and Ashraf, who are prominent critics of how IOK has developed, identify the lack of sufficiently dealing with epistemological and methodological challenges associated with the synthesis as the main problem with the IOK movement (Nasr 2010).

Traditionalism has several different, but related, conceptual manifestations (Pieper 2008; Shils 1971). Within Islamic discourse, the idea of traditionalism, or traditional Islam, asserts the importance of being connected to a chain of transmission of scholarship, *silsilah*, through which the tradition has been passed down in order to understand the authentic teachings and practices of the religion. Educationally, this translates into teaching using the framework of past scholarship and employing teachers connected to a chain of scholarship that goes back to Prophet Muhammad (pbuh). This theoretical framework is in many ways an extension of the concept of *tajdid*, or revival, within classical Islamic scholarship. The concept of *tajdid* is based on the belief that humanity has to cyclically realign its understanding and experiences to the true understanding of the sacred tradition as embodied in the teachings of Prophet Muhammad (pbuh). In contrast to views of modernization, human progress and development are not viewed as linear and evolutionary, but rather as a process of recalibration to the principles of revelation throughout human history, culminating with Islam. However, this recalibration is not a literal following of a formula, but rather a reinterpretation and situational application of these principles by legitimated scholars (Rahman 1970; Schimmel 1973).

Modernization theory is an evolutionary perspective that defines human progress based on economic growth and places material betterment and mass consumption as the ultimate goal of human development (Inkeles & Smith 1974; Nasr 1987; Portes 1973; Prickett, 2009; Rostow 1991). Modernization theory has been divided into two major categories: the psycho-cultural perspective with a focus on individual beliefs, attitudes, and behavior necessary for modernization, and the structural-functional perspective with a focus on the institutional changes needed to bring about modernization (Inkeles & Smith, 1974; Scott, 1995). Most, if not all, of the individual characteristics of the 'modern' man has been defined in opposition to the 'traditional' man with the perception of authority as a central area of difference. Whereas the traditional individual uses the standards of religion, tradition, and the sacred to evaluate his/her experiences, the modern individual uses the standards of rationality, technical competence, and modern culture to place value on his/her experiences (Inkeles & Smith 1974; Rostow 1991; Scott 1995). This results in the modern individual placing higher value on formal education and science over religion and the sacred (Inkeles & Smith 1974).

On the structural side, emphasis on technology, specialization of labor, and a factory system have all been identified as the institutional characteristics associated with modernization. However, modern mass education is the single most important institution correlated with the modern society. Furthermore, research suggests that more than the curriculum, the function, structure, and operation of the modern educational institution are most closely correlated with development of modern characteristics (Inkeles & Smith 1974). It is believed that modern educational institutions prepare students by instilling in them modern behavior, modern values, and modern ways of knowing (Fuller 1991; Lipset 1994), and societies adopt modern educational institution to signal legitimacy (Meyer & Ramirez 2000).

The concept of IOK provides a primary prism for discussing the Zaytuna College case study. The constructs of traditionalism and modernism provide a more nuanced understanding of the associated challenge and opportunities that the case of Zaytuna College introduces to the discussion of operationalizing the aims of Islamization in higher education.

SPECIFIC CHARACTERISTICS OF ZAYTUNA COLLEGE

Zaytuna College's hybrid identity is composed of Islamic, modern, and distinctly Western characteristics. The Islamic identity of the College is manifested in several ways. The goal of the College to develop a moral, religious, and spiritual person through the integration of a sacred Islamic worldview in all aspects of the educational experience forms the primary Islamic identity of the College. Reliance of the College on the concept of *ijma* or consensus of scholars as a tool to determine religious orthodoxy for religious subjects, and the College's emphasis on having professors who are connected to the tradition by way of having *ijaza* are two important methodological aspects of the College that are uniquely Islamic. Emphasis on Islamic contribution to subjects such as science, history, political thought, and astronomy is another pedagogical approach that adds to the College's Islamic identity. Finally, the creation of an Islamic environment for all aspects of student life, including an all-Muslim student body, prayer facilities, and student activities outside of the academic schedule provides an Islamic atmosphere for the students of the College.

Adopting a professionalized academic management system with bureaucratic procedures that are geared toward evaluations, appeals to professional standards, and most importantly accreditation gives Zaytuna College several distinctive features of a modern organization. Standards are seen as providing vigor, objectivity, and critical thinking. The College is adamant about ensuring the transferability of the diploma for continuation of education in other institutions of higher education. Although utility and transferability of a diploma is not strictly a modern manifestation, its application in higher education, especially its tie to accreditation, makes this an important part of the College's modern identity. The need to address challenges associated with a modern diverse society is another important characteristic of the College's modern identity. The College emphasizes the need to prepare students who understand diverse interpretations within the Islamic tradition, as well as the need for a more gender-balanced system that prepares orthodox female scholars. In regards to gender, it seems that the College has taken a very active and conscious role in ensuring gender equity as one of its unique characteristics. Nine out of the fifteen students in the first cohort at Zaytuna College were female, and the gender representation within the published documents of the College for that year was evenly balanced.

The commitment to the structure of the modern public university is most visible in the catalog of the College. There is very little divergence observed in terms of the structure of course offerings, admission processes, student services, grading policies, honor codes, or tuition and fees. The few instances where divergence is observed are in relation to the honor code where there is an appeal to the Muslim ethos and the "light of prophecy" as the foundations for academic integrity. The policy itself is not different than what would be found at other colleges, especially faith-based institutions, except for the Islamic nature of the codes themselves. In the first years of the College there was more insistence on using modern methods of teaching and not relying on 'traditional methods'. This can be interpreted as a manifestation of commitment to modern structures of education, as well as a mechanism to seek legitimacy within the field of higher education. With the passing of time and maturation of the institution, it seems that the College is experimenting with greater divergence from the dominant public university model. Class schedules are restricted to the mornings, students are restricted to a limit on the number of classes they take, and there are more classes offered by individuals who do not have Western academic credentials.

It is important to differentiate between Zaytuna College's modern and Western identities, because these two are not necessarily synonymous. The College models its curriculum on the two Western traditions of liberal arts and that of the Great Books program. The College's focus on liberal arts is grounded on the classical trivium and quadrivium, which were staples of the classical medieval Western universities. The trivium consists of grammar, formal logic, and rhetoric. The quadrivium consists of arithmetic, geometry, music, and astronomy. Traditionally, these seven subjects were considered essential for a free person in classical antiquity to know in order to participate in civic life. Students at Zaytuna take four courses in Arabic grammar, two courses in logic, two courses in rhetoric, one course in mathematics (which combines arithmetic and geometry), and one course in astronomy. Out of the seven liberal art subjects, music is not taught at the College.

The Great Books program emphasizes reliance on primary sources that are considered as constituting the foundations of Western culture. The catalog elaborates that Zaytuna's challenge is to "provide its students a foundation in the intellectual heritage of not one, but two major world civilizations: the Western and the Islamic." The concept of the Great Books program is operationalized in the College through reliance on both Western and Islamic classics, such as writings of Aristotle and Ghazali and having guest lectures on Islamic classics, such as the Gulistan and Bustan of the Persian poet Sa'di.

DISCUSSION

A significant criticism of the Islamization of Knowledge movement has been the limited number of cases where the praxis of moving from epistemology to methodology is realized. The case of Zaytuna College provides one example where the struggle to synthesize modern knowledge under an Islamic paradigm can be observed and analyzed.

Traversing from discussions of Islamic epistemology to its praxis and its manifestation in methodology has been a fundamental challenge that most works on Islamization have struggled with. Zaytuna College's experience shows one effort where this challenge is being negotiated.

The focus of Zaytuna College on a Western liberal arts curriculum, including a focus on the Great Books, introduces an interesting dimension to the Islamization discourse. Historically, a lot of the Islamization discussion has implicitly equated modernity with Western culture. Adopting a traditional liberal arts curriculum that focuses on the trivium, quadrivium, and the Great Books has helped Zaytuna differentiate between modernity and nonmodernist Western approaches to education and has helped Zaytuna introduce greater nuance to the conversation. This approach allows the College to draw upon the experiences of other communities and institutions that have rejected the dominant epistemology in higher education and have opted for more sacred epistemologies as the foundation of their teaching. This broadening of the field provides the opportunity for more collaborative work with other traditions that have closer epistemologies to Islam than that of modernism, allows for learning from their gains, makes room for the Islamization efforts to influence the greater discourse on alternative methodologies, and also helps in moving the discourse of Islamization from an isolated community to a greater community of similar-minded efforts.

A good number of strategies that Zaytuna has adopted are very similar to strategies that other faith-based institutions in the United States have used in dealing with the challenge of reconciling between the authority of empirical knowledge and the authority of sacred scripture. Zaytuna College has a remarkable grassroots approach from which it draws both financial and general support; the entirety of students, professors, and administration of the College, including the board of directors, is composed of individuals from within the Islamic tradition who are interested in the restoration and preservation of the Islamic identity of the College; the environment of the College is clearly in line with the tradition and ethos of Islam; and the College is using multiple avenues for teaching the tradition, including required courses, a parallel traditional curriculum in the Living Links program, and electives for further enhancement for students. All these strategies are evident in other faith-based institutions.

The emphasis on having teachers with verified chains of transmission, *silsilah*, and the traditional license to teach, *ijaza*, in order to establish legitimacy of scholarship is a unique additional dimension that Zaytuna adds to the praxis of moving Islamic epistemology to methodology. The criterion of the *silsilah* moves beyond a purely philosophical debate on the authority of knowledge and adds a dimension based on human connection. This human connection to determine legitimacy of knowledge can possibly open up areas of reconciliation between sacred authority and empirical observation that might seem theoretically impassable. The use of *silsilah* and *ijaza* at Zaytuna as a mechanism to preserve the tradition is still in its nascent stage, with the College using these two criteria informally. As the College matures, it is important that this aspect becomes more theorized and formalized as a unique contribution to the preservation of tradition.

Literature on modernization asserts that the structure and form of modern institutions of learning have a strong influence in instilling modern characteristics in students irrespective of the content of the curriculum (Fuller 1991; Inkeles & Smith 1974; Lipset 1994). Furthermore, structuration theory claims that institutional forms are adopted not only for the purposes of effectiveness and efficiency but are partly predetermined by the larger structure of organizational fields (DiMaggio & Powell 1983). Zaytuna College's structure is very much that of a modern university. It functions as a corporation, operates based on a rationalized and professionalized academic management system, relies on bureaucratic procedures that are geared toward evaluations, and appeals to professional standards and credentials. Based on DiMaggio and Powell's (1983) arguments, there are many pressures upon institutions like Zaytuna for convergence toward the dominant model of the public university.

Arguments from the structural-functional perspectives of modernization and DiMaggio and Powell's concept of organizational isomorphism suggest that in the long run, Zaytuna College will further resemble the modern university and potentially lose the strength of its unique Islamic identity. However, Zaytuna is challenging these notions and claiming that the structure of the modern university does not necessarily produce one kind of student and that it can be manipulated by having clearly defined goals and objectives to produce students with alternative worldviews. Additionally, Zaytuna's approach highlights the fact that the structure of the modern university is multifaceted and nuanced. While Zaytuna has adopted some central elements of the modern university, at the same time, it is clearly operating based on theistic goals and within the framework of a sacred epistemology.

Zaytuna College's experience reveals that both modernism and Islamic education are extremely nuanced and evolving concepts. The post-modern era has rejected the grand narrative of modernization that human development is linear and should be measured solely on the basis of economic growth. In such an environment, the structural-functional notions lose their vigor with more institutions turning to alternative narratives of higher education and the organizational field of the modern university making room for such alternatives. Additionally, the results of this study reveal that the Islamic concept of education is not rigidly defined and can take many forms. Zaytuna College's experience clearly shows that a general merger between the two concepts is certainly possible. However, because Islamic higher education in general, and Zaytuna College in particular, is a relatively new phenomenon in the United Stated, there are many opportunities to grow and expand the conversation of Islamization.

Zaytuna is the Arabic word for the olive fruit. The founders of Zaytuna College say they chose this name because the olive tree is considered a blessed tree in all Abrahamic traditions, the olive tree has long roots that sink into the earth to draw water, and the olive fruit unlike other fruits has to be treated with experienced human hands to become edible. All three reasons have clear symbolic value that capture the desires articulated in both the College's literature and in the interviews conducted for this chapter. Zaytuna College is envisioned as the olive tree that is nourished by its connection to the sacred sources of Islamic scholarship serving as a bridge to synthesize Western and modern advances under an Islamic worldview, therefore lighting a light that is neither of the East nor of the West (Quran 24:35).

BIBLIOGRAPHY

Al-Attas. 1979. Preliminary thoughts on the nature of knowledge and the definition and aims of education. In Al-Attas (ed.), *Aims and objectives of Islamic education* (pp. 19–47). London: Hodder & Stoughton.

American Islamic College. 2014. AIC website. Retrieved June 14, 2011, from http://www.aicusa.edu

Beaty,B., Lyon, L., & Mixon, S.L. 2004. Secularization and national universities: The effect of religious identity on academic reputation. *The Journal of Higher Education, 75*(4): 400–419.

Benne. 2001. *Quality with soul: How six premier colleges and universities keep faith with their religious traditions*. Grand Rapids, Michigan: William B. Eerdmans Publishing Company.

Boyle, H. 2006. Memorization and learning in Islamic schools. *Comparative Education Review, 50*(3): 478–495.

Bull, C. 1994. Who should pass judgment? *Tribal College, 5*(4): 25–28.

Cardoba University. 2014. Cardoba University website. Retrieved June 14, 2011, from http://www.cordobauniversity.org

Clitheroe, H. 2010. Academic accreditation and the postmodern condition: A critical analysis of practices in postsecondary education. *Journal of Integrated Studies, 1*(1): 1–10.

Dillon, T. E. 1995. Coming after U.: Why colleges should fear the accrediting cartel. *Policy Review,* 72: 39–42.

DiMaggio, P. J., & Powell, W. W. 1983. The iron cage revisited: Institutional isomorphism and collective rationality in organizational fields. *American Sociological Review, 48*(2): 147–160.

Dovre, P. J. (Ed.). 2000. *The future of religious colleges: The proceedings of the Harvard conference on the future of religious colleges*. Grand Rapids, Michigan: William B. Erdmans Publishing Company.

Fuller, B. 1991. *Growing-up modern: The Western state builds Third-World schools*. New York: Routledge.

HEFCE. 2008. *International approaches to Islamic Studies in higher education*. Retrieved from http://www.hefce.ac.uk/media/hefce/content/pubs/indirreports/2008/re0708/rd07_08.pdf.

Inkeles, A., & Smith, D. 1974. *Becoming modern: Individual change in six developing nations*. Cambridge, MA: Harvard University Press.

Khoja-Moolji, S. S. 2011. *An emerging model of Muslim leadership: Chaplaincy on university campuses*. Cambridge, MA: Harvard University.

Kurzman, C., & Ernst, C.W. 2009. *Islamic Studies in the U.S. universities*. Paper presented at the The production of knowledge on world regions: The Middle East, The University of North Carolina at Chapel Hill.

Lipset, S. M. 1994. The social requisites of democracy revisited. *American Sociological Review, 59*: 1–1.

Meyer, J., & Ramirez, F. 2000. The world institutionalization of education. In J. Shcriewer (Ed.), *Discourse formation in comparative education* (pp. 111–132). Frankfurt: Peter Lang.

Nasr, S. H. 1987. *Traditional Islam in the modern world*. London: Kegan Paul International.

Oguntoyinbo, L. (2010). First Muslim college in the U.S. to launch this fall. *Diverse Issues in Higher Education, 27*(7): 10.

Parker, J., Beaty, M., Mencken, F. C., & Lyon, L. 2007. The professionalization of faculty at religious colleges and universities. *Journal for the Scientific Study of Religion, 46*(1): 87.

Pieper, J. 2008. *Tradition : Concept and claim* (E. C. Kopff, Trans.). Wilmington, Delware: ISI Books.

Portes, A. 1973. Modernity and development: A critique. *Studies in Comparative International Development* 8(3): 247–279.

Prickett, S. 2009. *Modernity and the reinvention of tradition*. Cambridge: Cambridge University Press.

Rachel, Z. 2009, May 18. Muslim plan for U.S. college moves ahead. *USA Today*. Retrieved from http://www.usatoday.com/news/religion/2009-05-18-islamic-college_N.htm

Rahman, F. 1970. Revival and reform in Islam. In P. Holt, A. Lambton & B. Lewis (Eds.), *Islamic society and civilization* (Vol. 2B, pp. 632–656). Cambridge: Cambridge University Press.

Ramirez, F. O. 2006. The rationalization of universities. In M. L. Djelic & K. Sahlin-Anderson (Eds.), *Transnational governance: Institutional dynamics of regulation* (pp. 224–245). Cambridge: Cambridge University Press.

Rostow, W. W. 1991. *The stages of economic growth: A non-communist manifesto* (Third ed.). Cambridge: Cambridge University Press.

Schimmel, A. 1973. The sufi ideas of Shaykh Ahmad Sirhindi. *Die Welt des Islams, 14*(1/4), 199–203.

Schuman, S. 2009. *Seeing the light: Religious colleges in twenty-first-century America*. Baltimore: Johns Hopkins University Press.

Scott, C. V. 1995. *Gender and development: rethinking modernization and dependency theory*. Boulder: Lynne Rienner Publishers Inc.

Shils, E. 1971. Tradition. *Comparative Studies in Society and History, 13*(2): 122–159.

Wilshire, B. W. 1990. *The moral collapse of the university: Professionalism, purity, and alienation*. Albany, NY: State Univ of New York Press.

11 The 'Hadith of Gabriel'

Stories as a Tool for 'Teaching' Religion

Steffen Stelzer

> *And I say, what benefit is there in the reform of the tongue without the reform of the heart? Have you seen the one who is content with speech without station, and with speech without action? Does the tongue make you independent of trust, and does news make you independent of seeing? Allah knows best.*
>
> Sh. Alawi, *Knowledge of God*, p. XXVIIf

Describing an educated person in our time will probably not yield the image of a human being well versed in stories. If storytelling is at all recommended as a valid contributor to learning, it is often limited to the education of young children or is reserved a special place under 'therapeutic' methods addressing the constitution of personal identity. In both cases, there is a noticeable reluctance to give storytelling more space, at least as much as would be required for it to help develop differing facilities of the student or a sense of identity more comprehensive than the one often assumed in modern educational systems. Within religious teaching and dialogue, the idea of 'story' as *metaphor* and *moral vision* have been dealt as perennially synonymous. In what follows, we will attempt to explore the value of storytelling as religious pedagogy, with special reference to Islam. What we mean by this is that 'the place of storytelling in Islamic education' is less relevant to this discussion than the possibility of 'thinking about teaching religion' itself as through the medium of story. There are of course several, and often controversial, consequences to such a claim. Among these being a philosophical critique, which would warn against taking (and relating) knowledge from such ambiguous sources. There is also the methodological consideration that if the intention of religious education is to 'learn' religion and not just to learn 'about it' then how does such learning take place? Thinking more broadly about the concerns and the aims of the present book, stories seem to be unstable ground upon which to settle notions of an Islamic philosophy of education.

THE TRADITION OF STORY IN ISLAM

Let us first consider, in illustrating the importance and perhaps need of storytelling within the Islamic tradition, one of the most well-known narrations (*hadīth*) of the Prophet of Islam

Umar ibn al-Khattab said: One day when we were with God's messenger, a man with very white clothing and very black hair came up to us. No mark of travel was visible on him, and none of us recognized him. Sitting down before the Prophet, leaning his knees against his, and placing his hands on his thighs, he said, "Tell me, Mohammed, about submission." He replied, "Submission means that you should bear witness that there is no god but God and that Muhammad is God's messenger, that you should perform the ritual prayer, pay the alms tax, fast during Ramadan, and make the pilgrimage to the House if you are able to go there. The man said, "You have spoken the truth." We were surprised at his questioning him and then declaring that he had spoken the truth. He said, "Now tell me about Faith." He replied, "Faith means that you have faith in God, His angels, His books, His messengers, and the Last Day, and that you have faith in the measuring out, both its good and its evil." Remarking that he had spoken the truth, he then said, "Now tell me about doing what is beautiful."

He replied, "Doing what is beautiful means that you should worship God as if you see Him, for even if you do not see Him, He sees you." The man said, "Tell me about the Hour." The Prophet replied, "About that he who is questioned knows no more than the questioner." The man said, "Tell me about its marks." He said, "The slave girl will give birth to her mistress, and you will see the barefoot, the naked, the destitute, and the shepherds vying with each other in building." Then the man went away. After I had waited for a long time, the Prophet said to me, "Do you know who the questioner was, 'Umar?" I replied, "God and His messenger know best." He said, "He was Gabriel. He came to teach you your religion.

(Bukhari, 37)

This story, referred to as the 'hadīth of the Angel Gabriel,' is well known in Islamic lore and has been amply commented upon as a concise description of the constituents of "*dīn*," namely, *Islam*, *Iman*, and *Ihsan*.[1] Our interest here is, however, not with points of doctrine, but rather with the *teaching* of religion: "He came to teach you your religion (*atākum yu'allimukum dīnakum*)" is how the narration ends. It is therefore of great importance to investigate it as a story, with the desire to 'teach' religion. We may use this *hadīth* as a means to explore the pedagogic relation of 'teacher-student' through storytelling. In order to do so, we can identify the component elements of the story found in the *hadīth* of Gabriel.

a) The Teaching

First, there is the process of teaching or 'what takes place' through the story and consists of what can be witnessed as well as what may not be observed. Neither one is identified as being an aspect of teaching *while it takes place*, but only once it has occurred, suggesting the possibility of witnessing without knowing what is witnessed. In other words, one may say, in the context of the hadith, that:

1. Teaching occurs through *words* (questions and answers), through *appearance* (through the appearance of someone who is identified as teacher), and through *gesture*.
2. The exchange of words, if one may call it an exchange, is not between the teacher and the taught, i.e., the companions of Prophet (*saḥaba*). In the case of the *hadīth* cited, it is between teacher and a third party (the Prophet), while those who are taught are made to witness.
3. Furthermore, the purpose of questioning is not that the questioner finds an answer necessarily. It is to make the *truth heard* (cf. 'Umar's surprise about the questioner both asking and knowing the answer). And it matters that the 'taught' does not become involved in the question-answer process. The answers can, therefore, not be taken as the result of a student's intellectual prowess. The element of capriciousness, which may accompany intellectual effort, is thereby not given room.
4. Finally, the teaching referred to here does not transfer 'from other than you to yourself.' It is a cyclical, supra-hermeneutic disclosure of knowledge as it gives 'from you to you.' In one sense this may be understood as learning what you have known and offers a nondiscriminatory insight into an Islamic pedagogy based upon the idea that *fitra,* often translated as 'nature' also infers a primordial self, which in Islamic theology knew God before being instantiated in the world of matter. To realize your reality (*haqiqa*) is the aim of such a pedagogy.

b) The Taught

The 'taught' are the ones addressed as 'you.' The *companions* (*saḥaba*) of the Prophet in the story are both witnesses and addressees. It is important to notice that they are not characterized by a word indicating *what* they are (their *being*) but by a word indicating whom they are with (their being-*with*). They, the taught, are considered by whom they are with. The relevance of this remark becomes clearer when we remember to what extent reflections on education are guided by concepts of human beings formed in view of their age.[2] If the Prophetic *hadith* of the Angel Gabriel is a story of the teaching of religion, then it is remarkable that the 'taught ones' are not characterized by age, for instance, or any other marker other than being 'companions.'

c) The Teacher

The teacher in the narrative is known as such only after having left. However, there are features chosen (or remembered and told) by 'Umar of his description that shed light on the meaning of naming 'a man' (*rajulun*) 'teacher.' The Angel is described as "a man with very white clothing and very black hair came up to us. No mark of travel was visible on him, and none of us recognized him." Whiteness is usually interpreted in the Islamic tradition as a sign of 'cleanliness.' This teacher would, then, be someone of great purity. The color of hair indicates familiarity, while keeping, at the same time, through the extreme degree of its hue a trace of the unfamiliar. Both the attribution of extreme white and extreme black may also be a way of praising. The perplexity that this teacher causes through being both familiar (man) and unfamiliar (unknown in the city of Medina) finds perhaps its most poignant formulation in the traveler who bears no signs of travel. It is the perplexity resulting from something or someone who is very far and very intimate at the same time.

Let us consider again the aspect of the *hadīth* that describes the teacher sitting down before the Prophet, leaning his knees against his, placing his hands on his thighs, and saying "tell me, Mohammed." The attention paid to the way this teacher sits with the one who serves his teaching (i.e., the Prophet) echoes, of course, a culture in which gestures (and, among these, ways of 'sitting') are highly significant. The touching of knees and, even more so, the placing of hands on someone's thighs are gestures of a familiarity that must have left the companions—that is, those who already enjoy a high degree of familiarity—speechless. But there is, in this perplexity, a profound lesson concerning teaching. For the connection between Angel (teacher) and Prophet is not only established through words (question-answer) but also, and maybe even more so, through what we may call 'the discipline of the bodies.' For there to be teaching (and learning), one has to be, literally, 'in touch.'[3] To sum up these indicators, we may surmise from this important narration some pedagogic dispositions concerning the teaching of religion, namely, that

- The teaching of religion comes from a source that is both far and close.
- The teaching of religion is not only, or mainly, conveyed through words, which are pronounced and heard, but just as much through the gestures and postures of 'bodies' or the physicality of spatial learning.
- The teaching of religion encourages learning that helps to advance in the service of God (*'ibāda*) and not in the performance of mental feats attributable to oneself.
- For teaching to take place, the teacher does not need to be instantly known to the one taught, nor does the fact that he is teaching him need be made ostensible, breaking the accepted ideas of 'student-teacher' dichotomy in a novel way. The presence of the Angel Gabriel is not only relevant for the particular situation of learning described in this Prophetic tradition, but it is also constitutive for all religious education, especially when such education claims to be 'Islamic.'

These points of consideration are important when thinking about the role of story and narration in Islamic education and the possibilities of their translation into actual situations of teaching. To repeat, the hadīth of Gabriel does not only tell a 'story of' teaching, it also intends 'to teach.' If we can agree to call the Hadīth of Gabriel a 'story' in the widest sense and without being, for the moment, too sure of what constitutes the ontological status or the *being* of narrative,[4] the way is open for more extensive reflection. Such reflection will first have to take a step toward the *linguistic* nature of religious teaching, paying particular attention to the linguistics of storytelling, and then take another step toward some of its formulations in an Islamic context. To do so, we shall consider the importance of storytelling for the constitution of meaning in religion and religious education.

LITERARY CRITIQUE AND STORYTELLING

For the acclaimed critic Northrop Frye, it is the "verbal part of . . . culture and civilization" from which stories are primarily derived. Argumentative discourse is only a secondary development to this initial consideration.[5] To understand the character of language and meaning in religion or, at least, in the religion that has shaped his culture, namely, Christianity, Frye traces in *The Double Vision: Language and Meaning in Religion* the "relations of the Bible to secular culture" in order to describe the multileveled paths through which stories "advance in meaning" (Frye 1991, 77). The steps he identifies denote various levels of reading a story or rather, *the* Story, that is, the Bible and includes

- A *metaphorical-literal level* whereby "simply stories [help to suspend] judgement of the imagination without relation to the area we vaguely describe as 'truth.' "
- *The allegorical level* wherein the story "'really means' something expressible in discursive language . . . But the discursive element in allegory keeps something of the divisive 'I must be right and you must be wrong' quality in it . . ."
- *The moral or tropological level* is one in which "the reading of the Bible takes us past the story into the reordering and redirecting of one's life. The clearest example of this kind of meaning is probably the parables of Jesus, explicitly fictions, but fictions that end with "Go, and do thou likewise (Frye 1991, 76–78)."

The advance of the layers of meaning in a story has quite clearly educative connotations. It is understood by Frye as a path in the course of which "natural man" (who "has a body") transforms into a "spiritual being" (who "*is* a body") via inhabiting the various levels of meaning of the narrative (Frye 1991, 53). The levels of advancement here are modeled on the medieval canon of rhetoric. Yet the fact that we live in a culture described as 'secular' does not make this tradition irrelevant. The secular, for Frye, does not make the biblical element of narrative disappear, it only modulates the way it occurs and plays out through it. Although 'the secular' and 'the religious' tend to be addressed separately and sometimes in opposition, it would, therefore, be more appropriate to speak of 'secular-religious education.'

Frye's thesis that our culture and civilization[6] remains, even in its own self-assessment as 'rationalistic' or argumentative, still 'mythic' and 'story-based' has a number of implications for the educationalist and specifically for one thinking of religious education as 'story,' namely, that:

- The educative process of man advances through levels of 'story' in order to reach what we may call supra-rational or 'spiritual' levels of educative meanings that create a "world that the spirit can live in but (. . .) does not make us spiritual beings."[7]
- Education, specifically religious education in a secular context, is education of *a being* called 'man.' The path through which he advances is a path of gradual unfolding, which leads from a being of nature to a spiritual being. Secular-religious educational contexts help man to go through the changes necessary to become fully the being he is meant to be. Consequently, its story of education addresses someone who is on the path from immaturity (childhood) to maturity. It is a circular story in which a detached 'secularized' being returns through a second detachment 'home.'[8]
- Finally, to be truly 'educative,' that is, to go toward "the area we vaguely describe as 'truth,' "[9] a story has to go beyond itself. The most educative story, or the most educative reading, is "the reading of the Bible that takes us past the story."[10]

Let us, with these findings, return to the hadīth of Gabriel and ask if the presence of the Angel Gabriel is only relevant for the particular situation of learning described in this Prophetic tradition or if it is constitutive for all religious education that claims to be 'Islamic.' Given the fact that the angel is said to have come "to teach you your religion," it is at least advisable to assume this. Such a step leads to another question; namely, if we assume that both the 'secular-religious' tradition of education and another one we may call 'religious-religious' are drawn from the same pool of 'storytelling,' can the storytelling of the latter be described in the same terms as the former?

To further an understanding of this question, a citation from Burhān al-Dīn al-Zarnūjī's famous medieval treatise, *Instruction of the Student: The Method of Learning*, proves fruitful:

> It further behooves not to sit near to the teacher during the lecture except under necessity, rather it is essential that the pupils sit in a semi-circle at a certain distance from the teacher, for indeed it is more appropriate to the respect due (to the teacher). And it is necessary in the quest

> of knowledge to be on one's guard against shameful traits of character, for these are the howling dogs of the spirit. The Messenger of God has said: "The angels do not enter a home in which is a dog or a picture." Verily, man only learns through the medium of an angel (*wa innamā yat'allim al-insān bi wāsiṭa al-malā'ika*).
>
> (Al-Zarnūjī *trans.* 2010, 123)

If all learning takes place "through the medium of an angel," as suggested here, then religious education is shaped in every respect by the presence of the 'invisible.' The ascription of particular places to those involved in it, their manners and attitudes toward each other, the very possibility of the transmission of knowledge should be considered in view of it. Further, as important as words may be for it, this education is not defined through or concentrated in its 'verbal part,' as the verbal part is not the main locus of meaning. Knowledge is as much and even more so transmitted through 'being in company' (*soḥba*)—that is, ways of sitting, appearing, and even disappearing. And where it is of importance, the verbal part does not necessarily carry meaning in itself, as it can just as well serve to hold the attention of the students, while the invisible teaching communicates through 'other channels' of perception.

STORYTELLING: AN APPRAISAL FROM CLASSICAL ISLAMIC LITERATURE

It appears that we have to be cautious in applying linguistic-rhetorical concepts of 'story' when we speak of religious education in general and Islamic education in particular. For what should be gained from an understanding of a 'heavenly' religion, that is, of a religion that claims to be of heavenly 'origin,' when the only possible access to it is via a secularized state, that is, in its being moved out of place and brought 'down to earth.' The maxim that 'things are true only in their place' should therefore be applied especially to the analysis of religion under the dictate of the secular. If the teaching of one's religion requires the medium of an angel, then we have to go much further away for the understanding of 'story' than our accustomed categories of literature allow. Much further, that is, and much closer at the same time. We may even have to travel with the traveler who bears no visible "mark of travel" on him and whom "none of us recognized" as the *hadīth* implies. We may have to 'accompany him' to the place of all the Qur'anic stories. For this teacher is, after all, the Angel of Revelation, the angel who, in the Islamic narrative, brought-taught the Qur'an to the Prophet Muhammad. The Qur'an continues:

> All that we relate to thee of the stories of the messengers, with it We make firm thy heart: in them there cometh to thee the Truth, as well as an exhortation and a message of remembrance to those who believe.
>
> (11:120)

This statement and sentiment are clear, yet when reading through the literature that comments on the relevance of Qur'anic stories for learning the religion of Islam, one is, at first, struck by the diversity of responses. They range from a very low appreciation of storytelling, as in al-Ghazali's *Jewels of the Qur'an*, to very high accolades of the purposes of the story of the Prophets, as in the cases of Ibn 'Arabi, al-Tha'labi, and others.

The differences, or rather, the criteria for distinguishing stories, are instructive. For al-Ghazali (d. 1111 AD) the "knowledge of the stories (narrated) in the Qur'an" belongs to the lowest and outermost level of the scale of Qur'anic sciences he establishes in his *The Jewels of the Qur'an.* [11] The positions of the sciences are determined according to the image of the pearl and its shell. Each science is ranked on the shell and on the pith according to its distance from 'the pearl.' It is clear, however, that this ranking is not only determined by the various positions of 'sciences' in respect of their object, but that the positioning itself is based on a concept of knowledge. 'Knowledge,' for al-Ghazali, means ultimately a 'knowledge of God' and this knowledge has a certain character. One is forced to assume, therefore, that "the knowledge of the stories" is not just the furthest away from the knowledge of God because it gives only the faintest gleam but also because it corresponds least to the *idea* of knowledge leading to such a system of classification. For al-Ghazali, the 'knowledges' (*'ulum*) that follow "the knowledge of the stories" include *'ilm al-kalām* (theology), *fiqḥ (*jurisprudence), and following right through to the "knowledge of God" appear to be built on the concept of knowledge familiar from the so-called exoteric or 'rationalist' sciences. In lieu of this classification, al-Ghazali does not, therefore, see great intellectual feats performed by those who tell stories. This is, in itself, significant as it points to the important relation of storytelling with knowledge and to the fact that the relevance ascribed to stories for the transmission of knowledge depends to a great extent on our concepts of knowledge.[12] However, contrary to this position, when asking about the role of storytelling for religious education, we should not forget that it was the Prophet to whom the stories were told; "we relate to *thee* the stories of the messengers" as the Qur'an mentions. It is, therefore, important to try to understand *why* God, in the Quranic narrative, chose to teach His Prophet through stories.

Al-Tha'labī (d. 1036 AD) mentions in the introduction to his classical collection on the *Lives of the Prophets* 'five reasons or insights' why, according to the sages, "God related to the Chosen One the tales of the prophets," and numerates them as follows:

1. In order to manifest his prophethood (the Prophet "had no recourse to any tutor or teacher").
2. To provide models and examples (to follow "the conduct of the prophets").
3. To confirm him and to make known his nobility and his people's worth.

4. To tell the *stories* "as instruction and guidance for his (the Prophet's) people."
5. "To keep [the preceding prophets' and saints'] memory alive," as keeping their memory alive carries award in itself (Al-Tha'labī *trans.* 2002, 3).

As regards the Prophet, we could say that these 'reasons' confirm him in his prophethood, that is, in the role chosen for him. They give him divine assurance concerning his mission where his humanity may make him doubt by placing him under the instruction of the invisible (the angel) and linking him to a chain of human beings. If we listen, for a moment, to what is conveyed in these 'insights' we can assume that God taught him, or better, that He taught him by telling him stories. The importance in the process of learning, in Islamic contexts, of 'chains of transmission' (*isnād* in the transmission of hadīth or *silsila*, as the chain of masters or 'inheritors' of knowledge) is relevant here, as the story itself stands to act as a kind of perennial transmission. There are also reasons mentioned by al-Tha'labi that seem to be reserved for teaching the companions of the Prophet or, more generally, those with him ("his people"). Yet these reasons can equally apply to whoever hears them. For in hearing and reciting the "you" of "We relate to thee," as the Qur'an mentions, one cannot prevent oneself from feeling addressed, if only for a moment, before acknowledging that the "you" here is the Prophet. It is a "you" of *qiṣṣaṣ*, of storytelling, that invites one into the company of those whose stories you are told, by way of your care or *love* for them. In this sense, and *through that love*, we can say that education through the stories of the Prophet is also an 'education.' That learning without tutor and teacher is also learning and that through these stories we are invited to follow the conduct of those whom we love.

Al-Tha'labi's fifth insight locates the benefit of storytelling in itself. To tell stories is an act of remembrance, and remembrance keeps and strengthens the companionship of the faithful with the Invisible:

> He told him the stories of the preceding prophets and saints to keep their memory and legacy alive, so that those who do well in keeping the saints' memories alive assure themselves thereby a speedy reward in this world, in order that the saints' good renown and legacy may remain forever.
>
> (Al-Tha'labī *trans.* 2002, 5)

This list of al-Tha'labi's reasons for God telling stories could be considered complete if it were not for another purpose of storytelling, namely, to keep the preceding prophets' and saints' "memory alive." Al-Tha'labi continues that 'men are tales' and that "no man dies but mention of him revives him" (Al-Tha'labī *trans.* 2002, 5). In this reading, the life of humankind, namely, the life of this world and the life of the next, is told, rehearsed, and mythologized, not because we *tell* stories to each other or do not or because we may *use* stories for education or not, but rather because we *are* tales.

We pointed earlier to how closely our various concepts of education—and education itself—are tied to what I would call the question of 'our humanities'; that is, the question that asks wherein the humanity of man lies. One may answer it by saying that man is a storyteller and that he becomes most humane through an education advancing in the levels of understanding the meaning of 'story.' In the case of al-Tha'labi's addition, he does not suggest that man should tell stories and advance in their comprehension but that men are stories, which poses the question of who then tells their story? Within Islamic thought it would seem that it is the One who told the Prophet and that whoever tells stories, for as long as men do tell stories in this spirit, we do not have to worry about Islamic education marginalizing the role of the 'story.'

The question of the place of meaning in regard to stories deserves to be looked at again. The great mystic and thinker, Muḥyiddīn Ibn 'Arabi (d. 1240 AD), writes in his *Unveiling from the Effects of the Voyages* (*Kitāb al-isfār 'an natā'ij al-asfār*) regarding his own particular way of reading Qur'anic stories that:

> I only speak of it in regard to my essence/self. I'm not trying to give an exegesis of their actual story (in the Qur'an). For these journeys are only bridges and passageways set up so that we can cross over them (or "interpret" them) into our own essences/selves and our own particular states. They are beneficial to us because God has set them up as a place of passage for us: "Everything that We recount to you of the stories of the messengers is so that We might strengthen your heart through that. For through this there has come to you the Truth and an admonishment, and a Reminder to all the worlds" (Qur'an 11:120). And how eloquent is His saying that "there has come to you through this the Truth" and "a Reminder" of what is within you and in your possession that you have forgotten, so that these stories I have recounted to you will remind you of what is within you and what I've pointed out to you! For then you will know that you are everything, in everything, and from everything.
>
> (1995, 105)[13]

This reading of 'story' as providing a bridge to oneself, or to one's Self, is comparable to Frye's view of man as advancing from the "man of nature" to man as a "spiritual being" insofar as both authors try to propose ways for finding meaning through stories. The difference, in Ibn Arabi's case, is, however, that meaning is not sought in the story but in the one to whom the story leads ("in my essence/self," *fī dhātī*). This 'human being' is separated in himself and from himself and is, therefore, in need of being 'bridged.' He cannot, however, provide by himself the means to make this connection. What connects is, according to the Islamic mystical tradition, the God-*sent* that is the story. But as stories still need to be told, the connection must be realized and the bridge has to be *crossed*. Ibn 'Arabi gives detailed descriptions of this 'crossing' (*'ubūr*) in many places. When, for example, he praises the divine eloquence of the phrase "there has come to you through this the Truth," he indicates that the interpretation of the Qur'anic story does not search for meaning *in the story*, but this means 'taking truth sent to its addressee' and that storytelling is the way to do this. It is for this reason that stories are bridges and that interpreting them is an important, perhaps the most important, pedagogic exercise, as the Qur'an states, "So relate the stories that perhaps they may *reflect (fa-qṣiṣ al-qaṣaṣ la'allahum yatafakkarūn)*" (7:176).

CONCLUSION

This chapter has attempted to explicate the importance and contribution of storytelling as a means of teaching religion. Using the '*hadith* of Gabriel' as a case study, a close reading of its narrative structure, its lessons, and insights on audience help to rethink traditional ways of understanding student-teacher relations and knowledge-flow in a pedagogic environment. Although opinion differs as to the efficaciousness of such a tool, brought to light from interjections from no less a figure than al-Ghazali, who placed the activity of storytelling at the lowest rung of the intellectual ladder, its historical importance is made clear through the *hadith* itself. How this may translate into contemporary approaches to pedagogy is a thought experiment to be performed and one, which offers exciting possibilities for modern education. Doing so requires, as with Frye's work, to first rethink what we mean by story as a means of relating meaning. In doing so there ought to be a distinction made between what one may call normative or 'mere' storytelling on the one hand and the elaborate search for meaning from stories on the other. This distinction need not ensue an evaluation of one activity as 'higher' and the other as 'lower' necessarily, but rather the appreciation of the role the intellect and heart have in the search of knowledge. Although both engage and encourage different kinds of learning, the act of storytelling in the prophetic instance is perhaps a way of moving inside a tradition and to appreciate it from 'within.' It is this meaning that we may draw from the *hadith* of Gabriel as a path toward understanding the world of 'religious meaning' and be reminded that formal learning remains significant but that, interestingly, the Qur'an does not mention such activities while it imperatively states "tell the stories (*fa-qṣiṣ al-qaṣaṣ*)" (7:176).

NOTES

1 Cf., among more recent examples, Murata and Chittick whose *The of Vision of Islam* is in its completeness an interpretation of this prophetic tradition (Sachiko Murata and William C. Chittick, *The Vision of Islam*, [I. B. Tauris, London, 2006], p. XXV).

2 That is, education of *what* they are: what we call 'children' or what we call 'grown-ups'?

3 It must be stressed, again, that the hadith of Gabriel does not describe this contact as the one to exist between teacher and taught, but between teacher and Prophet.

4 Such insecurity forbids us to claim for our remarks on storytelling in this text the status of a 'narratology.' Mieke Bal has given a concise formulation of the problem of narratology when she says "But it seems that with the growth of the study of narrative, interest in what makes narratives 'be' or 'come across' as narrative has only declined. Partly, narratology is to blame for this discrepancy . . . " (Mieke Bal, *Narratology, Introduction to the Theory of Narrative,* 3rd edition [University of Toronto Press, Toronto, 2009], p. XIV).

5 "Man doesn't live nakedly in nature the way that animals do. He lives inside a transparent envelope that we call his culture or his civilization. The verbal part of that culture or civilization consists of stories that express his central concerns about himself, his destiny, and his nature, and also about the origin of his society. These become theological or political arguments later on, but they begin as stories in a culture where everything is concrete. When the arguments develop, they often repress the fact that they are in fact later developments of stories." "Storytelling," Interview No. 56, in: *Interviews with Northrop Frye: The Collected Works of Northrop Frye*, Vol. 24, ed. by Jean O' Grady (University of Toronto Press, Toronto, 2008), p. 512.

6 Which implicitly or explicitly means always 'Western' or 'Christian.'

7 N. Frye, *The Double Vision*, op.cit., p.16. The latter is the function, precisely, of another kind of stories, "the New Testament myths": "The literary language of the New Testament is not, like literature itself, simply to suspend judgement, but to convey a vision of spiritual life that continues to transform and expand our own. That is, its myths becomes, as purely literary myths cannot, myths to live by; its metaphors become, as purely literary metaphors cannot, metaphors to live in." (N. Frye, *The Double Vision*, op.cit. p. 17f.)

8 One can call the loss of "the vision of Gods," with its ensuing installment of the "world of facts and demonstrations and reasonings" a first detachment. The second detachment, the literary one, detaches through its metaphoric language in turn from this world. Finally, in a third stage of development, foreshadowed for Frye in William Blake's poetry, "the vision of gods comes back in the form of identity with nature, where nature is not merely to be studied and lived in but lived and cherished, where place becomes home" (Frye, *The Double Vision*, op.cit., p.83f.).

9 Cf. footnote 10.

10 Cf. footnote 12.

11 That is, the level of "knowledge of the stories (narrated) in the Qur'an and of what is related to the prophets, to the deniers (of God) and to His enemies. Storytellers, preachers, and some oft he Traditionists (*al-muḥaddithūn*) are responsible for this kind of knowledge. The need for this knowledge is not universal." (*The Jewels of the Qur'an*, Al-Ghazali's Theory, transl. by Muhammad Abul Quasem, [Kegan Paul International, London, 1983], p. 38.)

12 Al-Ghazali himself is a prime example for the changes our understanding of what presents 'knowledge' may go through. If it were possible, one should address the question about the value of "the knowledge of stories" again to the writer of the *Munqidh min al-Dalal* (The Deliverance from Error).

13 English translation by James Morris of a passage from the French translation of *Ibn 'Arabi: Le dévoilement des effets du voyage*. Texte arabe édité, traduit et présenté par Denis Gril; Editions de l'Eclat, 1994, p. 50. Morris's translation occurs in his review of this book in *Journal of the Muhyiddîn Ibn 'Arabî Society*, vol. XVII (1995), pp. 103–105.

BIBLIOGRAPHY

Al-Zarnūjī. 2010. *Instruction of the Student: The Method of Learning* transl. by G.E. von Grünebaum & Theodora M. Abel in *Classical Foundations of Islamic Educational Thought,* selected and introduced by Bradley J. Cook, Brigham Young University Press, Provo, Utha.

'Arā'is al-Majālis fī Qiṣaṣ Al-Anbiyā' or "Lives of the Prophets" as recounted by Abū Ishāq Aḥmad Ibn Muḥammad Ibn Ibrāhīm al-Tha'labī, transl. and annotated by William M. Brinner; Brill, Leiden, 2002.

Bal, Mieke. 2009. *Narratology: Introduction to the Theory of Narrative*; 3rd edition. Toronto, Canada: University of Toronto Press.

Fyre, Northrop. 1991. *The Double Vision: Language and Meaning in Religion.* Toronto, Canada: University of Toronto Press.

The Jewels of the Qur'an. 1983. Al-Ghazāli's Theory, transl. by Muhammad Abul Quasem, Kegan Paul International, London.

Murata, Sachiko and Chittick, William C. 2006. *The Vision of Islam.* I.B. Tauris, London.

O'Grady, Jean (ed.). 2008. "Storytelling: Interview No. 56." In *Interviews with Northrop Frye*; *The Collected Works of Northrop Frye*, Vol. 24, pp. 521–517. Toronto, Canada: University of Toronto Press.

Part IV

Contemporary Debates

12 Principles of Democracy in American Islamic Schools

Susan Douglass and Ann El-Moslimany

Binary discussions about whether Islam is capable of accommodating 'secular' schooling or is compatible with 'democracy' will not yield much insight. The issue can only be understood against a social-historical background of Islamic education in the United States and an exploration of what is meant by 'democratic' education, how it fares in the public schools, and how it relates to Islam and Islamic education. Giving specific examples from U.S. Islamic schools, we will show that the most basic understanding of living as Muslims—tawhid (unity), taqwa, (God-centeredness), fitrah (God-endowed human nature), khilafa (the intended role of humanity as representatives of God), and salam (peace)—when applied to educating Muslim children encompasses many of the same principles endorsed by the advocates of democratic public schools. The schools that we portray are not unique. They were chosen because we happen to be familiar with them through our own work in Islamic education over the past several decades.

ISLAMIC EDUCATION IN THE UNITED STATES

A typical Islamic school in North America is professionally oriented, has fewer than one hundred students, is less than six years old and growing, and is independently governed. Most teachers are certified and despite their recent founding, many schools are accredited. Principals are usually expected to have considerable experience and an advanced degree (Keyworth 2011).

Aside from these general similarities, Islamic schools in the United States vary considerably. At one extreme, there are a few schools patterned loosely on the South Asian madrassa system, which emphasizes memorization of the Qur'an and a limited range of basic subjects. On the other end of the spectrum is a small group of schools similar to progressive, private-education models, comparing most closely to some charter or alternative schools. At the center, and in the majority of some two hundred Islamic schools in the United States, are those that closely model their curriculum upon what is taught in the local public schools. Islamic schools, like those other religious schools, append classes in religion, offer opportunities to worship during the school day, and infuse their value system with moral and ethical training within the school's culture and across the curriculum.

The considerable variation in Islamic schools largely reflects the diversity in the backgrounds of American Muslims. The relative influence of representative stakeholders is a major factor in determining the educational philosophy of each individual school. Many Islamic schools were established or are primarily supported through donations by immigrant Muslims, often technical professionals, doctors, and engineers who are financially well established. Personal reawakening of religious values was part of the immigrant experience and has motivated them to establish Muslim institutions for their children. Further motivation comes from the fear that their children will lose knowledge of and loyalty to Islam if sent to public schools and that they will be culturally lost to the temptations of gender-permissive American society. As refugees from political and economic stagnation, these immigrants often adopt a critical stance toward their homelands. However, this is unlikely to extend to an alternative vision of education. Many equate quality education with the standardization based on the colonial models of their home countries, dependent on memorization and rigorous testing. They are likely to value the education—preferably in a technical field—that they themselves received. They tend to transfer this valuation to trusting the model of public education in their adopted country. Progressive educational models may seem like a risky and uncertain, if not frivolous, venture.

More than one-fourth of Muslims in the United States are African American. They include multigeneration Muslim families whose paths to Islam are varied. A significant proportion came to Islam—sometimes several generations ago—through the heterodox Nation of Islam (NOI). In the 1930s, the NOI founded the first Islamic schools in North America. The primary purpose was to teach African American children to know, love, and help themselves in an atmosphere away from the oppression of the public schools where they were shut out from the mainstream of American society. Following the death of the NOI founder Elijah Muhammad, the succession of his son Warith al-Din, and the move toward more traditional Islam, these schools, originally called the University of Islam, but actually elementary and secondary schools, were renamed the Clara Muhammad Schools in memory of the wife of Elijah Muhammed who had been the first teacher (Rashid & Muhammad 1992). The concern regarding social ills—particularly within urban public schools—and the importance of a solid education for economic advancement and sustainability are held in common with immigrant Muslims. However, unlike immigrant Muslim parents, their skepticism toward public education models opens them to more innovative forms of education.

Another smaller group includes first-generation converts to Islam among Euro-Americans, many of whom are active in Islamic education. Because of their conscious decisions to accept a new way of life and their own experiences with the public schools, they are inclined to be more critical of public education and postcolonial school systems. Additionally, they are less likely to indiscriminately assume that how things are done in any particular Muslim country is the 'Muslim way.' Among the African Americans, the white converts and the adult descendants of immigrants who are raising their own children and generally have a broader view of education than their technology-riveted parents, there is sufficient common ground for reconsidering the models within which Islamic education functions and rethinking its philosophy. Schools in which these groups dominate often teach in a way that is consistent with those Islamic values that also align with democratic ideals (Douglass 2015).

'DEMOCRATIC' EDUCATION

The primary purpose of the public school is said by many to have been instilling the practice of democracy in American children (Goodlad 2005; Kovalik 1997; McDonnell, et al., 2000; Tyler 2005). These advocates agree that, although content is important, merely teaching about democracy is not sufficient. More important is to have the structures, processes, and environment that bring democracy to life within the school. There is agreement among those who actively promote democratic education that democratic schools must have a holistic view of the child, of the world, and of humanity; that cooperative, project-based learning prevails over individualism and competition; and that assessment, also, is noncompetitive, ongoing, and individualized. There is general agreement that the democratic educational experience requires choice, freedom, equity, communities of varied age, and an integrated curriculum with deep learning (Apple & Beane 2007; Beane 1997, 2005; Darling-Hammond 2010; Goodlad et al., 2004; Meier 2003; Sizer 2013).

Some would disagree that the primary purpose of public schools was to instill democracy (Callahan 1962; Gatto 2000; Katz 1976). They have argued that it is more accurate to identify capitalism as the foundation of early public education, with schools established and managed on a factory-based model to train compliant workers for wealthy industrialists. This early system was gradually replaced by what Brady (2010) has called the corporatization of our schools and what Henderson and Gornik (2006) referred to as the Standardized Management Paradigm (SMP).

Whatever the original purpose, very few public schools today can be considered democratic schools in the sense discussed earlier. The top-down, externally imposed standardized curriculum, the preparation for and administration of increasing numbers of tests have squeezed teachers into a system that not only labels students but is also linked to their own lack of autonomy, job security, and school funding. Beane (2005, 15) lamented,

> If it seems that there is less room for local educators to make curriculum decisions . . . if it feels like teaching has lost its moral meaning, if it feels

> like there are more mandates and fewer resources, . . . if it feels like the school is becoming a corporate hierarchy . . . then welcome to the brave new world where the new accountability movement is taking us . . .

Jeremy Henzell-Thomas (2005), a well-known Muslim educator in the United Kingdom, has described British government schools in a way that bears a striking resemblance to Beane's depiction of U.S. public schools. He spoke of "a gradual process of attrition, constriction and ultimate strangulation, culminating in a sterile, standardized, bureaucratic system that demoralizes students and teachers alike . . ."

ISLAMIC AND DEMOCRATIC EDUCATION COMPARED

In spite of the authoritarian regimes that govern much of the Muslim world, there is no basis for assuming that democracy is alien to an Islamic worldview. Abou El Fadl (2004) noted that important Qur'anic values are best achieved through a democratic form of governance. These include (1) the pursuit of justice, (2) a consultative methodology, and (3) the institutionalization of mercy and compassion. Feldman (2004) reviewed the opinions of a wide-ranging group of Muslim scholars who promote democracy. Although they differed on many details, all agreed that Islam requires justice, equality, human dignity, pluralism, consultation, the rule of law, the selection of rulers by the ruled, and that specific conditions must be in place to protect the minority from an unjust majority. Obviously the primary goal of Islamic schools is not to instill democracy per se but to encourage the beliefs, practices, understanding, and commitment to living as a Muslim in today's world—principles that, however, neither negate nor fundamentally differ from democratic principles but encompass many of the same values endorsed by the advocates of democratic public schools. Moreover, under the present strict controls that govern the public schools, Islamic and other private schools have considerably more freedom to teach according to their ideals.

MODELS OF DEMOCRATIC/ISLAMIC EDUCATION

There are a number of individuals, organizations, and pedagogical systems that currently provide models of democratic/Islamic education. Particularly significant is the work of Dawud Tauhidi. In 1980, as a young American convert to Islam, Tauhidi returned to the United States after graduating from the Islamic university Al-Azhar in Egypt. He found that children leaving Islamic schools often knew a great deal about Islam but not how to live as Muslims. He devoted the remainder of his life to developing the Tarbiyah Project, an Islamic vision that aligns closely with the ideals of democratic education. He stressed the importance of hands-on activities, higher-order thinking skills, choice, authentic assessment, and real-world connections and applications. He stated that effective Islamic education must address the real concerns and needs of students, spiritually, emotionally, intellectually, and physically, and be integrated across time, place, culture, and range of topics. He attributed to these integrative aspects:

> the far-reaching potential of truly enhancing the power of Islamic teaching and learning (and thus making it genuinely tawhidic [based on the unity of God]) . . . This view is rooted in belief that the mission of Islam is to positively effect and transform the world, and the purpose of Islamic education is to prepare young men and women capable of carrying out this mission.
>
> (Tauhidi, 2001)

Tauhidi's project, although never published in complete form due to his untimely death, is known and held in high esteem by the body of Muslim educators and is prominently featured on the web page of the Islamic Schools League of America (ISLA 2015). Significant progress was made toward implementing this system through the efforts of Sommieh Flowers at Crescent Academy in Canton, Michigan, who worked out practical means of realizing these ideas.

Several complete systems of education are described as holistic, because they look at the world, humanity, knowledge—and especially the child—as a whole. The holistic approach that characterizes them has an equivalent in the unity inherent in Islam. The advantage of adopting a methodology that can accommodate an Islamic approach is that a specific program in which training, materials, manuals, and conferences are available is far more accessible than a theoretical concept. Among these holistic pedagogies is the Montessori system. Evidence of a move toward Islamic/democratic values can be seen in the growing number of Islamic Montessori schools. Founders and administrators give as the reason for their choice a number of ideals consistent with Islam. The Islamic concept of fitrah is most often mentioned. It is a fundamental tenet of Islam that children are born pure and close to their Creator prepared to live as God intends. Montessori has fully incorporated this concept into her whole philosophy of education, viewing the child as good and pure and in need only of gentle guidance, physical protection, and the right environment for development. She aptly described the Islamic concept of fitrah when she said:

> . . . hidden in their hearts is something deep, common to all. All have a tendency, however vague and unconscious, to raise themselves up; they aspire to something spiritual . . . there is a tiny light in the unconscious of mankind, which guides it toward better things.
>
> (Montesssori 1965, 209)

Such an understanding promotes trust, allowing students to take responsibility for their own learning, assume active roles within the school community, and to participate in decision making.

Fitrah comes to be realized by the individual's acceptance of the role as vicegerent of God (the Qur'anic meaning of the term khalifah). Similarly, Montessori taught that unlike other elements of creation that automatically fulfill their God-given roles, humanity has been given the task of improving the world. She emphasized that it is the responsibility of each person to fulfill his or her "cosmic role." Montessori's notable emphasis on peace and peace education is based on the concept of the unity of humanity.

Many individual Muslim educators are contributing to models that apply basic principles of Islam and in the process make our schools more democratic. Here we specifically identify examples of men and women who, often in the face of great difficulty, have remained constant in their promotion of the pedagogical practices that encompass Islamic and democratic principles. Mary El-Khatib founded and ran the El-Iman school in Virginia in the year 2000. Over the years of innovating on her own, she became drawn to and then committed to Montessori. She developed a model of Islamic Montessori education in her classroom, and took up formal Montessori training at the Barry School in Maryland. She now runs her own small, independent Islamic Montessori school. Susan Douglass worked with her as teacher and curriculum developer to build a middle and high school program that, while not based on Montessori methods, sought to integrate the school subjects and place responsibility for learning in the students' hands. Salahuddeen Abdel Karim is an educator with long experience and deep affiliation with Islamic school development, administration, and teaching throughout the DC area. He initiated many activities designed to build civic awareness, critical thinking, and participatory democracy. Matthew Moes has devoted himself to many years in Islamic education as teacher, founder, principal, and now as a consultant. He has been a strong advocate of applying the most basic of Islamic principles to how we teach Muslim children. Sommieh Flower, long-time principal at the school founded by Dawud Tauhidi worked with teachers to breathe life into his model developing training and assessment. She continues her work in a small school in India. Nadeem Memon in Toronto and Karen Keyworth in Michigan have each originated programs to further the improvement of Islamic education. Karen was an originator of the Islamic Schools League that brings educators of Islamic schools together through a listserv and conferences. Nadeem has originated a program, the Islamic Teacher Education Program (ITEP), centered in Toronto. ITEP trains teachers for Islamic schools and offers online webinars. A third organization, Council of Islamic Schools in North America (CISNA) also holds regular national conferences for educators. Many of the examples that we give originated from the efforts of these individuals.

CIVIC ACTION

In addition to course work in civics and U.S. history, students in Islamic schools throughout the United States are involved in political activity. Several Islamic schools have participated in voter registration drives. Others have traveled to state and federal capitals to meet their representatives. Urban schools often make use of public transportation to visit a city council meeting or to take a trip to the courthouse to observe legal proceedings. Regular and routine debate sessions are common.

New Horizons School (NHS) in Pasadena, California, is well known at city hall because of frequent field trips to observe local democracy in action. They have also reached out to civic organizations, presenting a plaque to their local fire department. Miftaahul Uloom Academy in Jersey City, Mohammad School in Atlanta, and Al Fatih in Reston, Virginia, are regular participants in mock U.N. meetings, as well as in mock trials sponsored by state bar associations. In a mock trial, students play the roles of attorneys and witnesses preparing and presenting evidence for a hypothetical case in a real courtroom. The *Dallas Morning News* published an article on the Qur'anic Academy in nearby Richardson. The article reads in part, "While civics lessons teach about democracy, in schools themselves, orders come from above," said Matthew Moes, principal of the Quranic Academy, an Islamic school in Richardson. "It's really too bad. It's a really big irony," he said. Mr. Moes wants his kindergarten through ninth-grade school to be different. The academy and six others in Texas are members of First Amendment Schools, a national network that aims to get students involved in community decisions, usually through a bigger role in school administration.

In an era when the hot question is, "How are students' test scores?" the nation's 101 First Amendment Schools ask, Do students understand their rights? Can they think critically about real-world problems? Can they work together on policies that affect them? Each First Amendment School decides for itself how best to emphasize freedom of speech, religion, press, petition, and assembly. As head of an Islamic academy, Mr. Moes is aware of his school's connection to America's democratic principles, particularly freedom of religion. 'The First Amendment is at the heart of what makes the Muslim community live and flourish peacefully,' he said. 'It's exciting for us to . . . show how a Muslim school can embody those democratic principles' (Schreier 2006).

Muslims embrace their role as loyal citizens of this country, but as in all schools based on religious teachings, their first allegiance is to God. NHS has modified the pledge of allegiance, putting God before all else, but at the same time pledging loyalty to family and their government:

> As an American Muslim, I pledge allegiance to God and His prophet. I respect and love my family and my community, and I dedicate my life to serving the cause of truth and justice. As an American citizen with

> rights and responsibilities, I pledge allegiance to the flag of the United States of America, and to the Republic for which it stands, one nation under God, indivisible, with liberty and justice for all.
>
> (So 2006)

AUTHENTIC ASSESSMENT

Democratic schools are urged to use authentic assessment, employing project-based learning in which students design and perform real-world tasks that apply their understanding and skills. Students should always be involved in evaluating their own work, as it is only in this way that they develop the ability to judge their mastery of any task. Those Islamic schools affiliated with Montessori are naturally committed to authentic assessment. Intrinsic motivation is encouraged. Competition, judgment, punishment, and rewards are absent. Although there are no grades, assessment is an ongoing process with close written daily observations. The hands-on learning materials have been designed to be self-correcting. The child easily sees any error and is able to make the corrections without any help.

One way to encourage authentic assessment is through presentations and debates. Salahuddin Abdel Kareem has developed debating techniques over his long teaching career. Debate is one area that exemplifies a real-world task that requires application of skills and understanding. Successful debate requires learners to become critical evaluators and analysts of what they hear and see in the mass media and in the real world. It provides deep exposure to less prominently featured news stories and an environment that welcomes diverse perspectives, emphasizes speaking and writing, develops self-confidence, and encourages the students to stay abreast of local and global news. A rubric for assessing students on debating might include all of the skills and understanding that debating is expected to develop.

INTEGRATION OF THE CURRICULUM

Beane (1997) has characterized curriculum integration as "the core of a democratic school," emphasizing, as did Tauhidi, that the curriculum should be based on real concerns of personal and social significance. The integrated curriculum is the logical result of applying the fundamental Islamic belief in the unity of knowledge. Knowledge in real life doesn't exist in disjointed unrelated fragments but is complex, interconnected. Writing, science, history, geography, politics, current events, "Islamic Studies," and even math, naturally became a part of most themes as the artificial boundaries between subjects dissolved.

Although Muslim educators are well aware that religious and secular knowledge are not separate entities in Islam, the majority of Islamic schools remain committed to the separate study approach of Western education, even using textbooks designed for public schools. There has, however, been considerable progress in recent years toward integrating Islam throughout the curriculum. Amira Al-Saraff, principal of the Pasadena NHS, described how she wove a part of California history, the accomplishments of Cesar Chavez, into an Islamic Studies class.

The children at Nur Montessori worked within a theme on gardening. They prepared a budget, planned advertising, and raised money by conducting yard sales and auctioning their artwork to buy garden supplies, including a worm composter and a rain barrel. Their physical education was tilling the soil, pulling and digging weeds, carrying water, and acting out seed germination to music. Designing and making ceramic stepping-stones and markers, learning to arrange flowers, recording through sketching was their art. They tested soil, measured the area and perimeter for fencing and soil. They studied parts of the seed and the life cycle of plants and pollinators and investigated controversies around pesticides and GMO organisms. They carried out their own research to determine (1) which parts of various plants are edible, (2) which plants discourage pests, (3) the global spread of edible plants, and (4) the use of the "three sisters"—corn, beans, and squash by the Native Americans. This way of studying what today we classify as 'science' exemplifies the Islamic (and Montessori!) view of creation, the intricate cause and effect networks that exist among all physical entities—the ayat (signs) of God; signs that the Qur'an urges humanity over and over again to seek, contemplate, understand.

The Islamic School of Seattle (ISS), an Islamic Montessori school with which Ann El-Moslimany was involved on many levels, also had a thematic curriculum. To go on extended field trips as part of their themes, the middle-school students raised money by holding bake sales, pizza sales, and by selling popcorn and drinks at free weekly films that were open to the public. A study of glaciers, ice ages, and the poles culminated with a trip to Mt. Rainier National Park, where they explored real glaciers, following the streams that emerged from them to the river and then to the sea. On two consecutive years, the children spent several days at Olympic National Park enrolled in a special program for schoolchildren. One year this took place in conjunction with a theme on rivers. They hiked to two dams in the Olympic Mountains that were soon to be torn down to allow the return of spawning salmon. While at the park, the children visited a nearby reservation of Native Americans who were anxiously anticipating the return of the salmon that are such a basic part of their culture. A theme on 'the Restless Earth,' plate tectonics, earthquakes, and volcanoes was climaxed with a trip to the Mt. St. Helens volcano. Field trips result in deep learning. Whereas a teacher might have used the time to cover considerably more material, the impact of these experiences trumps covering information by passive reading or listening, which rarely becomes a part of long-term memory. Not every school has access to spectacular national parks, but each locality has something to offer. Schools in the DC area are blessed with being close to the hub of national government and to national organizations and often take advantage of all this has to offer. Students at the Muslim Community School (MCS) with Salahuddin participated in a program, "Forty Community Leaders in Forty Schools," in which national leaders came into schools to meet with the students. El-Iman students accompanied a mayor from a small village in Palestine to Congress to present pinwheels for peace they had made, requesting protection for a kindergarten that was under demolition orders. It remains standing and operating to this day.

DIVERSITY AND EQUALITY

A classroom that prepares students for democracy . . . values and thrives on the kind of diversity on which a healthy democracy also thrives" (Goodlad, et al., 2004, 87). The Islamic concept of the unity of humanity is equivalent to the fundamental democratic principles of diversity and equality. The Qur'an says, "O Humanity! I have made you separate tribes and nations only that you may come to know one another." These words govern the attitude of Muslims toward others. An Eid celebration, or a Friday mosque in a large city, will reveal Muslims from all over the world. Muslim schools mirror this. This may be very unlike their own parents' experiences in their home countries, and with conscious guidance, this diversity can foster democratic understandings and behavior.

Diverse opinions and views are also part of a democratic classroom and welcomed in most Islamic schools. Students learn to honor different ways of thinking in a positive way. At Nur Montessori, students resolve conflicts with each other at the Peace Corner using steps that are proactively taught and modeled. Students learn to recognize and express their feelings and speak assertively to defend their rights and the rights of others. The teacher is involved only at the request of the students.

Islamic schools also make conscious efforts to involve their students with children outside of the Muslim community informally or through local, state, or national activities for school-age children—for the educational content, but also for the positive impact of interaction among children from different backgrounds. Nur Montessori is participating with other schools in collecting native seed to protect the Chesapeake Bay Watershed. ISS had a special relationship with Nova, an alternative public high school across the street. Once the middle-school children were invited for a vegan lunch prepared and served by the Nova students, some of whom were tattooed and pierced. As they walked back to the school, one of the girls was asked what she had learned. "Well," she said, "I learned what vegan is and that although some of those kids look really weird they are still, in lots of ways, just like us."

Islamic schools also make a practice of meeting on an equal basis with those of other faiths. Beginning in kindergarten, children from two Pasadena faith-based schools—one Jewish and one Muslim—get together. They stay in touch as they progress through school. Louis Cristillo (2009), in his study of Islamic schools in New York City, noted that all three Islamic high schools offered courses in comparative religion. They meet with students from other faith-based schools and hold interactive assemblies. Al Fatih children in Virginia have worked with the Mennonite Church assembling relief kits and letters of prayer for children in Iraq and with the interfaith community at Washington National Cathedral. Salahuddeen Abdel Karim took high school students to Georgetown University to listen to a lecture by then Cardinal Theodore E. McCarrick, who had just returned from an interfaith fact-finding trip to Europe during the crisis in Bosnia in the 1990s. Following the 9/11 tragedy, his students at the Muslim Community School in Maryland (MCS) sponsored a forum in which local government officials, community members, and leaders representing at least four major religious communities came together to offer their condolences to family members and others whose loved ones were victims of that disturbing moment in American history.

RESPONSIBLE COMMUNITIES OF LEARNING

Apple and Beane (2007, 11) described those involved in democratic schools as participants in diverse communities of learning, including people "who reflect differences in age, culture, ethnicity, gender . . . class and abilities." Islamic schools are generally small, and there is a family-like atmosphere with considerable mixing of ages. Children may socialize with teachers, as well as with classmates and their families outside of the school environment. Because Islamic schools are not under the direct control of the state or school districts, there is naturally a more level form of governance fostering cooperation among teachers, between teachers and the administration, and between parents and the school. In general, Islamic schools actively reach out to the local community, as well as to the global community. Guest speakers as well as other visitors are common.

In Islamic schools that have chosen to pattern themselves on Montessori pedagogy, the classrooms themselves are mixed age. At Nur Montessori, students take turns leading the morning meeting and a weekly gathering in which they acknowledge each other's caring or achievements, bring up concerns, and agree upon solutions as a community. They set their own weekly academic and personal goals. The teacher and student meet together to review goals and plan their work contracts for the upcoming week.

Community extends beyond the school to their neighborhoods and cities. It is especially important for Muslims, as a largely misunderstood minority, not to isolate themselves but to be a part of their surrounding community. Neighbors may feel uncomfortable when a new mosque or Islamic school is proposed. This was the case when NHS was being built in a residential neighborhood. One family that dubbed themselves "the Urban Homestead" was particularly apprehensive. Those at the school learned that this family was caring for the environment in a very fundamental way, to an extent far beyond what most Muslims are doing. The description from their web page describes their project,

> . . . , a family operated . . . real-life working model for sustainable agriculture and eco-living . . . For over a decade, we have proved that growing ones' own food can be sustainable, practical, successful and beautiful in urban areas. We harvest 3 tons of organic food annually from our 1/10 acre garden while incorporating solar energy and bio-diesel . . . to reduce our footprint . . .
>
> (Urban Homestead 2015)

As stewards of the earth, it is common for children in Islamic schools to participate in recycling and composting, but here was an opportunity to move far beyond these simple efforts. As the school community reached out, the family at the Urban Homestead overcame their reservations. Today the children meet four days a week with the homesteaders on a project called "From Farm to Table" in which the children learn about sustainable use of the land, lessons they are applying to their own school garden. The home-steading family meanwhile is becoming acquainted with Islam through their almost daily association with these very open and outgoing children.

For more than thirty years ISS students participated in the annual Seattle Martin Luther King Day activities, attending workshops and joining the parade, even carrying the banner at the lead. They also marched in demonstrations and participated in celebrations with other groups. Each spring they held a successful carnival for both the neighborhood and the Muslim community. These efforts have resulted in more than acceptance. At one time the Seattle School District attempted to take over the ISS property through eminent domain. The neighbors, completely on their own, circulated and presented a petition to the city council stating that the school was integral to the neighborhood and that they opposed its removal.

The results became particularly significant after the terrible events of September 11, 2001. When the ISS children returned to school, they found the parents, teachers, and students from the public high school across the street lining the entryway. As each child, parent, or teacher entered, they were handed a rose. Meanwhile, the Seattle Council of Churches patrolled the neighborhood, and two street musicians parked their camper in front of the school and slept there for days, keeping watch. In the following months, educators from several private and public schools asked to exchange visits. The most horrifying event in recent U.S. history had given these children the opportunity to come to know one another as fellow American children.

A large number of non-Muslim neighborhood children attended the low-cost, quality preschool at ISS. Several remained for elementary school.

Shortly after September 11, 2001, the administration was invited to attend services at a poor, predominantly African American Church. In spite of struggling to move from their rented building, they had taken up a collection to help a group suffering from the events of September 11. They chose ISS in thanks for its commitment to the neighborhood children.

THE QUEST FOR JUSTICE

Apple and Beane (2007, 13) emphasized the importance of democratic schools taking a stand "against racism, injustice, centralized power, poverty and other gross inequities in school and society" (13). Recognizing and fighting injustice is of course fundamental to Islam. The Qur'an admonishes, "O you who believe! Stand up firmly for justice . . . even against yourselves, or your parents, or your kin."

Islam teaches that faith alone is never sufficient but must be accompanied by action. The very purpose of humankind to assume the role of vicegerent or khalifah of God is primarily accomplished through seeking justice, justice for all of humanity, as well as for the rest of creation.

In every community there are those who have devoted their lives to working for justice and are happy to come and share their stories with children. MCS in Maryland invited the former chairperson of the United States Commission on Civil Rights. She shared with the students the importance of working for justice for everyone, regardless of their race, religion, culture. She answered questions, listened to what the students had to say, and offered suggestions. Later, the students had the opportunity to join her for lunch. To further students' understanding of the struggles faced by African Americans, the director of African and African American Studies from George Mason University was invited to the school, helping the students understand an important part of American history that is often downplayed.

U.S. history themes at ISS were usually presented from the point of view of minorities. A theme focusing on groups who have been mistreated because of their ethnicity or beliefs culminated in a trip to the WWII-era prison camp in Minidoka, Idaho, accompanying the local Japanese community, some of whom had been held there during World War II. The children became acquainted with their Japanese traveling companions and heard their stories. Although the theme did not directly address Islamophobia, a refrain heard throughout the trip was, "We will never let it happen to you."

Within Islamic schools, scouting, service learning, global education, programs emphasizing justice and democracy abound. Some have specific community service organizations. Medina Academy in Bellevue, Washington, has their Sadaqa (charity) organization; Crescent Academy in Michigan their Children of Charity; Al Fatih in Reston, Virginia, calls their group Kids Giving Salam. Some schools have formed chapters of larger service organizations. Al-Noor school in Flushing, New York, has a branch of Key Club International. Miftaahul Uloom Academy has a branch of the Beta Club, another national service organization. Universal Academy near Chicago has a school chapter of the Chicago-area Inner-City Muslim Action Network (IMAN), which means faith in Arabic. Within each of these programs, children develop projects to help those in need. Students in schools without specific service-oriented organizations volunteer in food banks, take part in neighborhood cleanups, collect warm clothing, and participate in flood or earthquake relief. Often these projects involve working with other community and interfaith groups.

We have shown through examples of Islamic schools that many democratic principles are also Islamic principles. The examples we have given here of Muslim educators working to instill Islamic values in the children they teach and those educators we have cited as being committed to 'democratic' schools have much in common. Both groups are devoted to the principles they hold dear, both have thought deeply about their goals and how best to attain them in spite of considerable obstacles. Moreover, both groups are aware that teaching through example and practical experience triumphs over merely teaching facts—about democracy or Islam.

BIBLIOGRAPHY

Abou El Fadl, K. 2004. *Islam and the Challenge of Democracy.* Princeton University Press.

Apple, M. & Beane, J. 2007. *Democratic Schools, Second Edition: Lessons in Powerful Education* (2nd ed.). Heinemann.

Beane, J. 2005. *A Reason to Teach: Creating Classrooms of Dignity and Hope Paperback*. Heinemann.

Beane, J. 1997. *Curriculum Integration: Designing the Core of Democratic Education.* Teachers College Press.

Cristillo, L. 2009. The Case for the Muslim School as a Civil Society Actor, pp. 67–83. In F. S. Y. Haddad, *Educating the Muslims of America.* Oxford University Press.

Darling-Hammond, L. 2010. *The Flat World and Education: How America's Commitment to Equity Will Determine Our Future.* Teachers College Press.

Douglass, S. L. 2015. Developments in Islamic Education in the United States, pp. 237–250. In Yvonne Y. Haddad and Jane I Smith, *The Oxford Handbook of American Islam.* New York: Oxford University Press.

Feldman, N. 2004. The Best hope. In K. Abou El Fadl, & J. C. Chasman (Ed.), *Islam and the Challenge of Democracy* (pp. 59–68 Koshu COHEN). Princeton University Press.

Goodlad, J. 2004. *A Place Called School.* McGraw Hill.

Goodlad, J. 1994. *What Schools Are For* (2nd ed.). Phi Delta Kappa Intl Inc.

Goodlad, J., & Goodlad, C. M.-B. 2004. *Education for Everyone: Agenda for Education in a Democracy*. Jossey-Bass.

Henzell-Thomas, J. 2003. *Identity and Dialogue: Spiritual Roots and Educational Needs.* 10th Annual International. Conference on Education, Spirituality and the Whole Child. University of Surrey Roehampton. London.

Islamic Schools League of America, 2015. Accessed January 8. http://theisla.org/.

Karp, S. & Christensen, L. 2003. *Rethinking School Reform, Views from the Classroom.* Rethinking Schools Press.

Keyworth, K. 2011. *Islamic Schools of the United States: Data-Based Profiles. Institute for Social Policy and Understanding.* 2011 Institute for Social Policy and Understanding.

Kovalik, S., & Wolgemuth, K. O. 2005. *Exceeding Expectations: A User's Guide to Implementing Brain Research in the Classroom by Susan J. Kovalik, Karen D. Olsen and Kathleen Wolgemuth* (3rd ed.). Susan Kovalik & Associates, Inc.

Manzoor, S. P. 1991. Studying Islam Academic, pp. 40–57. In Z. E. Sardar, *How We Know, Ilm and the Revival of Knowledge.* London.

Meier, D. 2002. *The Power of Their Ideas: Lessons for America from a Small School in Harlem Paperback by Deborah Meier (Author).* Beacon Press.

Nature Bridge, 2015. Accessed January 8. http://www.naturebridge.org/school-group-environmental-science-olympic

Rashid, H. M.–1. 1992. The Sister Clara Muhammad Schools: Pioneers in the Development of Islamic Education in America. *The Journal of Negro Education* 61 (2), 178–185.

Schreier, L. 2006. "Islamic School's Focus is Rights, Community, Democracy." *Dallas Morning News,* August 20.

Sizer, T. Sizer, N. F. & Meier, D. 2013. *The New American High School.* Jossey-Bass.

So, H. 2006. "Muslim School Reaches out to its Community." Retrieved May 7, 2015, from New Horizon School, Pasadena: newhorizonschool.org. July 5.

Tauhidi, D. 2001. "The Tarbiya Project, an Overview." Retrieved from Islamic Schools League of America.

Urban Homestead, 2015. Accessed January 8. http://urbanhomestead.org/.

13 Religious Pluralism and Islamic Education

Addressing Mutual Challenges

Sarfaroz Niyozov

This chapter attempts to analyze the developments, challenges, and possibilities that emerge from the encounter between religious pluralism and Islamic education. My analysis is grounded in research, teaching, and community activities that have centered on Islamic education in the last ten years. I have highlighted a number of themes, issues, and questions that I see as critical to establishing a deep or maximalist pluralist religious education. I build on Waghid's (2014) concept of maximalist pluralism as a discourse of reflexive engagement of competing epistemologies, difficult knowledges, and tensions reflected by critical pluralist religious educations.

I start with a brief description of pluralism as a concept due to the recent emphasis on it as the new panacea of addressing diversity and equity. Next I present a sketch of achievements and gaps in how Canadian public education addresses religious diversity through its multicultural framework in Ontario. Next I highlight some international pluralist efforts in religious education, including Islamic education. I consider both Canadian and international efforts as minimalist approaches to religious diversity because of their gaps in addressing the key tensions between Islamic education and pluralism. I take the reader through four interlinked sets of challenges and tensions between religious education and pluralism: (i) epistemological/ontological, (ii) political/economic, (iii) pedagogical-structural, and (iv) global. Without resolving these tensions, pluralist Islamic education will remain as another abstract idea with little relevance, practicality, and sustainability. I conclude that a successful project of pluralist religious education has to be maximalist (engage critically and constructively the foundational beliefs, values, and practices), comprehensive (i.e., embody all of the forms of religious education), consistent across all religious communities (not just Muslims), and harness the religious-secular and the local-global cooperation.

THE PLURALIST TURN IN EDUCATION

Pluralism has become a new global catchword in the era of globalization. Pluralism is tasked to ensure the productive coexistence of not just diverse, but even antagonistic positions and attitudes held by individuals, religious, cultural, and ideological groups; acculturate these groups and institutions toward moderation and avoidance of extremist positions; engender sustainable development; and create inclusive, peaceful, and just education and society.

As the further development to similar frameworks such as internationalism, multiculturalism, and cosmopolitanism, pluralism supposedly subsumes the advances previous progressive scholarship and policy making on all imaginable differences and divergences, including gender, class, age, and sexuality. Pluralism claims the status of a new grand narrative with policy or pedagogical implications. According to Eck (2002) pluralism:

(i) is not diversity alone, but *the energetic engagement with diversity*. Diversity can and has meant the creation of religious ghettoes with little traffic between or among them. Whereas religious diversity is a given, pluralism is not, and needs to be achieved;

(ii) is not just tolerance, but *the active seeking of understanding across lines of difference*. Tolerance is a virtue, but it does not require Christians and Muslims, Hindus, Jews, and secularists to know anything about one another. Tolerance is too thin a foundation for a world of religious difference and proximity. It does little to remove our ignorance of one another, and leaves in place the stereotype, the half-truth, the fears that underlie old patterns of division and violence;

(iii) is not relativism, but *the encounter of commitments*. Pluralism does not require us to leave our identities and our commitments behind, for pluralism means the encounter of these commitments, the holding our deepest differences, even our religious differences, not in isolation, but in relationship to one another.

(iv) is *based on dialogue, give and take, criticism and self-criticism*. Dialogue means both speaking and listening, and that process reveals both common understandings and real differences. Dialogue does not mean everyone at the "table" will agree with one another.

Pluralism's key feature has been addressing religious diversity and creating a field called religious pluralism, which can be defined as an attitude or policy regarding the diversity of religious belief systems coexisting in society (Silk 2007), and as "respecting the otherness of others" and accepting the given uniqueness endowed to the created world (Waghid 2014). It can indicate (i) a worldview according to which one's religion is not the sole and exclusive source of truth; (ii) an acceptance of the concept that two or more religions with mutually exclusive truth claims are equally valid; (iii) the exclusive claims of different religions turn out, upon closer examination, to be variations of universal truths that have been taught since time immemorial. Legenhausen (2005) found two types of Muslim religious pluralist discourses: (i) Reductive, which builds on common and positive aspects of all religions, echoes the ecumenical position, subsuming Christians, Jews, and even Zoroastrians into an ecumenical discourse. Here all these communities represent different paths to the same God (Boase 2005); and (ii) non-reductive, which portrays Islam as tolerant and pluralistic and respectful of other religions, yet at the same it being God's first and final, true and absolute religion and therefore other faith adherents are invited to join it before it is too late for them to redeem. Both reductive and non-reductive strands draw from Qur'an, hadith, and other sources within their tradition (Ayoub 2005). Importantly, Muslim scholars see no problem in this second, exclusivist approach, because they believe their judgment of others is based on the absolute sources of truth (e.g., Aasi 2009). There is an abundance of rhetorical pronouncements about pluralism in Islam and among Muslim leaders and scholars, which substitute the reality of Muslim societies, regretfully filled with anti-pluralistic, intolerant practices toward every imaginable other: non-Muslims, women, Muslims of different racial, linguistic, and ethnic backgrounds (Doumato & Starrett 2006). Rhetorical statements such as "Islam has always been cognizant of diversity and has addressed it before and better than the West has done"; "Islam understood religious pluralism long before the Western world, and the reason the Western world is having such problems with pluralism is due to the westerners never having understood religious pluralism" (Hofmann 2005, 240–241; see also Sachedina 2001; Sardar 2011, 235–244), are not sustainable in the face of contradicting realities that indicate the triumph of non-pluralist positions across most Muslim societies. Overall, most of the discussions on Islamic pluralism are the 'ought to' or call for, rather than the reality on the ground. This rhetoric-reality gap is noticed by the Aga Khan (2008) who is a key supporter of, and investor, in Islamic pluralism:

> [we] are seeing more and more around the world, no matter what the nature of the conflict is, that ultimately there is a rejection of pluralism as one of the components, whether it is tribalism, whether it is conflict amongst ethnic groups, whether it is conflict amongst religions. The failure to see value in pluralism is a terrible liability.
>
> (145)

In sum, genuine pluralism in the Muslim context remains a hope, grounded in seeds from their traditional textual sources and historical precedents.

THE CONTEXT OF CANADIAN PLURALISM

Canadian policy makers and educators have accepted pluralism as the advancement of multiculturalism. Bramadat and Seljak (2005) highlighted the contradictory effects of the secular multiculturalism of Canadian schools as a response to accommodate religious pluralism. They pointed out that the current liberal approach to both multiculturalism and religious diversity has flaws such as (i) lack of consensus over the goals and ends of multicultural education; (ii) the heightened concerns for individual rights, presumably violated by the presence of religion in the schools; and (iii) the possibility of students becoming entrenched into their particular identity.

Secular multiculturalism in Canada and the United States primarily implied de-Christianization of public schools with the hope to avoid hurting other cultural groups and developing a sense of common civic-secular national citizenship through public schools. To the surprise of Canadian policy makers, these minorities wanted not removal of religions, but the extension of these privileges to them. They wanted their religions and cultures to be reflected in the public schools while their faith-based schools were to be funded in ways similar to the Catholic schools (Memon 2012). Seljak (2005) furthered that the study of religions disappeared with the secularization, even from subjects such as history and society. This led to the distortion of Canadian history, as well as to religious illiteracy (Sweet 2002). As a result, we have children who do not understand their religion, the religions of their fellows, and are unable to understand the religious underpinnings of world events. "Children are taught to respect what they don't understand" (Seljak 2005, 188).

These and other assertions have apparently signaled the need for acknowledging the presence of religion in the Canadian public sphere. Islamic education scholars have argued that religion is deeply intertwined with affect, practices, relationships, and ways of life, areas that require engagement through an enabling school environment, where students are not discriminated against for their religiously motivated dress code, behaviors, and relationships with each other and their teachers.

The reality of Canadian education shows that there is a lot of religious activity going on in schools. There is abundant evidence from the existing research (Niyozov 2015) to say that the secularization has not pushed the religious out of public schools. First, Catholic schools have not vanished, despite some calls to abolish them. They are strongly supported by the Canadian state across almost all the provinces, except Newfoundland. Ontario Catholic board schools are viewed as offering better education than the secular schools in terms of quality, safety, community outreach, and extra-curriculum support. Many Muslim parents have enrolled their children in these Catholic schools. Second, not just students, but even some of teachers in the public schools are highly religious and do not leave their religiosity at the school doors (Zine, 2008).

Like Sweet's (1997) participants, participants in my research also brought God to their classrooms; spoke about creationism and considered evolution as a theory/perspective rather than the truth; taught students to abstain from active sexual activity; discouraged them from dating; asked them to not revolt against their conservative parents; shared their religious views in the classroom and respectfully challenged those religious voices when they arose, and continuously learned about Islam from their students, parents, the school board consultants, the Internet and broader literature. They had high opinions and expectations from most of their Muslim students; supported them against bullying and Islamophobia; disliked the media's negative portrayals of Muslims; did not support Western interventions and wars in Muslim-majority countries; helped their Muslim students succeed academically and socially; and taught them how to deal with police and law; included topics about Muslims and Islam in their teaching through students' individual projects (i.e., students' projects about Prophet Muhammad, Avicenna, Jinnah, the Aga Khan), current affairs (e.g., war in Afghanistan), and Muslim literature (The Kite Runner; Naguib Mahfooz); debated about gender equality (e.g., the case of Aqsa Pervez); exposed their monotheistic students to a variety of Islamic interpretations, cultures, and ways of life and to different and difficult knowledge from Greek mythology, to Shakespeare, to racism, discussed the questions of terrorism, domestic violence, and sexuality; insisted to parents that their children have to visit a theatrical show; allowed students to bring the idea of creationism into the classrooms; asked them to tolerate homosexuality and not judge others; and accommodated their students' parents' fears about overnight trips and theater visits. Muslim students are permitted to be exempt from classes during their religious holidays, have access to halal food, and be exempt from physical education activities where girls and boys may touch each other physically. Muslim students are allowed to pray at schools' cafeterias or prayer rooms, attend mosques, and leave for hajj; they are allowed to observe their dress codes such as hijab, grow beards, and wear a kufi. Since 2012, the Ontario Education Ministry declared February as Muslim month. During this month, Muslims proactively suggest to their schools speakers, books, shows, and other activities to present the positive side of Islam and Muslims' achievements.

There are, however, serious gaps between the policies regarding accommodation. Students' and community needs and policy pronouncements are not easily and proactively fulfilled in all schools. There are few special structures and resources in place. It takes Muslim students, their associations, the support of Muslim and supportive non-Muslim teachers, and the pressures from parents to move things beyond policies. There might be very few (if there are any at all) public schools where there is a designated prayer or meditation space. There are forces and groups in Canadian society and schools who openly oppose religious intrusion in the 'secular' schools. One such well-publicized resistance occurred in 2011 against the use of a school cafeteria in a public middle school in Toronto. The demonstrations and the polarized media debated the value and wisdom of using the secular public school for Muslim prayers, the way girls participated in prayer, the prayers' impact on non-Muslims and Muslims with different prayer practices, the content of the prayer and the Friday sermon conducted by an Imam from a nearby mosque, and whether Muslims were being overaccommodated over other cultural-religious groups (Friesen & Hammer 2011; Globe and Mail 2011).

Whereas reasonable accommodation is rooted in the struggle of the religious communities against anti-religiousness, prejudice against the newcomers, and Islamophobia, it has also been critiqued as a weak concept that reifies the *us versus them* divisions and does not tackle the hierarchical inequalities, power relations, internal divisions, and discriminations within the cultural communities (Beaman 2012).

RELIGIOUS EDUCATION INSIDE CLASSROOMS: THE CASE OF WORLD RELIGIONS

In addition to the aforementioned accommodations, academic engaging about religion has been another policy development. As early as in 1960s, the Ontario government's commission examined the situation and recommended that moral education ('character building'), information about and respect for all religions, and a *formal course* of study dealing with the world's principle religions with pre-service and in-service training in moral or values education and in religious education be provided (Watson 1990). Accordingly, almost all Canadian provincial education ministries and school boards have introduced an academic subject entitled *World Religions* in classrooms at the secondary level. An examination of the *World Religions* syllabus for Ontario Grade 11, university/college preparation reveals the following ideas relevant to religious pluralism: At the level of *objectives*, the course aims to enable students to discover what others believe and how they live, and to appreciate their own unique heritage. Students are expected to learn about the teachings and traditions of a variety of religions, connect religion and development of civilizations, and study the place and function of religion in human experience and contemporary society. Thematically, the course areas include: (i) religious beliefs; (ii) historical backgrounds; (iii) practices, rituals, symbols, and festivals; (iv) social structures, religions, and human experience; (v) significant figures; (vi) present and future roles of religion; and (vii) research and inquiry skills. Within these themes, the overall and specific expectations are identified. For example, within the area of *religious beliefs*, the relevant overall expectations include an analysis of the similarities and differences between the central beliefs of various religions. In the specific area of *historical background*, the expectations include the identification of the influential personalities such as Abraham, Baha'ullah, Christ, Confucius, Dalai Lama, Guru Nanak, Moses, Muhammad, Siddhartha Gautama, and Zoroaster and a summary of their contributions to the development of selected religions (Watson 1990, p. 128). In the area of *practices, rituals, symbols, and festivals* the overall expectations include *the categorization of the practices and rituals of various religions* (e.g., call to prayer, almsgiving, asceticism, atonement, anointing, covenant, sacrifice, holy days, dietary laws, vision quest) and identification of the origin and significance of these various practices, rituals, symbols, and festivals. Within the social structures, the overall expectations include (i) an understanding of *religious pluralism as a defining feature of contemporary Canadian society*; (ii) identification of the ways *in which religion is reflected in specific works of art, architecture, music, literature, dance, and in dress and cuisine, and how to interpret their religious significance*; and (iii) listing the diverse religions represented in Canada and analyzing how the high degree of religious pluralism in the population is reflected in Canadian society and culture (130). Under the theme of *religion and the human experience*, the overall expectations include *the recognition of prejudices associated with, and misconceptions about, various religions, beliefs, and traditions* and an understanding of a variety of belief systems (e.g., secular humanism, materialism, agnosticism, atheism). In the area of prejudices and misconceptions, the specific expectations include identification of religious leaders who used religion to oppose prejudice and discrimination (e.g., Martin Luther King Jr., Mohandas K. Gandhi, Marcus Garvey, Jesus Christ, Guru Nanak, Muhammad) and how they opposed these prejudices, as well as analysis of how positive and negative attitudes within religious traditions have been used to justify local and global prejudices and biases. A critical look at the aforementioned shows that, whereas a lot of pluralism-related themes and expectations are formulated, the assumption is that there are no contentious issues and no contradictions will emerge from the comparisons and exposure.

An analysis of the textbook on *World Religions: Canadian Perspectives* in my graduate course showed that it provides rich basic information about religions such as Zoroastrianism, Buddhism, Jainism, T(D)aosim, Hinduism, Buddhism, Sikhism, Judaism, Christianity, and Islam. The textbook is illustrated, interesting, and provides personal stories of how the adherents of these religions practice their faith in Canada. The overall message is that religions are positive and important factors in the individual and communal lives in Canada. All these religions are portrayed as preaching peace, harmony, and interfaith dialogue. Critically, my students found the textbook to be scholastic, lacking diversity, avoiding tensions and controversies, and presenting the dominant views. Another textbook, *World Religions: Peoples and Faiths* (published in 1994) has its fifth chapter on Islam called *Islam in Trafford*. This chapter moves around the life of a Muslim high schoolboy, Hanif, a goalie of his high school team, who, in response to the negative remarks and curious questions about Islam and Muslims from his colleagues, undertakes the project of deeper understanding of Islam and presenting it. The result is a Sunni–Arab-centric narrative. Even though it is a rich response to Hanif's non-Muslim friends and foes, it predominantly marginalizes and demeans non-Arab and non-Sunni Muslims (e.g., negatively describes Shi'as, Iranians, Hezbollah, and Ahmadis, while remaining silent on the Salafis, al-Qa'ida, and Afghan Mujahedins). In sum, Canadian efforts at meeting diverse religious demands, including the recent reasonable accommodations, have been producing some positive effects, but have fallen short of a pluralist approach.

PLURALIST ISLAMIC EDUCATION: FROM TENSIONS TO POSSIBILITIES

The first set comprises epistemological-ontological problems of defining pluralism and understanding it. Pluralism is often confused with terms such as plurality, diversity, tolerance, multiculturalism, cosmopolitanism, and spirituality. Internally, there are secular and religious, maximalist and minimalist, reductive and inclusive, deep and thin pluralisms. Whereas all these definitions prove the inevitability of diversity, they challenge the possibility of arriving at consensus on the concept, as Eck suggested earlier. Is it possible that the plurality of pluralism subverts its own promise of a committed engagement? How can one assert that religious pluralism is a divine injunction in the face of absolutist and excusive claims to truths and ethics? How can we move beyond viewing deep pluralism as a minorities' trick of survival, recognition, and self-legitimization? How can we rely on a universal understanding that pluralism, when it as a social construct, might be a tool for the survival for some and control for other groups? In sum, how can we pluralistically develop a consensus on pluralist religious education in the predominantly post-modern and post-structuralist intellectual conditions? Pluralism undermines positivist thoughts, established truths, and absolutist categories, notions of unity, monotheism, and ultimate reality. It has never been easy to acknowledge theological and sectarian divergences in any religion, including Islam. Acceptance of plurality of truths and considering them as provisional as a key quality of deep pluralism would suggest that every Islamic concept, beginning from the nature and meaning of God to his attributes, to prophecy and authority, and every other tenet of Islam is contested, multiple, and, at times, contradictory. This may imply accepting that there is no single but many Islams. How do we differentiate between single sacred reality and its multiple interpretations? What are the implications for Muslim scholarship, especially educational, to acknowledge the non-positivist methodological and epistemological approaches that suggest that knowledge is an imperfect human construction and that human's individual and social-contextual constructions of multiple meanings, i.e., multiple Islams, are inevitable (Geertz 1971; Sardar 2011).

Pluralism acknowledges human agency in interpretation of religion and democratizes the process. This challenges the *ulama* and *imams*' monopoly of interpretation of the foundational sources (Sardar 2011), but it may also undermine established criteria for judging what is right and wrong to individualism and relativism, destabilizing the structural-functionalist features of the Muslim identity and community.

Muslim educators need help with addressing post-modern questions such as "there is no objective reality"; or "all knowledge is a social and linguistic construction, inherently containing within itself the ideological assumptions of whoever constructed that knowledge" (Jackson 2004b, 62). El Fadl (2002) proposed that religious pluralism "does not mean that Muslims are required to regard other faiths and belief systems as equally true in the theological sense." Rather, he suggests, Muslims should accept that holders of other faiths or of no faith have a right to assert the validity and truth of their basic beliefs and values, and even claim it as the only true way, just as Muslims can. No faith community should be forced in any way to compromise the integrity of its belief system in order to be part of this admirable code of coexistence and mutual respect for the choices of fellow human beings (Fadl 2002, 147–48). El Fadl does not address the possibility that a young Muslim student may (similar to non-Muslims' conversions to Islam), by choice or deliberation, decide to modify or change his religion. How then could such change be tackled within the principles of *bid'a* (innovation) of *ridda* (apostasy)? In addition, El Fadl's idealistic suggestion of the coexistence does not admit that faithful Muslims may develop antagonistic understandings toward the other and subsequently act on their understanding; for acting on one's belief is a clear Islamic message. In sum, how energetic is the engagement with this theological diversity; the move beyond the doctrinaire pronouncements; the reflexivity about one's bias; and the inability to see the dichotomy and complexity among Islamic scholars, religious and community leaders as Eck (2002), Sardar (2011), and Waghid (2014) propose?

The second set of challenges is political—economic. Religious differences and truth claims are not just about meanings but also power, politics, and economics, hierarchy and structure that benefit some and exclude others. Religious leaders accrue enormous political and economic benefits from their communities. Pluralism at its deep level may lead to the switch of one's allegiance, which may result in a loss of economic and political power for these religious-political leaders. Most of Muslim scholars and leaders have taken the minimalist pluralism, i.e., allowing for pluralism as long as it does not challenge the held beliefs, structures, and power. How much are Muslim and other religious leaders prepared to accept the possibility that their followers become non-followers or shift their loyalties?

The third set includes pedagogical paradoxes, such as the dearth of pluralistic texts, materials, and strategies about religious ideas in the face of the abundance of non-pluralist (at times extremist) education materials on Islam and Muslims online. Whereas there are some genuine attempts, such as the U.S.- based materials on Islam and Muslims developed by the Council for Islamic Education, led by Susan Douglass's lateral world history approach; school-friendly texts for primary and early secondary age texts by Rukhsana Khan, Debora Ellis, and Ludmila Zeman in Ontario; and an innovative secondary curriculum by the institute of Ismaili studies in London, these resources follow minimalist pluralism, such as listing diverse Muslim groups, mostly present non-theological diversities, and sterilize controversial topics. Similarly, public schoolteachers need guidance in how to choose 'proper' education materials from the vast ocean of information on the Internet, because they feel unprepared to conceptualize the multiple and contradictory layers of religious diversity (e.g., individual students' perspectives, students' ethno-communal perspectives, and global theological perspective). One of my study's participants indicated that he prefers to engage students' personal perspectives:

> Encountering [Muslim students] as Muslims is the worst kind of stereotyping. As far as I'm concerned, it is racist. It is racism no matter how well meaning it is. Encountering them as Islamists is totally ridiculous because most of these young people have no philosophical and theological foundations. Who would? What young Christian has studied theology? I mean, yes, many young Muslims have learned how to recite the Qur'an, but that doesn't make them masters of Islam. I encounter them as young people that want to be educated and successful in their lives. I'm not there to validate their faith, to make the assumption that they are only Muslims and nothing else. I'm there to provide them with the healthiest set of coping strategies I can, and by and large, I do.

Fear of and punishment from taking a risk, as well as, the historical guilt of racism and colonization add to the teachers' and principals' minimalist and politically correct approaches of engaging students' individual and communal diversities and backgrounds. A teacher in my study mentioned that an attempt to discuss September 11 by his colleague spilled out of control to the degree that the students complained to their parents and the parents took the issue to the school principal and board. The teacher was rebuked, which led him and other teachers to avoid similar controversies in the classroom for many years to come.

Yet, for a genuine pluralism, Islamic education needs to move from a minimalist perspective on cosmopolitanism (uncritical acceptance of Islamic beliefs and practices) to a maximalist cosmopolitanism (i.e., examine these beliefs and practices in terms of their implications), as well as reject rote learning in favor of deliberation. Waghid and Davids (2014) suggest that Muslim practices have to transform into ones that are not patriarchal, acknowledge difference and diversity, and criminalize ethnic stereotyping, hate speech, and racism; Islamic education should educate for thinking and acting for others' justice not just one's own and one's community's, develop broader loyalty beyond umma, and condemn the use of religion for crimes against humanity. Muslim's inability and fear of engaging critically and reflexively with their Muslimness are perhaps the key reasons for tensions inherent in Islam. Muslims should uptake pedagogy of encounter, which does not predetermine who Muslims are supposed to meet and what they are supposed to learn. It is a pedagogy that is open to uncertainty, unsettling knowledge, and unsettling individuals. Waghid (2014) furthers that:

> . . . [e]ducation cannot be education if people do not engage with one another's differences—the very end of education is to establish opportunities for one to engage others in their otherness. Only if people engage

> one another though their differences might they have a real chance to learn from one another and to respect one another.
>
> (333)

This echoes the saying of a public schoolteacher in my study (herself a fundamentalist Christian) that Muslims should stay in the public schools rather than chose to segregate themselves into Islamic schools. It is through the challenge of encountering non-Muslims and other Muslims that students can strengthen their Muslimness and show what their faith stands:

> If you have friends that have other faiths, your faith becomes much more robust because you have that dialogue, and you have those questions about it. [For example,] when your friend looks at you and says, "Am I going to hell?" Well, if you've gone to a Christian school or Muslim school or whatever, you've been sheltered from those sorts of questions, your faith doesn't have to stand up to anything. Then there's this, the question of being the light to the others or being an influence on others. And, there are lots of questions there. I think that the reason that Islamic schools are so controversial is that people are afraid about terrorists and that's part of the hysteria. I don't think it really has much to do with the faith itself. So if Muslims stay in public school, others can talk to them and meet them. Who can show what Muslims are if they all chose to leave public schools?

Muslim students and parents in both public and Islamic schools also need some clarity around the stark discrepancy between the non-pluralistic, indeed non-tolerant, depictions of the other in the Muslim-majority countries and the avoidance of this negativity at home in the West. Waghid (2014) suggests that Muslim students should analyze the reasons for why prayer is sacrosanct and scrutinize the central tenets of the faith and move from seeing the purpose of Islamic education as biased toward defending Muslim community patriotically and blindly into considering every human being, irrespective of his/her cultural, religious, socioeconomic, political, and other differences as worthy of respect.

Earlier we described how positive and sterilized versions of all religions are depicted in the Canadian *World Religions* textbooks. Such sterilization of materials is clearly problematic given that there is a sheer amount of alternative depictions of these textbooks in themes elsewhere. Muslim parents and students in public and Islamic schools need to know why textbooks and media in South Asia (Lall 2008; Talbani 1996) and the Middle East (Doumato & Starrett 2006) and the books of the Muslim classics (many of which are accessible to students online and through school libraries) provide many negative and polarizing messages (e.g., Aasi, 1999; Kermalli 2008) about non-Muslims. Equally important is the question of intra-Muslim negativity that has become the foci of scholarship and global politics after the Islamic revolution in Iran, the civil war in Lebanon, the Shia–Sunni conflicts in Pakistan, Iraq, and, more recently, Bahrain, Syria, and Yemen. Asani (2003), Sardar (2011), and Waghid (2014) have taken a critical and reflexive stance on the whole idea of Muslims' internal pluralism. They have noted that any pluralistic education of Muslim students implies engaging inter-subjectivity within us and others.

Within Muslim-majority countries, Saudi Arabian textbooks, based on Wahhabi ideology, consider non-Wahhabi Sunnis, all of the Shias, Sufis, and Ahmadis as bad Muslims, polytheists, and infidels (Doumato 2006). Turkish textbooks give very limited space to the Alawis and Kurds (see Kayamakcan 2007). Some Shia officials consider Sunni Islam as oppressors' Islam. Panjwani (2005), in his examination of the syllabi in England's and Wales' community schools noted that with, some exception, the syllabi and the books failed to portray the rich internal diversity among the Muslims. This monolithic portrayal permeates the presentation of the meaning of Islam, the places of worship, revelation, authority, gender, and practices and beliefs, signs and symbols. Panjwani concludes:

> Unless a society arrives at a *consensus on its basic procedural values* through which it can negotiate differences and interests, there is a constant threat that the most politically and/or economically dominant group may impose its values on others. Procedural values provide safeguards to all, most of all to the least powerful. The challenge is how to arrive at them.
>
> (388, italics mine)

Muslim academic and education scholarship rarely engage these negative portrayals and confine the question of diversity to ethnic, linguistic, and geographic, leaving theological, gender, and social diversities out. When such rare challenges happen such as those Shia studies that challenge the Sunni sources on theological grounds, the key purpose of this challenge might be to carve space for their alternative, but again, non-pluralist position (Dakake 2014). There is almost no discussion of sexuality and class oppression with the literature of pluralism and diversity (Sardar 2011). The scholarship, with some exceptions (Fadl 2002; Waghid 2014), also avoids any discussion on how the traditional sources are employed to incite violence. The conventional responses to the groups that incite violence in the name of Islam are that they are (i) not Islamic, (ii) they misunderstand and misuse religion, or (iii) they are doing it in response to an aggression. Controversial concepts such as jihad, polygamy, gender inequality, and female genital mutilations are explained through contextualization (i.e., confining an act's value to a place and time), interfaith comparison (i.e., other faiths also incite violence), or rejection (i.e., seen as aberrations of true Islam (e.g., Sajoo 2009, Chapter 3).

Admittedly, the violent events committed in the name of Islam against non-Muslims (such as 9/11) and Muslims (e.g., Afghanistan, Iraq, Syria,

Yemen) and the subsequent international pressure and the internal perils of 'dancing with the extremists,' have forced many of the Muslim states to reform their curriculum 'to fight extremism' and enable their children to successfully participate in the modern globalized economy. Researching Islam and Muslims and offering ideas about curriculum reforms in not just secular but also religious schools has become a new field of Western foreign aid, comparative and international education (Hefner and Zaman 2007). This reform project, however, instead of critically engaging the problematic portrayals of the other and development of critical and reflexive attitudes through discussing the difficult knowledge, opted for removing all the uncomfortable incidents, religious topics and producing romanticized versions of Muslim thought, culture, and history (see Hugh 2007 for a critique).

Muslim educators, scholars, and policy makers also need to take pluralism across all forms of Islamic education, far beyond the official public education system. Muslim children also attend other forms of religious education, such as formal Islamic (e.g., Islamic schools and madrassas, homeschooling) and informal (e.g., weekend and evening religious instructions, online learning, and daily socialization through mosques and events) (Douglass and Shaikh 2004). The limited research shows that Muslim students are getting contradictory messages across these spaces. I found in the Islamic school of my research that while teachers expose students to certain concepts such as evolution, independent decision making, homosexuality, music, dance, and coeducation, they inject the 'Islamic' perspective, which abrogates these as un-Islamic. Without directly imposing, these students are reminded that the Islamic perspective, as the perfect and divinely ordained, should overrule. My graduate students from Jewish and Catholic education have also confirmed that their school approaches are not much different. There needs to be a mutually agreed upon strategy and cooperative talk about pluralist religious education across the secular-religious divide (Habermas 2006).

The last, fourth set of challenges to pluralist Islamic education consists of examining the effects of global forces such as Islamophobia, Orientalism, and neoliberalism. The current literature on neoliberalist globalization suggests that it has created standardization, homogeneity, and control more than pluralism. Structures and procedures such as PISA (Programme for International Student Assessment), standardization, human capital, and privatization focus on subjects that are needed for the economy and the financial market to the detriment of social sciences and humanities (Masemann 1995). At times, some Islamic movements (both Sunni and Shia) have coalesced with neoliberal ideologies to erase diversity and plurality within their folds: These entail eliminating indigenous practices as blameworthy innovations and erasing multiple identities (such as ethnic, linguistic, cultural) in favor of a singular Islamic identity. Within this job and test framework, there is little if any space and time for engaging cultural and religious diversity. Muslim educators committed to pluralism, therefore, need to question the dichotomy between neoliberalist talk about pluralism and its anti-pluralist actions. Pluralism cannot grow in a nondemocratic context; it cannot grow in a context where social and humanities subjects are denigrated in favor of economic and financial subjects. The Aga Khan (2008) pointed this out as follows:

> [t]he inability of human society to recognize pluralism as a fundamental value constitutes a real handicap for our development as a serious danger for our future . . . . Groups that seek to standardize, to homogenize or, if you will allow me, to normatize all that and those around them must be actively resisted through countervailing activities. (p. 9) move to global

The current Islamophobic sentiments in the West find Muslims' religiously grounded accommodation demands excessive. Muslims are construed as a post-Cold War foe, uninterested in integrating, disloyal and nonproductive citizens, unwilling to live by democratic principles, and, in fact, taking over the West. Orientalist portrayals persist that Muslims' problems are solely stemming from their faith, culture, rigidity, and physiological traits. An increasing number of Western leaders and policy makers blame Muslims for multiculturalism's failure in their countries. Muslims are now used for setting limits for the dichotomized description of civilized (Western) and noncivilized (Muslims) human beings (Ahmed 2000; Bakht 2012; Jiwani 2012). Such conditions create a sense of siege and self-preservation, rather than opening up and pluralism.

CONCLUSION

Religious (including Islamic) pluralist education appears to be a work in progress at best. The efforts remain minimalist because of theological limits and communal risks, the global anti-Islamic geopolitics, lack of pluralist educational resources, weak teacher preparation, lack of broader institutional support, absence of political will, and the negative global effects. Deep or maximalist pluralism, as suggested by Eck, Waghid, and others may be threatening to the already 'otherized' and marginalized faith community (Jiwani 2012). Islamic education cannot become pluralistic, while other education approaches remain monistic (Meijer et al. 2009). For a full-scale pluralist education to occur, the deep theological and ontological assumptions and sacred truths need to be creatively engaged and mutually adaptive solutions found.

Any religious education should start with the question of what kind of a learner-citizen it wants to produce and what is the purpose of education in the 21st century. If the purpose is to nurture a more devout person, deeply fossilized into the creed, dogmas, and practices of that particular faith (which is the predominant case of religious education now), then the next question is what are the practical implications for pluralism that is grounded in self-critical thinking and constructivism? Pluralism is weak if it is about just adding one more viewpoint to the tapestry without critically examining them or allowing for different approaches to reach the one truth or even about allowing questions to be asked and critical thinking applied as long these do not challenge the established regimes of truths that could be tolerated. A key to successful pluralist religious education is to have competing perspectives peacefully coexist within one person's mind, body, soul, and actions as a way of life of embodied knowledge.

BIBLIOGRAPHY

Aasi, G. H. (1999). *Muslim understanding of other religions: A study of Ibn Hazim's Kitab al- fasl fi almilal wa al-ahwa' wa al-nihal.* Islamabad, Pakistan: International Institute of Islamic Thought and Islamic Research Institute Publications.

Aga, Khan (2008). *Where hope takes root: Democracy and pluralism in an interdependent world.* Vancouver: Douglas & McIntyre.

Ahmed, S. (2000). *Strange encounters: Embodied others in post-coloniality.* London: Routldege.

Apple, M. (2006). *Educating the "right" way: Markets, standards, God, and inequality.* 2nd edition. New York: Routledge.

Arkoun. M. (1994). *Rethinking Islam: Common questions, uncommon answers.* London: Westview Press.

Asani, A. S. (2003). So that you may know one another: A Muslim American reflects on pluralism and Islam. *The Annals of the American Academy of Political and Social Science,* 588, 40–51.

Ayoub, M. (2005). The Qur'an and religious pluralism. In Boase, R. (Ed.), *Islam and global dialogue. Religious pluralism and the pursuit of peace* (pp. 273–284). England: Ashgate Publishing Limited.

Bakht, N. (2012). Veiled objections: Framing public opposition to the niqab. In Beaman, L. (Ed.). *Reasonable accommodation: Managing religious diversity* (pp. 70–108). Vancouver and Toronto: UBC Press.

Boase, R. (2005). Ecumenical Islam: A Muslim Response to Religious Pluralism. In R. Boase (ed.), *Islam and global dialogue. Religious pluralism and the pursuit of peace* (pp. 247246). England: Ashgate Publishing Limited.

Bramadat, P. (2005). Beyond Christian Canada: Religion and ethnicity in multicultural society. In Bramadat, P., Seljak, D. (Eds.), *Religion and ethnicity in Canada* (pp. 1–29). Toronto: University of Toronto Press.

Bramadat, P., & Seljak, D. (2005). Toward a new story about religion and ethnicity in Canada. In Bramadat, P., & Seljak, D. (Eds.), *Religion and ethnicity in Canada* (pp. 222–234). Toronto: University of Toronto Press.

Beaman, L. (Ed.) (2012). *Reasonable accommodation: Managing religious diversity.* Vancouver and Toronto: UBC Press.

Beyer, P. (2012). Religion and immigration in a changing Canada: the reasonable accommodation of "reasonable accommodation"? In Beaman, L. (Ed.), *Reasonable accommodation: Managing religious diversity* (pp. 14–31). Vancouver and Toronto: UBC Press.

Bouchard, G., & Taylor, C. (2008*). Building the future: A time for reconciliation. Commission de Consultation sur les practiques d'acoodement reliiees aux differences culturelles.* Quebec City: Quebec Government Printing Office.

Carper, J. (1998). History, religion, and schooling: A context for conversation. In James Sears and James C. Carper (Eds.), *Curriculum, religion and public education: Conversations for an enlarging public square* (pp. 11–24). Teachers College Press.

Dakake, M. M. (2014). Writing and resistance: The transmission of religious knowledge in early Shi'ism. In Daftary, F., & G. Miskinzoda (Eds.), *The study of Shi'i Islam: History, theology and* law (pp. 181–202). London: I.B. Tauris.

Douglass, S., & Shaikh, M. (2004). Islamic education: Differentiation and application. *Current Issues in Comparative Education* 7 (1), 5–18.

Doumato, A. E. (2006). Saudi Arabia: From "Wahhabi" roots to contemporary revisionism. In E. Doumato and G. Starrett (Eds.), *Teaching Islam. Textbooks and religion in the Middle East* (pp. 103–124). Boulder, CO: Lynn Rienner Publishers.

Doumato, E. A., & G. Starrett. (Eds.). (2006) *Teaching Islam. Textbooks and religion in the Middle East* (pp. 103–124). Boulder, CO: Lynn Rienner Publishers.

Eck, D. (2002). *A new religious America: Managing religious diversity in a democracy: Challenges and prospects for the 21st century Kuala Lumpur, Malaysia.* Retrieved from https://www.pcc.edu/resources/illumination/documents/article-a-new-religious-america..pdf on February 10, 2016.

El Fadl, Abou Khaled. (2002). The place of tolerance in Islam. In K. A. Fadl (Ed.), *The place of tolerance in Islam* (pp. 3–26). Boston: Beacon Press Books.

Friesen, J., & Hammer, K. (2011). School prayer debate creates unlikely allies. *The Globe and Mail,* June 08, 2011. Retrieved from http://www.theglobeandmail.com/news/toronto/school-prayer-debate-creates-unlikely- allies/article556662/. August 17, 2014.

Geertz, C. (1971). *Islam Observed, Religious Development in Morocco and Indonesia.* Chicago: University of Chicago Press.

The Globe and Mail. (2011, November 25). *Globe editorial: Prayer in public schools needs to respect all students.* Retrieved from http://www.theglobeandmail.com/globe- debate/editorials/prayer-in-public-schools-needs-to-respect-all-students/article4201101/

Gosh, R., & Abdi, A. (2013). *Education and the Politics of Difference: Canadian Perspectives,* 2nd edition. Toronto: Canadian Scholars Press.

Government of Canada (2010). *Study: Projections of the diversity of the Canadian population.* Retrieved from http://www.statcan.gc.ca/daily-quotidien/100309/dq100309a-eng.htm

Ibrahim, A. (2012). Contemporary Islamic thought: A critical perspective. *Islam and Christian- Muslim Relations*, 23(3), 279–294.

Ipgrave, J. (2010). Including the religious viewpoints and experiences of Muslim students in an environment that is both plural and secular. *Journal of International Migration and Integration*, 11, 5–22.

Jackson, R. (2004a). Editorial: Religious education and plurality in the common school. *British Journal of Religious Education*, 26(1), 3–6.

Jackson, R. (2004b.). *Rethinking religious education and plurality: Issues in diversity and pedagogy.* London and New York: RoutledgeFalmer, Taylor & Francis Group.

Jiwani, Y. (2012). Colluding hegemonies: Constructing the Muslim other post 9/11. In Zine (Ed.), *Islam in the hinterlands: Muslim cultural politics in Canada* (pp. 208–236). Vancouver: UBC Press.

Habermas, J. (2006). Religion in the public sphere. European *Journal of Philosophy*, 14, 1–25.

Hefner, R., & Zaman, M. Q. (2007). *Schooling Islam: The culture and politics of modern Muslim education.* Princeton University Press.

Kassam, T. (2003). Teaching religion in the twenty-first century. In B. Wheeler (Ed.), *Teaching Islam* (pp. 191–215). New York & Oxford: Oxford University Press.

Kayamakcan, R. (2007). Pluralism and constructivism in Turkish Religious Education: Evaluation of recent curriculum of religious culture and ethical knowledge lesson. *Educational Sciences: Theory & Practice,* 7 (1), 202–210.

Kermalli, J. (2008). *Islam, the absolute truth: A contemporary approach to understanding Islam's beliefs and practices.* Sanford, USA: Zahra Foundation.

Legenhausen, M. (2005) A Muslims non-reductive religious pluralism. In R. Boase (Ed.), *Islam and global dialogue. Religious pluralism and the pursuit of peace* (pp. 51–76). England: Ashagate Publishing Limited.

Madelung, W. (2014). Introduction. Theology. In Daftary, F., & G. Miskinzoda (Eds.), *The study of Shi'i Islam: History, theology and law* (pp. 455–464). London: I.B. Tauris.

Masemann, V. (1995). Canada: the Prospects for pluralistic educational forms. In Roeder, P. Richter, I., & H-P. Fussel (Eds.), *Pluralism and education: Current world trends in policy, law and administration* (pp. 131–146). Berkley: Institute of Governmental Studies Press, University of California.

Mc Andrew, M. (2010). The Muslim community and education in Quebec: Controversies and mutual adaptations. *Journal of International Migration and Integration*, 11(1), 41–57.

Meijer, W. J., & Miedema, S., & der-Welde, A. L. (Eds.) (2009) *Religious education in a world of religious diversity*. Munster: Waxman.

Memon, N. (2012). From mosques to madrassas: Civic engagement and the pedagogy of Islamic schools. In Zine, J, (Ed.), *Islam in the Hinterlands: Muslim cultural politics in* Canada (pp. 185–207). Vancouver: UBC press.

Moghissi, H., Rahnema, S., & Goodman, M. (2009). *Diaspora by design: Muslims in Canada and beyond.* Toronto: University of Toronto Press.

Niyozov, S. (2010). Teachers and teaching Islam and Muslims in pluralistic Societies: Claims misunderstandings, and responses. *Journal of International Migration and Integration* (Special Issue, edited by M. Andrew & J. Ipgrave), 11 (1), 23–40.

Niyozov, S. (2011). Easier Said than Done: Taking Religious and Cultural Dimensions Seriously. In Rolheiser, C., Evans, M., & Gambir, M. (Eds.), *Inquiry into practice: Reaching every Student through inclusive curriculum* (pp. 27–29). Toronto: OISE Publications.

Niyozov, S. (forthcoming). *The challenges and opportunities of Islamic Education in Toronto's public school.*

Ontario Ministry of Education (2000). *The Ontario Curriculum Grades 11 and 12.* Social Sciences and Humanities. Retrieved from http://www.bing.com/search?q=wolrld+religions+in+the+cirriculum&qs=n&form=QBE&pq=wolrld+religions+in+the+cirriculum&sc=0–17&sp= 1&sk=&cvid=fe3dd6a6bd5945fa91e4e09adfa99b35

Panjwani, F. (2005). Agreed Syllabi and un-agreed values: Religious education and missed opportunity for fostering social cohesion. *British Journal of Educational Studies*, 53(3), 375–393.

Ramadan, T. (2004). *Western Muslims and the future of Islam*. New York: Oxford University Press.

Razack, S. (2004). Imperilled Muslim women, dangerous Muslim men, and civilized Europeans: Legal and social responses to forced marriages. *Feminist Legal Studies,* 12(2), 129–174.

Sachedina, A. (2001). *The Islamic roots of democratic pluralism*. New York: Oxford University Press.

Sajoo, A. (2009). *Muslim ethics: Emerging vistas*. London. I.B. Tauris.

Sardar, Z. (2011). *Reading the Qur'an: The contemporary relevance of the sacred text of Islam*. Oxford & New York: Oxford University Press.

Selchuk, S., & Fine, M. (2008). *Muslim American youth: Understanding hyphenated identities through multiple methods*. New York: New York University Press.

Silk, M. (2007). Defining Religious Pluralism in America: A Regional Analysis. *The ANNALS of the American Academy of Political and Social Science*, 612, 62–81.

Sweet, L. (1997). *God in the classroom: the controversial issues of religion in Canada's schools*. Toronto: McClelland & Stewart.

Sweet, L. (2002). *Religious literacy: An antidote to extremism. Negotiating pluralism: Religion and Education Conference*. Waterloo: Wilfred Laurier University.

Talbani, A. (1996). Pedagogy, power and discourse: transformation of Islamic education. *Comparative Education Review,* 40(1), pp. 66–82.

Tan, C. (2011). *Islamic education and indoctrination: the case of Indonesia*. London: Routldege.

Waghid, Y. (2014). Islamic education and cosmopolitanism: a philosophical interlude. *Studies in Philosophy of Education* 33, 329–342.

Waghid,Y., & Davids, N. (2014). On the (im)possibility of democratic citizenship education in the Arab and Muslim world. *Studies in Philosophy of Education*, 33, 343–351.

Watson, G. (1990). *The Report of the Ministerial Inquiry on Religious Education in Ontario Public Elementary Schools*. Toronto: Government of Ontario.

Zine, J. (2008). *Canadian Islamic schools*. Toronto: University of Toronto Press.

14 Islamization and Democratization of Knowledge in Postcolonial Muslim-Oriented Contexts

Implications for Democratic Citizenship Education

Yusef Waghid and Nuraan Davids

In taking into account the political implications of Islamization for Muslims, the central concern of this chapter is to explore the conditions that ought to be in place if Islamization, as an instance of democratization, were to flourish in Muslim-majority and minority countries. We contend that it is not Islamization itself that is problematic. Rather, it is the deficient conditions that have truncated its implementation. In addressing these deficiencies—as reflected in the treatment of women, minority groups, or religious, ethnic, and cultural differences—we argue for a new imaginary of democratic citizenship. To this end, we argue for a democratic citizenship that cultivates participation, freedom of conscience, belonging, and dignity among and across multiple and diverse identities. A new imaginary of democratic citizenship characterized by these traits has the best chance of ensuring a curriculum that fulfills the ideals of recognition and inclusivity and yet allows for dissensus and otherness.

ISLAMIZATION OF KNOWLEDGE

For Ismail al-Faruqi, 'Islamization of knowledge' offers a comprehensive framework for society and individuals through which to amend and reinterpret knowledge through an Islamic worldview (1982, 30). In its broadest sense, it refers to the process by which varying forms of (often secular) knowledge are tempered and acclimatized by Islamic thought. As such, Islamization of knowledge, as proposed by al-Faruqi, was a direct response to what he defined as the malaise of the *ummah* (community). Conceptually, Islamization offered an alternative to modern secular society and what is perceived to be its negative impact on the Islamic world. Al-Faruqi's (1988) proposal of Islamization involved a detailed, twelve-step work plan, which incorporates the mastery of modern disciplines, the mastery of an Islamic legacy, a survey of the *ummah's* (Muslim community's) major problems, and recasting the disciplines under the framework of Islām and the dissemination of Islamized knowledge. The objective of his understanding of Islamization was to re-approach the disciplines—such as sociology, economics, and anthropology—so that Islām is foregrounded. To him, Islamization means the recasting of every discipline on the principles of Islām—its methodology, its strategy data, its problems, and its objectives, as well as its aspirations.

Islamization, as both an ideological and epistemological construct, has undoubtedly assumed its forms in relation to the (de)secularization of knowledge. Whereas in some instances it seems to have emerged in juxtaposition with secularization, which is mostly perceived to be posited as 'Western' knowledge, in other instances, Islamization has been couched in stark opposition to and a dismissal of the secular. Rahman (1982) emerged as a proponent of Islamization as a form of knowledge construction that does not dismiss what can be perceived as secular and argued vehemently for the 'modernization' of knowledge within Muslim societies—that is, to integrate all forms of knowledge (including the 'secular') with important concepts of Islam. In other words, higher forms of learning, irrespective of where they come from, had to be integrated with Islamic values for both individual and social life and such knowledge also had to be subjected to Quranic interpretation or a view of Islamic metaphysics. Thus, for Rahman (1988, 4), all forms of knowledge, including secular knowledge, can be considered as having been Islamized if subjected to these principles. The 'desecularization' of knowledge propounded by al-Attas (1980) involves "the deliverance of knowledge from its interpretations based on secular ideology; and from meanings and expressions of the secular" (45). Similarly, whereas Abushouk (2008, 39) understands it as a revivalist response to modernity and its secular impact on Muslim society, Nasr (2010, 270–271) describes Islamization as the application of the intellectual and spiritual principles of the Islamic tradition to counter the challenges and premises of modernism, which are viewed as a threat to the principles of Islam. Although the aforementioned understandings of Islamization seem to be different at first glance, there is some synergy between the two explications in that both Rahman and al-Attas do not denounce secular or Western knowledge in its entirety. Rather they advocate accentuating principles such as religion (*dīn*), man (*insān*), justice (*'adl*), and right action (*adab*), which should infuse Muslims' acquisition of knowledge (Wan Daud 1997, 12).

However, not all scholars have been in agreement with the objectives of Islamization or whether it is at all attainable. In labeling the Islamization project as incoherent, Farid al-Attas (2008) is of the opinion that Islamization of knowledge has more to do with an epistemological framework than with an actual discipline. The inconsistency of understandings regarding Islamization would begin to explain why little progress has been made in terms of 'Islamizing' disciplines and why the extant work lies between a tendency of being too abstract or rather obscure. Other criticisms include that Islamization has been too preoccupied with concepts of Western secularized education, yet clear principles for an Islamic epistemology or methodology have still to be articulated. There are also those such as Wan Daud (2009) who, as Rahman, believe that the conception of Islamization has little to do with the reworking of textbooks or the restructuring of academic disciplines but fundamentally to do with the reconstitution of the right kind of human being, specifically referring to al-Attas's person of *adab* (right action). According to Wan Daud, Islamic epistemology recognizes that knowledge "stripped of the faulty opinions, doubts, and conjectures, as well as negative influence of the various human interests generally termed as *hawa*, is indeed universal" (8). This universality rests on two central contentions related to knowledge in Islam. The first is that whereas knowledge is extracted from two distinct knowledge forms, namely, *'ulum al-aqli* (knowledge of the rational, human, and sciences) and *'ulum al-naqli* (knowledge of the revealed sciences) as encapsulated in the primary sources of the Qur'an and *Ahādīth* (Prophetic utterances and conduct), these two forms are not mutually exclusive. This is so because in terms of the epistemologies of *tarbiyyah* (socialization), *ta'līm* (critical engagement), and *ta'dīb* (social activism), any conceptualization of knowledge ought to have intellectual, judgmental, and ethical ramifications. Second, to have knowledge of the physical world and the self is to have knowledge of God. It is on this premise that the religion of Islam propagates the seeking of knowledge as a religious obligation.

However, irrespective of whether the Islamization of knowledge has some relation with the (de)secularization of knowledge, its insistence that knowledge be aimed at enhancing both individual and social development confirms its internal connection to democratization. When knowledge is democratized, it is recognized that interpretations of such knowledge are subjected to critical deliberation and scrutiny by others. Rahman's open-ended approach to knowledge construction, in that interpretations are not monolithic and inflexible, and al-Attas's position that further elaboration and application of knowledge are inherent in Islamic metaphysics corroborate the argument that there is always more to know and more with which people should engage. The Qur'an, for instance, as Abu Zayd (2010, 282) explains, responded both explicitly and implicitly to a particular historical context and within a particular intellectual milieu. To this end, it is therefore quite possible, and necessary, to discern between that which can be understood as the universal component of the Qur'an and that which is particular to a specific community. At the core of the democratization of knowledge is that there are no absolutes and that understandings are flexible and always subjected to critical scrutiny by others in deliberation with one another. This means that the construction of knowledge is always open and responsive. Islam, as every other religion, is shaped and impacted upon by other communities and other forms of knowledge, which means, says Abu Zayd (2010, 283), that Islam is the result of the interpretation and experiences of real people.

Such has been the tradition of exegetical scholars, whose commentaries on and interpretations of the traditions of the Prophet (*Sunnah*) and the Qur'an have always been subjected to examination and scrutiny by other authoritative scholars. By implication, the Islamization of knowledge cannot and has not been the reserved ownership of a few, and knowledge construction should be associated with democratization, because the Qur'an positions itself clearly as a text for all times and places. As such, contends Davids and Waghid (2014, 1490), its (con)textual manifestations will always be subjected to (re)interpretations as Muslims endeavor to live their lives in ethical conduct and obedience to the dictates of its primary sources. Therefore, we contend that Islamization of knowledge is another instance of how knowledge can be democratized. Having explicated these conceptual problems with Islamization, the chapter now turns toward a discussion of the progress of Islamization in some postcolonial, Muslim-majority countries, focusing on the Gulf States and Saudi Arabia, Iran and Malaysia, as well as in a Muslim-minority country such as South Africa.

ISLAMIZATION OR NOT: KNOWLEDGE IN SELECTED MUSLIM-MAJORITY COUNTRIES

It is important to initially note that in the Gulf States and Saudi Arabia, the fusion of traditional and Western knowledge has been less apparent, considering the concentration of the applied sciences as well as on oil and water economics, geopolitics and further have no established history of higher educational institutes where debates may occur (Shaw 2006, 41). The curriculum for school and college education does not always prepare students, therefore, adequately for employment, as the job market requires mostly people in applied sciences, maths, and technology (Shaw 2006, 44). Considering the fact that the social sciences and humanities predominate in schools and colleges, the upshot is that curriculum reform integrating the Islamic epistemic traditions within such disciplines has yet to be devised imaginatively (Shaw 2006, 48). This lack of an integrated curriculum questions the Islamizing and, therefore, democratizing of the curricula.

Islamization of the curriculum in schools and universities after the Cultural Revolution in Iran (post-1980) was instigated by the Ayatollah Khomeini, who vehemently denounced Western curricula on the basis that the latter alienated students from their Islamic roots (Levers 2006, 159). In school textbooks, the emphasis on Iranian nationalism and identity was minimized and importance was given to Islamic identity with "concepts such as justice, equality, morality, devotion to family, absence of malice and avarice, and cooperation with the state . . . advocated as attributes of an Islamic society" (Levers 2006, 166). Significantly, the commensurability between Islamization and politicization (more specifically democratization) was clearly accentuated in textbooks, and the idea that religion ought to be segregated from politics was denounced as a 'Western' concept alien to Islam. Despite the fact that the Islamic Republic of Iran regarded the Islamization of education as important to the political, cultural, societal, and economic transformation of society away from the Pahlavi regime's

(1921–1979) emphasis on Westernization, it is recognized that there still is a lack of space for individuality, self-expression, and critical thinking in the school curriculum, coupled with an overemphasis on overtly ideologically driven curricular content that undermines creative thought (Levers 2006, 172). Similarly, under the Islamic Republic, 'Islamized' curriculum changes at universities were accelerated by the compulsory introduction of a series of Islamic texts to supplement the existing curriculum, most notably the books *Introduction to Islam* and *Islamic Revolution and Its Roots*, which became part of the curriculum for all faculties. These books accentuate the importance of questioning and challenging aspects of autonomy that break with doctrinaire understandings of Islam. Although Islamic texts on themes such as the family in Islam, psychology from an Islamic viewpoint, Islamic economics, Islamic law, and Islamic political thought were introduced in specific faculties in universities to supplement the existing curriculum in the social sciences, university textbooks for scientific and technical subjects remained unaltered (Levers 2006, 161). By implication, the envisaged Islamization in the aftermath of the revolution has not had the desired consequences, more specifically at the levels of fusion between the traditional and 'modern' curriculum. It can be argued that Islamization thus emerged as a supplementary discourse, rather than as a tenable, integrated initiative to democratize the new curriculum.

The Islamization agenda in Malaysia, pioneered by the Muslim Youth Movement (*ABIM*) in the 1970s and 1980s, was influenced primarily by Syed Muhammad Naquib al-Attas's intellectual, academic, and historical aspirations to transform the lives and thoughts of the majority-Muslim Malay community and had a strong sociocultural impetus. During this phase of Islamization, *ABIM* strongly advocated a discourse of Islamic universalism and its significance for a pluralistic Malaysia, which involved adhering to the democratic teachings of Islam, promoting equal and complementary roles for men and women, and promoting social justice for all, irrespective of ethnic and religious affiliation (Bakar 2009, 38). The main focus of *ABIM's* Islamization programs were education through their nationwide network of kindergartens and schools (and later Islamic teacher training colleges and universities) through which they advanced the idea of the Islamization of modern knowledge. In the meanwhile, non-Muslim Malaysians did not feel threatened because of Islamization's commitment to intellectual and social conscientization, despite the fact that the programs for the Islamization of knowledge were all directed exclusively at the Malay Muslim community. However, after the Islamization agenda under the leadership of Mahatir Mohammad became politicized and was adopted as government policy by his ruling United Malays National Organisation (UMNO) party, it was strongly opposed by many non-Muslims:

> Although his Islamisation programme was mainly directed at the Muslim community, seeking to transform their minds and attitudes to be

> in line with the requirements of Islam and modernity, his policy of the inculcation of Islamic values in economic development and in the government machinery as well as the creation of a national administration guided by Islam, directed at all Malaysians, was seen by non-Muslims as impinging on their own religious and cultural values.
>
> (Bakar 2009, 41)

Despite the suspicions harbored about political Islamization, the majority-Muslim Malay community recognized the concept as important to the country's economic, scientific, and technological developments, thus acknowledging that Islamization has both a sociocultural and politico-economic impetus. This is evident in the Islamization policy of Mahatir's successor, Abdullah Badawi. His policies, commonly referred to as *Islam Hadhari*, advocated the principles of faith and piety in Allah, a just and trustworthy government, a free and independent people, mastery of knowledge, balanced and comprehensive economic development, a good quality of life, protection of the rights of minority groups and women, cultural and moral integrity, safeguarding the environment, and strong defenses (Bakar 2009, 42). The Malaysian example represents a maximal form of Islamization, considering that sufficient emphasis was placed on an integrated Islamized curriculum in schools and universities under the auspices of a government intent on promoting the idea of Islamization of knowledge. In the 1990s, the government initiated curricular reforms and launched an integrated curriculum for secondary schools in order to inculcate universal religious values in all young people (Hwang 2008, 159). Through the educational efforts of *ABIM*, the state's curriculum for Malay Muslims became integrated with an Islamic philosophy of education in schools (Hwang 2008, 160). Likewise, at the higher education level, *ABIM*'s members became influential in the development of the International Islamic University of Malaysia (IIUM), which was largely influenced by the Islamization agenda of Ismail al-Faruqi, as well as the International Institute of Islamic Thought and Civilisation (ISTAC) under the then directorship of Syed Muhammad Naquib al-Attas. For the majority-Muslim Malays, Islamization meant that the curriculum in secondary schools and universities was organized to produce citizens who were intellectually, spiritually, emotionally, and physically balanced and harmonious, with a strong belief in God (Hashim 1996, 8).

In summary of the progress of Islamization in the three major Muslim-majority regions in the world—the Gulf States and Saudi Arabia, Iran and Malaysia—it can be claimed that Islamization has been implemented along a continuum from not having been implemented successfully (having assumed a supplementary orientation) to having been maximally implemented as an integrated curriculum. There are several Muslim-majority countries, such as Turkey, Egypt, Indonesia, and Pakistan that have responded to the Islamization idea in different forms, but suffice it to add that these countries have either adopted a supplementary or integrated curriculum approach to the idea of the Islamization of knowledge. Consequently, these countries would not necessarily be in a position to offer an understanding of how Muslim-majority countries that have responded to the Islamization agenda have actually embraced the idea. Their understandings would be limited to one of three positions: having adopted an undesirable stance, as in the case of the Gulf States and Saudi Arabia; a supplementary position, as in the case of Iran; or a maximally integrated approach as encountered in Malaysia.

We are more concerned in this chapter with the political implications of Islamization for Muslims in the world, in particular the conditions that ought to be in place if Islamization, as an instance of democratization, were to flourish in Muslim-majority and minority countries that have responded to the theoretical and practical features of Islamization. Continuing this theme, we examine how a minority-Muslim country such as South Africa, which has been influenced by the Islamization agenda as espoused earlier, has responded to this agenda. It is our contention that certain aspects of the Islamization agenda developed in Muslim-majority countries have had an impact on the way Muslims as a minority in South Africa enacted their curricular reforms and as such our examination focuses cursorily on private Muslim schooling.

MANIFESTATION OF ISLAMIZATION AT PRIVATE MUSLIM SCHOOLS IN SOUTH AFRICA

The existence of private or independent Muslim schools is neither a recent phenomenon, nor one that emerged specifically from a post-apartheid discourse. Muslim schools, as other faith-based schools, were a prominent feature of the apartheid landscape, with many being established as a protesting response to the ideologies of the apartheid state. Muslim missionary schools, as they were commonly known, just like other mission school systems, were subsidized by the apartheid state and served as the primary type of schooling for 'blacks,' 'coloureds,' and 'Indians'—the racial demographic categories in terms of which people were classified under apartheid. Whereas the primary objective for the establishment of the Muslim missionary schools was to preserve Muslim identity and practices, Tayob (2011, 42) describes their purpose as twofold. On the one hand, they provided employment for Muslim teachers, who could not find posts at Christian-dominated schools. On the other hand, they also provided schooling for Muslim children, whose parents were concerned about the dominant Christian ethos at both state and missionary schools. Muslim schools therefore were free to employ their own teachers and design a curriculum that met the religious needs of their community. An added advantage was that learners would not have to attend *madrassah* after school hours, because the *madrassah* curriculum would form part of the school curriculum—an indication that Muslim schools initially adopted a supplementary approach to curriculum design.

The establishment of private Muslim schools during apartheid, therefore, while partly in protest against apartheid, also served the particular religious needs of a particular Muslim community.

The culturally and religiously specific character of private Muslim schools did not shift in post-apartheid South Africa. If apartheid fulfilled its objective of segregating communities, then it would appear that Muslim schools in post-apartheid South Africa became even more isolationist (Davids 2014, 229). The proliferation of private Muslim schools (a total of seventy-three in 2014) can be ascribed directly to the provision for public and independent (including faith-based) schools as stipulated in the South African Schools Act (Act no. 84 of 1996) (Tayob 2011, 43). This served the agenda of Muslim schools well, as it gave impetus to the view that public schools could not be trusted to cultivate and transmit the values and traditions that are core to the respective religious beliefs. Waghid (2013) explains that there are many reasons that account for the continuing emergence of independent private Muslim schools. One is the broadly held perception of educational associations, parent-teacher organizations, and Muslim societies that Muslim schooling contributes overwhelmingly to the shaping of learners' faith-based identities.

The idea of Islamization has been familiar to Muslim schools since the 1970s and took root at a number of schools when a Cape Town–based school hosted the Sixth International Education Conference on Islamization of Knowledge in 1996. Discussions and ideas from this conference led to a number of schools agreeing, in principle, to implement an Islamized curriculum. The Islamized curriculum, however, needed to be integrated with the South African national curriculum, which at that time was grounded on an outcomes-based approach to education, leading to various interpretations and adaptations of an 'Islamized' curriculum. On the one hand, an outcomes-based approach to education resonated with a particular philosophy of Islamic education that prejudices the prescriptiveness of knowledge and postulates that learners should be molded into agents of critical thinking. On the other hand, outcomes-based education was a new educational approach that responded positively to diversifying a curriculum. Hence, it seems as if the new post-apartheid education system provided an adequate framework to implement an integrated curriculum. Whereas certain schools in the Western Cape, such as Islamia College, prided themselves on following a particular integrationist philosophy of Islamization, others, such as the Mitchell's Plain Islamic School, changed its name to the more 'Islamized' Darul Arqam and set out to instill an Islamic ethos on a supplementary basis.[1] This ethos, while still aligned with the stipulations of the public school curriculum, consisted of the promotion of Islamic values and the daily recitation of the Qur'an, culminating in a monthly completion of a *khātam*—that is, completion of the recitation of the whole Qur'an in a specific period of time. Although it appears that schools like Islamia College adopted an integrationist approach to an Islamized curriculum, others such as Darul Arqam that adopted a supplementary approach to an Islamized curriculum predominated, especially in light of having biased the national school curriculum. Islamic subjects were introduced to supplement the formal national school curriculum and examinations were based on the requirements of the national Ministry of Education.

The Springs Muslim School in Gauteng aspires toward being "a progressive institution of learning experience by offering quality education based on an Islamic ethos that aims to serve humanity" (Springs Muslim School 2014). This Islamic ethos is defined by the core Islamic values of sacrifice, morality, accountability, respect, and trust. It hopes to achieve its vision of a progressive institution by developing Allah consciousness and providing an integrated curriculum. Darul Falaah College in KwaZulu-Natal describes itself as a "multifaceted organisation which caters for the diverse needs of the Muslim Ummah in general and the Nation as a whole" (Darul Falaah College 2010). Among its core values are "an awareness of the Almighty and merciful Allah; developing and acquiring the right knowledge, skills, values and attitudes." Although the private Muslim schools advocate an allegiance to an integrated Islamized curriculum, in reality their curricular changes are commensurate with that of a supplementary approach to Islamization. This intimates that Islamization has not been realized maximally in these schools—a view that is corroborated by the minimal way in which Islamization has in fact been practiced at these schools. In other words, for these schools—despite making claims to being progressive and forward looking—Islamization implies supplementing the national state curriculum, better known as the National Curriculum Statement (NCS), with Islamic subjects. For example, the sciences and mathematics are still taught as prescribed by the NCS, but only extended to include subjects with an Islamic orientation. Such minimal efforts toward the realization of an authentic form of Islamization are a vindication that the concept of knowledge has yet to be understood and practiced in the Muslim community. And, considering that several of the private Muslim schools are under the hegemonic control of conservative Deobandi (a traditionally dogmatic sect among Muslims in South Africa) religious leaders (*'ulama*), it seems very unlikely that a defensible form of Islamization will manifest in these schools, because these leaders advocate strongly for the implausible bifurcation of traditional Islamic sciences and rational secular sciences. It therefore would not be erroneous to claim that Islamization has not gained momentum in many of the Deobandi-controlled private Muslim schools.

The majority of private Muslim schools (sixty-eight of seventy-three) are registered with the Association of Muslim Schools of South Africa, which was established in 1989. The vision of the association is "to provide quality services, which will enable our schools to deliver an Islamically-based education of the highest standard and quality" (Association of Muslim Schools 2014). It aims to advance, promote, and represent the interests of private Muslim schools; to encourage cooperation between schools; and to organize activities for schools. But, just as it is difficult to garner a clear understanding of the curriculum on offer from the limited information available on the Association of Muslim Schools' (SA) website, especially concerning its academic programs, it is equally problematic to do so in relation to the other Muslim schools—an indication that the Islamization of knowledge is not deemed as important enough to espouse. One of the most commonly shared features of private Muslim schools appears to be the commitment to community involvement and outreach.

It is worth noting that, in terms of the South African Schools Act (Act no. 84 of 1996), Muslim schools, like all other faith-based schools, whether public or private, are mandated to follow the National Curriculum Statement (NCS) as prescribed by the Department of Basic Education. In addition, the school governing bodies (SGBs) of these schools are allowed to make decisions on the extramural curriculum, specialist subjects, and support in relation to the broad curriculum. In this instance, subjects such as Islamic Studies, Quranic studies, and Arabic will be optional and might not be examinable. The compulsory element of the NCS at Muslim schools has meant the prioritizing thereof—with a number of teachers conceding that the idea of Islamization was limited to mere enactments of rituals, such as starting and ending the day with a prayer, enforcing strict dress codes, particularly for girls, or celebrating particular Islamic festivals at school. Whereas other interpretations have focused on introducing specific examples from Muslim societies, or presenting Islamic perspectives, it is hard to determine whether any of the teachers at these schools have received any training in Islamization or what it means to offer an 'Islamized' curriculum.

There are a number of possible reasons for the lack of consensus on an 'Islamized' curriculum or the implementation thereof. On the one hand, teachers have not been trained in teaching an 'Islamized' curriculum. On the other hand, the educational qualifications of teachers are varying and, at times, nonexistent. Whereas some might have a formal qualification in education, others might have a qualification as a *madrassah* teacher or a certificate in Arabic or *fiqh*, or others may be teachers by virtue of being *hafiz* (one who has memorized the Qur'an). The other issue facing private Muslim schools is their location in a compulsory South African curriculum, which has seen significant changes since the onset of democracy. Changes to a once apartheid-endorsed Christian National Education have included the introduction of outcomes-based education (OBE), implemented through Curriculum 2005; then the development of the National Curriculum Statement, which would later become the Revised National Curriculum Statement; and, most recently, the Curriculum Assessment Policy Statement (CAPS). So, besides being expected to implement an 'Islamized' curriculum, Muslim schools have also been expected to accommodate all the changes accompanying three revisions of a post-apartheid curriculum. It might also be that, whereas many Muslim schools regard the compulsory element of the NCS—(mistakenly) considered by Muslim schools as being the secular component of education at their schools—as the obstacle to the implementation of an 'Islamized' curriculum, the NCS might very well be used in the implementation of an 'Islamized' curriculum, and hence the enactment of democratization.

Returning, then, to our earlier contention that the Islamization of knowledge is another instance of how knowledge can be democratized, we would like to offer a reconsidered view of the 'secular' understanding of the NCS. Through the values stipulated in the NCS policy documents, learners are expected to be exposed to the principles of social transformation; outcomes-based education; high knowledge and high skills; integration and applied competence; progression; articulation and portability; human rights, inclusivity, environmental and social justice; valuing indigenous knowledge systems; and credibility, quality, and efficiency. Waghid (2013, 3) describes the aforementioned as the knowledge, skills, and values associated with democratic citizenship education. By merging the principles of the NCS with the values and objectives of Muslim education—which is to enact a form of social justice (Waghid (2013, 4)—it would seem as if Muslim schooling not only integrates two different forms of education—that is Muslim education and public democratic citizenship education—but that the two educational discourses are in fact not irreconcilable, but in consonance.

By way of concluding, we now focus our attention on what conditions ought to be in place for more 'maximal' forms of postcolonial Islamized curricula to be implemented in educational institutions. Earlier we alluded to the importance of cultivating democratic citizenship education as a framework in terms of which Islamization of the curriculum might just be more favorably—maximally, we would argue—implemented in schools and universities. Considering that Islamization has been presented in this chapter as a form of democratization, it is inconceivable that the notion will be realized if autocracy, exclusivism, and inequality are not undermined in the societal practices of Muslims—all practices that work against any form of democratic citizenship.

AGAINST AUTOCRACY, EXCLUSIVISM, AND INEQUALITY: TOWARD A NEW IMAGINARY OF DEMOCRATIC CITIZENSHIP

Whereas Muslim scholars are in agreement that conceptions of justice and equality are cardinal to the teachings of Islam, interpretive versions of justice and equality in Muslim-majority countries, however, continue to undermine these values through practices of autocracy, exclusivism, and inequality. Consequently, it would be reasonable to argue that what Islam needs to realize its own social/ethical/religious/legal vision is a democratization of its knowledge base. If this argument appears to be too simplistic, then consider that whatever type of democratization is enacted through Islamization has to be one that ably meets the demands of Islam today, while also remaining cognizant of, and loyal to, the religious integrity of a profoundly diverse *ummah* (community). Indeed, it would appear that the demands of Islam can only be met through the acknowledgment and recognition of a profoundly heterogeneous *ummah*—one that places value on encountering the other. *Ta'aruf*, or encountering the other, is considered as a condition of good living, as espoused in the following Quranic verse:

> O mankind! We created You from a single (pair) of a male and a female, and made you into nations and tribes, that Ye may know each other (Not that ye may despise each other).
>
> (*Surah Al-Hujurāt* 49, 11)

What the aforementioned verse clearly reveals is that differences among people, whether along the lines of race, ethnicity, language, religion, or culture, cannot be used to exclude and marginalize others. This is so because exclusion and marginalization can easily lead to the subjugation and oppression of others. The idea of encountering the other, as other, holds significant implication not only for a maximal description of citizenship through Islamic education but also offers renewed explorations into the potential role of Islam, Islamic education, and Muslim communities in relation to a (post) secular context.

To this end, enactments of deliberation and belonging can be attained through unconstrained notions of *shura* (consultation) and *ikhtilāf* (disagreement)—ultimately striving toward cultivating peaceful human coexistence, not only among a diverse *ummah* but also among all other people who are not Muslim. The idea of a maximalist Islamic education shifts beyond mere participation toward deliberative engagement, thereby bringing diverse groups of people into relations of trust and recognition on the basis of extending agency toward one another. As such, people engage in public deliberation without dismissing the otherness of others and without imposing their views on others in an authoritative manner. Again, the Qur'an is replete with messages and injunctions toward peace and peaceful coexistence:

> (Naught) but the saying: Peace, (and again) Peace.
>
> (*Surah Al-Wāqia* 56, 26)

> Of those We have created are people who direct (others) with truth, and dispense justice therewith.
>
> (*Surah Al-'Arāf* 7, 181)

> Indeed We have sent Our Messengers with clear proofs, and revealed with them the Scripture and the Balance (justice) that humankind may keep up justice. And We brought forth iron wherein is mighty power

> (in matters of war), as well as many benefits for humankind, that Allah may test who it is that will help Him (His religion), and His Messengers in the unseen. Verily, Allah is All-Strong, All-Mighty.
>
> (*Surah Al-Hadīd* 57, 25)

Intrinsic to the religious integrity of Islam is to understand maximally that violations in the form of exclusivism, inequality, and autocracy—even in their least minimalist forms—cannot be accepted as a defining legacy of Islam. The fact that social customs, propagated as Islamic values, continue to restrict women from voting in most of the Gulf States is not only a commentary on a particular patriarchal form of exclusivism but also casts a dark shadow on the glaring gap between an exegetical understanding of Quranic text and its contextual implementation. Similarly, the series of eruptions—commonly known as the Arab Spring (2010/2011)—from Tunisia, Egypt, Algeria, and Libya, to Jordan, Kuwait, Yemen, and Morocco are a staggering reflection of the manipulation of Islamic discourse. What the Arab Spring has brought to the fore is a distressed call for a reformation not of individual countries, but of the ideologies that have contributed to the social, political, and educational malaise of Muslim-majority countries.

CONCLUSION

In our analysis of the varied ways in which postcolonial Muslim-majority and minority countries have attempted to 'Islamize' their curricula, we have shown that, whereas some countries have adopted a minimally supplementary and others a maximally integrated approach to the Islamization of knowledge, neither of the two approaches has shed much light on the political implications of Islamization for Muslims or the particular conditions that ought to be in place if Islamization as an instance of democratization were to flourish in Muslim-majority and minority countries. In arguing, then, that it is not Islamization that has failed, but rather the deficient conditions that have truncated its implementation, how may we argue for a new imaginary of democratic citizenship?

Perhaps we may first seek a new imaginary of democratic citizenship that looks beyond citizenship as dictated to by gender. In the Muslim-majority world, it is quite apparent that political and social development do not depend only on removing barriers between men and women but also on establishing structures, procedures, and processes that enable men and women to become citizens in development, rather than 'gendered citizens' (Issan 2013, 166). In the Muslim-majority world, women are seen as keepers of morality and often encounter obstructive social and family environments, which envelop many of them in the fallacy that a woman's destiny is the home, whereas learning and careers are the domain of men (Issan 2013, 164). The view of women as the custodians of morality is, of course, one that echoes in the majority of world religions and no less so in the three monotheistic traditions of Judaism, Christianity, and Islam:

> In the context of the Enlightenment, urban-industrialisation and the formation of a class society, 'separate spheres' for men and women emerged to impose domestic ideology as a heavily religious and moral discourse on angelic confinement from the public sphere. Historians have placed religion as central to the lives of middle-class women of the nineteenth century as they developed identity and a moral agency over their own destinies, as well as developing a 'space' in religious, temperance and philanthropic organisations within which they cultivated a worldly role.
>
> (Brown 2009, 59)

Despite the social advances that women have made in the past century there is still much that needs to be achieved and not least that which can be provided for by Islamization of knowledge approach to learning. Similarly, as O'Connor (1989, 112–114) argues that as women are rereading, reconceiving, and reconstructing religious traditions, so too are they gaining a renewed self-consciousness. This involves a process of revisiting both the sources and suppressed visions of the various religious traditions. A new imaginary of democratic citizenship is creating a discourse of commitment to constitutional rights for gender equality, universal education at all levels, increasing visibility of women in managerial and decision-making positions; increasing training and educational opportunities for women, and the establishment of authorities and organizations for women (Issan 2013, 165).

Second, a new imaginary of democratic citizenship requires attention being paid to participation and dignity in the midst of multiple/inclusive identities; public trust and solidarity, which trump fragmentation and incivility; and freedom of conscience, which involves either rejection or the choice to distinguish good from bad through debate and dissent (Turner 2008, 55). In a way, a new imaginary of democratic citizenship is focused not only on the right of people to belong but also to participate as equal adults in their political communities (Yuval-Davis 2011, 77). For instance, women are still not allowed to vote in Saudi Arabia, which highlights their lack of full participation in the political system of a Muslim-majority country. What a new imaginary of democratic citizenship has in mind is a politics of belonging that contests exclusionary and hierarchical social relations regarding women and ethnic, religious, and sexual minorities. This also implies that the practices of many Muslims today have to transform into ways of life that are not patriarchal and that acknowledge difference and diversity, and that Muslim-majority countries ought to enforce legislation to criminalize ethnic stereotyping, hate speech, and racism (Turner 2008). And for this to happen, a new imaginary of democratic citizenship ought to be cultivated through avenues that are not merely political but also sociocultural. If a new imaginary of democratic citizenship were to be realized in postcolonial Muslim-majority countries, the possibility of an integrated Islamized curriculum might be enhanced and would be in becoming.

In conclusion, it is our argument that it is not Islamization that has failed. Rather, it is the deficient conditions that have truncated its implementation. What is necessary to address these deficient conditions is a new imaginary of democratic citizenship that facilitates and ensures the participation, freedom of conscience, and a sense of belonging of multiple identities, including that of women. A new imaginary of democratic citizenship, which takes into account the rights and dignity of all—whether majority or minority groups—has the greatest potential of transforming not only patriarchal constructions but also ensuring an Islamized curriculum, which is politically, socially, and culturally inclusive.

NOTE

1 South Africa has nine provinces, which include the Western Cape, Gauteng, and KwaZulu-Natal.

BIBLIOGRAPHY

Abushouk, A.I. 2008. "World History from an Islamic Perspective: The Experience of the International Islamic University of Malaysia." In *Global Practice in World History*, edited by P. Manning, 39–52. Princeton, NJ: Princeton University Press.

Abu Zayd, N. 2010. "The Qur'an, Islam and Muhammad." *Philosophy & Social Criticism* 36: 3–4: 281–294.

Al-Attas, F. 2008. "Interview on Islam and Education." *Islamic Perspective Journal* 1(2): 7–16.

Al-Attas, S.M.N. 1980. *The Concept of Education in Islam*. Kuala Lumpur: Muslim Youth Movement of Malaysia.

Al-Faruqi, I.R. 1982. *Islamization of Knowledge: The General Principles and the Workplan*. Herndon, VA: International Institute of Islamic Thought.

Al-Faruqi, I.R. 1988. Islamization of Knowledge: Problems, Principles and Prospective. *Islam: Source and Purpose of Knowledge*. Accessed January 4, 2010. http://www.epistemology.net.

Association of Muslim Schools. 2014. Accessed March 12. http://www.islamicfocus.co.za/index.php?option=com_content&task=view&id=410&Itemid=24.

Bakar, O. 2009. "Religious Reform and the Controversy Surrounding Islamization in Malaysia." In *Muslim Reform in Southeast Asia: Perspectives from Malaysia, Indonesia and Singapore*, edited by S.F. Alatas, 31–45. Singapore: Muslim Ugama Islam Singapura.

Brown, G., C. (2009), *The Death of Christian Britain: Christianity and Society in the Modern World* (Routledge, London).

Darul Falaah College. 2010. Accessed March 13, 2014. http://www.darulfalaah.org.za/College/dfcollege.html.

Davids, N. (2014) Muslim schools in post-apartheid South Africa: Living with an apartheid past? *Education as Change*, 18(2): 227–236.

Davids, N. & Waghid, Y. (2014) Beyond the indigenous/non-indigenous knowledge divide: The case of Muslim education and its attenuation to cosmopolitanism. *South African Journal of Higher Education,* 28(5): 1485–1496.

Hashim, R. 1996. *Educational Dualism in Malaysia: Implications for Theory and Practice.* Oxford: Oxford University Press.

Hwang, J.C. 2008. "Education and Social Cohesion in Malaysia and Indonesia." In *Religious Diversity and Civil Society: A Comparative Analysis*, edited by B.S. Turner, 143–66. Oxford: The Bardwell Press.

Islamia College. 2013. "Our school website." Accessed April 25. www.islamia college.co.za.

Issan, S.A. 2013. "Gender and Education in the Arabian Gulf States." In *Education in the Broader Middle East: Borrowing a Baroque Arsenal*, edited by G. Donn and A. Manthri, 145–70. Oxford: Symposium Books.

Levers, L.Z. 2006. "Ideology and Change in Iranian Education." In *Education in the Muslim World: Different Perspectives*, edited by R. Griffin, 149–90. Oxford: Symposium Books.

Nasr, S.H. 2010. *Islam in the Modern World: Challenged by the West, Threatened by Fundamentalism, Keeping Faith with Tradition.* Washington, DC: HarperOne.

O'Connor, J. 1989. "Rereading, reconceiving and reconstructing traditions: Feminist research in religion." *Women's Studies* 17(1): 101–123.

Rahman, F. 1982. *Islam and Modernity.* Chicago: The University of Chicago Press.

Rahman, F. 1988. "Islamization of Knowledge: A Response." *The American Journal of Islamic Social Sciences* 5(1): 3–11.

Shaw, K. 2006. "Muslim Education in the Gulf States and Saudi Arabia: Selected Issues." In *Education in the Muslim World: Different Perspectives*, edited by R. Griffin, 26–41. Oxford: Symposium Books.

Springs Muslim School. 2014. Accessed March 13. http://www.springsmuslim school.co.za/wmenu.php.

Tayob, A. 2011. "Islamization for South African Muslim independent schools." In *Muslim Schools and Education in Europe and South Africa: Religionen im Dialog*, edited by A. Tayob, I. Niehaus & W. Weisse, 39–54. Berlin: Waxmann Verlag.

Turner, B.S. 2008. "Religious Diversity and the Liberal Consensus." In *Religious Diversity and Civil Society: A Comparative Analysis*, edited by B.S. Turner, 42–72. Oxford: Bardwell Press.

Waghid, Y. 2011. *Conceptions of Islamic Education: Pedagogical Framings.* New York: Peter Lang Publishing.

Waghid, Y. 2013. "Muslim Education and Democratic Citizenship Education in South Africa: The Case of Islamia College." Paper presented at the Conference on Madrasah Education, Singapore, March 15–16.

Wan Daud, W.M.N. 1997. "Islamization of Contemporary Knowledge: A Brief Comparison Between al-Attas and Fazlur Rahman." *Al-Shajarah* 2(1): 1–19.

Wan Daud, W.M.N. 2009. "Dewesternization and Islamization: Their Epistemic Framework and Final Purpose." Paper presented at the International Conference on Islamic University Education, Kazan, Russia, September 27–30.

Yuval-Davis, N. 2011. The Politics of Belonging: Intersectional Contestations. Los Angeles: SAGE.

15 Teaching Islam

Are There Pedagogical Limits to Critical Inquiry?

Farah Ahmed and Ibrahim Lawson

Muslims in the United Kingdom have been systematically setting up educational programs for children and adults for the last fifty years or more, beginning with mosque-based study circles and evening classes for children of school age and gradually extending to a full range of provision from homeschooling to independent Islamic schools, a handful of which have succeeded in becoming state funded. Among the oldest Islamic schools are the *Darul Ulooms*, independent boarding schools for boys, mainly, which teach a traditional curriculum of Islamic Studies and constitute an extension of the Deobandi project into the late-modern Western European context. Although Islamic schools are generally small, their numbers have been increasing, and there are now over 150 across the United Kingdom, usually based in inner-city locations where there is a high proportion of Muslims. Due to developing controversies surrounding Islam, Islamic education is becoming increasingly controversial. As the state extends its control over schooling and curriculum, Islamic schools are struggling to find ways to survive and remain proactive in working out the role of Islam in a post-Christian, neoliberal society. This chapter will showcase on two very different responses to this challenge that nevertheless share similar underlying concerns. The first is a project to develop the Prophetic practice of *Halaqah* with young children in two independent Islamic primary schools in the London area, England. The second is part of a higher Islamic education course for adults studying the traditional Islamic sciences in a Deobandi-origin institution also in London.

Furthermore, in order to answer the question of our title, it is important to clarify and problematize three initial concepts: 'teaching Islam,' 'pedagogical limits,' and 'critical inquiry.' The discourse in this chapter takes into account both Islamic paradigms and where they differ from dominant educational discourses, i.e., the challenge of 'freedom of thought' and 'critique' in the pedagogical relationship between teacher and learner. It is only through problematizing these three terms that the two emerging pedagogical models of critical inquiry can be appreciated and understood.

TEACHING ISLAM AND PEDAGOGICAL LIMITS: A DISCUSSION OF TERMINOLOGIES

To begin with, what do we mean by 'teaching Islam?' If the word Islam is defined as attaining peace through submission (to the will of Allah), there immediately appears a challenge to the notion of 'criticality' or critical distance through such education. However, further exploration of what Islam requires in relation to submission, i.e., that it comes through a free choice made by an autonomous individual, takes us immediately to an inherent aporia in Islam. Through its creedal premise of *tawhid* (unity), Islam ignores what are usually perceived in the Western mind as dichotomies and thus, in the Islamic worldview, freedom from self (*nafs*) and others (*an-nas*) is attained through submission to Allah who is *Ahad* (the ultimate Unity). Furthermore, although Allah exhorts *insaan*, human beings, to use their *'aql* (intellect), the use of this uniquely human faculty leads to a recognition of the limits of the human intellect in that Allah and the *ghayb* (unseen) cannot be properly known by it alone. Thus, whereas *'aql* has been created in order for the human being to recognize Allah through his *ayat* (signs), recognizing them as such leads to a recognition of human feebleness, thereby leading to an acceptance of the need to become *Muslim*, which in the Arabic is to submit to *as-Samad* (the Absolute). Such a view is inherently contradictory to a humanist basis as evolved within European thought and which underpins much of contemporary 'Western' thought. In Islamic discourses, free will and *'aql* are the two distinctly human qualities that elevate the human being above the rest of creation and which allow human beings to exercise their autonomy in choosing to become *Muslim* (one who submits). Thus when we are talking about teaching 'Islam,' are we talking about teaching a learner to submit to Allah? There are many ways to answer this question, but for the purposes of this chapter, we will accept the conceptualization of 'teaching Islam' as this definition goes to the heart of the problem given in our title, in a way that teaching *about* Islam may not. Further, it is this concept of confessional 'Islamic education' that is considered controversial and indoctrinatory.

The verb 'teach' is also at the heart of the problem given in the title in that it immediately implies authority. For how can there be teaching without authority? For this reason, the word has been sidelined in contemporary educational settings, so that educators now talk about 'delivering' a lesson as opposed to 'teaching.' This new term partly arises from the 'learner-centered' pedagogies built on Piagetian and Vygotskian constructivist and social-constructivist epistemologies that dominate contemporary educational discourse. Yet for many involved in traditional Islamic education, sacred knowledge comes from Allah and is *not* constructed by human beings: *ta'lim* (teaching) is transmission of sacred knowledge, and the teacher as transmitter of this sacred knowledge is central to Islamic pedagogy. Combining the definition of Islam with this definition of teaching it is easy, yet fallacious, to conclude that Islamic education is pure indoctrination.

Nevertheless, even in this definition of *ta'lim* there is complexity: The primary duty of the Islamic teacher is to develop the character of the learner and thus the teacher-learner relationship is not just about transmission of sacred knowledge but about the close relationship and interaction between student and teacher. It is through this relationship that sacred knowledge, reflective wisdom, and moral character are built and traditionally thought to have developed. So the learner is not an empty vessel but very much an active agent, a seeker of knowledge who is looking for something from this particular teacher. Thus 'teaching Islam' has a complexity wherein dichotomies such as teaching and learning are carefully balanced and unified through a *tawhid* worldview. Further, there are other ways of defining Islamic education, as will be shown in this chapter, furthering nuance to the already complex classical understanding of *ta'lim*.

We also need to examine what we mean by 'pedagogical limits.' The phrase 'pedagogical limits' raises the challenge of teaching as a paradoxical practice in that it can potentially limit other or broader understandings which may be supplanted by teacher-intended understandings. This exists in all conceptualizations of education, even learner-centered ones, and it is what Bonawitz et al. describe as the 'double-edged sword of pedagogy' (Bonawitz et al., 2011). In their work with preschool-aged children, looking at how explicit instruction affects learning through exploratory play, they found that, although pedagogical instruction will speed up children's understanding of the function of a toy, it can also hinder further exploration of a toy by very young children, thereby restricting the learning benefits of exploratory play. They conclude that a combination of the efficiency of pedagogical transmission with encouragement toward exploratory play should maximize learning in the short and long term. Scaling this up to the teacher-learner relationship in traditional Islamic education, a clear practical solution emerges that requires *skillful* teaching, that is, a pedagogical repertoire that is both teacher-led and learner-led. Skillful teaching would involve encouraging questioning, criticality, an awareness of differing arguments, and personal reflection in students, combined with the effective and precise transmission of sacred knowledge to the student through direct teaching and instruction. Whereas at the level of practice the earlier argument addresses the question of the pedagogical limits of critical inquiry, it does not address the more fundamental contradiction between teaching sacred knowledge and personal freedom in questioning sacred truths, which is the concern of this chapter. In this instance, surely, there are pedagogical limits to critical inquiry; that is, a learner is not permitted to be critical about matters of creed or dogma. At this level, it could be argued that criticism of Islamic education as indoctrination remains and that, ultimately, such education fundamentally relies on an authority that limits autonomy.

THE TEACHER-LEARNER RELATIONSHIP BETWEEN AUTHORITY AND AUTONOMY

Traditional educational authority lies both with the teacher and the text. Whereas learner autonomy is recognized, as argued earlier, the authority of the teacher as interlocutor within a chain of transmission from the Prophet remains paramount for Islamic education. The teacher is a necessary spiritual and intellectual guide who enables the learner to submit as a Muslim through an intellectual understanding of the text, to appreciate the truth of Islam, and, through reflective self-knowledge, attain to spiritual submission to Allah. In this context, the question of 'pedagogical limits' would be one of how far any authority, however strong, can teach this type of submission without the learner making an active choice. Without the learner's autonomous choice, the act of submission becomes meaningless. Does this mean that authority and autonomy are actually mutually defining? Rather than being a matter of either/or, is it not rather that both are necessary to achieve the objective of Islamic education? In the case of an adult who has converted to Islam and sought out a teacher that she wishes to learn from, there is a conscious choice, and the relationship between authority and autonomy is accepted; yet what may be said for a young child being taught in a *madrasah*. How far does she exercise any kind of autonomy? Does she really *choose* to submit?

It could be argued, as has been famously done by Amartya Sen (1985), that there is a limit to all our choices; a child newly born has no choice but to accept the authority of her parents, and she is limited in many other ways, such as by gender, class, the language and culture of the family home, etc. Furthermore, the concept of choice only applies when a person has the capacity to choose, which itself requires the ability to think, to envisage alternatives, and to be aware of one's own feelings, in other words, to have a mind that is aware of itself, has experiences, and has beliefs about the world. Is it not the role of education to facilitate the development of such an individual? Accordingly, should not Islamic education aspire to create these skills and this capacity or has the goal of personal autonomy been neglected in Islamic education? As in all educational communities, these issues have been reflected on by a range of contemporary Muslim thinkers (Sahin 2013; Waghid 2011; Attas 1979). It has already been stated earlier that, theoretically at least, it can be argued that Islamic education is about enabling the flourishing of the human being's autonomy until she, as an active agent, chooses to be Muslim; therefore, as with any educational process, the possibility of an outcome that is not intended is inevitable. That is, she could choose to exercise her agency to reject Islam. This is a given within the Islamic worldview of human accountability in the *akhira* (hereafter) for choices made in this life. As Imam Al-Ghazali says:

> O Son! Live your life as you see fit, for you will surely die. Desire what you want, for you will surely depart. Do what you want, for you will

> surely pay for it. Gather up what you want for, for you will surely leave it behind.
>
> (Ghazali 2010, 94)

In further exploring what is meant by 'critical inquiry' and elaborating two pedagogical responses to the relation of critical inquiry to Islamic education in contemporary classrooms, we need to acknowledge the question as to what extent there is any room for criticality in relation to the authority of the teacher and the authority of the text in Islamic education. Regarding the teacher, there is no doubt that, as the possessor of sacred knowledge, the teacher holds an eminent place in Islam. Nevertheless, in classical Islamic education, students choose their teachers and thus have the right to select based on judgments of quality, character, intellect, etc. This already shows that it is the student's opinion that establishes the authority of any given teacher, and classical Muslim scholarship has commented in varying ways the agency of the student in the activity of learning (Günther 2006). This suggests the possibility of a kind of deep, critical inquiry that can be conducted at every level of education and with pupils of all ages. Wherein lies the reality of that autonomy that makes submission to authority authentic if it is not within ourselves? Two potential ways in which contemporary Islamic educators are developing a pedagogic approach to the teaching of critical inquiry in practice will be briefly examined, first in the context of primary and then adult education in the United Kingdom.

CASE STUDY I: DEVELOPING CRITICALITY AND AUTONOMY THROUGH HALAQAH

The use of a Halaqah as a dialogic pedagogy with primary-aged children in United Kingdom goes beyond the role of critical *thinking* and incorporates ideas such as critical pedagogy (Freire 1970), culturally relevant education (Ladson-Billings 1995), and Attas's work on the relationship between knowledge, the self, and Allah (Attas 1980). The practice of Halaqah in UK primary schools has been specifically developed as a culturally relevant pedagogical approach for the education of Muslim children in the 21st century to promote *shakhsiyah* (Ahmed 2012). Shakhsiyah is defined in this context as individuals who, through their own autonomous and critical thought, have chosen to adopt an Islamic worldview and Islamic identity, which they are able to exercise in a Western secular-liberal society. In this sense, a capability approach to freedom informs practice during daily 'Halaqah' in these schools. This is through both a critical pedagogy approach, empowering religious and cultural autonomy, *and* a sociocultural, dialogic approach, empowering personal autonomy by developing the skills of critical and reflective thought.

Since 1998, Halaqah has been a daily practice in a range of Muslim homeschooling collectives, which eventually turned into two registered UK independent primary schools known as Shakhsiyah Schools (ISF 2015). Since 2005, a curriculum for Halaqah has been in place, while secondary homeschooling collectives continue to operate on a more flexible basis; a curriculum for secondary schools is planned for development. Halaqah, in this context, consists of young children or young adults sitting on the floor in a circle with a teacher who will briefly introduce a topic or concept and then open a discussion. Teachers skillfully choreograph dialogue that includes critical questioning to arrive at a deeper understanding of the topic or concept. Teachers receive extensive training on how Halaqah differs from a teacher-led lesson and how it draws on Islamic educational theory and practice. This practice of Halaqah is underpinned by a well-developed pedagogical theory that drawings on classical and contemporary Muslim scholarship on education to develop classroom practice appropriate for the 21st century UK context. Our research on Halaqah has identified four pedagogical strands that can be attributed to the Prophet, *hifz*, *tarbiyah*, *ta'lim*, and *ta'deeb*.

As the strands of *hifz* and *ta'deeb* are not directly relevant to this discussion, I will focus on *tarbiyah* and *ta'lim*, which, I argue, share conceptual elements with critical pedagogy and critical inquiry, respectively. *Tarbiyah* is a very broad term; indeed, Abdullah Sahin argues that it encompasses all other Islamic terms for education and is inherently critical—he describes it as the "critical-dialogical process of becoming" (Sahin 2013, 167). In Shakhsiyah Schools, Halaqah involves personalized shakhsiyah development, i.e., supporting children to become self-reflective learners focused on the ongoing development of their own character and 'self.' *Tarbiyah* in Halaqah is also theorized as a process of developing social and political awareness, "a pedagogy of hope" (Freire 1994) built on the Prophetic model of challenging injustice. Prophetic Halaqah led not only to the pursuit of personal development and *haqq* (truth) but also communal and societal nurturing toward *haqq* in its broader sense encompasses social justice.

> The Prophets' . . . teaching . . . often involving heated debates and discussions . . . aiming largely at the adult, the oppositional, the disappointed and the marginalized. It spoke about the social injustices, and daily issues, using the language of religion and poetry. It was informal and integrative of words and actions . . . To that end, Islamic education of the period of revelation was radical.
>
> (Niyozov and Memon 2011, 8)

In Shakhsiyah Schools, *tarbiyah* is theorized as understanding the *active* dimension of Islam within a real-life context: children learning Islam within their own unique context as individuals with hybrid identities and within the more complex multilayered realities of Muslim and British society. During Halaqah, they actively ask questions about their role as Muslims in the current world and the social issues that they see around them, such as racism, poverty, and environmental issues. This social awareness has a spiritual dimension and is interwoven with a broader teaching of the Islamic way of life and how it can be realized in a contemporary UK context. Through developing a reflective and complex but nevertheless strongly Islamic identity, there is a natural emphasis on the role of Islam in social reform and the call for social justice. For example, in discussing the Islamic concept of *amanah*, children will contemplate what it means that the earth has been 'entrusted' to human beings. They may consider how much pollution local factories release and how that relates to the concept of the earth as a trust (*amanah*). Children then consider what they can do to change the situation and whether they have a responsibility to act. However, as a religious pedagogy, Halaqah differs from traditional ideas of 'critical pedagogy' in that it subscribes to an Islamic worldview instead of a secular human rights one. There will naturally be contentions of gender and other issues that secular critical pedagogy considers important, yet despite these points of contention, Muslim educators draw on critical pedagogy to argue for a more transformative education (Ahmed 2012; Zeera 2001; Zine 2008).

In Shakhsiyah Schools, Halaqah also draws on the pedagogical tradition of education as *ta'lim*. In doing so, it recalls the early Islamic tradition of *sawal jawab* (question and answer), where students engaged in extensive questioning of a teacher and a dialogue ensued. The basis of this emphasis on critical reflection is the importance given to questioning and reflection in the Qur'anic narrative. In theorizing *ta'lim* in this way, a parallel is seen in sociocultural theory, which is the study of pedagogy from a Vygotskian purview, i.e., that learning takes place through dialogical interaction between teacher and learner or co-learners and that it involves an interdependent relationship that recognizes that opportunity that presents itself at the 'zone of proximal development.' Sociocultural education researchers work at the interface of the 'pedagogical limits' to any act of learning, examining where those limits are and how they can be broadened. They suggest that dialogue and criticality are the keys to enhanced learning in modern classrooms (Alexander 2008; Barnes 2008; Mercer & Littleton 2007). Teacher training on Halaqah in Shakhsiyah Schools includes training on Alexander's 'Dialogic Teaching' and Mercer's 'Exploratory Talk' as useful pedagogical models of generating classroom dialogue. Teachers understand that underpinning these kinds of pedagogical models in Halaqah is the Qur'anic pedagogy of questioning and reflection, a form of critical inquiry that was enacted through Qur'anic recitation in the Prophetic Halaqah as an impetus for critique of long-held beliefs and questions, raising the possibility of personal and societal transformation. The Qur'anic revelation spoke directly to the people of that time, asking them to consider a range of issues, referring directly to events and problems that concerned the people of the time. So the Qur'an asks:

> Have you seen the one who denies the recompense? For that is the one who drives away the orphan and does not encourage the feeding of the needy.
>
> (Qur'an 107:1–3)

> Certainly has Allah heard the speech of the one who argues with you, [O Muhammad], concerning her husband and directs her complaint to Allah. And Allah hears your dialogue; indeed, Allah is Hearing and Seeing.
>
> (Qur'an 58:1)

And in other verses, it asks people to reflect:

> Do you not see that Allah sends down rain from the sky and makes it flow as springs [and rivers] in the earth; then He produces thereby crops of varying colors; then they dry and you see them turned yellow; then He makes them [scattered] debris. Indeed in that is a reminder for those of understanding.
>
> (Qur'an 39:21)

> Are those who know equal to those who do not know?
>
> (Qur'an 39:9)

> Have you not considered how Allah presents an example, [making] a good word like a good tree, whose root is firmly fixed and its branches [high] in the sky? It produces its fruit all the time, by permission of its Lord. And Allah presents examples for the people that perhaps they will be reminded.
>
> (Qur'an 14:24)

Critical reflection is therefore an essential part of Islamic education, designed to encourage use of the exclusive human faculty of *'aql* (intellect). Questioning and dialogue are means of engaging in critical reflection. Thus children in Halaqah are encouraged to ask questions and to feel that Halaqah is a safe space for asking the most difficult questions. So, for example, during a classroom discussion, we were presented by a nine-year-old child who was a little hesitant but did feel that she could ask a question about the famous Hadith where Allah says: *"Pride is My cloak and greatness My robe, and he who competes with Me in respect of either of them I shall cast into Hell-fire."* Her question was that she felt that this statement lacked humility and *"isn't Allah being a bit arrogant here?"* She wanted to understand why Allah asks us to be humble but displays *"arrogance"* in statements like this. When prompted to reflect on this further, she herself concluded that *"Because He is the God and God is important and majestic . . . I don't think, actually I do think, that Allah thinks that he is better than everyone."* When asked why Allah is saying this, she said, *"So that people believe in Him and pray to Him."* It is through this kind of critical reflective dialogue conducted on a daily basis that Halaqah seeks to develop autonomous, critical young people who themselves are beginning to experience the choice to be Muslim.

UNDERSTANDING 'CRITIQUE' IN TEXTUAL HERMENEUTICS

In our second case study, we will look at the kinds of philosophical questions that arise in the context of Islamic higher education in the United Kingdom. At this level of adult education, there can be a more explicit focus on hermeneutics and the relation between textual authority and interpretation. Initially, it is important to explicate that, within the study of the philosophy of language, we begin with the recognition that all texts are commonly understood to have an 'objective' or 'authoritative' and meaning intended by the author that exists independently of 'interpretation.' This also applies to a sacred text such as that of the Qur'an. Nevertheless, we recognize that when we understand or interpret the meaning of a text, this understanding is always something we ourselves construct. We think of the task of hermeneutics as reconstructing the meaning of a text to produce an interpretation that accords as closely as possible with the meaning intended by the author. Thus there are three structural elements in the process of understanding: the meaning intended by the author, the text that encodes and conveys this meaning, and the meaning that we construct by decoding the text. This type of hermeneutics is considered to be conservative (Gallagher 1992), where the text has one final, fixed objective meaning ('out there,' in the world, represented in the text) that can be discovered.

However, Gallagher defines two other approaches to hermeneutics, moderate and radical. In moderate hermeneutics, the text has an objective meaning, but we can never know all of its variances. However, we can distinguish better, more accurate (true) interpretations from worse, less accurate (false) interpretations according to how close they come to the real objective truth of what the text means. The reason we can never understand it all is that all understanding is affected by contextual factors in the 'hermeneutic background' of the interpreter and so will be different according to time and place. According to Gallagher, this contingency is simply a fact about communication and the use of language or any system of communication in signs; it is not a theory of how things *might* be. So does it apply to the text of the Qur'an and other sacred texts?

We necessarily understand Allah's words on the basis of our 'background' knowledge, i.e., everything we already know, and this is different for every one of us and in every generation. Classical *mufassirun* (interpreters of the Qur'an) have also recognized this situation and have tended to place a constraint on interpretation through giving importance to the consensus of the interpreters and the body of knowledge they create/construct; but this brings us to the third far more challenging possibility. In *radical* hermeneutics there is no 'objective' meaning external to the text or, rather, the concept of *'objective'* makes no sense. This is because we are always 'stuck' within our own conceptual limits that we have been 'subjected' to and have no way of thinking outside these limits. Our subjectivity is always absolute for us and yet historically contingent; in fact, it is not really 'ours' at all, it has just been lent to us to use to understand things while we are here. The only thing that keeps the process stable is the contemporary, shared consensus of interpretation, which is what our individual hermeneutic 'backgrounds' essentially comprise.

The implication of this is that, as the consensus gradually changes over centuries, so does our understanding of texts. Ultimately, when interpreting a text from another completely different time and culture, all we have to go on is the hermeneutic consensus that we have inherited and which we have no way of standing outside of. In Derrida's words, there is no *hors texte*, no outside the text, no universal objective standpoint. At the same time, we cannot escape the fact that this consensus is also subject to continuous (re)interpretation in ways that we cannot stand aside from and assess. The upshot is that we have no way of knowing how and to what extent our contemporary understanding of traditional texts has changed and changed again. It is not that this is in any way *unfortunately* the case (because how nice it would be to have access to the absolute, universal, and timeless truth); this is just the way things are and they could not be any different.

Whereas this may seem far too radical - Muslims consider themselves to *know* that the Qur'an is *absolute truth* - it is, ironically, a very modern idea that the 'objective truth' about 'reality' can potentially be known in full. This does not mean that we cannot know *anything*, but only that the matter is not as simple or straightforward as we imagine. In practice, we can never escape from the conditions that make knowledge and understanding possible in the first place, and what is necessary, therefore, is to become as aware of these as possible and to discriminate critically in choosing what to accept.

What then does criticality entail if it is not a matter of uncovering the 'objective' truth encoded in a text? Critical inquiry is one of a number of expressions conveying a range of meanings, all based on the idea of critique or criticism. The origin of these words is the Greek *krites*, a judge or umpire, and *krinein*, to discern, separate, or decide. The word 'criticism' and its cognates are frequently used in English to imply making a negative judgment, even minimally in the sense of having standards that may be unnecessarily high; being critical is not always appropriate or appreciated. In the more formal sense, however, 'criticality' refers to the positive virtue of being discerning. The distinctions between the various compound uses of 'critical' in the text that follows can be thought of as relating to the *object* of criticism and, by extension, to the methodology entailed in each case.

Critical *thinking* has been defined as "the effort to examine any belief or supposed form of knowledge in the light of the evidence that supports it and the further conclusions to which it tends" (Thomson 2009, 3). Other authors suggest that "the prime tools of Critical Thinking are the skills of formal and informal logic, conceptual analysis, and epistemology" (Burbules & Berk in Popkewitz & Fender 1999, 46).

Can we, however, understand the purpose of critical *inquiry* as something that goes beyond critical thinking and critical theory into the space opened up by Heidegger, for example, who defines questioning as the *"the piety of thought"* (Heidegger 1982, 35) and as the resolve to *"know . . . to stand in the manifestation of being, to endure [withstand] it . . . [and] to be able to learn"* (Heidegger 1959, 21). This suggestion is one that sees critical inquiry as inevitably turning reflexively toward the being of the inquirer for whom 'being' itself comes into question. If the ultimate purpose of critique is to get to the bottom of things, then we must eventually arrive at the source of the critique in the person of the subject; you could say that the 'object becomes the subject.' This is the starting point of Heidegger's revival of ontology in which he proposes that *"only as phenomenology, is ontology possible"* (Heidegger 1978, H36). In other words, if to understand being (both in the sense of the difference between what is and what is not as well as what it means for something to be such as it is) is the ultimate inquiry and "the most far-reaching . . . the deepest, and finally . . . the most fundamental of all questions" as Heidegger claims elsewhere (Heidegger 1959, 2), then our methodology must be such that we turn our full attention to things *as they appear to us*. Crucially, however, this appearing is not to be understood as referring to the way in which we can be mistaken about what something 'really' is, as when we are taken in by appearances, but to indicate the being of entities precisely as that which shows itself to us, i.e., as a phenomenon or coming to light. This does not mean, on the other hand, that phenomena are always fully obvious or transparent in their being, hence the need to develop an explicit understanding of the being of beings.

The aforementioned range of interpretations of criticality from critical thinking as argument analysis through the application of critical theory to the ideological structure of society and the social construction of subjectivity ended with the suggestion that the deepest focus of criticality, in the sense of discernment, is with the reality of the self-experiencing of being at the level of a fundamental ontological understanding. This would clearly have implications for education and the requirement to *know oneself* as a precursor to, or precondition of, properly understanding anything else.

CASE STUDY II: DEVELOPING CRITICAL CONTEMPLATION OF BEING AND SELF-REALIZATION IN UK ISLAMIC HIGHER EDUCATION

In forty years of experience as an educator, a key question that continues to push forward is how one's meaning as a person is informed by the practice of being a teacher/learner; I would go as far as to say that all education is a means to this end of self-realization. As a teacher of Islam, it is even clearer that he "who knows himself, knows his Lord" and that this is the ultimate goal and purpose of the being human. This traditional saying is a gloss on the Qur'anic verse in which Allah explains, "I did not create jinn and man except to worship Me" (Qur'an 51: 56), and hence this worship, which amounts to properly knowing, is the essence of what it means to be human. A similar tradition passed down by the Sufis, the mystics of Islam, is purported to be a hadith *qudsi*, a statement made by Allah that is not part of the Qur'anic text, to the effect that *"the whole of My creation cannot contain me but the heart of My believing slave contains me."* Thus the movement of one who seeks direct, experiential knowledge of God is toward understanding the mysteries of the heart as an organ of spiritual understanding that connects us to the divine. There is a direct parallel here with Heidegger's 'Being question.'

During the last twenty years, I have had the opportunity to pursue this interpretation of education through the teaching of philosophy to adults, most recently as part of an Islamic higher education course in London, England. The students are adults who are following a traditional Islamic Studies curriculum using Arabic texts from the Qur'an through to classical works in *tafsir, hadith, fiqh,* and *'aqidah*, while developing their mastery of the Arabic language. In this context, criticality can sometimes be misunderstood. The students are young adults, most of whom are British, seeking a traditional Islamic education but nevertheless feeling themselves entirely at home in a modern Western environment, especially multicultural, metropolitan London. This is a cultural setting that is almost overloaded with aporia, that is, contradictions (or impossible necessities) whose dialectical interplay forcibly creates an open space for inquiry and the generation of new thinking. Into this lifeworld created by the multiple forces of late modernity, many of which are threatening to the sustainability of both the individual and society, locally and globally, the students are projecting possibilities for an understanding and implementation of Islam that brings the authority of past tradition into a relation with the demands of an unpredictable future. As Muslims in the United Kingdom, they experience Islam as increasingly contested by 'mainstream' society, which might encourage a defensive or apologetic tendency that immediately construes criticism as negative. It seems natural that, when much scrutiny of Islam, its practices, and beliefs becomes mainstream, a normal reaction would be to close ranks and protect the tradition, rather than submit it to forms of criticality. Yet this reactive conservatism also moves to inhibit intelligent critique and a deeper understanding of the issues involved, withdrawing instead to simple certainties that remain comfortably unexamined. Most of the students recognize that this kind of defensive retreat is not a solution to the difficulties experienced by many Muslims today in Western or westernized contexts. If their knowledge of Islam is to be applied successfully, they must learn to read not only the texts they are studying but also the contexts in which they will be called upon to act.

To begin this process, in our lessons, we examine the ways in which Greek philosophy has developed over the last twenty-five hundred years or so and especially how metaphysics has eventually failed to account for every part of what it means to be human. We illustrate this with a study of the arguments proposed for the rationality of theism, we learn how to evaluate reasoning, to think critically, and what the limits of logic and science are as ways of explaining the world. Moving on through a case study of the apparent contradictions between religion and science, we turn to language, phenomenology, and hermeneutics in the search for helpful answers. Motivated by our concern for justice in society, which is an inseparable element of Islamic education, as much as by our search for a deep understanding of Islam as the human relation with the divine, we look at the way in which metaphysics, colonialism, and capitalism combine in the modern worldview to counter traditional religious and spiritual ways of understanding and produce a technological nihilism, reducing the human being to a biological object in an essentially meaningless physical world of matter and energy. This helps in two ways: it enables us to identify the obstacles to a renewed understanding of Islam, such as Orientalism and Islamophobia on the one hand and the defensive conservatism they provoke on the other; and we also come to challenge the metaphysical foundations of Western thought and the almost hidden influence that has had on the development of the Islamic sciences. By finally arriving at Heidegger's philosophy and its post-philosophical tendencies as well as developments such as post-structuralism and deconstruction, which fall within the Heideggerian project, we are able to raise important questions regarding the ways in which Islam as a text, in the broadest sense, can be read in the 21st century.

The essential pedagogy involved is one that has been developing over the last few decades. It can be thought of as student centered, as a form of critical inquiry, as higher-order questioning of thinking, or as a mode of self-discovery. The methodology is recognizably philosophical in the sense that it takes traditional philosophical texts and arguments as its starting point and a good deal of time is necessary to allow students to become familiar with this style of inquiry. It soon becomes apparent, however, that philosophy as a discipline is very strange: It is not a science, but it cannot be restricted to logical analysis either; it is not a form of literature, although great philosophers create their own original style. What we begin to realize after a few months is that philosophy concerns itself with things that somehow precede and make possible any formal style of inquiry. How then can we deal with these things? In feeling our way through this question, we begin to realize also that others have been here before, trying to formulate what cannot be grasped by any of the tools of thinking we are familiar with. Is this not, in fact, the direction in which the Qur'an is pointing, neither bound by logical dialectic nor yet 'merely' a form of poetry? If philosophy as metaphysics fails to provide a basis for the interpretation of religious principles and we are not ready to conclude that God is finally dead, as Nietzsche feared, what kind of new thinking, new forms of inquiry, will reveal themselves? As we reflect on this, on our own experience of life and on the exploding train wreck that is Western modernity, we begin to sense that these are not just questions for Muslim scholars but for humanity in general, that there are no limits to critical inquiry in Islam and the questions confronting not only us as Muslims but all human beings.

CONCLUSION

In this chapter, we have argued that there is no clear answer to what could or should be the pedagogical limits to critical inquiry in teaching Islam. The question posed in this way suggests that criticality and Islam are mutually exclusive at some point. However, education, including Islamic education, necessarily encompasses both authoritative and critical elements, although the degree of each will vary according to the context. In our view, criticality is increasingly important for Muslim students in that the Islamic worldview is under constant challenge, and without engaging with personal beliefs critically, young Muslims will struggle to make sense of their place in a fast-changing world. Strong critical inquiry skills enable young Muslims to constructively engage in personal reflection and contribute with confidence to their own communities, to civic life, and to the wider society. Moreover, we make the case that profound critical reflection, or questioning, leads reflexively to the core reality of what we were created for, both in Qur'anic terms and in those of the emerging realization in the West of the deep existential connection between human being and the world.

BIBLIOGRAPHY

Ahmed, Farah. 2012. "Tarbiyah for Shakhsiyah (educating for Identity): Seeking out Culturally Coherent Pedagogy for Muslim Children in Britain." *Compare: A Journal of Comparative and International Education* 42 (5): 725–49. doi:10.1080/03057925.2012.706452.

Attas, Syed Muhammad Naquib. 1979. *Aims and Objectives of Islamic Education*. Hodder and Stoughton.

Attas, Syed Muhammad Naquib. 1980. *The Concept of Education in Islam: A Framework for an Islamic Philosophy of Education*. Makkah, Saudi Arabia: Muslim Youth Movement of Malaysia.

Alexander, Robin J. 2008. *Toward Dialogic Teaching: Rethinking Classroom Talk*. 4th edition. Dialogos.

Barnes, Douglas. 2008. "Exploratory Talk for Learning." In *Exploring Talk in School*, edited by Neil Mercer and Steve Hodgkinson, 1–17. London, UK: SAGE.

Bonawitz, Elizabeth, Patrick Shafto, Hyowon Gweon, Noah D. Goodman, Elizabeth Spelke, and Laura Schulz. 2011. "The Double-Edged Sword of Pedagogy: Instruction Limits Spontaneous Exploration and Discovery." *Cognition* 120 (3): 322–30. doi:10.1016/j.cognition.2010.10.001.

Freire, Paulo. 1970. *Pedagogy of the Oppressed*. Herder and Herder.

Ladson-Billings, Gloria. 1995. "But That's Just Good Teaching! The Case for Culturally Relevant Pedagogy." *Theory Into Practice* 34 (3): 159–65. doi:10.1080/00405849509543675.

Freire, Paulo, and Ana Maria Araújo Freire. 1994. *Pedagogy of Hope: Reliving Pedagogy of the Oppressed*. Continuum.

Gallagher, S. (1992). *Hermeneutics and Education*. SUNY Press.

Ghazali, Abu Hamid Muhammad. 2010. "O Son!" In *Classical Foundations of Islamic Educational Thought: A Compendium of Parallel English-Arabic Texts*, edited by Bradley J. Cook and Fatḥī Ḥasan Malkāwī, translated by Dacid C. Reisman, 88–107. Brigham Young University Press.

Günther, Sebastian. 2006. "Be Masters in That You Teach and Continue to Learn: Medieval Muslim Thinkers on Educational Theory." *Comparative Education Review* 50(3): 367–88. doi:10.1086/503881.

Heidegger, M. (1959). *An Introduction to Metaphysics* (1st edition). New Haven and London: Yale University Press.

Heidegger, M. (1978). *Being and Time* (New Ed edition). Wiley-Blackwell.

Heidegger, M. (1982). *The Question Concerning Technology, and Other Essays*. HarperCollins.

Islamic Shakhsiyah Foundation, 2015. Accessed April 20. http://isf.education.

Mercer, Neil, and Karen Littleton. 2007. *Dialogue and the Development of Children's Thinking: A Sociocultural Approach*. Routledge.

Niyozov, Sarfaroz, and Nadeem Memon. 2011. "Islamic Education and Islamization: Evolution of Themes, Continuities and New Directions." *Journal of Muslim Minority Affairs* 31(1): 5–30. doi:10.1080/13602004.2011.556886.

Popkewitz, T., & Fendler, L. (Eds.). (1999). *Critical Theories in Education: Changing Terrains of Knowledge and Politics*. New York: Routledge.

Sahin, Abdullah. 2013. *New Directions in Islamic Education: Pedagogy and Identity Formation*. Kube Publishing Limited.

Sen, Amartya. 1985. "Well-Being, Agency and Freedon: The Dewey Lectures 1984." *The Journal of Philosophy* 82(4): 169–221.

Thomson, A. (2009). *Critical Reasoning 3e: A Practical Introduction*. Routledge.

Waghid, Yusef. 2011. *Conceptions of Islamic Education: Pedagogical Framings* (1st New edition). New York: Peter Lang Publishing Inc.

Wake, P., & Malpas, S. (2013). *The Routledge Companion to Critical and Cultural Theory*. Routledge.

Wittgenstein, L. (2013). *Tractatus Logico-Philosophicus*. Routledge.

Zeera, Zahra al. 2001. *Wholeness and Holiness in Education an Islamic Perspective*. IIIT.

Zine, Jasmin. 2008. *Canadian Islamic Schools: Unravelling the Politics of Faith, Gender, Knowledge, and Identity*. University of Toronto Press.

Contributors

Farah Ahmed is Visiting Research Associate, Centre for Research and Evaluation in Muslim Education, UCL Institute of Education and PhD candidate, Faculty of Education, University of Cambridge, UK.

Talal Al-Azem is Junior Research Fellow, Pembroke College, Faculty of Oriental Studies, University of Oxford, UK.

David B. Burrell is Theodore Hesburgh C.S.C. Professor Emeritus in Philosophy and Theology at the University of Notre Dame, USA.

Nuraan Davids is Lecturer of Philosophy of Education in the Department of Education Policy Studies, Faculty of Education at Stellenbosch University, South Africa.

Susan Douglass is K–14 Education Outreach Coordinator at the Center for Contemporary Arab Studies, Georgetown University, and a doctoral candidate at George Mason University, Fairfax, Virginia, USA.

Ann El-Moslimany is Founding Director of the Islamic School of Seattle, USA.

Sebastian Günther is Professor and Chair of Arabic and Islamic Studies at the University of Göttingen, Germany.

Ibrahim Lawson is the Director of Research at Ebrahim College, London, UK.

Shaikh Abdul Mabud is Associate Professor of Islamic Spirituality, Ethics, and Education at the Sultan Omar 'Ali Saifuddien Centre for Islamic Studies, Universiti Brunei Darussalam, Brunei.

Nadeem A. Memon is the Director of Education at Razi Education, Canada.

Seyyed Hossein Nasr is University Professor of Islamic Studies at George Washington University, USA.

Sarfaroz Niyozov is Associate Professor at the University of Toronto, Canada.

Omar Qargha is a doctoral student at University of Maryland's International Education Policy program, USA.

Omar Anwar Qureshi is a PhD candidate at Loyola University (USA) in Cultural and Educational Policy Studies Program and Principal of Islamic Foundation School at Villa Park, Illinois, USA.

Steffen Stelzer is Professor and Chair of the Department of Philosophy, The American University in Cairo, Egypt.

Abdullah Trevathan is currently Headteacher of the Al Akhawayn School and formerly a Senior Lecturer of Education at Roehampton University and Lecturer in Comparative Religion at Al Akhawayan University, Morocco.

Yusef Waghid is Professor of Philosophy of Education in the Department of Education Policy Studies, Stellenbosch University, Executive Member of the International Network of Philosophers of Education and Fellow of the Academy of Science of South Africa.

Tim Winter is Shaykh Zayed Lecturer in Islamic Studies, Faculty of Divinity, University of Cambridge and College Dean, The Cambridge Muslim College, UK.

Mujadad Zaman is Visting Research Fellow at the Center for Islamic Theology, University of Tübingen, Germany.

Index